牛津小学生
彩图英汉双解词典

OXFORD ILLUSTRATED ENGLISH-CHINESE DICTIONARY FOR PRIMARY STUDENTS

英语原文（English text）：R·霍尔特（R. Holt）
汉语译文（translation）：关品枢（Guan Pinshu）

全新版

Completely New Edition

上海远东出版社
牛津大学出版社

图书在版编目(CIP)数据

牛津小学生彩图英汉双解词典/(英) 霍尔特(Holt, R.)编;关品枢译.—上海:上海远东出版社,1999

ISBN 7-80613-867-6

Ⅰ.牛… Ⅱ.①霍… ②关… Ⅲ.英语-双解词典-英、汉 Ⅳ.H316

中国版本图书馆 CIP 数据核字(1999)第 28321 号

牛津小学生彩图英汉双解词典

〔英〕R·霍尔特 编著 关品枢 译

出版	上海远东出版社 (上海冠生园路 393 号 邮编 200233) 牛津大学出版社
发行	上海远东出版社
经销	全国新华书店
印刷	上海市印刷七厂
开本	787×960 1/16
印张	19
千字	485
版次	1999 年 8 月第 1 版
印次	1999 年 8 月第 1 次
印数	1-50000

ISBN 7-80613-867-6 / H·113

图字:09-1999-212 号

定价:25.00 元

Note for Parents and Teachers

致家长和教师

《牛津小学生彩图英汉双解词典》是牛津英汉词典系列中专为小学生编写的工具书，所收录的3800多个单词和短语、5000多条例句、1000多帧图片，均经过牛津大学出版社词典专家们的精心挑选及编排，有助于以英语为第二语言的学生正确了解和运用英语。

在内容方面，为使小学生从小养成良好的双语学习习惯，本词典每一词目均有简明准确的英语释义和汉语释义。例句的内容生活化，全部以英汉对照的方式列出，形象说明每一词目的具体含义和确切用法。同时，注意介绍常与有关词目并用的其他词语和短语，以利于学生提高阅读英语及以英语思考的能力。本词典还根据小学生的认知特点，精心设计了大量生动的情景、精美的插图，令小学生学习时兴趣盎然，印象深刻。

在语音方面，本词典采用的方式，是先把词目按音节断开，注明须重读的音节，再列出其国际音标，务求以双重方式令学生快速记忆及掌握词语的正确读音。

在语法方面，每个词条均提供大量资料，包括词目的词类，词目作名词、动词、形容词或副词使用时的不规则变化等，方便学生以英语写作时参考之用。其中，常用的不规则词语自成独立词目。另有不少词目列有同义词、反义词或用法说明。

附录部分以精美插图按不同主题如家庭、学校等编排而成，为学生提供了大量英汉对照生词，另附有不规则动词表和常用口语表，既实用又富趣味性。

《牛津小学生彩图英汉双解词典》内容丰富、功能齐全、品牌优质，不仅可为小学生学习英语提供极大的帮助，而且，对于广大内地学生而言，其知识含量可延伸至初中，有效使用周期较长。

为配合我国的英语教学改革，我社从牛津大学出版社引进《牛津小学生彩图英汉双解词典》，在内地出版发行简化汉字版。出版前，经牛津大学出版社同意，我们对原书的文字和图片作了少量技术处理，使之更符合内地学生的学习习惯。

愿《牛津小学生彩图英汉双解词典》成为广大小学生学习英语的好伙伴。

上海远东出版社

1999年8月

Contents 目录

Key to IPA Phonetic Symbols 国际音标符号

Vowels and diphthongs 元音和双元音

1	iː	as in	**see** /siː/	11	ɜː	as in	**fur** /fɜː(r)/
2	ɪ	as in	**sit** /sɪt/	12	ə	as in	**ago** /ə'gəʊ/
3	e	as in	**ten** /ten/	13	eɪ	as in	**page** /peɪdʒ/
4	æ	as in	**hat** /hæt/	14	əʊ	as in	**home** /həʊm/
5	ɑː	as in	**arm** /ɑːm/	15	aɪ	as in	**five** /faɪv/
6	ɒ	as in	**got** /gɒt/	16	aʊ	as in	**now** /naʊ/
7	ɔː	as in	**saw** /sɔː/	17	ɔɪ	as in	**join** /dʒɔɪn/
8	ʊ	as in	**put** /pʊt/	18	ɪə	as in	**near** /nɪə(r)/
9	uː	as in	**too** /tuː/	19	eə	as in	**hair** /heə(r)/
10	ʌ	as in	**cup** /kʌp/	20	ʊə	as in	**pure** /pjʊə(r)/

Consonants 辅音

1	p	as in	**pen** /pen/	13	s	as in	**so** /səʊ/
2	b	as in	**bad** /bæd/	14	z	as in	**zoo** /zuː/
3	t	as in	**tea** /tiː/	15	ʃ	as in	**she** /ʃiː/
4	d	as in	**did** /dɪd/	16	ʒ	as in	**vision** /'vɪʒn/
5	k	as in	**cat** /kæt/	17	h	as in	**how** /haʊ/
6	g	as in	**got** /gɒt/	18	m	as in	**man** /mæn/
7	tʃ	as in	**chin** /tʃɪn/	19	n	as in	**no** /nəʊ/
8	dʒ	as in	**June** /dʒuːn/	20	ŋ	as in	**sing** /sɪŋ/
9	f	as in	**fall** /fɔːl/	21	l	as in	**leg** /leg/
10	v	as in	**voice** /vɔɪs/	22	r	as in	**red** /red/
11	θ	as in	**thin** /θɪn/	23	j	as in	**yes** /jes/
12	ð	as in	**then** /ðen/	24	w	as in	**wet** /wet/

Abbreviations Used in the Text 本词典略语表

Abbreviation 略语	Meaning 字义	Example 例子
adj.	adjective — a word that tells you what a noun is like 形容词	big 大的 An elephant is a *big* animal. 象是体形庞大的动物。
adv.	adverb — a word that tells you how, when or where something is done 副词	quickly 快速地 The children walked *quickly* to school. 孩子们急步向学校走去。
art.	article — word before a person or thing 冠词	the 那；这 The dinner is on *the* table. 晚饭就放在这桌子上。
conj.	conjunction — a word that joins two other words 连词	and 和 Peter likes chicken *and* fish. 彼得喜欢吃鸡和鱼。
int.	interjection — a word that you use as an exclamation 感叹词	oh! 噢! *Oh!* I've lost my purse! 噢！我丢了钱包!
n.	noun — a word that is the name of a thing 名词	cat 猫 The *cat* caught a mouse. 那猫儿抓了一只老鼠。
prep.	preposition — a word that is used before a noun to show where, when or how 介词	under 在下面 Peter sat *under* the tree. 彼得坐在那棵树下。
pron.	pronoun — a word that is used instead of a noun 代词	she 她 Where is Mary? *She* is late. 玛丽在哪里？她迟到了。
v.	verb — a word that tells you what someone or something is or is doing 动词	run 跑 Sally *ran* to school. 萨莉奔向学校。
opp.	opposite — a word that is entirely different from another word 反义词	\`above' and \`under'
syn.	synonym — a word that means almost the same thing as another word 同义词	\`above' and \`over'
p.t.	past tense 过去式	ate p.t. of eat eat的过去式
p.p.	past participle 过去分词	been p.p. of be be的过去分词
pres.p.	present participle 现在分词	being pres.p. of be be的现在分词

Eight Parts of Speech 英语八大词类

adjective 形容词
adverb 副词
conjunction 连词
interjection 感叹词
noun 名词
preposition 介词
pronoun 代词
verb 动词

How to Use the Dictionary

本词典用法说明

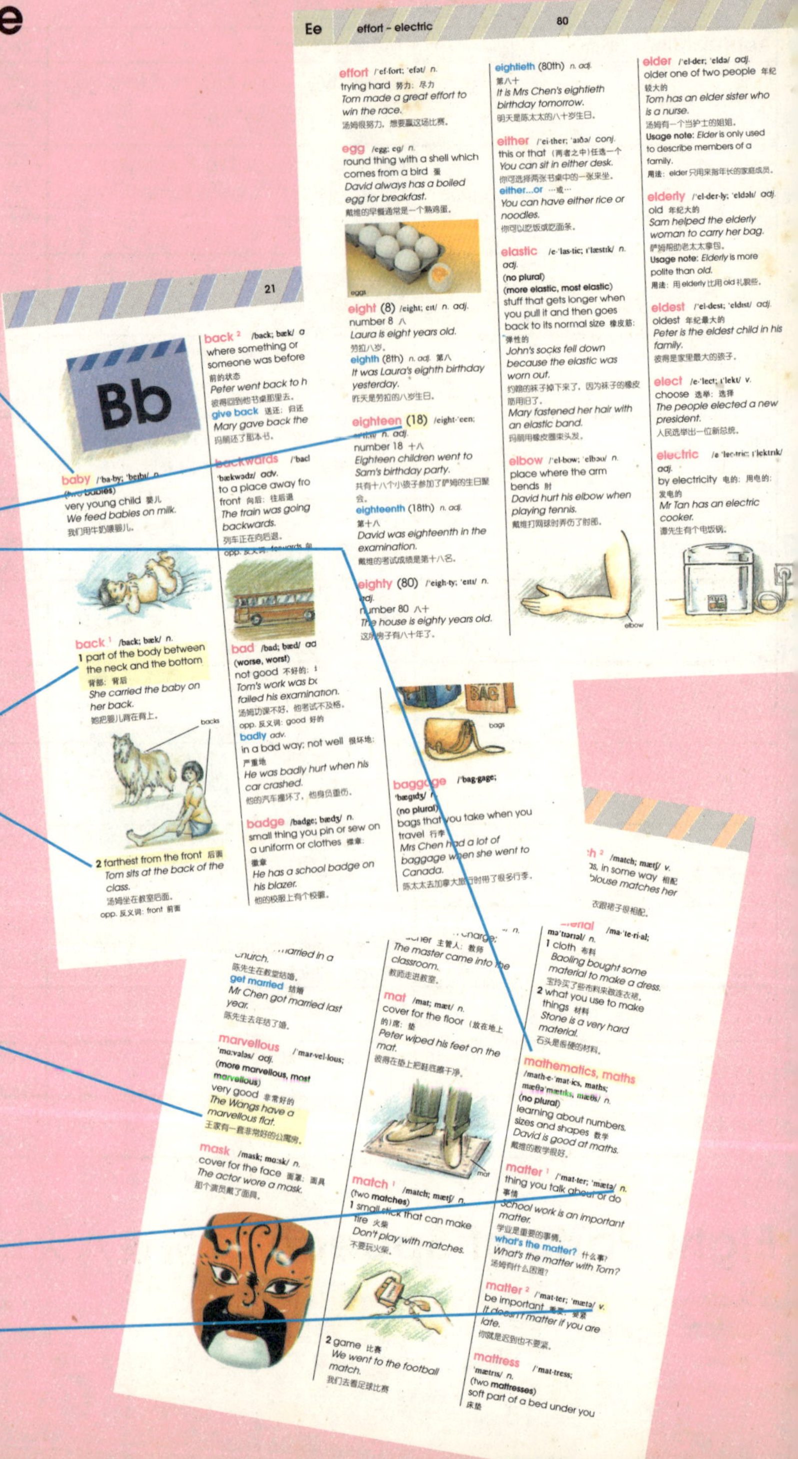

词目 ●以红色标示。编排方法是按词目的字母在字母表中的顺序排列先后；
●词目后的括号内为表示该词的符号或缩写；
●两个单词并列为一个词目，表示它们意思相同，可以通用。

解释 英汉对照；如词目的解释多于一个，则较常用的解释排在前面。

例句 英汉对照；题材生活化。

词类 词目和派生词后面均有列明所属的所有词类。如一词作不同词类使用时用法有明显分别，则按其词类分列为若干独立词条。

各种词类的不规则变化　列出名词复数、形容词及副词的比较级及动词时态的不规则变化。

用法　英汉对照，并附例句；内容包括语法资料(如介词、冠词的运用)，词语的习惯用法、特殊解释及使用等等。

插图　附精美彩图及照片，有助学生理解词义。

读音　“/　/”号内为读音资料。前半部分把词目字母按读音的音节划分，用圆点断开，重音节前注有“ˈ”号；后半部分采用国际音标(IPA)注音。

短语、习语、复合词和派生词附汉语翻译及英汉对照例句。

同义词，反义词　反义词附汉语翻译。

Aa

a, an /a, an; ə, ən/ *art.*
(**a** banana, **some** bananas)
1 one 一个
I ate a banana and an apple.
我吃了一只香蕉和一个苹果。
2 every 每一
We eat three meals a day.
我们每天吃三顿饭。
Usage note: You should use *an* before words beginning with a vowel sound, such as *a, e, i, o* or *u*.
用法：以 a、e、i、o 或 u 等元音音素开头的词，前面要用 an。

abacus /'a·ba·cus; 'æbəkəs/ *n.*
(two **abacuses**)
wood and metal thing with beads for counting and arithmetic 算盘
He added up the bill on an abacus.
他用算盘把账单里的各项价目加起来。

abbreviation
/ab·bre·vi·'a·tion; əbri:vɪ'eɪʃn/ *n.*
short way of writing a word
缩写
Mon. is an abbreviation for Monday.
Mon. 是 Monday 的缩写。

able /'a·ble; 'eɪbl/ *adj.*
can do something 能够；会
She is able to read and write.
她会看书和写字。
opp. 反义词：unable 不能够；不会
ability *n.* 能力
He has the ability to pass his examinations.
他有能力通过考试。

aboard /a·'board; ə'bɔ:d/ *adv. prep.*
on or onto a boat or plane
上(船或飞机)；在(船或飞机)上
He went aboard the ship.
他上了船。
There are twenty men aboard.
船上共有二十人。

about [1] /a·'bout; ə'baut/ *adv.*
1 near 差不多；大约
I have about a hundred dollars.
我大约有一百港元。
2 in different places; here and there 到处；在…各处
John leaves his clothes lying about.
约翰把他的衣服到处放。

about [2] /a·'bout; ə'baut/ *prep.*
of 关于
I saw a film about cowboys.
我看了一部关于牛仔的电影。
Usage note: You can use *on* in the same way as *about* — *Sam read a book about China. Sam read a book on China.*
用法：有些句子里，about 和 on 可以互相通用，例如 Sam read a book about China 也可以写成 Sam read a book on China。

above /a·'bove; ə'bʌv/ *prep.*
over; higher than 在…之上；高于
An aeroplane flew above the city.
一架飞机在这城市上空飞。
syn. 同义词：over
opp. 反义词：under, below 下面；在…之下
Usage note: You can use *over* in the same way as *above* — *The bedroom is above the kitchen. The bedroom is over the kitchen.*
用法：有些句子里，over 和 above 可以互相通用，例如 The bedroom is above the kitchen 也可以写成 The bedroom is over the kitchen。

abroad /a·'broad; ə'brɔ:d/ *adv.*
to or in another country
去外国；在外国
Peter goes abroad for his holidays.
彼得去外国度假。

absent /'ab·sent; 'æbsənt/ *adj.*
not here 不在场；缺席
Baoling was absent from school.
宝玲没有上学。

syn. 同义词：away
opp. 相反词：present 在场

absence *n.* 不在；没有来
The teacher noticed Baoling's absence.
老师注意到宝玲没有到。

accept /ac·'cept; ək'sept/ *v.*
take something that someone gives you 接受
Mrs Chen accepted the present.
陈太太接受了礼物。

accident /'ac·ci·dent; 'æksɪdənt/ *n.*
bad things that happen by chance 意外；事故
David was hurt in a road accident.
戴维在一次交通事故中受伤。

according to /ac·'cor·ding to; ə'kɔːdɪŋ tuː/ *prep.*
from what is said 根据
According to the weather forecast, it is going to rain.
根据天气预报，今天会有雨。

accurate /'ac·cu·rate; 'ækjərət/ *adj.*
(more accurate, most accurate)
right; correct 准确的；正确的
This watch is always accurate.
这块手表永远走得很准确。
opp. 反义词：wrong 错误的

accuse /ac·'cuse; ə'kjuːz/ *v.*
(accusing, accused, accused)
say that someone has done something wrong 指责；控告
Mrs Brown accused Peter of breaking the window.
布朗太太指责彼得打破了玻璃窗。

ache /ache; eɪk/ *v.*
(aching, ached, ached)
gives you a pain 痛
My head aches.
我头痛。

achieve /a·'chieve; ə'tʃiːv/ *v.*
(achieving, achieved, achieved)
do well; get something by hard work 获得；取得；达到
The children achieved good results in the exams.
孩子们在考试中取得良好的成绩。

achievement *n.* 成就；成绩
Climbing the mountain is a great achievement.
登上那座山是一项重大的成就。

across /a·'cross; ə'krɒs/ *adv. prep.*
1 on the other side of 在…的另一边
The cinema is across the road.
电影院在马路的另一边。
2 from one side to the other 横过；横渡
He swam across the river.
他游到河的对岸。

across 2

act /act; ækt/ *v.*
1 take a part in a play or a film 扮演
Peter acted in the play.
彼得在戏剧中扮演一个角色。

2 do something 行动
The firemen acted quickly and put out the fire.
消防员很快地行动起来，把火扑灭。

action /'ac·tion; 'ækʃn/ *n.*
doing something 动作；行动；行为
Their brave action saved the girl from the fire.
他们勇敢的行动把女孩从大火中救出。

active /'ac·tive; 'æktɪv/ *adj.*
(more active, most active)
moving around a lot 活跃
Mr Chen is very active.
陈先生非常活跃。

activity /ac·'tiv·i·ty; æk'tɪvətɪ/ *n.*
(two **activities**)
something you do 活动
Xiaofang's favourite activity is swimming.
小芳最喜爱的活动是游泳。

actor /'ac·tor; 'æktə/ *n.*
someone who acts in a play or film 男演员
Peter was the best actor in the play.
彼得是这出戏剧中最好的男演员。

actress /'ac·tress; 'æktrɪs/ *n.*
(two **actresses**)
woman or girl who acts in a play or film 女演员
She was the best actress in the film.
她是这部电影中最好的女演员。

add /add; æd/ *v.*
1 put numbers together to make a bigger number 加起来
If you add 2 and 3 you get 5.
如果把2和3加起来，就等于5。

2 put one thing with another 加进去
He added more salt to the soup.
他在汤里面多放了些盐。

add up *v.* 加起来
The waiter added up the bill.
服务员把账单里的各项价目加起来。

addition *n.*
adding one thing to another 加

address /ad·'dress; ə'dres/ *n.*
(two **addresses**)
number and name of the place where you live 地址
Peter's address is 2 Ming Court.
彼得的地址是明阁2号。

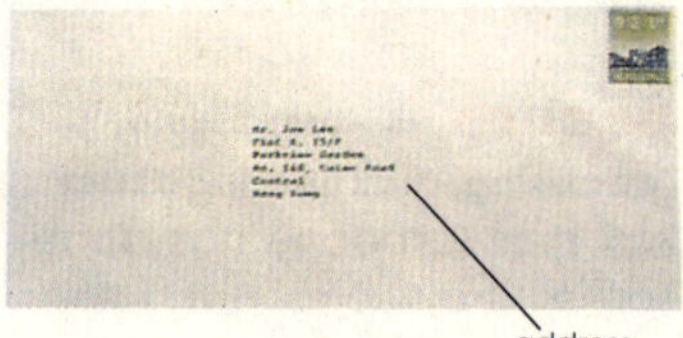
address

adjective /'ad·jec·tive; 'ædʒɪktɪv/ *n.*
word that tells you about someone or something 形容词
The words 'small' and 'happy' are adjectives.
small和happy都是形容词。

admire /ad·'mire; əd'maɪə/ *v.*
(**admiring, admired, admired**)
to think a person or thing is very good 赞赏；羡慕
Peter admired John's bicycle.
彼得羡慕约翰的自行车。

admit /ad·'mit; əd'mɪt/ *v.*
(**admitting, admitted, admitted**)
agree with something bad about yourslf 承认
John admitted that he broke the window.
约翰承认是他打破了玻璃窗。

adult /'a·dult; 'ædʌlt/ *n.*
person who is grown up 成年人
The tickets are $2 for adults and $1 for children.
成年人票价二港元，儿童一港元。
opp. 反义词：child 儿童

adventure /ad·'ven·ture; əd'ventʃə/ *n.*
exciting thing that you do 奇遇；冒险的经历
Our camping holiday was a great adventure.
我们的假日露营充满了惊险和刺激。

adverb /'ad·verb; 'ædvɜːb/ *n.*
word that tells you how, when or where 副词
The words 'quickly', 'now' and 'here' are adverbs.
quickly, now和here都是副词。

advertise /'ad·ver·tise; 'ædvətaɪz/ *v.*
(**advertising, advertised, advertised**)
tell people about something to buy 登广告
Mr Li advertised his car in the newspaper.
李先生在报纸上登广告卖他的汽车。

advertisement *n.*
something that tells you about things to buy 广告
You see advertisements on TV and in newspapers.
你在电视和报纸上都可以看到广告。

advice /ad·'vice; əd'vaɪs/ *n.*
(**no plural**)
something that tells you what you should do 劝告
David listened to the teacher's advice and worked harder.
戴维听从老师的劝告，努力学习。

advise /ad·'vise; əd'vaɪz/ *v.* **(advising, advised, advised)**
tell someone what they should do 劝告
The teacher advised David to work harder.
老师劝告戴维要努力学习。

aeroplane /'aer·o·plane; 'eərəpleɪn/ *n.*
machine that flies 飞机
We went by aeroplane to Canada.
我们乘飞机去加拿大。

affect /af·'fect; ə'fekt/ *v.*
make a difference to 影响
Mary's illness affected her work.
玛丽的病影响了她的功课。

afford /af·'ford; ə'fɔːd/ *v.*
have enough money to pay for something 负担得起
Tom could not afford to go to the cinema.
汤姆没有足够的钱去看电影。

afraid /a·'fraid; ə'freɪd/ *adj.*
having fear of something 害怕
Xiaofang is afraid of snakes.
小芳怕蛇。
syn. 同义词: frightened, scared
Usage note: *afraid* is usually followed by *of* — *Sam is afraid of snakes.*
用法: afraid 后面通常用 of, 例如 Sam is afraid of snakes.

after /'af·ter; 'ɑːftə/ *prep.*
1 later than something 在…之后
We play football after school.
我们上完课之后去踢足球。
2 in a place behind something 在…后面
In the alphabet, 'y' comes after 'x'.
在字母表里，y 在 x 之后。
opp. 反义词: before 在…之前; 在…前面

afternoon /af·ter·'noon; ɑːftə'nuːn/ *n.*
the time between midday and evening 下午
What shall we do this afternoon?
我们今天下午做什么?
syn. 同义词: p.m.
opp. 反义词: a.m., morning 上午; 早上

afterwards /'af·ter·wards; 'ɑːftəwədz/ *adv.*
later 后来; (时间) 在…之后
Peter finished his homework and went out to play afterwards.
彼得做完了家庭作业，然后出去玩。

again /a·'gain; ə'gen/ *adv.*
once more 再次
The sum is not right. Please do it again.
总数不对，请你再做一遍。

against /a·'gainst; ə'genst/ *prep.*
1 next to; upon 靠着
He put the ladder against the wall.
他把梯子靠着墙放好。
2 the other side from someone in sport or a fight (在体育比赛或打斗中) 对…
Our school plays football against other schools.
我们学校和别的学校比赛足球。

age /age; eɪdʒ/ *n.*
how old someone or something is 年龄; 年纪
John is 12 years of age.
约翰十二岁。
aged *adj.* 年龄是…岁
The children in the class are all aged eight.
这一班的小孩年龄都是八岁。
old age *n.* 年纪很大
My grandmother lived to an old age.
我的祖母活到很大年纪。

ago /a·'go; ə'gəʊ/ *adv.*
time before now 以前
Baoling left school a year ago.
宝玲一年以前离开了学校。

agree /a·'gree; ə'griː/ *v.* **(agreeing, agreed, agreed)**
think like someone else 同意
I agree with you.
我同意你的意见。
opp. 反义词: disagree 不同意

ahead /a·'head; ə'hed/ *adv.*
in front 在前面
David finished the race ahead of Peter.
戴维到达终点时，跑在彼得的前面。
opp. 反义词：behind 在后面

air /air; eə/ *n.*
(**no plural**)
1 what we breathe 空气
Let's go out for some fresh air.
我们到外面去呼吸点新鲜空气吧。

2 sky 天空
The bird flew in the air.
鸟儿在天空中飞翔。
by air 乘飞机
Tom went to America by air.
汤姆乘飞机去美国。

air-conditioner
/'air·con·di·tioner; 'eəkəndɪʃənə/ *n.*
machine for cooling or warming air （冷暖）空调
This room is hot. Switch on the air-conditioner.
房间很热，把空调打开吧。

aircraft /'air·craft; 'eəkrɑ:ft/ *n.*
(two **aircraft**)
machine that has wings and can fly 飞机
Three aircraft flew over us.
三架飞机在我们上空飞过。

airline /'air·line; 'eəlaɪn/ *n.*
company which runs a plane service 航空公司
Hong Kong has many airlines.
香港有很多家航空公司。

airmail [1] /'air·mail; 'eəmeɪl/ *n.*
(**no plural**)
letters and parcels sent by aeroplane 航空邮件
It is quicker to send a letter by airmail.
寄航空信会快一点。

airmail [2] /'air·mail; 'eəmeɪl/ *adj.*
carried by aeroplane 航空邮寄的
Peter got an airmail letter from Canada.
彼得收到了一封加拿大寄来的航空信。

airport /'air·port; 'eəpɔ:t/ *n.*
place where aeroplanes land and take off 飞机场
We went to the airport to catch a plane.
我们到机场去赶搭一班飞机。

alarm /a·'larm; ə'lɑ:m/ *n.*
noisy machine or a sound that warns you about danger
警钟；警报
When the alarm rang, the children left the building.
警钟响了起来，孩子们立即离开那座建筑物。
alarm clock *n.* 闹钟
Mary set the alarm clock for six o'clock.
玛丽把闹钟拨到六时。

album /'al·bum; 'ælbəm/ *n.*
book for photographs or stamps 相片簿；集邮簿
Susan put some new stamps in her album.
苏珊把一些新邮票贴在集邮簿里。

alike /a·'like; ə'laɪk/ *adj.* *adv.*
almost the same 相似；差不多一样
Twins often look alike.
双胞胎的相貌常常很相似。
opp. 反义词：different 不一样；不同
Usage note: You cannot use *alike* before a noun.
用法：alike 不能用在名词之前。

alive /a·'live; ə'laɪv/ *adj.*
living 活着的；健在的
All my grandparents are alive.
我的祖父母和外祖父母都健在。
opp. 反义词：dead 已死的
Usage note: You cannot use *alive* before a noun.
用法：alive 不能用在名词之前。

all /all; ɔ:l/ *pron.* *adj.* *adv.*
1 everyone 人人；所有的人
They all went to school.
他们全都上学去了。
2 the whole 全部
We ate all the rice.
我们把饭全都吃光了。
opp. 反义词：none 一个也没有
all over 到处都是
There was rubbish all over the beach.
海滩上到处都是垃圾。
all round 走遍了
The tourists went all round Hong Kong.
游客们走遍了香港各处。

all right /all·'right; ɔ:l 'raɪt/ *int.* *adj.*
1 yes, I agree 好吧
All right, you can go.
好吧，你可以走了。
2 safe; not hurt 安然无恙的；还好
He fell, but he was all right.
他掉了下来，不过还好(没有受伤)。

allow /al·'low; ə'laʊ/ *v.*
say that someone can have or do something 准许；允许
My parents allowed me to go to the birthday party.
我的父母准许我参加生日聚会。

almost /'al·most; 'ɔ:lməʊst/ *adv.*
nearly 差不多；几乎
Baoling almost had an accident.
宝玲差点儿出了意外。

alone /a·'lone; ə'ləʊn/ *adj.*
without anyone 单独；独自
Xiaofang never goes out alone at night.
小芳晚上从来不单独外出。
Usage note: *Alone* is not always the same as *lonely*. *Alone* does not suggest unhappiness, while *lonely* suggests that someone does not want to be alone and is unhappy. *Alone* is not used before a noun.
用法：alone 和 lonely 的意思有些不同：alone 没有"不开心"的意思；lonely 则表示不愿意独自一人，有"不开心"的意味。alone 不能用在名词的前面。

along /a·'long; ə'lɒŋ/ *prep.*
from one end of a place towards the other 沿着
He walked along the road.
他沿着路走。

along

aloud /a·'loud; ə'laʊd/ *adv.*
so that people can hear 高声地
Baoling read the story aloud.
宝玲朗诵这个故事。
opp. 反义词：silently 不作声地；静默地

alphabet /'al·pha·bet; 'ælfəbet/ *n.*
all the letters used to write a language 字母
We are learning the English alphabet.
我们在学英语字母。
alphabetical *adj.* 按字母顺序的
A dictionary has words in alphabetical order.
词典里的词都按字母的次序排列。

already /al·'read·y; ɔ:l'redɪ/ *adv.*
before now 已经
The train has already left.
火车已经开走了。

also /'al·so; 'ɔ:lsəʊ/ adv.
too; as well 也；又；亦
Peter speaks Chinese. He also speaks English.
彼得会说汉语，也会说英语。

although /al·'though; ɔ:l'ðəʊ/ conj.
word you use when you are starting to say something different 虽然；虽则
Although he was clever, he failed the test.
虽然他聪明，但是测验却不及格。
syn. 同义词：though

altogether /al·to·'geth·er; ɔ:ltə'geðə/ adv.
with everyone or everything 全部；总共
Altogether I have sixty books.
我一共有六十本书。

always /'al·ways; 'ɔ:lweɪz/ adv.
at all times 经常；永远；总是
I always wear a seat-belt in a car.
我坐汽车时总是扣上安全带。
opp. 反义词：never 永不；绝不

a.m. /a·'m; eɪ'em/
in the morning; before midday 上午
I get up at 7 a.m.
我上午七时起床。

am /am; əm/ v.
1st person singular present tense of **be** be 的第一人称单数现在式
I am a Primary 6 student.
我是小学六年级的学生。

ambulance /'am·bu·lance; 'æmbjʊləns/ n.
special van for sick or injured people 救护车
The ambulance took the injured man to hospital.
救护车把受伤的人送去医院。

America /A·'mer·i·ca; ə'merɪkə/ n.
the United States of America 美国
They had their summer holiday in America.
他们在美国度过了暑假。
American adj. n. 美国的；美国人
Sam has an American friend.
萨姆有一个美国朋友。

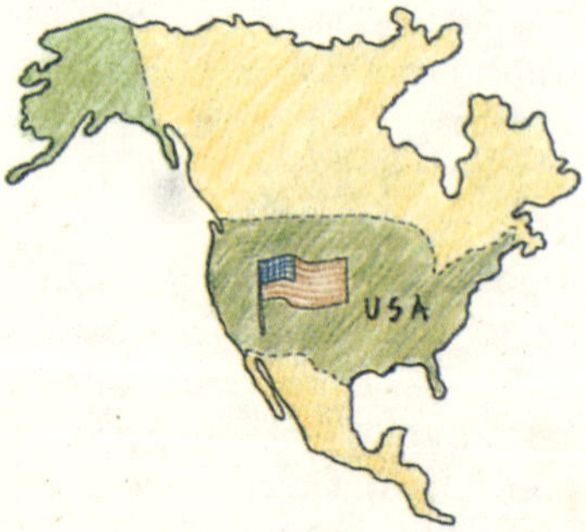

among /a·'mong; ə'mʌŋ/ prep.
in the middle of 在…中间
The park was among a lot of tall buildings.
公园位于许多高楼大厦中间。
Usage note: You should use *among* for groups — *Sam shared his sweets among the class.* For people and things who are not a group, use *between — She divided the sweets between her three children.*
用法：among 用于一群的人或物之间，例如 Sam shared his sweets among the class。在各自独立的人或物之间则用 between，例如 She divided the sweets between her three children。

amount /a·'mount; ə'maʊnt/ n.
how much there is 数量
David only had a small amount of money.
戴维只有很少的钱。

amuse /a·'muse; ə'mju:z/ v.
(amusing, amused, amused)
make someone laugh or smile 使人发笑；使…开心
He amused the children with his stories.
他给孩子们说故事，逗他们开心。
amusing adj. 使人发笑的；有趣的
His amusing stories made the children laugh.
他那些有趣的故事使孩子们大笑。

ancestor /'an·ces·tor; 'ænsestə/ n.
someone who was in the family a long time ago 祖先；先人
Baoling's ancestors lived in Guangzhou.
宝玲的祖先住在广州。

ancient /'an·cient; 'eɪnʃənt/ adj.
(more ancient, most ancient)
very old 古代的
They found an ancient tomb at Xi'an.
他们在西安发现了一座古墓。
opp. 反义词：modern 现代的

and /and; ənd/ *conj.*
word that joins two other words 和；及；与
Peter likes chicken and rice.
彼得喜欢吃鸡和饭。
Usage note: You can use *and* instead of *to* after some verbs — *Come and see my new bike. Go and find Tom.*
用法：有些句子里，and 可以用来代替 to, 例如 Come and see my new bike 和 Go and find Tom。

angle /'an·gle; 'æŋgl/ *n.*
corner 角
David measured the angles of the triangle.
戴维量那三角形三只角的度数。

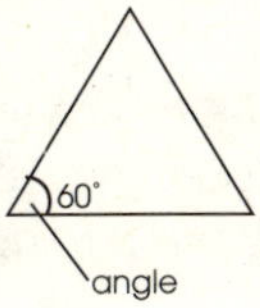

angry /'an·gry; 'æŋgrı/ *adj.*
(angrier, angriest)
very unhappy 生气；愤怒
He was angry when his bicycle was stolen.
他的自行车被偷走了，他非常生气。
opp. 反义词：happy 高兴；快乐
angry at 对…生气
Mr Tan gets angry at the traffic in Hong Kong.
谭先生因香港的交通情况而生气。
angry with 对(…人)生气或恼火
The teacher never gets angry with the children.
老师绝对不会对孩子们生气。
anger *n.* 愤怒
angrily *adv.* 愤怒地

animal /'an·i·mal; 'ænıml/ *n.*
living creature 动物；兽类
A wolf is a wild animal.
狼是一种野生动物。

animals

ankle /'an·kle; 'æŋkl/ *n.*
the part between the foot and the leg 足踝
John hurt his ankle while playing football.
约翰踢足球的时候把足踝扭伤了。

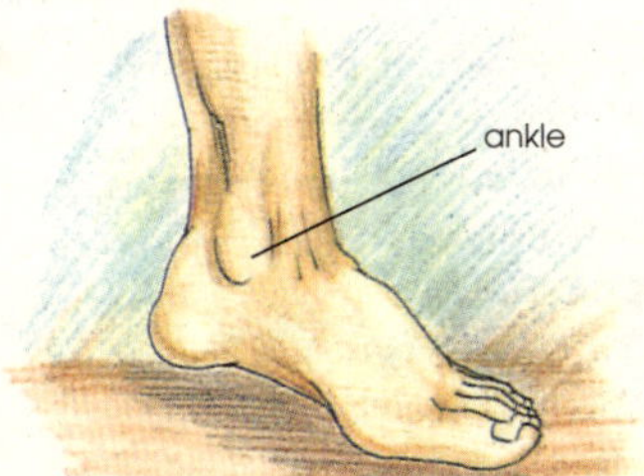

annoy /an·'noy; ə'nɔı/ *v.*
make someone angry 使人烦恼；使人生气
A loud radio annoyed the people on the beach.
海滩上收音机的声音放得太大，使人厌烦。
annoying *adj.* 使人烦恼的；使人生气的
The loud noise was annoying.
大声吵闹使人厌烦。

annual /'an·nu·al; 'ænjuəl/ *adj.*
every year 每年的
The Dragon Boat Festival is an annual event in Hong Kong.
在香港，端午节是一年一度的盛事。
annually *adv.* 每年地
He goes to Shanghai annually.
他每年都去上海。

another /an·'oth·er; ə'nʌðə/ *adj.*
1 one more 再一个
Would you like another cake?
再吃一块蛋糕好么？
2 a different one 另一个
I don't like black. Have you another colour?
我不喜欢黑色。有另一种颜色的没有？

answer [1] /'an·swer; 'ɑːnsə/ *n.*
something you say in reply 答案；答复
John knew the answer to the question.
约翰知道这问题的答案。
syn. 同义词：reply
opp. 反义词：question 问题

answer [2] /'an·swer; 'ɑːnsə/ *v.*
to say something in reply 回答；回复
John answered the question.
约翰回答了这个问题。
opp. 反义词：ask 问

ant /ant; ænt/ *n.*
small insect 蚂蚁
The grass was full of ants.
草地上到处都是蚂蚁。

ants

any /'an·y; 'enɪ/ *adj. pron. adv.*
one; some 任何一个；一些
Peter hasn't any money.
彼得一点儿钱也没有。
any longer; any more
再长一点(多指时间)；再多一点
It's late. We can't stay any longer.
已经很晚了，我们不能再待着不走了。
Usage note: You can use *any* in questions — *Have you any sweets?* You can also use *any* to answer *no* — *I haven't any sweets.* Use *some* to answer *yes* — *I have some sweets.*
用法：any 可用于问句中，例如 Have you any sweets? any 也可用于否定句中，例如 I haven't any sweets。在肯定句中要用 some，例如 I have some sweets。

anybody, anyone
/'an·y·bo·dy, 'an·y·one; 'enɪbɒdɪ, 'enɪwʌn/ *pron.*
any person 任何人
Do you know anybody who lives in Shatin?
你认识住在沙田的人吗？
opp. 反义词：nobody, no one 没有人

anything /'an·y·thing; 'enɪθɪŋ/ *pron.*
any thing; something 任何东西；一些东西
Is there anything to eat?
有什么东西吃吗？
opp. 反义词：nothing 没有什么东西

anyway /'an·y·way; 'enɪweɪ/ *adv.*
in any case 不管怎样；无论如何
I can't come out. Anyway, it's late.
我不能出来。不管怎样，也太晚了。

anywhere /'an·y·where; 'enɪweə/ *adv.*
at, in or to any place
在任何地方
I didn't go anywhere yesterday.
昨天我什么地方也没有去。
opp. 反义词：nowhere 没有地方

apartment /a·'part·ment; ə'pɑ:tmənt/ *n.*
home on one floor of a building 一套公寓房
The Wang family have a big apartment.
王家住的公寓房面积很大。
syn. 同义词：flat

ape /ape; eɪp/ *n.*
large monkey 猿
We saw an ape in the zoo.
我们在动物园里看到一只猿。

apologize, apologise
/a·'pol·o·gize, a·'pol·o·gise; ə'pɒlədʒaɪz, ə'pɒlədʒaɪz/ *v.*
(**apologizing, apologized, apologized**)
say you are sorry 道歉
Susan apologized for being late.
苏珊因为迟到而道歉。

appear /ap·'pear; ə'pɪə/ *v.*
1 come so that you can see it 出现
A rainbow appeared after the rain.
雨后天空出现了一道彩虹。
opp. 反义词：disappear 消失；失踪
2 seem to be 看来好像；似乎
That child appears to be lost.
那小孩看来是不见了。
appearance *n.* 外表
His appearance is very untidy.
他的外表很不整洁。

apple /'ap·ple; 'æpl/ *n.*
round red or green fruit 苹果
He was eating an apple.
他在吃苹果。

April /'A·pril; 'eɪprəl/ *n.*
fourth month of the year 四月
It often rains in April.
四月经常下雨。

apron /'a·pron; 'eɪprən/ *n.*
cloth you wear to keep your front clean 围裙
Mary wears an apron when she is cooking.
玛丽烧饭时总是穿上围裙。

arch /arch; ɑ:tʃ/ *n.*
(two **arches**)
curved part in a building 拱门
The building has an arch at the front.
这座建筑物的正面有一道拱门。

arch

architect /'ar·chi·tect; 'ɑ:kɪtekt/ *n.*
person who designs buildings 建筑师
The architect designed the new building.
建筑师设计这座新建筑。

are /are; ɑ:/ *v.*
present tense plural of **be**
be 的复数现在式
We are students.
我们是学生。
opp. 反义词: are not, aren't 不是

area /'a·re·a; 'eərɪə/ *n.*
part of a town, place, or country 地区；区域
The school is in a quiet area of the town.
学校位于城里一处幽静的地区。

aren't /aren't; ɑ:nt/ *v.*
are not 即 are not
They aren't here.
他们不在这里。

argue /'ar·gue; 'ɑ:gju:/ *v.*
(**arguing, argued, argued**)
talk angrily with a person because you think they are wrong 争论
We argued with the waiter about the bill.
我们与服务员为账单而争论起来。

argument *n.* 争论；辩论
He had an argument with his teacher.
他与老师争论起来。

arithmetic /a·'rith·me·tic; ə'rɪθmətɪk/ *n.*
(**no plural**)
work with numbers 算术
Peter is good at arithmetic.
彼得的算术很好。

arm /arm; ɑ:m/ *n.*
the part of the body from the shoulder to the hand 手臂
He carried his newspaper under his arm.
他把报纸夹在手臂下。

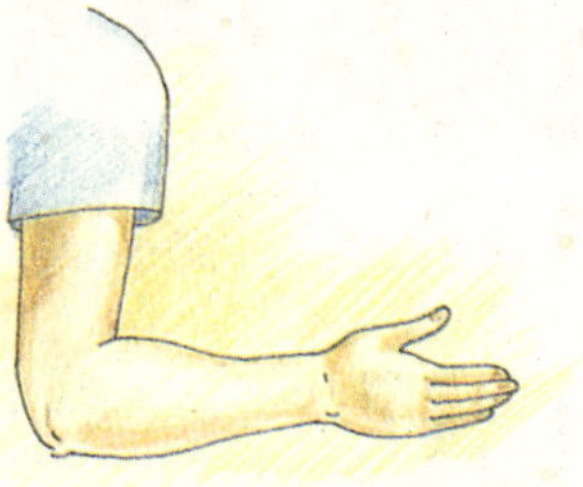

armchair *n.* 扶手椅
I sit in an armchair to read.
我坐在一张扶手椅上看书。

army /'ar·my; 'ɑ:mɪ/ *n.*
(two **armies**)
people in uniform (who fight on land) 军队；陆军
The army needed soldiers.
陆军需要士兵。

army

around /a·'round; ə'raʊnd/ *adv.*
1 round someone or something 四周；围绕着
There are flowers around the house.
房子四周都是花。

2 here and there 到处都是
There was paper all around the classroom.
教室里到处都是纸张。

arrange /ar·'range; ə'reɪndʒ/ *v.*
(**arranging, arranged, arranged**)
1 put things somewhere neatly 排列整齐；摆放好
Xiaofang arranged the furniture.
小芳把家具摆放好。
2 make a plan 安排；计划
I arranged to meet Peter at the cinema.
我安排好了在电影院和彼得见面。

arrest[1] /ar·'rest; ə'rest/ *v.*
stop someone and make him a prisoner 拘捕
The policeman arrested the thief.
警察拘捕了那个小偷。

arrest[2] /ar·'rest; ə'rest/ *n.*
making someone a prisoner
拘捕(行动)
The policeman made an arrest.
警察作了一次拘捕行动。

arrive /ar·'rive; ə'raɪv/ *v.*
(arriving, arrived, arrived)
come to a place 到达
David arrived at school.
戴维来到学校。
syn. 同义词: reach
opp. 反义词: leave, depart 离开

arrow /'ar·row; 'ærəʊ/ *n.*
thin, sharp stick you shoot from a bow 箭
He shot an arrow at the target.
他向着靶射出一枝箭。

art /art; ɑːt/ *n.*
(no plural)
drawing, painting, etc. 艺术; 美术
Mr Chen loves art.
陈先生喜爱艺术。
artist *n.* 艺术家
Mr Chen is a good artist.
陈先生是个优秀的艺术家。

as /as; əz/ *conj. prep.*
1 while; when 当…的时候
He arrived as the bus was leaving.
正当公共汽车要开的时候，他赶到了。
2 because 因为
Peter can't go to school as he is ill.
彼得因为生病，不能上学。
as...as...
like; the same amount
和…一样
Peter is as tall as John.
彼得和约翰一样高。
as if, as though
like 好像
He behaves as if he were very important.
他的举止行动好像他是个大人物似的。
as well
too 也; 亦
as well as
also; and 也是; 和
He has a house as well as a flat.
他除了拥有一套公寓房外，还有一所房子。

Asia /'A·sia; 'eɪʃə/ *n.*
one of the seven continents
亚洲
Asia is a huge continent.
亚洲是个很大的大陆。
Asian *adj. n.* 亚洲的; 亚洲人
Mr Chen has visited several Asian countries.
陈先生到过几个亚洲国家。

ask /ask; ɑːsk/ *v.*
want to know why 问
He asked a lot of questions.
他问了许多问题。
opp. 反义词: answer 回答

ask for 要求; 请求; 要
He asked for an apple.
他要求吃个苹果。
ask to 邀请; 邀约
I asked Susan to come to dinner.
我邀请苏珊来吃饭。

asleep /a·'sleep; ə'sliːp/ *adj.*
sleeping 睡着了
The body is asleep.
婴儿睡着了。
opp. 反义词: awake 醒着的

assembly /as·'sem·bly; ə'semblɪ/ *n.*
meeting 集会
The school has an assembly every morning.
学校每天早上都有集会。

assistant /as·'sist·ant; ə'sɪstənt/ *n.*
1 someone who works in a shop 店员
The shop assistant was very polite.
那个店员非常有礼貌。
2 someone who helps another person in a job 助手
The manager has two assistants.
经理有两个助手。

astronaut /'as·tro·naut; 'æstrənɔ:t/ *n.*
person who travels in space 太空人；宇航员
The astronauts travelled to the moon.
宇航员飞向月球。

at /at; ət/ *prep.*
1 word that shows where 在(指地方)
She left her bag at school.
她把书包遗留在学校。
2 word that shows when 在(指时间)
We finish school at 4 o'clock.
我们四时下课。
3 towards something 向着…
He threw a stone at me.
他向我扔出一块石头。
at last 最后；终于
At last Peter finished his homework.
彼得终于做完功课了。
at once 立即；马上
Tom! Come here at once!
汤姆！马上来！

ate /at; ət/ *prep.*
p.t. of **eat** eat 的过去式
I ate the apples.
我吃了那些苹果。

athlete /'ath·lete; 'æθli:t/ *n.*
someone who runs, jumps, etc. 运动员
Tom is a good athlete.
汤姆是个运动健将。
athletics *n.* 体育运动
John likes athletics.
约翰喜爱体育运动。

atlas /'at·las; 'ætləs/ *n.*
(two **atlases**)
book of maps 地图
He looked for where the city was in an atlas.
他在地图上找那城市在哪里。

atlases

attack [1] /at·'tack; ə'tæk/ *n.*
starting to fight 攻击；进攻
There was an attack on the city.
那个城市受到了一次攻击。

attack [2] /at·'tack; ə'tæk/ *v.*
start fighting or hurting a person or country 攻击；进攻
The army attacked the city.
军队进攻那城市。

attempt [1] /at·'tempt; ə'tempt/ *v.*
try to do something 尝试；企图
He attempted to climb the mountain.
他尝试登上那座山。

attempt [2] /at·'tempt; ə'tempt/ *n.*
trying to do something 尝试；努力
They failed in all their attempts to climb the mountain.
他们攀登该山的一切尝试都失败了。

attention /at·'ten·tion; ə'tenʃn/ *n.*
(**no plural**)
looking and listening carefully and with interest 注意；留心
The animal caught his attention.
那只动物引起他注意。
pay attention 注意；留心
Students should pay attention in class.
学生在上课时应该留心听。

attractive /at·'trac·tive; ə'træktɪv/ *adj.*
(**more attractive, most attractive**)
nice to look at 有吸引力的；漂亮的
She is a very attractive girl.
她是个很漂亮的女孩子。

(12)

audience /'au·di·ence; 'ɔ:dɪəns/ *n.*
people who have come to see and hear a concert, a play, etc. 听众；观众
There was a large audience at the concert.
音乐会听众很多。

August /'Au·gust; 'ɔ:gəst/ *n.*
eighth month of the year
八月
The weather is hot in August.
八月天气很热。

aunt /aunt; ɑ:nt/ *n.*
sister of our father or mother
姑母；姨母；婶母；伯母；舅母；阿姨
I went to visit my aunt.
我去看我姑母。

author /'au·thor; 'ɔ:θə/ *n.*
someone who writes books, plays, etc. 作者；作家
Tom is the author of two books.
汤姆是两本书的作者。

automatic /au·to·'ma·tic; ɔ:tə'mætɪk/ *adj.*
that can work by itself 自动的
Mrs Chen has an automatic washing machine.
陈太太有一台自动洗衣机。

autumn /'au·tumn; 'ɔ:təm/ *n.*
third season of the year 秋天
The leaves fall from the trees in autumn.
秋天树叶都从树上落下来。

average /'av·er·age; 'ævərɪdʒ/ *adj.*
not big and not small; ordinary 平均的；中等的
Mary is of average height.
玛丽身材中等(不算高，也不矮)。

avoid /a·'void; ə'vɔɪd/ *v.*
keep away from someone or something you do not like
避开；躲开
David avoided the big hole on the pavement.
戴维避开了人行道上的大坑。

awake /a·'wake; ə'weɪk/ *adj.*
not sleeping 醒着的
Mary is always awake early in the morning.
玛丽早上总是醒得很早。
opp. 反义词：asleep 睡着的
Usage note: You cannot use *awake* before a noun.
用法： awake 不能用在名词之前。

away /a·'way; ə'weɪ/ *adv.*
1 not here 不在
Tom is away from school.
汤姆不在学校。
syn. 同义词：absent
2 from here; from there
离这里(或那里)
Guangzhou is not far away.
广州离这里不远。
give away 送给
Peter gave away his old toys.
彼得把旧玩具都送给别人。
go away 走开
The fierce dog would not go away.
那只凶猛的狗不肯走开。
throw away 扔掉
Don't throw away those old clothes. Give them to someone.
不要把旧衣服扔掉，送给别人吧。

awful /'aw·ful; 'ɔ:fl/ *adj.*
(**more awful, most awful**)
very bad 可怕的
There was an awful accident yesterday.
昨天发生了一件可怕的意外事故。

axe /axe; æks/ *n.*
tool for cutting wood 斧子
Tom cut the tree down with his axe.
汤姆用斧把树砍倒了。

Bb

baby /'ba·by; 'beɪbɪ/ *n.*
(two **babies**)
very young child 婴儿
We feed babies on milk.
我们用牛奶喂婴儿。

back [1] /back; bæk/ *n.*
1 part of the body between the neck and the bottom
背部；背后
She carried the baby on her back.
她把婴儿背在背上。

2 farthest from the front 后面
Tom sits at the back of the class.
汤姆坐在教室后面。
opp. 反义词：front 前面

back [2] /back; bæk/ *adv.*
where something or someone was before 回复到以前的状态
Peter went back to his desk.
彼得回到他书桌那里去。
give back 送还；归还
Mary gave back the book.
玛丽还了那本书。

backwards /'back·wards; 'bækwədz/ *adv.*
to a place away from the front 向后；往后退
The train was going backwards.
列车正在向后退。
opp. 反义词：forwards 向前

bad /bad; bæd/ *adj.*
(**worse, worst**)
not good 不好的；坏的
Tom's work was bad. He failed his examination.
汤姆功课不好，他考试不及格。
opp. 反义词：good 好的
badly *adv.*
in a bad way; not well 很坏地；严重地
He was badly hurt when his car crashed.
他的汽车撞坏了，他身负重伤。

badge /badge; bædʒ/ *n.*
small thing you pin or sew on a uniform or clothes 襟章；徽章
He has a school badge on his blazer.
他的校服上有个校徽。

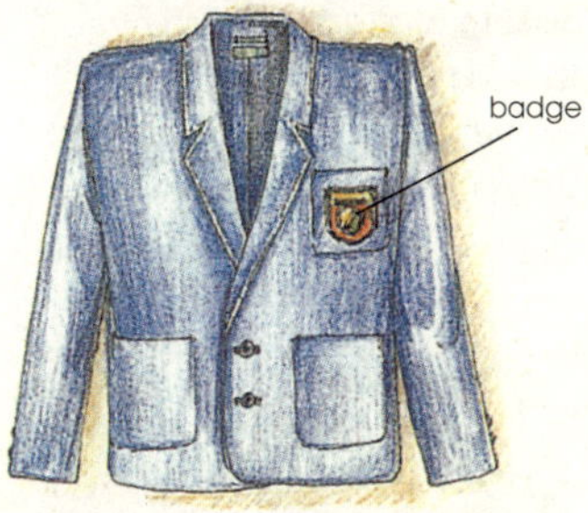

badminton /'bad·min·ton; 'bædmɪntən/ *n.*
(**no plural**)
game you play with rackets
羽毛球
Peter plays badminton.
彼得打羽毛球。

bag /bag; bæg/ *n.*
something for carrying things
袋；提袋；提包
He carries his things in a bag.
他把东西都放在一个袋子里带着。

baggage /'bag·gage; 'bægɪdʒ/ *n.*
(**no plural**)
bags that you take when you travel 行李
Mrs Chen had a lot of baggage when she went to Canada.
陈太太去加拿大旅行时带了很多行李。

bake /bake; beɪk/ *v.*
(**baking, baked, baked**)
cook in an oven 烤；烘
Mary baked a cake for Tom's birthday.
玛丽烘了一个蛋糕给汤姆为他祝贺生日。

baker *n.*
someone who makes bread and cakes 面包师傅；西点师傅

bakery *n.*
place where food, especially bread, is cooked in an oven
面包店；面包厂；西点店

balcony /ˈbal·co·ny; ˈbælkənɪ/ *n.*
(two **balconies**)
place outside a building above the ground 露台；阳台
The flat is small but it has a big balcony where we sit in the evening.
那套房间是小一点，但有个大阳台，每天傍晚我们总是在那里坐坐。

balconies

bald /bald; bɔːld/ *adj.*
with no hair on your head
秃头的
Mr Qian is bald.
钱先生是秃头的。

ball /ball; bɔːl/ *n.*
1 round thing you play games with 球
We could not play tennis because we did not have a ball.
我们没有球，不能打网球。

balls

2 dancing party 舞会
Cinderella went to the ball.
灰姑娘去参加舞会。

ballet /ˈbal·let; ˈbæleɪ/ *n.*
(**no plural**)
kind of dancing 芭蕾舞
Susan likes ballet.
苏珊喜欢芭蕾舞。

balloon /bal·ˈloon; bəˈluːn/ *n.*
light, round thing with air inside 气球
Mary blew up some balloons for her party.
玛丽为她的聚会吹好了一些气球。

balloons

ballpoint /ˈball·point; ˈbɔːlpɔɪnt/ *n.*
pen that has a small round end 圆珠笔；原子笔
Don't draw with a ballpoint pen. You can't rub it out.
不要用圆珠笔画画，擦不掉的。

bamboo /bam·ˈboo; bæmˈbuː/ *n.*
tall plant with long hard stems 竹；竹竿
They built a hut with bamboo and leaves.
他们用竹子和树叶筑了一间小屋。

bamboo shoot *n.* 竹笋
In the restaurant, Tom ordered a dish with bamboo shoots in it.
汤姆在餐馆里叫了一个有竹笋的菜。

banana /ba·'na·na; bə'nɑ:nə/ *n.*
long, yellow fruit 香蕉
The monkey was eating a banana.
猴子在吃香蕉。

bananas

band /band; bænd/ *n.*
1 group of people who play music together 乐队
Tom plays the piano in a band.
汤姆在一支乐队里弹钢琴。

2 thin, flat thing you put round things 带；布带
Mary put a rubber band round her hair.
玛丽用一只橡皮圈把头发束起来。

bandage /'band·age; 'bændɪdʒ/ *n.*
piece of cloth you tie round the part of your body that is hurt 绷带
When Peter cut his finger, I put a bandage on it.
彼得割破了手指，我用绷带把他的伤口包起来。

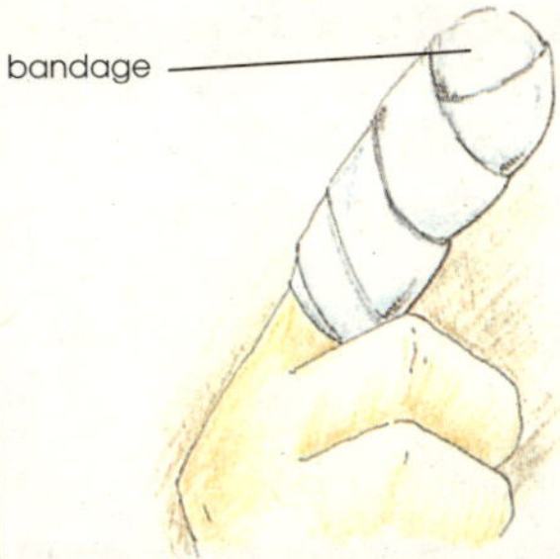

bang [1] /bang; bæŋ/ *v.*
hit something hard 用力敲打
The teacher banged on the table and we stopped talking.
老师用力敲打桌子，我们便不再讲话了。

bang [2] /bang; bæŋ/ *n.*
sudden, loud noise 砰然一声
The cars crashed with a loud bang.
砰的一声，两辆车撞在一起。

bank /bank; bæŋk/ *n.*
1 place where you can keep your money 银行
Mary has a thousand dollars in the bank.
玛丽有一千港元存在银行。

2 side of a river 河岸
John slipped down the bank into the river.
约翰从岸边溜下河里去了。

bar /bar; bɑ:/ *n.*
long piece of something hard 一条；一长块
Peter ate a bar of chocolate.
彼得吃了一块巧克力。

barbecue /'bar·be·cue; 'bɑ:bɪkju:/ *n.*
meal you cook over a fire outside 烧烤
In summer we often have a barbecue on the beach.
夏天的时候，我们常常去海滩烧烤。

barber /'bar·ber; 'bɑ:bə/ *n.*
someone who cuts men's hair 理发师
The barber cut Tom's hair very short.
理发师把汤姆的头发剪得很短。

bare /bare; beə/ *adj.*
(barer, barest)
with nothing on 光秃秃的
The island was bare rock.
那个岛是块光秃秃的大石头。
barefoot *adj.* 赤脚
The poor children were barefoot.
那些贫穷的孩子都赤着脚。

bargain [1] /'bar·gain; 'bɑ:gɪn/ *n.*
something that is cheap and good 便宜货
The car Mr Li bought was a bargain.
李先生买的车子是便宜货。

bargain [2] /ˈbar·gain; ˈbɑ:gɪn/ *v.*
try to get the best price when you are buying or selling something 讲价钱；讨价还价
When Susan goes to the market she always bargains.
苏珊去市场买东西时总要讨价还价。

bark [1] /bark; bɑ:k/ *n.*
1 outside part of a tree 树皮
If you take the bark off a tree it will die.
如果你把树皮剥掉，树就会死。
2 sound made by a dog 狗叫声
Our dog has a loud bark.
我们的狗叫的声音很大。

bark [2] /bark; bɑ:k/ *v.*
to make the sound of a dog 狗叫
A dog was barking last night. It woke me up.
昨天晚上一只狗在叫，把我吵醒了。

basket /ˈbas·ket; ˈbɑ:skɪt/ *n.*
hard bag made with thin sticks 篮子
Baoling put the fruit in a basket.
宝玲把水果放在篮子里。

basketball /ˈbas·ket·ball; ˈbɑ:skɪtbɔ:l/ *n.*
1 (**no plural**) game played by throwing a large ball into a high net 篮球运动
John plays basketball at school.
约翰在学校里打篮球。
2 the ball the game is played with 篮球
Laura threw the basketball to John.
劳拉把篮球抛给约翰。

bat /bat; bæt/ *n.*
1 small animal like a mouse with wings 蝙蝠
The bats flew out of the cave.
蝙蝠从山洞里飞出来。

2 piece of wood for hitting a ball 球拍；球棒
He hit the ball with his bat.
他用球拍击球。

bath [1] /bath; bɑ:θ/ *n.*
1 washing of the whole body 沐浴；洗澡
He takes a bath every morning.
他每天早上都洗澡。
2 thing you sit in to wash yourself 浴缸；浴盆
He filled the bath with hot water.
他把浴缸放满热水。

bathroom *n.* 浴室；洗澡间
Sam went to the bathroom to have a shower.
萨姆去浴室洗了个淋浴。

bath [2] /bath; bɑ:θ/ *v.*
take a bath or have a bath 洗澡
We should bath every day.
我们每天都应该洗澡。

bathe /bathe; beɪð/ *v.*
(**bathing, bathed, bathed**)
swim in the sea or in a river 游泳
Baoling likes to bathe in the sea.
宝玲喜欢到海里游泳。

battery /ˈbat·ter·y; ˈbætərɪ/ *n.*
(two **batteries**)
thing that you put in a car, torch or radio to make electricity 电池
I can't hear the radio. It needs new batteries.
我的收音机没有声音啦，要换些新电池了。

bauhinia /bau·'hin·i·a; bəu'hɪnɪə/ *n.*
sort of flower 紫荆花
There were several bauhinias in the park.
公园里有几株紫荆花。

bay /bay; beɪ/ *n.*
sea with land on three sides 海湾
There were a lot of ships in the bay.
海湾里有许多船。

be /be; bɪ/ *v.*
(**being**, **was** or **were**, **been**)
1 word that tells you about someone or something 是
Xiaofang will be twelve next month.
小芳下个月就是十二岁了。
2 happen 发生在
Her birthday is in October.
她的生日在十月。
3 word you use with another verb to show what happens to a person or thing 用这词加另一动词来说明某人(或物)接受了某一动作
The birthday cake was quickly eaten.
生日蛋糕很快地被吃光了。

beach /beach; bi:tʃ/ *n.*
(two **beaches**)
sand or stones along the edge of the sea 海滩
Peter had a swim and then lay on the beach.
彼得游了一会泳，然后躺在海滩上。

bead /bead; bi:d/ *n.*
small, round thing with a hole through the middle 小圆珠
An abacus has a lot of beads on it.
算盘有许多算珠。

beak /beak; bi:k/ *n.*
the hard part of a bird's mouth 鸟嘴
The bird had a fish in its beak.
那只鸟嘴上衔着一条鱼。

bean /bean; bi:n/ *n.*
seed used as food 豆子
I like red bean soup.
我喜欢喝红豆汤。

bean curd *n.*
soft food made from soya 豆腐

bean sprout *n.*
sort of vegetable 豆芽

bear [1] /bear; beə/ *n.*
big wild animal with thick fur 熊
The bear stood on its back legs to reach the honey.
那熊用后腿站了起来，去拿蜂蜜。

bear [2] /bear; beə/ *v.*
put up with 忍受；容忍
Mr Chen cannot bear loud music.
陈先生不能忍受声音太大的音乐。

beard /beard; bɪəd/ *n.*
hair on a man's chin and cheeks 胡子；须
The old man had a long, white beard.
那老人有一把长长的白须。

beast /beast; bi:st/ *n.*
fierce animal in stories; cruel man 野兽；凶恶的人
The children read a story called 'Beauty and the Beast'.
小孩们念了一个故事，叫做《美女与野兽》。

beat /beat; bi:t/ *v.*
(**beating**, **beat**, **beaten**)
1 hit someone hard and often 打；痛打
The cruel man was beating the horse.
那狠心的人在猛打那匹马。
2 hit something to make a noise 敲打
Tom was beating his drum loudly.
汤姆在打鼓，打得很响。
3 win a game or fight 胜过；打败
We beat the other team three goals to one.
我们以三比一的成绩打败了对方那一队。

beautiful /ˈbeau·ti·ful; ˈbjuːtɪfl/ *adj.*
(**more beautiful, most beautiful**)
someone or something you like to look at or listen to
美丽的；漂亮的
John painted a beautiful picture.
约翰画了一幅很美丽的画。
syn. 同义词：lovely
opp. 反义词：ugly 丑陋的；难看的
beautifully *adv.* 美丽地
The dress was beautifully made.
这件连衣裙做得好看极了。
beauty *n.*
what is nice to look at or listen to 美；美好
Usage note: You use *beautiful* for girls and ladies. *Handsome* is used for boys and men.
用法：形容女子或女孩子漂亮用 beautiful；形容男子或男孩子漂亮则用 handsome。

became /be·ˈcame; bɪˈkeɪm/ *v.*
p.t. of **become** become 的过去式
Peter went to university and then became a teacher.
彼得上过大学，然后成为教师。

because /be·ˈcause; bɪˈkɒz/ *conj.*
for the reason that 因为
Tom slipped because the floor was wet.
汤姆滑了一跤，因为地板很湿。
because of 因为；由于
We stayed indoors because of the rain.
由于下雨，我们要留在户内。

become /be·ˈcome; bɪˈkʌm/ *v.*
(**becoming, became, become**)
come or grow to be 成为；变为
Peter hopes to become a teacher when he leaves university.
彼得希望念完大学后成为教师。

bed /bed; bed/ *n.*
something you sleep on 床
Tom lay on his bed and went to sleep.
汤姆躺在床上睡着了。
bedroom *n.*
place where you sleep 卧室；睡房
Baoling's bedroom is very small.
宝玲的卧室很小。
bedtime *n.* 睡觉的时间
Nine o'clock is Susan's bedtime.
苏珊九时上床睡觉。

bee /bee; biː/ *n.*
flying insect that makes honey 蜜蜂
The flowers were covered with bees.
花朵上满是蜜蜂。

beef /beef; biːf/ *n.*
(**no plural**)
meat from a cow or an ox
牛肉
David likes fried beef with noodles.
戴维喜欢吃牛肉炒面。

been /been; biːn/ *v.*
p.p. of **be** be 的过去分词
Mary has been ill for a week.
玛丽已经病了一个星期了。

beetle /ˈbee·tle; ˈbiːtl/ *n.*
insect with hard covers on its wings 甲虫
There were a lot of beetles in the rubbish.
垃圾堆里面有许多甲虫。

before /be·ˈfore; bɪˈfɔː/ *adv. prep. conj.*
1 earlier; in the past 以前；从前
I have seen this film before.
我以前看过这部电影。
2 earlier than something
在…之前
Tom always has breakfast before he goes to school.
汤姆总是在上学之前吃早餐。
3 in front of something
在…的前面
'Been' comes before 'beetle' in this dictionary.
在这词典里，been 出现在 beetle 之前。
opp. 反义词：after 在…之后

beg /beg; beg/ *v.*
(**begging, begged, begged**)
ask for food, money or other things 乞求；恳求
The poor man begged for money.
那个贫穷的人向人乞钱。

beggar *n.* 乞丐
Mrs Chen gave the beggar a dollar.
陈太太给了那乞丐一港元。

begin /be·'gin; bɪ'gɪn/ *v.*
(beginning, began, begun)
1 start happening 开始
The film begins at 8 o'clock.
电影八时开始。
2 start doing something 开始（做某事）
We begin school at 9 o'clock.
我们九时上课。
opp. 反义词：stop, finish 停止；完毕

beginner *n.*
someone who is starting to do something 初学者

beginning *n.*
the first part 最初的部分；起点
We were late and missed the beginning of the film.
我们迟到了，没看到电影开头的部分。
Usage note: You can use *start* in the same way as *begin* — *The play begins at seven. The play starts at seven.*
用法：begin 和 start 的用法相同。The play begins at seven 可以写成 The play starts at seven。

behave /be·'have; bɪ'heɪv/ *v.*
(behaving, behaved, behaved)
be good or bad 行为
Tom was punished because he behaved badly at school.
汤姆因为在学校行为不好而受到惩罚。

behaviour *n.* 行为；品行
Tom was punished because his behaviour was bad.
汤姆因为行为不好而受到惩罚。

behind /be·'hind; bɪ'haɪnd/ *adv. prep.*
at the back of someone or something 在…的后面
Mary hid behind the curtain.
玛丽躲在窗帘后面。
opp. 反义词：in front of 在…前面

being /'be·ing; 'bi:ɪŋ/ *v.*
pres. p. of **be** be 的现在分词
I don't like being hungry.
我不喜欢饿着肚子。

believe /be·'lieve; bɪ'li:v/ *v.*
(believing, believed, believed)
think that something is true 相信
I don't believe in ghosts.
我不信有鬼。

bell /bell; bel/ *n.*
something that rings 钟；铃
At the end of a lesson the bell rings.
上完一堂课，铃就响了。

belong /be·'long; bɪ'lɒŋ/ *v.*
1 to be owned by someone or something 属于；是…所有的
This book belongs to John.
这是约翰的书。
2 be a member of a group, club, etc. 是…的成员
Tom belongs to a football club.
汤姆是足球俱乐部的成员。

below /be·'low; bɪ'ləʊ/ *prep.*
under someone or something 在…之下
We moved because our flat was below a noisy family.
我们搬了家，因为我们住在一个喧闹家庭的楼下。
syn. 同义词：under
opp. 反义词：above 在…之上

belt /belt; belt/ *n.*
long piece of material you put round your waist 腰带
The policeman had a gun on his belt.
警察的腰带上挂着手枪。

bench /bench; bentʃ/ *n.*
(two **benches**)
long seat made of wood, metal or stone 长凳
Peter sat on a bench in the park.
彼得坐在公园的长凳上。

bend [1] /bend; bend/ *v.*
(**bending, bent, bent**)
1 make a curve in something 弄弯
Tom bent the wire to make a hook.
汤姆把铁丝弯成一个钩。

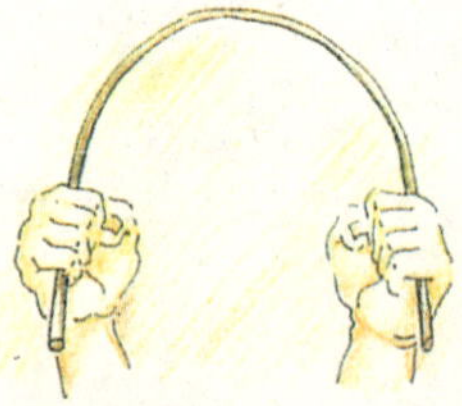

2 make a curve with your body 弯腰
He bent down to clean the floor.
他弯下腰来把地板擦干净。

bend [2] /bend; bend/ *n.*
a curve in something 弯曲
The bus came to a bend in the road.
公共汽车驶到一个拐弯处。

bent [1] /bent; bent/ *adj.*
not straight 弯的
The car aerial was bent.
汽车的天线弯了。

bent [2] /bent; bent/ *v.*
p.t. of **bend** bend 的过去式
Baoling bent down to put on her shoes.
宝玲弯下腰来穿鞋子。

berry /'ber·ry; 'berɪ/ *n.*
(two **berries**)
small fruit with seeds in it 莓；浆果
The birds were eating berries from the bush.
鸟儿在矮树丛中吃浆果。

berries

beside /be·'side; bɪ'saɪd/ *prep.*
at the side of someone or something 在…旁边
Come and sit beside me.
过来，坐在我旁边。
syn. 同义词：next to

besides /be·'sides; bɪ'saɪdz/ *prep.*
in addition to 除了…之外
Who will be there besides you and me?
除了你我之外，还有谁去？

best [1] /best; best/ *adj.*
very good 最好的
Xiaofang is the best student in the class.
小芳是班里最好的学生。
opp. 反义词：worst 最坏的；最差的

best [2] /best; best/ *adv.*
very well 最好地
Xiaofang works best in the morning.
小芳早上工作得最好。
opp. 反义词：worst 最差

better [1] /'bet·ter; 'betə/ *adj.*
1 more excellent 比较好；更好
Tom's work is better than Mary's.
汤姆的工作做得比玛丽好。
2 more healthy 好了点；健康较佳
Bill was ill, but he is better now.
比尔病了，不过现在好了点。
opp. 反义词：worse 更坏的；更差的

better [2] /'bet·ter; 'betə/ *adv.*
in a more excellent way 更好地
Tom works better than Mary.
汤姆做事比玛丽做得好。
opp. 反义词：worse 更差

between /be·'tween; bɪ'twi:n/ *prep.*
1 with someone or something on one side and someone or something on the other 在两个人(或物)中间
Tom sits between John and Peter.
汤姆坐在约翰和彼得中间。

between

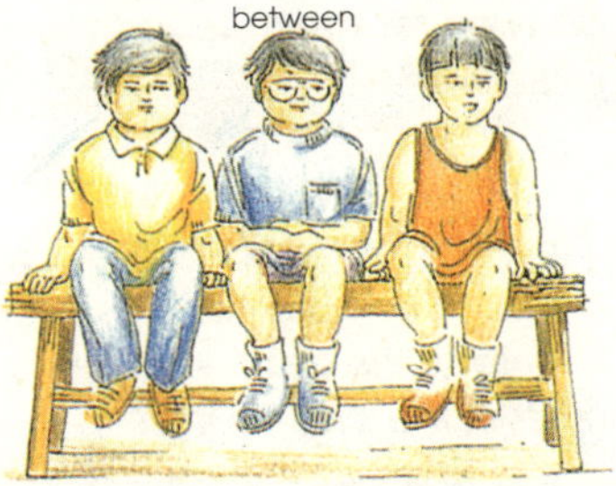

2 from one place to another 之间
There is a ferry between Central and Tsim Sha Tsui.
中区与尖沙嘴之间有渡轮往来。

3 to different people or things 给不同的人或物
She divided the sweets between the children.
她把糖果分给孩子们。

beware /be·'ware; bɪ'weə/ *v.*
be careful 提防；当心
Beware of the dog.
提防那只狗。

beyond /be·'yond; bɪ'jɒnd/ *prep.*
further than; on the far side of 在…的那一边；越过
The village is beyond the hill.
村子在山的那一边。

bicycle /'bi·cy·cle; 'baɪsɪkl/ *n.*
machine with two wheels that you ride 自行车；脚踏车；单车（方言）
Tom goes to school on his bicycle.
汤姆骑自行车上学。
syn. 同义词：bike

big /big; bɪg/ *adj.*
(bigger, biggest)
large 大的
An elephant is a very big animal.
象是很大的动物。
opp. 反义词：small, little 小的
Usage note: You can use *large* in the same way as *big* -- *They have a big house. They have a large house.* But *large* is not usually used to describe people.
用法： big 和 large 的用法大致相同。例如 They have a big house 可以写成 They have a large house。不过，large 一般都不用来形容人。

big

bike /bike; baɪk/ *n.*
short word for bicycle 自行车；脚踏车；单车（方言）
Tom rides his bike to school.
汤姆骑自行车上学。

bill /bill; bɪl/ *n.*
piece of paper that says how much you have to pay for something 账单
We finished the meal and asked for the bill.
我们吃完饭就要求开账单来。

bin /bin; bɪn/ *n.*
large container, especially for rubbish 箱子
Put your rubbish in the bin.
请你把垃圾丢在垃圾箱内。

bird /bird; bɜ:d/ *n.*
animal with feathers and wings 鸟；飞禽
The birds were singing in the trees.
鸟儿在树上唱歌。

birthday /'birth·day; 'bɜ:θdeɪ/ *n.*
the day when you were born 生日
Mary got a lot of presents for her birthday.
玛丽生日收到了许多礼物。

biscuit /'bis·cuit; 'bɪskɪt/ *n.*
small, thin, dry cake 饼干
Anna bought a packet of biscuits for her lunch.
安娜买了一包饼干做午餐。

biscuits

bit [1] /bit; bɪt/ *n.*
small piece of anything
一小片；碎片；少许
He gave the birds some bits of bread.
他给鸟儿喂些面包碎屑。

bit [2] /bit; bɪt/ *v.*
p.t. of **bite** bite 的过去式
The dog bit the postman.
那只狗咬了邮递员。

bite [1] /bite; baɪt/ *v.*
(biting, bit, bitten)
cut with the teeth 咬
If you hit the dog, it will bite you.
如果你打那只狗，它就会咬你。

bite [2] /bite; baɪt/ *n.*
piece of something cut off with your teeth （咬的）一口
He took a bite from the apple.
他把苹果咬了一口。

bitter /'bit·ter; 'bɪtə/ *adj.*
(more bitter, most bitter)
with a taste that is not sweet
苦的
Coffee without sugar has a bitter taste.
没有糖的咖啡有点苦味。
syn. 同义词：nasty
opp. 反义词：sweet 甜的

black /black; blæk/ *adj.*
very dark colour 黑色
Chinese people have black hair.
中国人有黑色的头发。
opp. 反义词：white 白色

blackboard /'black·board; 'blækbɔːd/ *n.*
piece of dark board or wall on which you write with chalk
黑板
The teacher wrote the sentence on the blackboard.
老师把句子写在黑板上。

blade /blade; bleɪd/ *n.*
the part of a knife that cuts
刀刃
The knife blade was very sharp.
这刀刃非常锋利。

blame /blame; bleɪm/ *n.*
(no plural)
say that a person or thing made something bad happen 责怪；责备
The teacher blamed the children for the mess in the classroom.
老师责备孩子们把教室弄得乱七八糟。
take the blame 对做错的事负责
Tom took the blame for the mess in the classroom.
汤姆承认教室里弄得乱七八糟是他的错。

blank /blank; blæŋk/ *n.*
empty space 空白；空格
The exercise was to fill the blanks in the sentences.
这个练习是要在句子的空白处填上字。

blanket /'blan·ket; 'blæŋkɪt/ *n.*
piece of thick cloth to cover someone 毯子；毛毯
When it is cold I put a blanket on my bed.
天冷时我在床上放了一条毛毯。

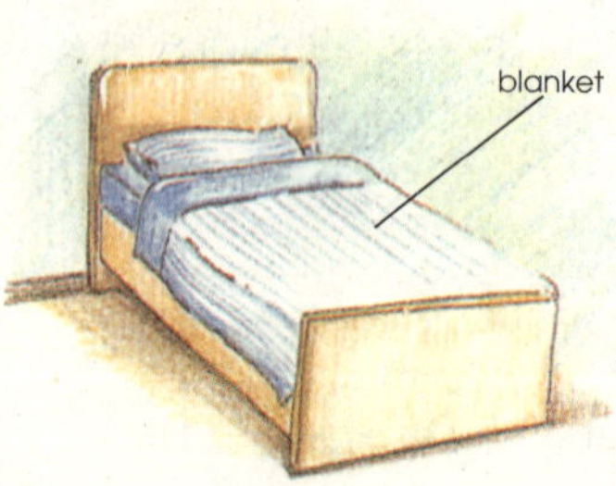

blazer /'bla·zer; 'bleɪzə/ *n.*
kind of jacket 宽松的外衣
Tom's school uniform is a blue blazer and grey trousers.
汤姆的校服是蓝色的宽松外衣和灰色的裤子。

bleed /bleed; bliːd/ *v.*
(bleeding, bled, bled)
have blood coming out 流血

The cut on John's finger was bleeding.
约翰手指上的伤口在流血。

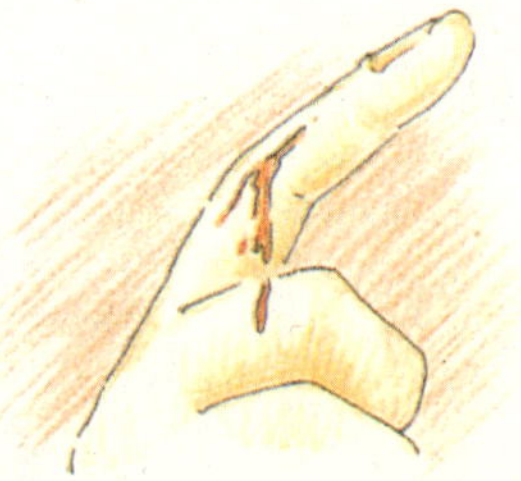

blew /blew; bluː/ *v.*
p.t. of **blow** blow 的过去式
The typhoon blew down the tree.
台风刮倒了那棵树。

blind [1] /blind; blaɪnd/ *adj.*
not able to see
盲的；瞎了的
Mary helped the blind man cross the road.
玛丽帮助那盲人过马路。

blind [2] /blind; blaɪnd/ *n.*
something you put on a window to keep out the sun
窗帘
Mrs Li closed the blinds.
李太太把窗帘拉上。

block [1] /block; blɒk/ *n.*
1 square piece of something
方块
The children were playing with building blocks.
小孩们在玩积木。

2 building 大楼；大厦
Peter lives in a big block of flats.
彼得住在一座很大的大厦里面。

block [2] /block; blɒk/ *v.*
not allow anything to go through 堵塞
A fallen tree blocked the road.
一棵倒下来的树把路堵塞了。

blood /blood; blʌd/ *n.*
(no plural)
red liquid inside your body
血液
Many people give blood for the hospitals.
许多人给医院献血。

blouse /blouse; blaʊz/ *n.*
piece of clothing a girl or a woman wears on the top of her body 女用短上衣；女装衬衫
Anna bought a new blouse to wear at school.
安娜买了一件新的短上衣，上学的时候穿。

blow [1] /blow; bləʊ/ *v.*
(blowing, blew, blown)
1 move like the wind 风吹
A strong wind was blowing.
正刮着大风。
2 send air from your mouth
吹气
Mary blew out the candles on her birthday cake.
玛丽把她生日蛋糕上的蜡烛都吹熄了。

blow up 爆炸；使充气
The firework blew up with a bang.
一声巨响，烟火给引爆了。
The children blew up the balloons.
小孩子们把气球充了气。
blow one's whistle 吹哨子
The teacher blew his whistle.
老师吹哨子。
blow one's nose 擤鼻子
Tom blew his nose loudly.
汤姆大声地擤鼻子。

blow [2] /blow; bləu/ *n.*
hard hit 打；击
The blow knocked the man down.
那个男人被人一拳打倒在地上。

blue /blue; blu:/ *adj.*
(**bluer, bluest**)
with the colour of a clear sky
蓝色
Mary has blue eyes.
玛丽有一双蓝眼睛。

blunt /blunt; blʌnt/ *adj.*
with an edge or point that is not sharp 钝的；不锋利的；不尖的
This knife is blunt. It won't cut.
这把刀钝了，不能切东西了。
This pencil is blunt. It won't write.
这枝铅笔钝了，不能写了。
opp. 反义词：sharp 锋利的；尖的

board /board; bɔ:d/ *n.*
flat piece of wood 木板
The workmen covered the hole with boards.
工人们用木板把洞盖好。
on board 在船上
John went on board the ship.
约翰上了船。

boast /boast; bəust/ *v.*
praise yourself and what you do or have 自夸；吹嘘
Sam was boasting about his new bicycle.
萨姆在炫耀他的新自行车。

boat /boat; bəut/ *n.*
something that can move on water 船；小艇
Peter travelled to Shanghai by boat.
彼得乘船去上海。

body /'bod·y; 'bɒdɪ/ *n.*
(two **bodies**)
all of a person or animal 身体
You should keep your body clean by bathing every day.
你应该天天洗澡，保持身体清洁。

boil /boil; bɔɪl/ *v.*
heat water or other liquid until there are bubbles in it
煮沸
Anna boiled some water to make tea.
安娜烧些开水来泡茶。
opp. 反义词：freeze 结冰；冻结

bone /bone; bəun/ *n.*
the hard parts of the body 骨
Tom fell down and broke a bone in his leg.
汤姆跌了下来，把一根腿骨摔断了。

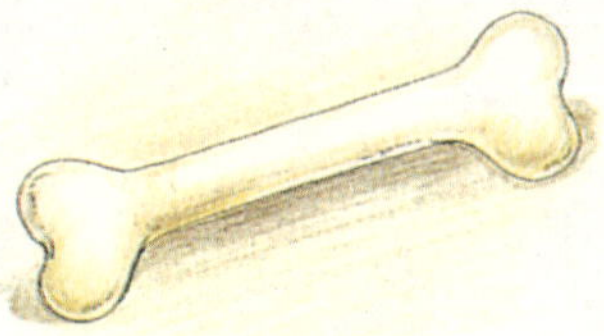

book [1] /book; buk/ *n.*
pieces of paper fixed in a cover 书
Xiaofang reads a lot of books.
小芳看很多书。

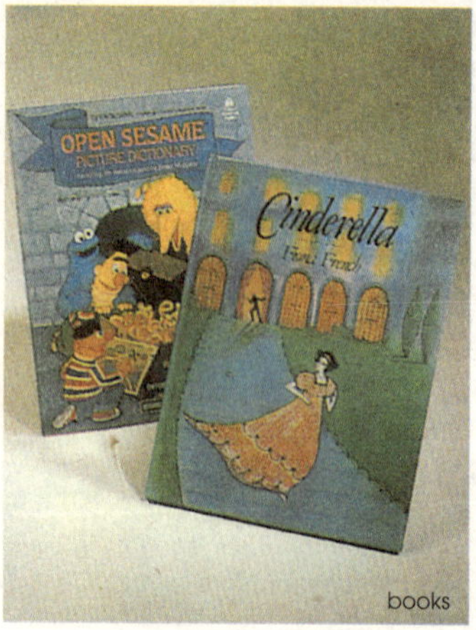

books

bookcase *n.*
a piece of furniture where you keep books 书架；书柜
bookshop *n.*
place where they sell books
书店

book [2] /book; buk/ *v.*
ask for a seat in a theatre or a room in a hotel before you need it 预定

Mary booked two seats for the concert.
玛丽预定了音乐会的两个座位。

boot /boot; bu:t/ *n.*
sort of heavy shoe 靴
During the cold, wet weather, Mary wore boots.
天气又冷又湿时玛丽就穿上靴子。

boots

border /'bor·der; 'bɔ:də/ *n.*
line between two countries 边界
David crossed the border into Canada.
戴维越过边界进入加拿大。

bored /bored; bɔ:d/ *adj.*
unhappy because you are not interested in something 厌倦；厌烦；无聊
John was bored because he had nothing to do.
约翰很无聊，因为他无事可干。
boring *adj.* 令人厌烦的
The programme was boring, so Peter switched off the television.
节目使人厌烦，所以彼得把电视机关上了。

born, be born
/born, be born; bɔ:n, bɪ bɔ:n/ *v.*
come alive 出生
Peter was born in China.
彼得在中国出生。
opp. 反义词：die 死亡

borrow /'bor·row; 'bɒrəʊ/ *v.*
ask for something and give it back later (向别人)借
Can I borrow your pencil?
我可以借你的铅笔吗?
opp. 反义词：lend 借…给别人

boss /boss; bɒs/ *n.*
(two **bosses**)
person in charge 老板；上司；主管
He is the boss of a big factory.
他是一家大工厂的老板。

both /both; bəʊθ/ *pron. adj adv.*
the two 两；双
Peter can write with both hands.
彼得两只手都可以写字。

bottle /'bot·tle; 'bɒtl/ *n.*
glass or plastic container for liquids 瓶子
Anna drank a bottle of water.
安娜喝了一瓶水。
bottle-opener *n.*
thing for opening bottles 开瓶器

bottles

bottom /'bot·tom; 'bɒtəm/ *n.*
1 the lowest part 底部
There are lots of shells at the bottom of the sea.
海底有许多贝壳类动物。
opp. 反义词：top 顶部
2 part of your body that you sit on 臀部
Peter slipped and fell on his bottom.
彼得滑了一跤，臀部着地摔倒了。

bought /bought; bɔ:t/ *v.*
p.t. of **buy** buy 的过去式
Mary bought a dress yesterday.
玛丽昨天买了一件连衣裙。

bounce /bounce; baʊns/ *v.*
(**bouncing, bounced, bounced**)
move up and down 弹跳；弹回
The ball bounced over the wall.
那球弹起来，越过了那堵墙。

bow [1] /bow; bəʊ/ *n.*
1 sort of knot 蝴蝶结
Mary had a red bow in her hair.
玛丽在头发上打了个红蝴蝶结。

2 thing you shoot arrows with 弓
A long time ago, soldiers had bows and arrows.
从前，士兵都佩带弓箭。

bow [2] /bow; baʊ/ *v.*
bend the head and body
鞠躬
The singer bowed to the audience.
演唱者向听众鞠躬答谢。

bow *n.*
bending your head in front of an important person 鞠躬
He made a bow when he met the emperor.
他见到皇帝时鞠躬。

bowl /bowl; bəʊl/ *n.*
deep, round dish 碗
John ate two bowls of rice.
约翰吃了两碗饭。

bowling /'bow·ling; 'bəʊlɪŋ/ *n.*
(**no plural**)
game where you try to knock down wooden pieces with a big, hard ball 保龄球
Tom goes bowling every week.
汤姆每星期都去玩保龄球。

box /box; bɒks/ *n.*
(two **boxes**)
container made of cardboard, wood, plastic, etc. 箱子；盒子
The shopkeeper put the shoes in a box.
店主把鞋放在盒子里。

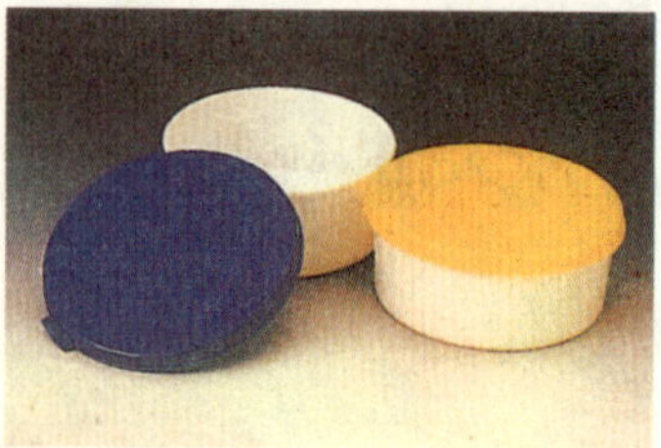

boxing /'box·ing; 'bɒksɪŋ/ *n.*
(**no plural**)
sport where you fight with your hands 拳击
Boxing is a dangerous sport.
拳击是危险的运动。

boxer *n.* 拳击手
The boxer was hurt.
拳击手受伤了。

boy /boy; bɔɪ/ *n.*
male child 男孩
Peter is a clever boy.
彼得是个聪明的男孩子。

bracelet /'brace·let; 'breɪslɪt/ *n.*
ring or chain that you wear round your arm 手镯；臂镯
Anna has a gold bracelet.
安娜有一只金手镯。

brackets /'bra·ckets; 'brækɪts/ *n.*
(**plural**)
marks you put round words 括号；括弧
Put the answer in the brackets.
把答案填在括号内。

brain /brain; breɪn/ *n.*
part inside your head that you use to think 脑
Boxing can damage the brain.
拳击运动可能伤害脑部。

branch /branch; brɑ:ntʃ/ *n.*
(two **branches**)
1 part of a tree with leaves growing on it 树枝
The bird was sitting on a branch.
鸟儿正在树枝上停着。

2 part of a company （公司的）分行；支行
The bank has many branches in Hong Kong.
这家银行在香港有许多分行。

brave /brave; breɪv/ *adj.*
(**braver, bravest**)
not afraid 勇敢的
The brave fireman rescued the children from the fire.
那勇敢的消防员从火场中把孩子们救出来。
bravely *adv.*
doing something with no fear
勇敢地
The fireman went bravely into the burning building.
那消防员勇敢地进入焚烧着的大厦。

bread /bread; bred/ *n.*
(**no plural**)
food made with flour and water and then baked 面包
Mary bought some bread to make sandwiches.
玛丽买了些面包来做三明治。

break [1] /break; breɪk/ *v.*
(**breaking, broke, broken**)
drop, hit or pull something so that it is in pieces 打破；打碎
The ball hit the window and broke it.
皮球打到玻璃窗上，把玻璃打碎了。
break down 坏了
The car broke down and Tom had to walk home.
车子坏了，汤姆只好步行回家。
break in, break into 擅自闯入；强行进入
The thieves broke into the house.
窃贼闯进房屋里。
break out (指灾害)突然发生
Fire broke out in the factory.
工厂突然发生火警。
break up 学期结束放假
School breaks up for the summer holidays in June.
学期六月结束，开始放暑假。

break [2] /break; breɪk/ *n.*
short rest from work 短暂的休息；小憩
The factory workers had a ten-minute break at 11 o'clock.
工厂工人在十一时有十分钟休息。

breakfast /'break·fast; 'brekfəst/ *n.*
first meal of the day 早餐
Peter has his breakfast at 7 o'clock.
彼得七时吃早餐。

breathe /breathe; bri:ð/ *v.*
(**breathing, breathed, breathed**)
take air into your nose and mouth and send it out again
呼吸
I like to go to the country parks to breathe the fresh air.
我喜欢到郊野公园去呼吸新鲜空气。
breath *n.* 呼吸
Tom arrived at school out of breath. He had run all the way.
汤姆到学校时气都喘不过来，他是一路跑来的。

brick /brick; brɪk/ *n.*
block of hard clay for building 砖
The wall was made of bricks.
这堵墙是砖砌的。

bride /bride; braɪd/ *n.*
woman on her wedding day
新娘
John met his bride in Hong Kong.
约翰在香港认识他的新娘。

bridegroom /'bride·groom; 'braɪdgru:m/ *n.*
man on his wedding day
新郎
The bridegroom was very nervous.
新郎非常紧张。

bridge /bridge; brɪdʒ/ *n.*
path or road over a river, road or railway 桥
There is no bridge from Hong Kong to Kowloon.
香港与九龙之间没有桥。

bright /bright; braɪt/ *adj.*
1 light; shining 光亮的；明亮的
It was a bright day with no clouds.
这是阳光灿烂的一天，没有云。
opp. 反义词：dark, dull 黑暗；沉闷
2 clever 聪明的
John is a bright boy.
汤姆是个聪明的男孩。
opp. 反义词：dull, stupid 笨，愚蠢

brightly *adv.*
with a lot of light 光亮地；明亮地
The sun shone brightly in a clear sky.
太阳在晴朗的天空中明亮地照着。

bring /bring; brɪŋ/ *v.*
(**bringing, brought, brought**)
carry something or someone from another place 带来；拿来
Mary brought her mother a cup of tea.
玛丽拿了一杯茶给妈妈。

broad /broad; brɔ:d/ *adj.*
far from one side to the other 宽阔
Near the sea, the river was very broad.
那河流的近海处，河面非常广阔。

broke /broke; brəʊk/ *v.*
p.t. of **break** break 的过去式
Peter fell and broke his arm.
彼得跌了下来，手臂跌断了。

broken /'bro·ken; 'brəʊkən/ *adj.*
1 in pieces 破碎了的
Broken bottles are dangerous. The pieces can cut you.
破瓶子很危险，碎片会割伤你。
2 not working 坏了的
Tom found a broken watch. It did not work.
汤姆找到一块不能走的坏表。

broom /broom; bru:m/ *n.*
brush for sweeping the floor 扫帚；扫把
Sam swept the yard with a big broom.
萨姆拿一把大扫帚扫院子。

brother /'broth·er; 'brʌðə/ *n.*
boy or man who has the same parents as another person 兄弟
Mary has a brother and a sister.
玛丽有一个兄弟和一个姐妹。

brought /brought; brɔ:t/ *v.*
p.t. of **bring** bring 的过去式
Peter brought a ball to school.
彼得带了一个球去学校。

brown /brown; braʊn/ *adj.*
colour of coffee or tea 棕色；褐色
Anna wears a brown skirt.
安娜穿了一件棕色的裙子。

bruise /bruise; bru:z/ *n.*
dark mark on your body where you have been hurt 青肿；淤痕；淤伤
After the match, Peter had a bruise on his leg.
比赛之后，彼得腿上有了一处淤伤。

brush[1] /brush; brʌʃ/ *n.*
(two **brushes**)
bunch of strong, short hairs fixed to a handle 刷子
We clean our teeth with a toothbrush.
我们用牙刷刷牙。

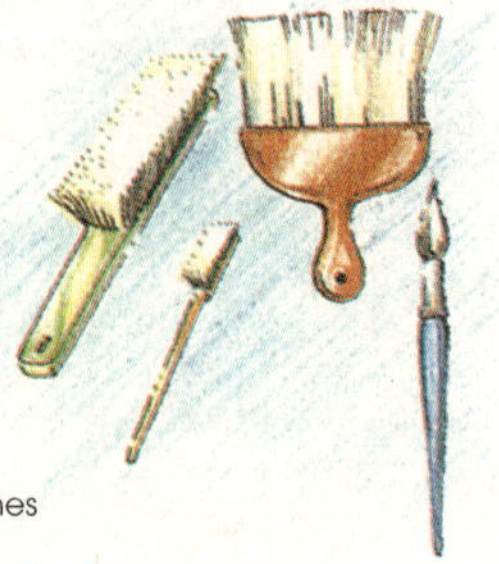
brushes

brush[2] /brush; brʌʃ/ *v.*
use a brush 刷
Mary brushed her hair.
玛丽用刷子刷头发。

bubble /'bub·ble; 'bʌbl/ *n.*
little ball of air or gas 气泡；水泡
Lemonade is full of bubbles.
柠檬汽水有很多气泡。

bubbles

bucket /'buck·et; 'bʌkɪt/ *n.*
container, with a handle, for carrying liquids 水桶；提桶
Anna filled a bucket with water.
安娜装满一桶水。

bucket

buckle /ˈbuck·le; ˈbʌkl/ *n.*
thing that fastens a belt 扣子
Sam has a big buckle on his belt.
萨姆的腰带上有一个大扣子。

bud /bud; bʌd/ *n.*
flower before it opens 花蕾
The plants were covered with buds.
那些植物长满了花蕾。

buffalo /ˈbuf·fa·lo; ˈbʌfələʊ/ *n.*
(two **buffaloes**)
large animal with horns 水牛
We saw some buffaloes in Chaozhou.
我们在潮州看到一些水牛。

build /build; bɪld/ *v.*
(**building, built, built**)
make something by putting parts together 建造；建筑
Tom built a hut with bamboo and leaves.
汤姆用竹子和树叶筑了一间小屋。
builder *n.* 建筑工人
The builders finished the house.
建筑工人盖好了那所房子。

building /ˈbuild·ing; ˈbɪldɪŋ/ *n.*
place where people live and work, etc. 建筑物；房屋
There were ten flats in the building.
这座建筑物里有十套房间。

building

built /built; bɪlt/ *v.*
p.t. of **build** build 的过去式
They built the school last year.
他们去年建好了那所学校。

bulb /bulb; bʌlb/ *n.*
round, glass thing that makes electric light 电灯泡
Tom changed the bulb in the lamp.
汤姆把电灯里的灯泡换了。

bull /bull; bʊl/ *n.*
male cow 公牛
The bull was very fierce.
那头公牛非常凶猛。

bump /bump; bʌmp/ *n.*
part that is higher than the other parts 地面隆起处
The car hit a bump on the road.
汽车撞到路上一处隆起的地方。
bump into 撞到；碰到
A truck bumped into the car.
一辆大卡车撞到小汽车上。

bun /bun; bʌn/ *n.*
small, round piece of bread 小圆面包
Tom and Mary ate all the buns.
汤姆和玛丽把小圆面包都吃光了。

bunch /bunch; bʌntʃ/ *n.*
(two **bunches**)
things you fasten together; things that grow together
一束；一把
John bought a bunch of flowers for his mother.
约翰买了一束花给妈妈。

bundle /ˈbun·dle; ˈbʌndl/ *n.*
things tied together 一捆；一扎
The man was carrying a bundle of sticks.
那人扛着一捆柴枝。

burglar /ˈbur·glar; ˈbɜːglə/ *n.*
someone who steals from a building 窃贼
The burglar stole the TV set.
窃贼偷走了电视机。
burglary *n.* 盗窃；盗窃案
There were three burglaries last night.
昨晚发生了三宗盗窃案。

burn /burn; bɜːn/ *v.*
(**burning, burnt, burnt**)
1 hurt someone or damage something with fire or heat
烫伤；烧伤
When you have a barbecue, be careful not to burn yourself.
你烧烤时要小心，别烫着了。
2 make flames or light 燃烧；发亮
Paper burns easily.
纸张容易燃烧。
The lights were burning.
电灯都是亮着的。

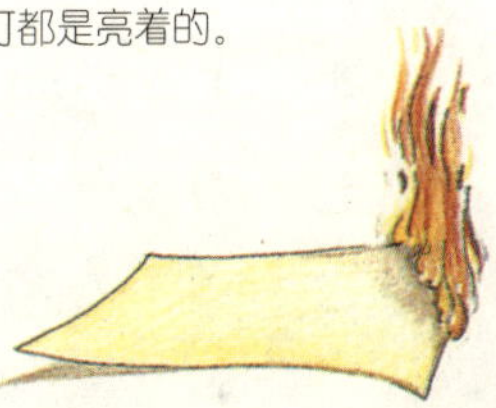

burst /burst; bɜːst/ *v.*
(**bursting, burst, burst**)
break open suddenly 爆破；炸开
The balloon burst.
气球爆炸了。

bury /'bur·y; 'berɪ/ *v.*
(**burying, buried, buried**)
put something in a hole in the ground and cover it 埋藏；埋葬
The dog buried a bone in the garden.
那只狗把一根骨头埋藏在花园里。

bus /bus; bʌs/ *n.*
(two **buses**)
kind of big car for carrying a lot of people 公共汽车；巴士（方言）
Peter goes to school by bus.
彼得乘公共汽车上学。

catch a bus 搭（乘）公共汽车
Peter catched a bus to school.
彼得搭公共汽车上学。

bus driver *n.*
someone who drives a bus
公共汽车司机

bus stop *n.*
place on a road where you get on and off buses
公共汽车站

bush /bush; bʊʃ/ *n.*
(two **bushes**)
plant like a small tree 矮树丛；灌木
The bird flew out of the bush.
那只鸟儿从矮树丛中飞了出来。

busily /'bus·i·ly; 'bɪzɪlɪ/ *adv.*
(**more busily, most busily**)
in a busy way 忙碌地
Tom was working busily.
汤姆忙碌地工作。

business /'busi·ness; 'bɪznɪs/ *n.*
buying and selling things; making things to sell 买卖；生意；商业
His shop is a good business.
他的店铺生意很好。

busy /'bus·y; 'bɪzɪ/ *adj.*
(**busier, busiest**)
working; with a lot to do 忙碌
Tom was busy with his homework.
汤姆忙于做他的家庭作业。

but /but; bʌt/ *conj.*
word you can use when you are starting to say something different 但是
Peter is small but he is strong.
彼得个子矮小，但很结实。

butcher /'butch·er; 'bʊtʃə/ *n.*
someone who sells meat
屠夫；肉食商
She bought some pork from the butcher.
她在肉食商那里买了些猪肉。

butter /'but·ter; 'bʌtə/ *n.*
(**no plural**)
soft, oily food made from milk 黄油；牛油（方言）
John likes toast with butter.
约翰喜欢吃烤面包涂黄油。

butterfly /'but·ter·fly; 'bʌtəflaɪ/ *n.*
(two **butterflies**)
insect with big, pretty wings
蝴蝶
There were a lot of butterflies on the flowers.
花丛里有很多蝴蝶。

button [1] /'but·ton; 'bʌtn/ *n.*
small, round thing on clothes
纽扣
Baoling fastened the buttons on her coat.
宝玲把外套的纽扣扣好。

buttonholes *n.* 纽孔；纽眼
Tom could not fasten his shirt because the buttonholes were too small.
汤姆扣不紧他的衬衣，因为纽孔太小了。

buttons

button [2] /'but·ton; 'bʌtn/ *v.*
fasten with buttons 扣好；扣紧
It's cold. Button your coat.
天气很冷，把你外衣的纽扣扣好。

buy /buy; baɪ/ *v.*
(buying, bought, bought)
get something by paying for it 购买
Xiaofang bought some new shoes.
小芳买了一些新鞋。
opp. 反义词：sell 卖

by /by; baɪ/ *prep.*
1 near or beside someone or something 靠近；在…的旁边
We live by the sea.
我们住在海边。
2 not later than 不迟于…时候
Mary always arrives at school by 9 o'clock.
玛丽总是九时以前到学校。
3 word that shows how 用…的方法
John goes to school by tram.
约翰乘电车上学。
4 past someone or something 经过
The buses go by the school.
公共汽车经过学校。

bye-bye /bye·ˈbye; baɪˈbaɪ/ *int.*
something you say when you leave someone 再见
Mary said 'bye-bye' to her mother.
玛丽对妈妈说"再见"。
syn. 同义词：goodbye

Cc

cabbage /ˈcab·bage; ˈkæbɪdʒ/ *n.*
vegetable with thick, green leaves 卷心菜；洋白菜；椰菜
Cabbage is Peter's favourite vegetable.
卷心菜是彼得喜欢吃的菜。

cable-car /ˈca·ble·car; ˈkeɪblkɑː/ *n.*
small car that hangs from a wire and takes you up and down hills 缆车
There are cable-cars to go up the mountain.
登山有缆车。

café /ˈca·fe; ˈkæfeɪ/ *n.*
place where you buy and eat food 咖啡馆；小餐馆
Peter had lunch in a café.
彼得在一家小餐馆吃了午饭。

cage /cage; keɪdʒ/ *n.*
place for keeping birds or animals 笼子
At the zoo, the animals are in cages.
在动物园，各种动物都关在笼里。

cake /cake; keɪk/ *n.*
sweet food made with flour, sugar, butter and eggs and then baked 西点；蛋糕；糕饼
Anna had a big cake for her birthday.
安娜过生日有一个很大的生日蛋糕。

calculator /ˈcal·cu·la·tor; ˈkælkjʊleɪtə/ *n.*
machine that can add, divide, etc. 计算器
Mr Chen uses a calculator to do his work.
陈先生用计算器来做他的工作。

calendar /ˈcal·en·dar; ˈkælɪndə/ *n.*
list of days, weeks and months of the year 日历
Susan marked her friends' birthdays on her calendar.
苏珊把朋友们的生日都记在日历上。

calf /calf; kɑːf/ *n.*
(two **calves**)
young cow 小牛
The cow had two calves.
母牛有两头小牛。

call [1] /call; kɔːl/ *n.*
1 shout 叫喊；呼喊
Anna heard a call for help.
安娜听见一声求救的叫喊。
2 phone-call 电话
Peter had a call from Mary.
彼得接到玛丽打来的电话。

call [2] /call; kɔːl/ *v.*
1 shout 叫；呼喊
Peter called to Tom.
彼得大声叫汤姆。
2 send a message to someone to come 叫…人来；召唤
Call the fire-brigade. There's a fire.
着火啦！叫消防队来吧。
3 give a name to a person or thing 给人或物起个名字
He is called Peter.
他叫彼得。

calm /calm; kɑːm/ *adj.*
1 quiet; not excited 镇定的；安静的
Susan was calm after the accident.
苏珊遇到了意外之后，表现得很镇定。
2 with no big waves （水面）平静的
The sea was flat and calm.
海面一片平静。
calmly *adv.* 镇定地
John calmly phoned for an ambulance.
约翰镇定地打电话去叫救护车。

came /came; keɪm/ *v.*
p.t. of **come** come 的过去式
A lot of children came to Tom's party.
许多小孩来参加汤姆的聚会。

camel /ˈcam·el; ˈkæml/ *n.*
large animal that lives in hot, dry places 骆驼
They call the camel 'the ship of the desert'.
人们把骆驼称为“沙漠之舟”。

camera /ˈcam·er·a; ˈkæmərə/ *n.*
machine that makes photographs 照相机；摄影机
Baoling put a new film in her camera.
宝玲把一卷新胶卷装到照相机里。

camp [1] /camp; kæmp/ *n.*
group of tents where people live for a short time 露营地
Peter goes to a camp in Sai Kung every summer.
彼得每年夏天都去西贡一个露营地度假。

camp [2] /camp; kæmp/ *v.*
stay in a tent for a short time 露营
Peter camps in Sai Kung every summer.
彼得每年夏天都去西贡露营。
go camping *v.* 露营
The scouts go camping every summer.
童子军每年夏天都去露营。

can [1] /can; kæn/ *n.*
metal container 金属罐；罐头
Mary bought a can of fruit.
玛丽买了一听水果。

can [2] /can; kən/ *v.*
(**could**)
1 able to do something; know how to do something 会；能够
Peter can swim.
彼得会游泳。
John can speak English.
约翰会说英语。
opp. 反义词：cannot, can't 不能够；不会
2 be allowed to do something 可以（表示请求）

Can I go swimming today?
我今天可以去游泳吗?

canal /ca·'nal; kə'næl/ *n.*
river made by people 水渠;运河
They dug a canal to bring water to the fields.
他们挖了一条水渠,把水引到田里。

candle /'can·dle; 'kændl/ *n.*
stick of wax that gives light when it burns 蜡烛;
Susan had ten candles on her birthday cake.
苏珊的生日蛋糕上有十支蜡烛。

candy /'can·dy; 'kændɪ/ *n.*
(two **candies**)
small piece of sweet food or chocolate 糖果
Too much candy is bad for your teeth.
吃太多糖果对牙齿有害。

canoe /ca·'noe; kə'nu:/ *n.*
light boat 轻舟;独木舟
Tom went down the river in a canoe.
汤姆乘着轻舟沿河划下去。

can't /can't; kɑ:nt/ *v.*
can not, cannot 即 can not 或 cannot
Laura can't swim.
劳拉不会游泳。

Cantonese [1] /Can·ton·'ese; kæntə'ni:z/ *adj.*
from Guangdong in China 广东的
John likes Cantonese food.
约翰喜欢吃广东菜。

Cantonese [2] /Can·ton·'ese; kæntə'ni:z/ *n.*
1 Chinese language spoken in Guangdong and Hong Kong 广州话;粤语
Most people in Hong Kong speak Cantonese.
大多数香港人说广州话。
2 (**no plural**) people from Guangdong 广东人
Xiaofang is a Cantonese.
小芳是广东人。

cap /cap; kæp/ *n.*
1 sort of soft hat 鸭舌帽;小软帽
Peter wears a cap and blazer for school.
彼得戴着鸭舌帽、穿着校服去上学。

2 cover for the top of a tube or bottle 盖子
Don't forget to put the cap back on the toothpaste.
不要忘记把牙膏盖旋好。

capital /'cap·i·tal; 'kæpɪtl/ *n.*
1 most important city in a country 首都
Paris is the capital of France.
巴黎是法国的首都。
2 large letters of the alphabet 大写字母
Names of people start with capitals.
人名的开头要用大写字母。

captain /'cap·tain; 'kæptɪn/ *n.*
1 leader of a team 队长
David is captain of his football team.
戴维是足球队队长。
2 chief person on a ship 船长
He is the captain of a large ship.
他是一艘大船的船长。

capture /'cap·ture; 'kæptʃə/ *v.*
(**capturing, captured, captured**)
catch and hold a person or animal 捕获;捉到
They captured a lion for the zoo.
他们替动物园捉到了一只狮子。

car /car; kɑ:/ *n.*
thing with four wheels and an engine that can carry a small number of people 汽车
Mr Tan goes to work by car.
谭先生开汽车上班。

car-park /'car·park; 'kɑ:pɑ:k/ *n.*
place where cars are left 停车场
Mr Tan always puts his car in a car-park when he goes to town.
谭先生进了城以后总是把车子停在停车场。

card /card; kɑ:d/ *n.*
1 piece of thick paper 厚纸片
Mary stuck the pictures on cards.
玛丽把那些图画粘在厚纸片上。
2 thing that you use in a game 扑克牌；纸牌
Tom and Peter like to play cards.
汤姆和彼得都喜欢玩扑克牌。
3 thing that you use for messages 卡片
Susan sent Anna a birthday card.
苏珊寄了一张生日卡给安娜。

cards

cardboard /'card·board; 'kɑ:dbɔ:d/ *n.*
(**no plural**)
sort of thick paper 厚硬纸板
Shoe boxes are made of cardboard.
鞋盒是用硬纸板做的。

cardigan /'car·di·gan; kɑ:dɪgən/ *n.*
woollen coat that fastens in front 开襟毛外衣
Mary wears a cardigan when it is cold.
天气冷时，玛丽穿上一件开襟毛衣。

care [1] /care; keə/ *n.*
(**no plural**)
trying to do something safely or well 小心；谨慎
Take care when you cross the road.
过马路时要小心。
take care at 照顾；看管；照料
Will you take care of my things while I have a swim?
我去游泳时，你替我看管一下我的东西好吗？

care [2] /care; keə/ *v.*
(**caring, cared, cared**)
feel that something or someone is important to you 关心
Tom cares about his school work.
汤姆很关心自己的功课。

careful /'care·ful; 'keəfl/ *adj.*
(**more careful, most careful**)
taking care 小心的；仔细的；谨慎的
His work is very careful.
他的工作非常仔细。
opp. 反义词：careless 不小心的；不仔细的
be careful 当心；小心
Be careful when you cross the road.
过马路时要小心。
carefully *adv.* 小心地
She carefully picked up the baby.
她小心地抱起婴儿。

careless /'care·less; 'keəlɪs/ *adj.*
(**more careless, most careless**)
not taking care 不小心的；不仔细的
Peter's work is sometimes careless.
彼得的工作有时不够仔细。
opp. 反义词：careful 小心的；仔细的
carelessly *adv.* 粗心大意地
Tom writes carelessly.
汤姆写字粗心大意。

caretaker /'care·ta·ker; 'keəteɪkə/ *n.*
someone who looks after a building 管理员
The caretaker made sure that the doors of the building were locked.
管理员查看这大厦所有的门，看看是否锁好。

cargo /'car·go; 'kɑ:gəu/ *n.*
(two **cargoes**)
things that a lorry, ship or aeroplane carries 装运的货物
The ship had a cargo of rice.
这艘船装的货物是大米。

carpenter /'car·pen·ter; 'kɑ:pəntə/ *n.*
someone who makes things out of wood 木匠
The carpenter made a door.
木匠做了一道门。

carpet /'car·pet; 'kɑ:pɪt/ *n.*
sort of big cloth that covers a floor 地毯
They had beautiful carpets on the floor.
他们家里的地板上铺了些漂亮的地毯。

carpet

carriage /ˈcar·riage; ˈkærɪdʒ/ *n.*

1 part of a train where you sit 火车的车厢

The Guangzhou train had ten carriages.

去广州的火车有十节车厢。

2 vehicle pulled by horses 马车

The princess rode in a carriage.

公主坐在马车里。

carried /ˈcar·ried; ˈkærɪd/ *v.*

p.t. of **carry** carry 的过去式

The woman carried her baby on her back.

那女人把她的婴儿背在背上。

carrot /ˈcar·rot; ˈkærət/ *n.*

long orange or yellow vegetable 胡萝卜

Tom likes carrot juice.

汤姆喜欢饮胡萝卜汁。

carrots

carry /ˈcar·ry; ˈkærɪ/ *v.*

(**carrying, carried, carried**)

take someone or something from one place to another 携带；载送；搬运

The bus carries a hundred passengers.

这辆公共汽车可载送一百位乘客。

carry on

go on doing something 继续

When the other children went out to play, Tom carried on working.

别的孩子出去玩耍时，汤姆继续工作。

cart /cart; kɑːt/ *n.*

sort of box on wheels pulled by a man or an animal

二轮车；手推车

The horse was pulling a cart.

这匹马拉着一辆二轮车。

cartoon /car·ˈtoon; kɑːˈtuːn/ *n.*

story or film made of drawings 漫画；卡通片；动画片

Peter likes to watch cartoons on television.

彼得喜欢看电视的卡通片。

case /case; keɪs/ *n.*

box or suitcase 箱子；盒子

Susan packed a case with clothes.

苏珊把衣服装到箱子里。

in case 万一；如果

Take your umbrella in case it rains.

请你带一把雨伞，以防万一下雨。

cash /cash; kæʃ/ *n.*

(**no plural**)

money in coins or notes

钱；现款

The shopkeeper kept his cash in a drawer.

店主把钱放在抽屉里。

cashier *n.* 出纳员；收款员

Mary paid the cashier for the dress.

玛丽付了买连衣裙的钱给收款员。

cassette /cas·ˈsette; kəˈset/ *n.*

small plastic case with a tape of music or words

卡式录音盒带

David had a lot of songs on cassettes.

戴维录了很多歌曲在盒带里。

cassette-recorder *n.*

machine for recording and playing cassettes 卡式录音机

castle /ˈcas·tle; ˈkɑːsl/ *n.*

big, strong building that kept people inside safe from their enemies 堡垒；城堡

Many soldiers lived in the castle.

城堡内住了许多士兵。

cat /cat; kæt/ *n.*
small animal with long tail, which lives with people 猫
The cat caught a mouse.
那只猫捉了一只老鼠。

catch /catch; kætʃ/ *v.*
(**catching, caught, caught**)
1 stop something which is moving and hold it 接住；抓住
Tom caught the ball.
汤姆把球接住了。

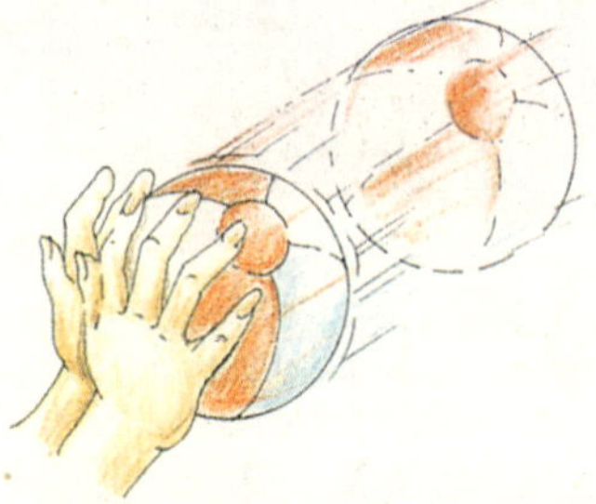

2 find and hold someone 捉住
The police caught the thief.
警察捉住了小偷。
3 get an illness 患病
Mary caught a cold.
玛丽患了感冒。
catch a bus, catch a train 赶上公共汽车或火车
Mr Chen catches a train to work.
陈先生及时赶上火车上班。
catch fire 着火；烧着
The man dropped a match and the grass caught fire.
那人掉了一根火柴在草地上，草地立刻烧起来。

caterpillar /'cat·er·pil·lar; kætəpɪlə/ *n.*
very small animal like a worm with hairs 毛虫
Caterpillars were eating the cabbages.
毛虫在吃卷心菜。

cattle /'cat·tle; 'kætl/ *n.*
(**no plural**)
cows and bulls (总称)牛
There were some cattle in the field.
田野里有些牛。

catty /'cat·ty; 'kætɪ/ *n.*
(two **catties**)
Chinese weight 斤
Xiaofang bought a catty of carrots.
小芳买了一斤胡萝卜。

caught /caught; kɔ:t/ *v.*
p.t. of **catch** catch 的过去式
David caught the bus to school.
戴维赶上了那辆公共汽车上学。

cauliflower /'cau·li·flow·er; 'kɒlɪflaʊə/ *n.*
white vegetable 菜花；花椰菜
Mary cooked some cauliflower for lunch.
玛丽午饭煮了些花椰菜。

cauliflower

cause [1] /cause; kɔ:z/ *n.*
person or thing that makes something happen 原因；起因
A barbecue was the cause of the fire.
烧烤是起火的原因。

cause [2] /cause; kɔ:z/ *v.*
(**causing, caused, caused**)
make something happen 引起；导致
A dog ran across the road and caused an accident.
一只狗跑过马路，引起了车祸。

cave /cave; keɪv/ *n.*
big hole in a hill or under the ground 山洞；洞穴
The wolves were living in a cave.
那些狼住在一个山洞里。

ceiling /'ceil·ing; 'si:lɪŋ/ *n.*
the part of the room above your head 天花板
A light was hanging from the ceiling.
天花板上吊着一盏灯。
opp. 反义词：floor 地板

cent (¢) /cent; sent/ *n.*
part of a dollar 一分钱
There are 100 cents in a dollar.
一港元相当于一百分钱。

centimetre (cm) /ˈcen·ti·me·tre; ˈsentɪmiːtə/ *n.*
measure of length 厘米
There are 100 centimetres in a metre.
一米相当于一百厘米。

central /ˈcen·tral; ˈsentrəl/ *adj.*
in the middle 中央的；中心的
He works in the central part of town.
他在城中心上班。

centre /ˈcen·tre; ˈsentə/ *n.*
the middle 中央；中心
Mary put the flowers in the centre of the table.
玛丽把花放在桌子中央。

century /ˈcen·tu·ry; ˈsentʃərɪ/ *n.*
(two **centuries**)
a hundred years 世纪
We are living in the twentieth century.
我们生活在二十世纪。

cereal /ˈce·re·al; ˈsɪərɪəl/ *n.*
food made from grains, usually eaten at breakfast 谷类食品
Susan eats cereal for breakfast.
苏珊早餐吃谷类食品。

cereals

certain /ˈcer·tain; ˈsɜːtn/ *adj.*
(**more certain, most certain**)
sure 肯定；确定
I'm certain I saw Peter at school.
我的确在学校看见过彼得。
certainly *adv.* 当然
I certainly saw Peter at school.
我当然在学校见过彼得。

certificate /cer·ˈtif·i·cate; səˈtɪfɪkət/ *n.*
piece of paper saying you have done something 证明书；奖状
Baoling got a certificate for winning the painting competition.
宝玲在绘画比赛中获胜，得了一张奖状。

chain /chain; tʃeɪn/ *n.*
many metal rings joined together 锁链；链子；项链
Xiaofang wears a gold chain round her neck.
小芳颈上戴了一条金项链。

chair /chair; tʃeə/ *n.*
something you sit on 椅子
Mary put six chairs round the table.
玛丽把六张椅子围着桌子摆好。
chairman *n.* 主席
Mr Li was the chairman of the meeting.
李先生是这个会议的主席。

chairs

chalk /chalk; tʃɔːk/ *n.*
soft stick for writing on a blackboard 粉笔
David cleaned the chalk off the blackboard.
戴维把黑板上的粉笔字擦掉。
Usage note: Use *pieces of chalk* for more than one — *Sam picked up two pieces of chalk.*
用法：如果粉笔的数量多于一枝，要用 pieces of chalk，例如 Sam picked up two pieces of chalk。

champion /ˈchamp·i·on; ˈtʃæmpɪən/ *n.*
someone who does better than all the others 冠军
David is the club tennis champion.
戴维是俱乐部里的网球冠军。

chance /chance; tʃɑ:ns/ *n.*
1 something that happens when you did not plan it 偶然
Mary met Susan by chance in the park.
玛丽在公园里偶然碰到苏珊。
2 time when you can do something; time when something can happen 机会
David had a chance to go to Canada.
戴维有一个机会去加拿大。

change [1] /change; tʃeɪndʒ/ *v.*
(changing, changed, changed)
1 become different 改变；转变
Susan's address has changed.
苏珊的地址更改了。
2 take or put one thing in place of another 更换；转换
Tom changes his clothes after school.
汤姆下课后更换衣服。
change places 换位置
Peter and David changed places.
彼得和戴维互换了位置。

change [2] /change; tʃeɪndʒ/ *n.*
1 **(no plural)** money you get back when you have paid too much 付款后找回的钱；找头
Peter gave the cashier $100 and got $20 change.
彼得给收款员一百港元，找回二十港元。
2 time when a difference comes 变化；转变
There was a change in the weather.
天气有了变化。

chapter /ˈchap·ter; ˈtʃæptə/ *n.*
part of a book 章；篇
David read the first chapter of the book for homework.
戴维做家庭作业，先阅读书的第一章。

character /ˈcha·rac·ter; ˈkærəktə/ *n.*
1 written Chinese words 汉字
Baoling knows thousands of characters.
宝玲认识几千个汉字。
2 person in a film, play or book（电影、戏剧或小说中的）角色
He played a bad character in the film.
他在这部电影里扮演一个坏人的角色。
3 what someone is like 性格
Susan has a good character.
苏珊性格善良。

charge /charge; tʃɑ:dʒ/ *v.*
(charging, charged, charged)
ask a price for something 要价
The shopkeeper charged Mary $2 for an apple.
店主卖了一个苹果给玛丽，收了两港元。
be in charge of 负责管理
The officer was in charge of the policemen.
警官负责管理警员。

chart /chart; tʃɑ:t/ *n.*
piece of paper with information on it 图表
The chart showed the number of children in each class.
图表显示每班孩子的数目。

chase /chase; tʃeɪs/ *v.*
(chasing, chased, chased)
run after someone or something 追赶
The dog chased the cat.
那只狗追那只猫。

cheap /cheap; tʃi:p/ *adj.*
not costing much money 便宜的；廉价的
This dress is cheap. It's only $20.
这件连衣裙很便宜，只售二十港元。
opp.反义词：expensive, dear 价钱贵的
cheaply *adv.* 便宜地
They were selling dresses cheaply.
他们的衣服卖得便宜。

cheat /cheat; tʃi:t/ *v.*
do something that is not honest 欺骗；作弊
You should never cheat in exams.
考试绝不能作弊。

check /check; tʃek/ *v.*
look carefully at something to see if it is correct 检查；核对
The teacher checked the answers to the test.
教师检查测验的答案。

cheek /cheek; tʃi:k/ *n.*
side of the face under the eye 颊；脸蛋
It was very hot. Tom had red cheeks.
热得很，汤姆脸颊通红。

cheer [1] /cheer; tʃɪə/ *v.*
shout to show you are pleased with someone 欢呼
The audience cheered the singer.
听众向演唱者欢呼。
cheer up
become happy; make someone happy 高兴起来；使…高兴
The little girl cheered up when her mother came home
妈妈回家，小女孩就高兴起来。

cheer [2] /cheer; tʃɪə/ *n.*
shout of joy 欢呼；喝彩
The audience gave a big cheer.
观众大声欢呼喝彩。

cheerful /'cheer·ful; 'tʃɪəfl/ *adj.*
(**more cheerful, most cheerful**)
happy 愉快的；快乐的
The children at the party were very cheerful.
参加聚会的孩子们都很快乐。
cheerfully *adv.* 愉快地；快乐地
The children played cheerfully.
小孩子们快乐地玩。

cheese /cheese; tʃi:z/ *n.*
(**no plural**)
sort of food made from milk 干酪；乳酪；芝士(方言)
Baoling does not like cheese.
宝玲不喜欢吃乳酪。

cherry /'cher·ry; 'tʃerɪ/ *n.*
(two **cherries**)
small, red fruit 樱桃
Tom bought a catty of cherries in the market.
汤姆在市场买了一斤樱桃。

cherries

chess /chess; tʃes/ *n.*
(**no plural**)
game where two people move small wooden or plastic pieces on a board
棋；国际象棋；西洋棋
David likes playing chess.
戴维喜欢下棋。

chest /chest; tʃest/ *n.*
front of the body between the neck and the waist 胸部
The ball hit Sam on the chest.
球打中了萨姆的胸部。

chew /chew; tʃu:/ *v.*
crush food in your mouth 咀嚼
The meat was hard to chew.
这块肉很难嚼。
chewing-gum *n.* 口香糖；橡皮糖；香口胶(方言)
The children cannot take chewing-gum to school.
小孩子们不许带口香糖上学。

chicken /'chick·en; 'tʃɪkɪn/ *n.*
1 young hen you keep to eat and for eggs 小鸡；鸡
There are many chickens on the farm.
农场里有很多小鸡。

chickens

2 meat from a chicken 鸡肉
David likes chicken and rice.
戴维爱吃鸡饭。

chief /chief; tʃi:f/ *adj.*
most important 主要的
The chief crops in Hong Kong are rice and vegetables.
香港主要的农作物是稻米和蔬菜。

child /child; tʃaɪld/ *n.*
(two **children**)
young boy or girl 小孩子；儿童
The children are playing in the park.
小孩子们在公园里玩耍。
opp.反义词：adult 成年人

chimney /'chim·ney; 'tʃɪmnɪ/ *n.*
sort of big pipe that takes smoke out of a building 烟囱；烟筒
Smoke was coming from the factory chimneys.
工厂的烟囱冒出烟。

chin /chin; tʃɪn/ *n.*
part of the face below the mouth 颏；下巴
Tom rested his chin on his hand.
汤姆一只手托住下巴。

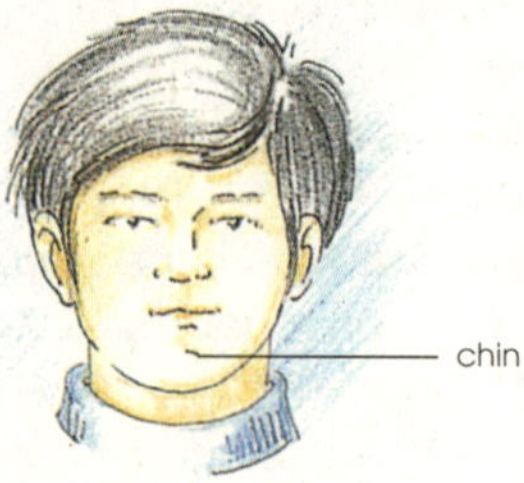

China /'Chi·na; 'tʃaɪnə/ *n.*
name of a country 中国
China is in Asia.
中国位于亚洲。

Chinese [1] /'Chi·nese; 'tʃaɪni:z/ *adj.*
from China 中国的
Baoling likes Chinese food.
宝玲喜欢吃中国菜。

Chinese [2] /'Chi·nese; 'tʃaɪni:z/ *n.*
1 language of China 汉语
Peter can speak Chinese.
彼得能说汉语。

2 (**no plural**) people from China 中国人
Many Chinese live abroad.
很多中国人在外国居住。

Chinese New Year *n.*
中国的新年；农历新年
We have a holiday at Chinese New Year.
农历新年我们放假。

chip /chip; tʃɪp/ *n.*
small piece of fried potato 炸薯条
Tom had hamburger and chips for lunch.
汤姆午餐吃了汉堡包和炸薯条。

chocolate /'choc·o·late; 'tʃɒklət/ *n.*
sweet food made from cocoa 巧克力；朱古力（方言）
Most children like chocolate.
大部分孩子都爱吃巧克力。
chocolates *n.* 巧克力糖
Mary bought a box of chocolates for her mother.
玛丽买了一盒巧克力糖给她妈妈。

choice /choice; tʃɔɪs/ *n.*
taking or naming what you like best 选择
David had a choice between a camera and a bicycle for his birthday present.
戴维可以选择要一架照相机或一辆自行车作为他的生日礼物。

choir /'choir; 'kwaɪə/ *n.*
group of singers 合唱团
David sings in the school choir.
戴维是学校合唱团的成员。

choke /choke; tʃəuk/ *v.*
(choking, choked, choked)
not be able to breathe
哽在喉中；卡住
The man almost choked on a fish bone.
那人几乎给一根鱼骨卡住了。

choose /choose; tʃu:z/ *v.*
(choosing, chose, chosen)
take or say what you like best
选择
David chose a bicycle for his birthday present.
戴维选了一辆自行车作为自己的生日礼物。

chop /chop; tʃɒp/ *v.*
(chopping, chopped, chopped)
cut something into pieces with an axe or knife 用刀切或斩开
The cook chopped up the meat.
厨师把肉切开。
chopper *n.* 砍刀
The cook cut up the chicken with a chopper.
厨师用砍刀把鸡斩开。

chopsticks /'chop·sticks; 'tʃɒpstɪks/ *n.*
(plural)
two long sticks for lifting food to the mouth 筷子
Baoling eats her food with chopsticks.
宝玲用筷子吃东西。

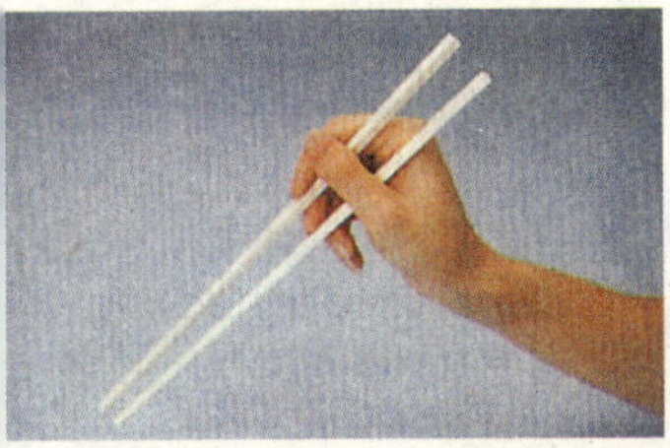

chose /chose; tʃəuz/ *v.*
p.t. of **choose** choose 的过去式
David chose a present for his mother.
戴维挑选了一件礼物送给妈妈。
chosen *v.* 挑选
Mary has chosen a blue dress to wear to the party.
玛丽已经选好了一件蓝色连衣裙去聚会时穿。

Christmas /'Christ·mas; 'krɪsməs/ *n.*
Christian festival 圣诞节
Christmas is in December.
圣诞节在十二月。

church /church; tʃɜ:tʃ/ *n.*
(two **churches**)
building where people pray
教堂
Some Christians go to church on Sundays.
有些基督徒逢星期日就上教堂。

cigarette /ci·ga·'rette; ˌsɪgə'ret/ *n.*
paper tube of tobacco 香烟
Smoking cigarettes is bad for your health.
吸烟对健康是有害的。

cinema /'cin·e·ma; 'sɪnəmə/ *n.*
place where you go to see films 电影院
Anna saw a good film at the cinema.
安娜在电影院看了一部好看的电影。

circle [1] /'cir·cle; 'sɜ:kl/ *n.*
round shape 圆圈；圆形
David used a coin to draw a circle.
戴维用一个硬币画了一个圆圈。
circular *adj.* 圆形的
The shape of a coin is circular.
硬币是圆形的。

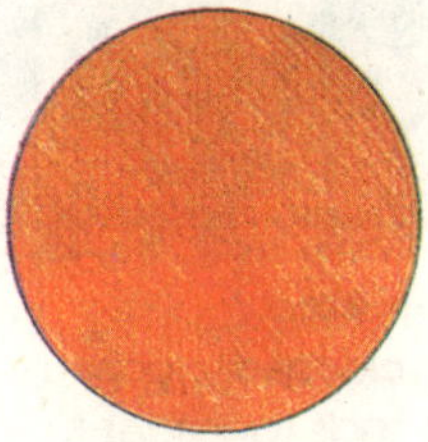

circle [2] /'cir·cle; 'sɜ:kl/ *v.*
(circling, circled, circled)
go round 环绕；盘旋
The plane circled the airport.
飞机绕着机场飞。

circus /'cir·cus; 'sɜ:kəs/ *n.*
(two **circuses**)
people and animals that you watch in a tent 马戏团；马戏表演
Mary saw an elephant at the circus.
玛丽在马戏表演中看到了一头大象。

citizen /ˈci·ti·zen; ˈsɪtɪzn/ *n.*
person who belongs to a country 公民
Sam is a Canadian citizen.
萨姆是加拿大公民。

city /ˈcit·y; ˈsɪtɪ/ *n.*
(two **cities**)
important town 城市
Shanghai is a large city in China.
上海是中国一个大城市。

clap /clap; klæp/ *v.*
(**clapping, clapped, clapped**)
hit your hands together to make a noise 拍手；鼓掌
The audience clapped the singer.
听众为演唱者鼓掌。

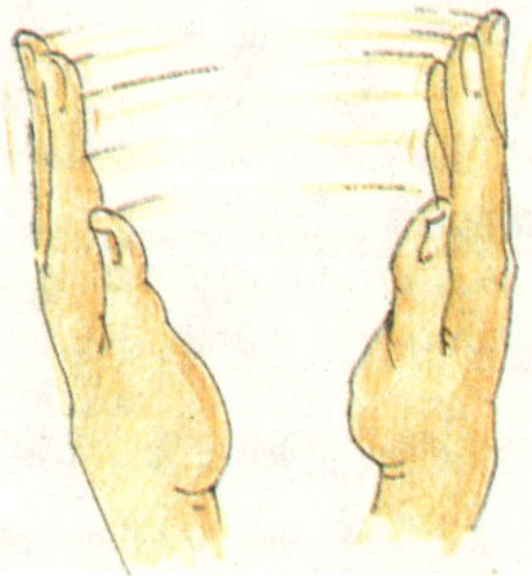

class /class; klɑːs/ *n.*
(two **classes**)
group of pupils who learn together 班；级
There were twenty classes in the school.
学校有二十个班。

classmate *n.* 同班同学
Tom plays football with his classmates.
汤姆和同班同学踢足球。

classroom *n.* 教室
There are thirty desks in the classroom.
教室里有三十张书桌。

clean [1] /clean; kliːn/ *adj.*
not dirty 干净；清洁
Anna put on a clean dress.
安娜穿上了一件干净的连衣裙。

clean [2] /clean; kliːn/ *v.*
make something clean 弄干净
Mrs Lin cleaned the windows.
林太太把窗子擦干净。

clean up 收拾干净；整理
Mrs Lin cleaned up the mess.
林太太把弄乱了的东西收拾干净。

clear /clear; klɪə/ *adj.*
1 easy to see, hear, or understand 清楚的
The answer to the question was clear.
这问题的答案是清楚的。
2 nothing there 畅通无阻的
The road was clear.
这路畅通无阻。

clearly *adv.*
in a clear way 清楚地
Please speak clearly.
请说得清楚些。

clerk /clerk; klɑːk/ *n.*
someone who works in an office 职员；文书
The clerk took the letters to the manager.
职员把信件送给经理。

clever /ˈclev·er; ˈklevə/ *adj.*
able to understand and learn quickly 聪明的
Baoling is a clever girl.
宝玲是个聪明的女孩子。
opp.反义词：stupid 愚蠢

cliff /cliff; klɪf/ *n.*
high, steep side of a hill 峭壁；悬崖
Tom climbed down the cliff to the beach.
汤姆爬下峭壁到了海滩。

climate /ˈcli·mate; ˈklaɪmɪt/ *n.*
the sort of weather a place has 气候
What sort of climate does Hong Kong have?
香港的气候怎么样？

climb /climb; klaɪm/ *v.*
go up or down something 爬
David climbed the ladder to the roof.
戴维爬梯子上了屋顶。

climber *n.* 登山运动员
The climbers reached the top of the mountain.
登山运动员登上山顶。

clinic /'clin·ic; 'klɪnɪk/ *n.*
place where people go to see a doctor or nurse or to get medicine 诊所；门诊部
Mrs Lin went to the clinic to see a doctor.
林太太去诊所看病。

clock /clock; klɒk/ *n.*
machine that shows you the time 钟
There was a clock on the classroom wall.
教室墙上挂了一只钟。

closkwise *adv.* 顺时针方向的
Turn the knob clockwise.
顺时针方向转动旋钮。

close [1] /close; kləuz/ *v.*
(closing, closed, closed)
1 shut something 关闭
Mary closed the window.
玛丽把窗子关上。

2 stop doing business
停止营业
The shops close at seven o'clock.
这些商店七时停止营业。

opp. 反义词：open 开；开始营业

closed *adj.* 关闭的
Peter went to the shop, but it was closed.
彼得去商店，但已经关门了。

Usage note: You can use *shut* in the same way as *close* — *Close the door, please, Shut the door, please.*
用法：shut 与 close 同义，例如 Close the door, please 可以写成 shut the door, please。

close [2] /close; kləus/ *adv.*
near 靠近
Tom lives close to the school.
汤姆住的地方靠近学校。

closely *adv.* 仔细地
Mrs Chen watched the baby closely.
陈太太仔细地守护着婴儿。

cloth /cloth; klɒθ/ *n.*
1 (no plural) material made by weaving 布；布料
Mrs Lin bought some cotton cloth to make a dress.
林太太买了一些棉布来做一件连衣裙。

cloth 1

2 piece of material 一块布
Mary wiped the floor with a cloth.
玛丽用一块布来抹地板。

tablecloth *n.* 桌布
The waiter put a clean tablecloth on the table in the restaurant.
在餐馆里，服务员把一块干净的桌布铺在桌子上。

clothes /clothes; kləuðz/ *n.*
(plural)
things you wear to cover your body 衣服
Dresses and shirts are clothes.
连衣裙和衬衣都是衣服。

clothing /'cloth·ing; 'kləuðɪŋ/ *n.*
(no plural)
clothes 衣服
The factory makes clothing.
这家工厂制造衣服。

cloud /cloud; klaʊd/ *n.*
white or dark shape that floats in the sky 云
The sun was covered by black clouds.
太阳给乌云遮盖着。
cloudy *adj.*
with clouds 多云的；密云的；阴的
The sky was cloudy.
天空是多云的。

clouds

clown /clown; klaʊn/ *n.*
man who wears funny clothes and makes people laugh 丑角；小丑
Tom saw some clowns at the circus.
汤姆在马戏表演中看到了一些小丑。

club /club; klʌb/ *n.*
group of people who like to do something 俱乐部；会所
David belongs to a football club.
戴维参加了一个足球俱乐部。

clue /clue; kluː/ *n.*
something that helps you to find the answer to a problem
线索；提示；端倪
I don't know the answer. Give me a clue.
我答不出来，给点提示吧。

coach /coach; kəʊtʃ/ *n.*
(two **coaches**)
1 bus for long journeys
长途旅游汽车
John took a coach from Hong Kong to Guangzhou.
约翰乘长途旅游汽车从香港去广州。
2 someone who teaches a sport（体育运动）教练
The football coach was very good.
这个足球教练很好。

coast /coast; kəʊst/ *n.*
land by the sea 海岸；沿岸地区
There are many beaches along the coast of Hong Kong.
香港沿岸有许多海滩。

coat /coat; kəʊt/ *n.*
something you wear over other clothes in cold or wet weather 大衣；长外衣
It was a cold day, so Anna put on a warm coat.
天气很冷，因此安娜穿上了一件暖和的大衣。

cobweb /ˈcob·web; ˈkɒbweb/ *n.*
thin net made by a spider
蜘蛛网
There were a lot of cobwebs in the room.
房间里有很多蜘蛛网。

cock /cock; kɒk/ *n.*
male chicken 公鸡
I hear a cock crow every morning.
每天早上我都听见公鸡啼叫。

cockroach /ˈcock·roach; ˈkɒkrəʊtʃ/ *n.*
(two **cockroaches**)
large, dark-brown insect 蟑螂
Cockroaches are very dirty insects.
蟑螂是非常肮脏的昆虫。

cocoa /ˈco·coa; ˈkəʊkəʊ/ *n.*
(no plural)
kind of drink 可可
At night, Mr Lin drinks a cup of cocoa.
林先生晚上总是喝一杯可可。

coconut /ˈco·co·nut; ˈkəʊkənʌt/ *n.*
big, brown nut that grows on palm trees 椰子
There were many coconut trees in the garden.
花园里有很多椰子树。

coconuts

code /code; kəud/ *n.*
secret signs or writing 密码
Tom wrote a message in code to Peter.
汤姆用密码写了一封信给彼得。

coffee /ˈcof·fee; ˈkɒfɪ/ *n.*
(**no plural**)
kind of drink 咖啡
In the morning, Mr Lin drinks a cup of coffee.
林先生早上总是喝一杯咖啡。
coffee shop *n.*
café in a hotel 旅馆里的小吃部

coin /coin; kɔɪn/ *n.*
round piece of metal money 硬币；钱币
David found a 50-cent coin.
戴维找到了一个五毛钱的硬币。

coins

cold [1] /cold; kəuld/ *adj.*
not hot 冷
The winters in Canada are cold.
加拿大冬天很冷。

cold [2] /cold; kəuld/ *n.*
illness that makes you cough and sneeze 感冒；伤风
Mary caught a cold.
玛丽患了感冒。

collar /ˈcol·lar; ˈkɒlə/ *n.*
the part of your clothes that goes round your neck 衣领
Baoling has a red dress with a white collar.
宝玲有一件白色衣领的红连衣裙。

collect /col·ˈlect; kəˈlekt/ *v.*
gather things together 收集；搜集
David collects stamps.
戴维收集邮票。

collection /col·ˈlec·tion; kəˈlekʃn/ *n.*
group of things gathered together 收藏品；搜集品
David has a large stamp collection.
戴维收藏了很多的邮票。

college /ˈcol·lege; ˈkɒlɪdʒ/ *n.*
place where students go to learn 大学；学院；专科学校
Peter goes to college.
彼得上大学了。

colony /ˈcol·o·ny; ˈkɒlənɪ/ *n.*
(two **colonies**)
country or territory ruled by a foreign people 殖民地
There aren't many colonies now.
现在殖民地已不多了。

colour [1] /ˈco·lour; ˈkʌlə/ *n.*
blue, red, yellow, etc. 颜色
What colour is Mary's dress?
玛丽穿的连衣裙是什么颜色的?

colour [2] /ˈco·lour; ˈkʌlə/ *v.*
put paint or crayon on something 涂上颜色；着色
Colour the picture in your book.
给你书里的图画着色。

coloured *adj.*
with a colour that is not black or white 有颜色的
This book has coloured pictures.
这本书有些彩色图片。
colourful *adj.* 色彩鲜艳的
The fireworks were very colourful.
这些烟火色彩鲜艳。

comb [1] /comb; kəum/ *n.*
thing to make your hair tidy 梳子
Anna always takes a comb to school to keep her hair tidy.
安娜总是带一把梳子上学，使头发保持整齐。

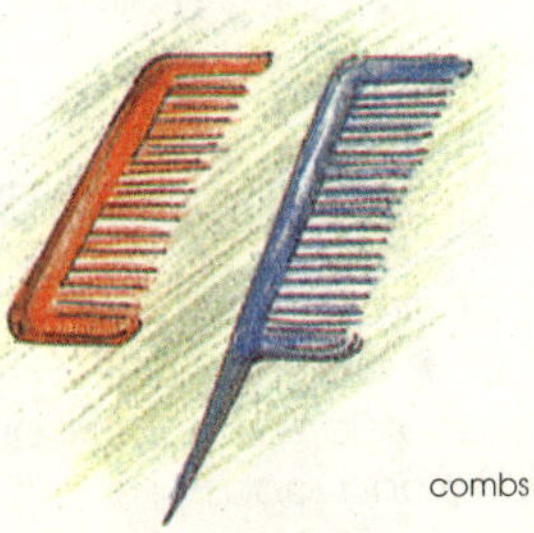
combs

comb [2] /comb; kəum/ *v.*
use a comb 用梳子梳
Anna combs her hair several times a day.
安娜每天梳几次头发。

come /come; kʌm/ *v.*
(**coming, came, come**)
1 move here; arrive 来；到
Tom came home late.
汤姆很晚才回到家里。
opp.反义词：go 去
2 be; happen 在；发生
'A' comes before 'B' in the alphabet.
在字母表中，A在B之前。
come along! come on!
hurry! 赶快！加把劲儿！

comfortable /'com·fort·a·ble; 'kʌmftəbl/ *adj.*
(**more comfortable, most comfortable**)
nice to sit on, lie on, or wear
舒服；舒适
These shoes are very comfortable.
这双鞋穿起来很舒适。
opp. 反义词：uncomfortable
不舒服

comic /'com·ic; 'kɒmɪk/ *n.*
children's magazine with stories in pictures 连环漫画
Peter likes reading comics.
彼得喜欢看连环漫画书。

comma /'com·ma; 'kɒmə/ *n.*
sign (,) that shows a short stop in a sentence 逗号

common /'com·mon; 'kɒmən/ *adj.*
happening often; usual
普通的；常见的
Accidents are common on Hong Kong roads.
在香港的马路上，交通事故是很常见的。

compact disc (CD)
/com·pact 'disc; kɒmpækt 'dɪsk/ *n.*
special kind of record 激光唱片
Mr Wang bought a compact disc player.
王先生买了一部激光唱机。

company /'com·pa·ny kʌmpənɪ/ *n.*
(two **companies**)
1 group of people who work together 公司；
Mr Lin works for a big company.
林先生在一家大公司工作。
2 being with other people
同伴；伴侣
David is good company when we go out.
我们出去玩的时候，戴维是个好同伴。

compare /com·'pare; kəm'peə/ *v.*
(**comparing, compared, compared**)
look at two or more things to see if they are different 比较
David and Peter compared their answers to the questions.
戴维和彼得比较他们对问题的答案。

compass /'com·pass; kʌmpəs/ *n.*
(two **compasses**)
thing with a needle that always points to the north
指南针；罗盘
The man used a compass to find his way in the desert.
那人用指南针在沙漠中寻找道路。

compasses /'com·passes; 'kʌmpəsɪz/ *n.*
(**plural**)
thing used for drawing circles
圆规；两脚规
Mary used her compasses to draw a circle.
玛丽用圆规画了一个圆形。

competition
/com·pe·'ti·tion; kɒmpə'tɪʃn/ *n.*
race or contest 比赛
Mary won the painting competition.
玛丽在图画比赛中获胜。
compete *v.* 比赛
Tom competed in the race.
汤姆参加了竞赛。

complain /com·'plain; kəm'pleɪn/ *n.*
say that you do not like something 抱怨；投诉
Mr Lin complained that his neighbours were very noisy.
林先生抱怨说他的邻居十分喧闹。
complaint *n.* 投诉；怨言
There were many complaints about rubbish on the beaches.
有许多投诉是关于海滩上的垃圾的。

complete[1] /com·'plete; kəm'pli:t/ *adj.*
whole; with all its parts 完整的；全部的
The tents made a complete circle.
那些帐篷围成一个完整的圆形。

complete[2] /com·'plete; kəm'pli:t/ *v.*
(**completing, completed, completed**)
finish doing or making something 完成
David completed his homework before going to play.
戴维做完家庭作业以后再去玩。
completely *adv.* 完全地；全部
The food was completely eaten.
食物全部吃光了。

complicated /'com·pli·ca·ted; 'kɒmplɪkeɪtɪd/ *adj.*
(**more complicated, most complicated**)
difficult 复杂
The questions were very complicated.
这些问题非常复杂。

composition /com·po·'si·tion; kɒmpə'zɪʃn/ *n.*
story that you write 作文；文章
Xiaofang wrote a composition about her holiday in Canada.
小芳写了一篇关于她去加拿大度假的文章。

comprehension /com·pre·'hen·sion; kɒmprɪ'henʃn/ *n.*
test of understanding 理解力
Baoling is good at English comprehension.
宝玲的英语理解力很好。

computer /com·'put·er; kəm'pju:tə/ *n.*
machine that stores information and finds answers quickly 电脑；电子计算机
David likes to play games on his computer.
戴维喜欢用他的电脑玩游戏。

concert /'con·cert; 'kɒnsət/ *n.*
music played or sung for many people 音乐会
The choir sang at the school concert.
合唱团在学校音乐会上演唱。

concrete /'con·crete; 'kɒŋkri:t/ *n.*
(**no plural**)
hard stuff for building 混凝土
The building was made of concrete.
这座建筑物是用混凝土建造的。

condition /con·'di·tion; kən'dɪʃn/ *n.*
(**no plural**)
how someone or something is 情况；状态
David's bicycle is in a good condition.
戴维的自行车一点毛病也没有。

conductor /con·'duc·tor; kən'dʌktə/ *n.*
1 person who collects fares on a bus or train 公共交通工具上的售票员
There are no conductors on the tram.
电车上没有售票员。
2 person who leads an orchestra or choir 乐队或合唱团的指挥
The conductor was pleased with the way the choir sang.
指挥对合唱团的演唱很满意。

cone /cone; kəun/ *n.*
biscuit for holding ice-cream 冰淇淋蛋卷筒；雪糕筒（方言）
Mary bought an ice-cream cone.
玛丽买了一个冰淇淋蛋卷筒。

confident /'con·fi·dent; 'kɒnfɪdənt/ *adj.*
(**more confident, most confident**)
feeling that you can do things well 有信心的
Laura was very confident before the exam.
劳拉考试前非常有信心。

confusing /con·'fu·sing; kən'fju:zɪŋ/ *adj.*
(more confusing, most confusing)
making something difficult to understand 混乱；混淆
The teacher's explanations are confusing.
老师的讲解令人困惑。

congratulations /con·grat·u·'la·tions; kəngrætʃʊ'leɪʃnz/ *int.*
word that tells someone that you are pleased about what they have done or had 恭喜！祝贺你！
Congratulations on your 10th birthday!
祝贺你十岁生日！
syn. 同义词：well done!
congratulate *v.* 祝贺
The teacher congratulated Mary on her good marks.
老师祝贺玛丽学习成绩优良。

connect /con·'nect; kə'nekt/ *v.*
join together 连接
The cross-harbour tunnels connect Hong Kong and Kowloon.
过海隧道把香港和九龙连接起来。

conquer /'con·quer; 'kɒŋkə/ *v.*
beat someone in a war 征服
The army conquered the whole country.
这支军队征服了整个国家。

consist of /con·'sist of; kən'sɪst əv/ *v.*
be made of 包含有…
The meal consisted of meat and vegetables.
这顿饭有肉和菜。

consonant /'con·so·nant; 'kɒnsənənt/ *n.*
the letters of the English alphabet that are not vowels 辅音；子音
There are 21 consonants in the English alphabet.
英语里有二十一个辅音字母。

construct /con·'struct; kən'strʌkt/ *v.*
build; make 建造；建筑
They constructed many new buildings.
他们建筑了许多新楼房。

contact lenses /'con·tact len·ses; 'kɒntækt lenzɪz/ *n.*
(plural)
small pieces of glass or plastic that you wear in your eyes to see better 隐形眼镜
Baoling wears contact lenses instead of glasses.
宝玲戴隐形眼镜而不是普通眼镜。

contain /con·'tain; kən'teɪn/ *v.*
have something inside 包含；含有；里面有
The box contained shoes.
这个盒子里面装了鞋。
container *n.* 容器；货柜
Baskets and buckets are containers.
篮子和水桶都是容器。
container ship *n.* 集装箱船
The container ship carried 100 containers.
这艘集装箱船装了一百个集装箱。

contented /con·'ten·ted; kən'tentɪd/ *adj.*
(more contented, most contented)
happy; pleased 满意的；满足的
He has a job and a house. He is very contented.
他既有工作，又有房子，他十分满足了。

contents /'con·tents; 'kɒntents/ *n.*
(plural)
things that are inside something else 内容；里面所有的东西
Tom emptied the contents of his desk.
汤姆把书桌里的东西全部拿了出来。

contest /'con·test; 'kɒntest/ *n.*
game, sport, or test where people try to win 比赛；竞赛
John won the fishing contest.
约翰赢了钓鱼比赛。
contestant *n.* 比赛者；竞赛者
There were twenty contestants.
参加比赛的有二十个人。

continent /'con·ti·nent; 'kɒntɪnənt/ *n.*
large area of land 大陆
Asia and Europe are continents.
亚洲和欧洲都是大陆。

continue /con·'tin·ue; kən'tɪnju:/ *v.*
(continuing, continued, continued)
1 keep doing something and not stop 不停
The rain continued for several days.
雨不停地下了几天。
2 start again after you have stopped 继续下去

After lunch, we continued our work.
吃完午饭，我们继续工作。

control [1] /con·'trol; kən'trəʊl/ *n.*
(**no plural**)
making someone or something do what you want 控制
Mr Tan lost control of his car and crashed into a tree.
谭先生的汽车失去控制，撞到一棵树上。

control [2] /con·'trol; kən'trəʊl/ *v.*
(**controlling, controlled, controlled**)
make someone or something do what you want 控制：
Tom controlled his bicycle very well.
汤姆骑自行车控制自如。

conversation /con·ver·'sa·tion; kɒnvə'seɪʃn/ *n.*
talking betwen people 谈话；对话
The teacher had a long conversation with Mrs Lin.
老师和林太太谈了很久。

cook [1] /cook; kʊk/ *v.*
make food ready to eat 烹调；烧饭；做菜
Tom cooked some sausages on the barbecue.
汤姆在烧烤炉上烤了些肉肠。

cook [2] /cook; kʊk/ *n.*
someone who cooks 厨师
Mary is a good cook.
玛丽是个很好的厨师。
cooker *n.* 锅
She cooks on an electric cooker.
她用电锅来烧菜。

cookery *n.* 烹调术；烹饪术
Sam learns cookery at school.
萨姆在学校学烹饪。
cooking *n.* 烹调；做菜
Baoling likes cooking.
宝玲喜欢做菜。

cool /cool; ku:l/ *adj.*
a little cold 凉的
It was a cool day so Mary wore a cardigan.
这天比较凉，因此玛丽穿了一件开襟羊毛外衣。
opp. 反义词：warm 温暖

co-operate /co·'op·er·ate; kəʊ'ɒpəreɪt/ *v.*
(**co-operating, co-operated, co-operated**)
work together 合作
The children co-operate very well.
小孩子们合作得很好。
co-operation *n.* 合作
Everybody's co-operation is needed to keep the city clean.
为保持城市清洁，需要人人合作。

copy [1] /'cop·y; 'kɒpɪ/ *n.*
(two **copies**)
something that looks like another thing 复写本；副本
Tom made a copy of the map.
汤姆把地图复印了一份。

copy [2] /'cop·y; 'kɒpɪ/ *v.*
(**copying, copied, copied**)
make something that looks like another thing 抄写；复制副本
Tom copied the map of China into his geography book.
汤姆把中国地图照样画在他的地理书上。

cork /cork; kɔ:k/ *n.*
thing you put in the top of a bottle to close it 软木塞
Peter put the cork back in the bottle.
彼得用软木塞把瓶子重新盖好。

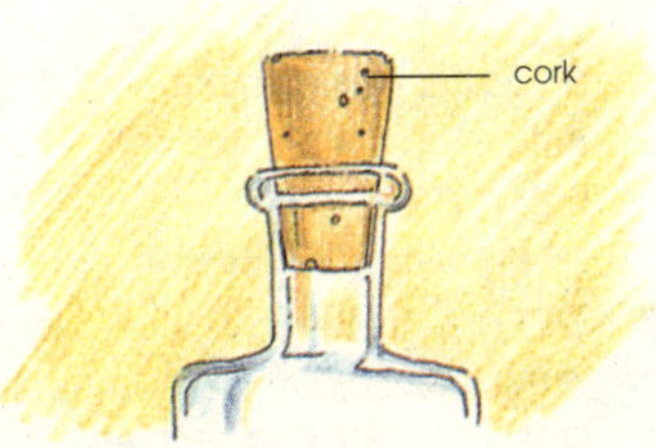

corn /corn; kɔ:n/ *n.*
(**no plural**)
kind of seed 玉米；玉蜀黍
Mrs Lin made chicken and corn soup.
林太太做了一个玉米鸡汤。

corner /'cor·ner; 'kɔ:nə/ *n.*
place where two lines, walls or roads meet 角；角落
Anna put the table in the corner of the room.
安娜把桌子放在房间角落里。

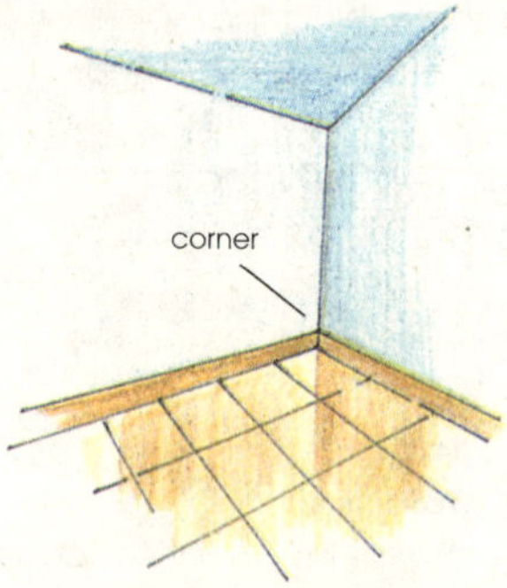

correct [1] /cor·'rect; kə'rekt/ *adj.*
(more correct, most correct)
right; with no mistake 正确；对的
David found the correct answer.
戴维找到了正确的答案。
opp. 反义词：wrong, incorrect 错误的；不正确的
correctly *adv.* 正确地
Tom answered the question correctly.
汤姆正确地回答了问题。

correct [2] /cor·'rect; kə'rekt/ *v.*
make something right 改正；修改
The teacher corrected the homework.
老师改正学生的家庭作业。

correction /cor·'rec·tion; kə'rekʃn/ *n.*
something made right 改正
There were a lot of corrections on Tom's homework.
汤姆的家庭作业上有老师的许多改正。

corridor /'cor·ri·dor; 'kɒrɪdɔ:/ *n.*
long, narrow way inside a building 走廊
The children walked along the corridor to their classroom.
孩子们沿着走廊走到他们的教室。

cost [1] /cost; kɒst/ *v.*
(costing, cost, cost)
be the price of something 花费；值
How much does the shirt cost?
这件衬衫值多少钱？

cost [2] /cost; kɒst/ *n.*
the price of something 价钱；费用
What is the cost of the shirt?
这件衬衫的价钱是多少？

costume /'cos·tume; 'kɒstju:m/ *n.*
special clothes that you wear 服装；戏服
The teacher made costumes for the play.
老师为那出戏剧做了一些戏服。

cot /cot; kɒt/ *n.*
small bed with high sides, for a baby 婴儿床
The baby was asleep in a cot.
婴儿在婴儿床里睡着了。

cottage /'cot·tage; 'kɒtɪdʒ/ *n.*
small house in the country 农舍；小房子
Mr Lin bought a cottage in a village.
林先生在乡间买了一间小房子。

cotton /'cot·ton; 'kɒtn/ *n.*
(no plural)
1 kind of cloth made from a plant 棉布
Cotton clothes are cool in summer.
夏天穿着棉布做的衣服是很凉快的。
2 thread made from the plant 棉线
Mary used some white cotton for her sewing.
玛丽用一些白棉线来缝衣服。
cotton-wool *n.* 棉花；药棉
Anna cleaned her cut fingers with cotton-wool.
安娜用药棉把受伤的手指擦干净。

cotton-wool

cough [1] /cough; kɒf/ *v.*
send air out of your mouth and throat in a noisy way
咳嗽
David coughed loudly.
戴维大声咳嗽。

cough [2] /cough; kɒf/ *n.*
noise you make when you have a bad cold 咳嗽
David had a bad cough.
戴维咳得很厉害。

could /could; kʊd/ *v.*
p.t. of **can** can 的过去式
Peter could not do his homework.
彼得不会做家庭作业。
opp. 反义词：could not, couldn't
不能；不会

couldn't /ˈcould·n't; ˈkʊdnt/ *v.*
could not 即 could not
I couldn't find my cap.
我找不到我的便帽。

count /count; kaʊnt/ *v.*
find out how much or how many 计算；数一数
The shopkeeper counted the money.
店主把钱数了一下。

counter /ˈcount·er; ˈkaʊntə/ *n.*
sort of long table in a shop
商店的柜台
The shopkeeper put the change on the counter.
店主把该找回的钱放在柜台上。

country /ˈcoun·try; ˈkʌntrɪ/ *n.*
(two **countries**)
1 nation 国家
China is a big country.
中国是个大国。
2 land that is not in a city or town 乡间
Mr Lin has a farm in the country.
林先生在乡间有一个农庄。

country park *n.* 郊野公园
There are many beautiful country parks in Hong Kong.
香港有许多风景优美的郊野公园。
countryside *n.* 乡村地区；郊区
Keep the countryside clean.
保持郊区清洁。

Usage note: *Country* should be used together with *the* to mean *land that is not in a city or town* — *My grandfather lives in the country.*
用法：country 如果解作“乡间”的时候，要和 the 连用，例如 My grandfather lives in the country。

couple /ˈcou·ple; ˈkʌpl/ *n.*
two people or things 一对；一双
The young couple bought a flat.
这对年轻的夫妇买了一套公寓房。

courage /ˈcour·age; ˈkʌrɪdʒ/ *n.*
(**no plural**)
bravery 勇气
You need courage to be a fireman.
当消防员要有勇气。

course /course; kɔːs/ *n.*
1 part of a meal 一道菜
There were ten courses for dinner.
晚宴有十道菜。
2 series of lessons 课程
Baoling is doing an English course.
宝玲正在攻读一个英语课程。
of course 当然
Of course I will come to your party.
我当然会参加你的聚会。

court /court; kɔːt/ *n.*
place where judges and lawyers work 法院；法庭
The thief had to go to court.
那个贼必须送法院受审。

cousin /ˈcous·in; ˈkʌzn/ *n.*
child of your uncle or aunt
堂兄弟；堂姐妹；表兄弟；表姐妹
Peter has three cousins.
彼得有三个堂兄弟。

cover [1] /ˈcov·er; ˈkʌvə/ *v.*
put one thing over another
遮盖
Tom covers his bicycle when it rains.
下雨时汤姆把自行车盖住。
opp. 反义词：uncover 揭开盖子；揭露

cover [2] /ˈcov·er; ˈkʌvə/ *n.*
thing that you put over another 遮盖物；盖子；封面
The book has a red cover.
这本书的封面是红色的。

cow /cow; kaʊ/ *n.*
big farm animal which gives milk 母牛；乳牛
The farmer milks his cows twice a day.
那个农民每天挤两次牛奶。

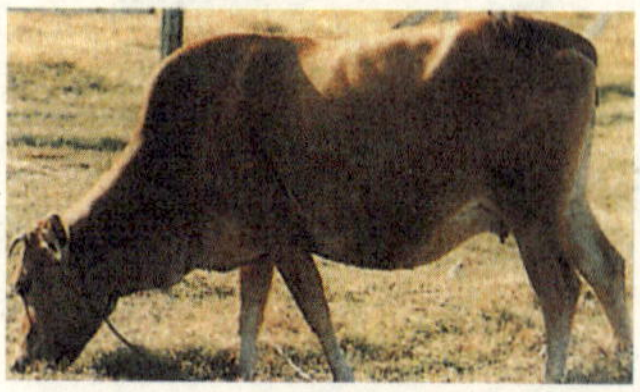

coward /ˈcow·ard; ˈkaʊəd/ *n.*
someone who is afraid of things 懦夫；胆小的人
A policeman must be brave. He cannot be a coward.
当警察必须勇敢，绝不能胆子小。

cowboy /ˈcow·boy; ˈkaʊbɔɪ/ *n.*
man who looks after cattle in America 牛仔
The cowboy rode after the cattle.
牛仔骑着马看管牛群。

crab /crab; kræb/ *n.*
sea animal with big claws 蟹
Crabs are good to eat.
蟹是好吃的。

crack [1] /crack; kræk/ *n.*
line where something has nearly broken 裂缝
There was a crack in the vase.
这个花瓶有一道裂缝。

crack [2] /crack; kræk/ *v.*
nearly break into pieces 破裂；打裂
David dropped the vase and cracked it.
戴维把花瓶掉在地上打裂了。

crane /crane; kreɪn/ *n.*
machine with a big arm for lifting things 起重机
The crane lifted the big box.
起重机把大箱子吊起来。

crash [1] /crash; kræʃ/ *n.*
(two **crashes**)
1 accident with a car, aeroplane or train, etc.
(汽车、飞机、火车等)失事撞毁
The two cars were in a crash.
两辆汽车撞在一起了。
2 noise made when something crashes 撞击发出的声响
The people heard a loud crash.
人们听见一声撞击的巨响。

crash-helmet *n.* 头盔；安全帽
Motor-cyclists wear crash-helmets.
驾驶摩托车的人都戴头盔。

crash[2] /crash; kræʃ/ *v.*
hit against something very hard 猛烈撞击
The car crashed into a tree.
汽车猛地撞到一棵树上。

crawl /crawl; krɔ:l/ *v.*
move slowly on your hands and knees 爬行
The baby was crawling on the floor.
那婴儿在地板上爬行。

crayon /ˈcray·on; ˈkreɪən/ *n.*
stick of coloured wax for drawing 蜡笔
Mary coloured the picture with crayons.
玛丽用蜡笔在图画上着色。

crayons

cream /cream; kri:m/ *n.*
(**no plural**)
thick part on top of milk 乳脂；忌廉(方言)
We use cream to make butter.
我们用乳脂来制造黄油。

credit card /ˈcre·dit card; ˈkredɪt kɑ:d/ *n.*
piece of plastic card that you can use instead of money 信用卡
Mr Chen used his credit card to buy the presents.
陈先生用信用卡购买一些礼物。

creep /creep; kri:p/ *v.*
(**creeping, crept, crept**)
move slowly and quietly
静悄悄地慢慢移动；爬行
Tom crept into the classroom, five minutes late.
汤姆悄悄地走进教室，他迟到了五分钟。

crew /crew; kru:/ *n.*
group of people who work together on a ship or aeroplane (船或飞机上的)全体工作人员
The crew went on board the ship.
全体船员都上了船。

cricket /ˈcrick·et; ˈkrɪkɪt/ *n.*
1 insect which makes a loud noise 蟋蟀
The cricket kept me awake.
那只蟋蟀吵得我睡不着。
2 (**no plural**) game played with a bat and ball 板球
David plays cricket.
戴维打板球。

cried /cried; kraɪd/ *v.*
p.t. of **cry** cry 的过去式
The baby cried when she fell down.
那个婴孩跌了一跤，哭了起来。

cries /cries; kraɪz/ *v.*
3rd person singular present tense of **cry** cry 的第三人称单数现在式
The baby sometimes cries.
这婴儿有时会哭。

crime /crime; kraɪm/ *n.*
something wrong that you must not do 罪行
Stealing is a crime.
偷窃是犯罪。
criminal *n.* 罪犯；犯人
The criminal went to prison.
罪犯入了狱。

crisp /crisp; krɪsp/ *n.*
thin slice of fried potato 炸薯片
Peter ate a packet of crisps.
彼得吃了一包炸薯片。

crocodile /ˈcroc·o·dile; ˈkrɒkədaɪl/ *n.*
large reptile with big jaws which lives in rivers 鳄鱼
The crocodile caught and ate a big fish.
那条鳄鱼咬住一条大鱼，把它吃了。

crooked /ˈcrook·ed; ˈkrʊkɪd/ *adj.*
(**more crooked, most crooked**)
not straight 弯曲的
The branches of the tree were crooked.
那棵树的树枝都是弯曲的。

crop /crop; krɒp/ *n.*
plants a farmer grows
农作物的收成
There was a good crop of rice.
稻米的收成很好。

cross [1] /cross; krɒs/ *n.*
(two **crosses**)
mark like an x 叉形(X)记号
The teacher puts crosses against wrong answers.
老师在错误的答案上打上叉号。

cross [2] /cross; krɒs/ *v.*
go from one side to the other 横穿
The ferry crosses the harbour.
渡轮横渡海港。

cross [3] /cross; krɒs/ *adj.*
angry 生气；发脾气
Mrs Lin was cross when she saw the untidy rooms.
林太太看见房间这么零乱就很生气。
crossly *adv.* 生气地
Mrs Lin spoke crossly to the naughty children.
林太太生气地把那些顽皮的孩子们骂了一顿。

crossing /'cros·sing; 'krɒsɪŋ/ *n.*
place where you can cross
横穿处
You should use pedestrian crossings to cross the road.
你应该沿人行横道过马路。

crossroads /'cross·roads; krɒsrəudz/ *n.*
place where two roads meet
十字路口
There are usually traffic lights at crossroads.
十字路口通常都有交通指挥灯。

crossword /'cross·word; 'krɒswɜ:d/ *n.*
test with clues to words which you write in a square 纵横字谜；填字游戏
Peter is good at crosswords.
彼得很会玩纵横字谜。

crow /crow; krəu/ *n.*
big, black bird 乌鸦
There were a lot of crows in the trees.
树上有许多乌鸦。

crowd /crowd; kraud/ *n.*
many people together 人群
There was a big crowd at the football match.
有很大的一群人来看这次足球比赛。

crowded *adj.*
having many people 拥挤的
In Hong Kong the pavements are usually crowded.
香港的人行道上通常都是拥挤的。

crown /crown; kraun/ *n.*
hat worn by a king or queen
王冠
There are many jewels in the Queen's crown.
女王的王冠上有许多宝石。

crown

cruel /cruel; kruəl/ *adj.*
(**crueller, cruellest**)
causing a person or animal pain 残忍的；狠心的
The cruel man hit his dog.
那狠心的人打他的狗。
opp. 反义词：kind 仁慈的
cruelly *adv.* 残忍地
The man beat the dog cruelly.
那人残忍地打那只狗。
cruelty *n.* 残忍
Cruelty to animals is against the law.
虐待动物是违法的。

crumb /crumb; krʌm/ *n.*
very small bit of bread or cake 面包或糕饼的碎屑
Peter gave some crumbs to the bird.
彼得拿了一些面包碎屑去喂鸟。

crush /crush; krʌʃ/ *v.*
make flat; break into pieces
压破；压碎
The car was crushed by the falling tree.
大树倒下来把汽车压坏了。

crutch /crutch; krʌtʃ/ *n.*
(two **crutches**)
stick to help you to walk 拐杖
The injured man used crutches to walk.
那个受伤的人扶着拐杖走路。

cry [1] /cry; kraɪ/ *v.*
(**crying, cried, cried**)
1 shout 喊叫
The man cried for help.
那人大声喊救命。
2 to be in tears 哭
The girl was crying because she fell down.
那女孩子跌了一跤，大哭起来。

Usage note: People can *cry* because they are happy or unhappy — *Peter cried out when he opened his present. The baby was crying because it was hungry.* You can also use *cry* in the same way as *say* — *'What's that?' cried David.*
用法：cry 可以是高兴或悲伤所引起的，例如 Peter cried out when he opened his present 和 The baby was crying because it was hungry。cry 与 say 的用法一样，例如 'What's that?' cried David。

cry [2] /cry; kraɪ/ *n.*
(two **cries**)
shout; speaking loud 喊叫声
The fireman heard cries for help.
消防员听见呼救的喊声。

cube /cube; kju:b/ *n.*
solid shape with six square sides 立方块
Anna put two cubes of sugar in her coffee.
安娜在咖啡里放了两块方糖。

cucumber /ˈcu·cum·ber; ˈkju:kʌmbə/ *n.*
long vegetable with green skin 黄瓜；青瓜（方言）
Janet made a salad with cucumber and tomatoes.
珍妮特用黄瓜和番茄做了一道凉拌菜。

cuff /cuff; kʌf/ *n.*
end of a sleeve that covers your wrist 袖口
David turned up the cuffs of his shirt and washed the dishes.
戴维卷起衬衣袖口，动手洗碟子。

cup /cup; kʌp/ *n.*
small bowl for drinking tea or coffee 杯
Xiaofang drank two cups of tea.
小芳喝了两杯茶。

cupboard /ˈcup·board; ˈkʌbəd/ *n.*
piece of furniture with shelves and doors 橱；柜
Anna put the cups and saucers in the cupboard.
安娜把杯子和碟子都放到碗橱里。

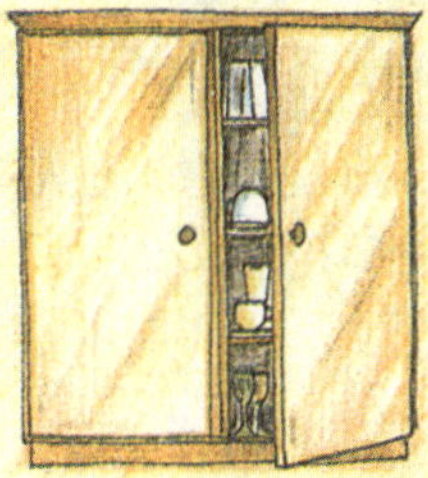
cupboard

cure /cure; kjʊə/ *v.*
(**curing, cured, cured**)
make a sick person well 治愈；治疗
A doctor cures sick people.
医生治疗病人。

curl /curl; kɜ:l/ *n.*
ring of hair 卷发
Mary's hair is full of curls.
玛丽的头上满是一圈一圈的卷发。
curly *adj.* 卷曲的
Mary has curly hair.
玛丽的头发是卷曲的。

curtain /ˈcur·tain; ˈkɜ:tn/ *n.*
piece of cloth that hangs in front of a window 窗帘
When it got dark, Mary closed the curtains.
天黑了，玛丽把窗帘拉上。

curtain

curve /curve; kɜːv/ *n.*
line or shape that is not straight 曲线；弯曲处
The car went round a curve in the road.
汽车在路上拐了一个弯。

cushion /'cu·shion; 'kʊʃn/ *n.*
soft thing to sit on 软垫子；坐垫
There were soft cushions on the chairs.
那些椅子上都有椅垫。

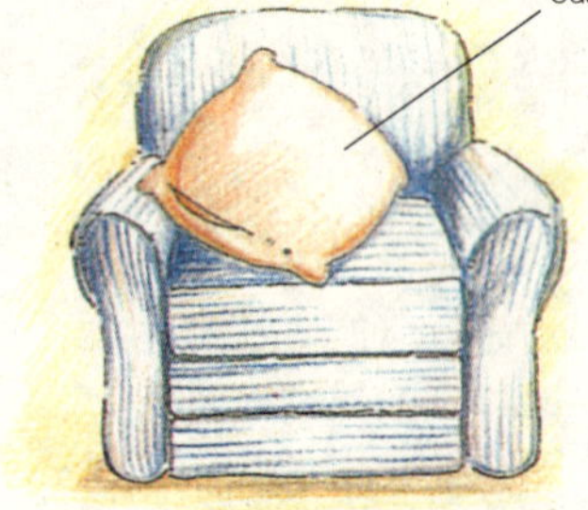

custom /'cus·tom; 'kʌstəm/ *n.*
what a group of people usually do 风俗；习惯
It's a custom to give presents at Christmas.
圣诞节互赠礼物是一种风俗。

customer /'cus·tom·er; 'kʌstəmə/ *n.*
someone who buys things in a shop 顾客
There were a lot of customers in the shop.
商店里顾客很多。

cut [1] /cut; kʌt/ *v.*
(**cutting, cut, cut**)
open or take a piece off something with a knife, scissors, etc. 切；割；剪
David cut the apple into pieces.
戴维把苹果切成小片。

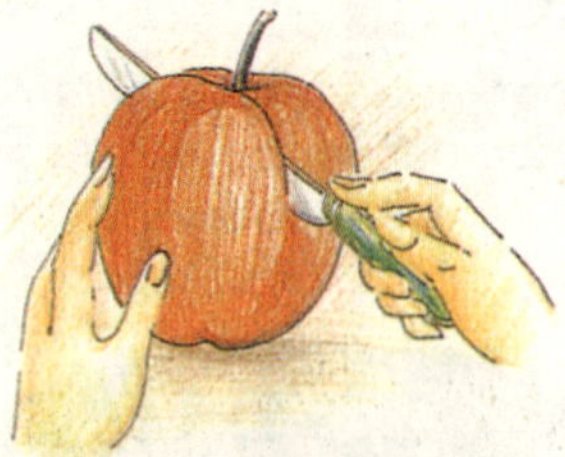

cut [2] /cut; kʌt/ *n.*
hole made by a sharp thing 伤口；切口
Peter has a cut on his finger.
彼得的手指上有个伤口。

cycle /'cy·cle; 'saɪkl/ *v.*
(**cycling, cycled, cycled**)
ride a bicycle 骑自行车
David cycles to school.
戴维骑自行车上学。
cyclist *n.* 骑自行车的人
David is a cyclist.
戴维是骑自行车的人。

Dd

Daddy, Dad /'Dad·dy, Dad; 'dædɪ, dæd/ *n.*
(two **daddies**)
father 爸爸
The child calls his father Daddy.
那小孩称他父亲为爸爸。

daily /'dai·ly; 'deɪlɪ/ *adj. adv.*
every day 每天的；每天
Anna reads a daily newspaper.
安娜在看一份日报。
Tom has four meals daily.
汤姆每天吃四餐。

dairy /'dair·y; 'deərɪ/ *n.*
(two **dairies**)
place where cows are milked 牛奶场
The dairy produces a lot of milk.
牛奶场出产许多牛奶。

dam /dam; dæm/ *n.*
wall built across a river, etc., to hold the water back 水坝
There was a lot of water behind the dam.
水坝拦住许多水。

damage [1] /'dam·age; 'dæmɪdʒ/ *n.*
(**no plural**)
harm done to something 损失

The typhoon caused a lot of damage.
台风导致巨大损失。

damage [2] /'dam·age; 'dæmɪdʒ/ *v.*
(damaging, damaged, damaged)
break or harm something 损毁；弄坏
Mr Lin damaged his car in an accident.
林先生在一次事故中把汽车撞坏了。

damp /damp; dæmp/ *adj.*
a little wet 潮湿的
Hong Kong has a damp climate.
香港气候潮湿。

dance [1] /dance; dɑ:ns/ *n.*
way of moving to music 舞；舞蹈
The children did a pretty dance.
孩子们的舞蹈很好看。

dance [2] /dance; dɑ:ns/ *v.*
(dancing, danced, danced)
move to music 跳舞
The children danced at the concert.
孩子们在音乐会上跳舞。
dancer *n.* 跳舞的人；舞蹈员
The children are good dancers.
孩子们的舞都跳得很好。
dancing *n.* 跳舞
The children like dancing.
孩子们喜欢跳舞。

danger /'dan·ger; 'deɪndʒə/ *n.*
(no plural)
chance of getting hurt or killed 危险
There is a lot of danger in rock climbing.
攀岩活动非常危险。

dangerous /'dan·ger·ous; 'deɪndʒərəs/ *adj.*
(more dangerous, most dangerous)
not safe 危险的
It is very dangerous to cross the road without looking.
不先看清楚就过马路是非常危险的。
opp. 反义词：safe 安全
dangerously *adv.* 危险地
The man drove dangerously.
那人驾驶得很危险。

dare /dare; deə/ *v.*
(daring, dared, dared)
be brave enough to do something 敢
Tom did not dare to touch the snake.
汤姆不敢触摸那条蛇。

dark [1] /dark; dɑ:k/ *n.*
(no plural)
time or place with no light or not much light 黑暗
Baoling is not afraid of the dark.
宝玲不怕黑。
darkness *n.* 黑暗
The light went out and the room was in darkness.
电灯熄灭了，房间一片漆黑。

dark [2] /dark; dɑ:k/ *adj.*
1 with no light or not much light 黑暗的
When the sun sets, it gets dark.
太阳下山，天就黑了。
opp. 反义词：bright 光亮的
2 with a colour that is nearly black 深色或暗色的
Anna wore a dark blue dress.
安娜穿了一件深蓝色的连衣裙。
opp. 反义词：light 浅色的

date /date; deɪt/ *n.*
day of the month or year 日期(指年、月、日)
What's the date today?
今天是几月几日?

daughter /'daugh·ter; 'dɔ:tə/ *n.*
girl child 女儿
Mrs Lin has two daughters and one son.
林太太有两个女儿和一个儿子。

dawn /dawn; dɔ:n/ *n.*
(no plural)
time when the sun comes up 黎明；天初亮时
At dawn, the sun comes up and the birds start to sing.
天初亮时，太阳升起，鸟儿开始歌唱。

day /day; deɪ/ *n.*
1 24 hours 一天；一日
There are seven days in a week.
一星期有七天。
2 time when it is light 白天；日间
During the day, Tom goes to school.
白天，汤姆在校上课。

syn. 同义词：daytime

opp. 反义词：night 夜里；晚上

one day 有一天

One day, we went to the zoo.

有一天，我们去动物园。

the other day 前几天

The other day, Anna went to the shops.

前几天，安娜去商店买东西。

daylight /'day·light; 'deɪlaɪt/ *n.*

(**no plural**)

light from the sun when it is daytime 日光

She could see daylight coming through the window.

她见到窗外透进来的日光。

daytime /'day·time; 'deɪtaɪm/ *n.*

(**no plural**)

time when it is light 白天；日间

We go to school in the daytime.

白天，我们去学校上课。

dead /dead; ded/ *adj.*

not alive 死的

Mary's grandfather is dead.

玛丽的祖父死了。

opp. 反义词：alive, living 在世的；活着的

death *n.* 死亡；去世

Grandfather's death was very sudden.

祖父的去世来得很突然。

deaf /deaf; def/ *adj.*

not able to hear 聋的

The old man was deaf.

那位老人是聋的。

deaf

dear /dear; dɪə/ *adj.*

1 expensive 贵的；昂贵的

The shoes were very dear.

那双鞋非常贵。

opp. 反义词：cheap 便宜的

2 that you love 亲爱的

Mary is my dear friend.

玛丽是我亲爱的朋友。

3 way to start a letter 信开头称呼对方的用语

Dear Peter, I'm having a birthday party on Saturday.

亲爱的彼得，我将在星期六开生日聚会。

December /De·'cem·ber; dɪ'sembə/ *n.*

last month of the year 十二月

Christmas is in December.

圣诞节在十二月。

decide /de·'cide; dɪ'saɪd/ *v.*

(**deciding, decided, decided**)

choose an idea or plan after thinking 决定

Anna decided to go to the cinema.

安娜决定去看电影。

decision *n.* 决心

Peter made a decision to work harder.

彼得下定决心要加倍努力。

decimal /'dec·i·mal; 'desɪml/ *adj.*

counting in tens or hundreds 十进的

The decimal system is easy to learn.

十进制易学。

deck /deck; dek/ *n.*

floor of a ship or bus 甲板；公共汽车的一层

The sailors lined up on the deck.

水手在甲板上排队。

decorate /'dec·o·rate; 'dekəreɪt/ *v.*

(**decorating, decorated, decorated**)

put things on something to make it look pretty 装饰

Peter decorated his room.

彼得把他的房间装饰一番。

decoration *n.* 装饰

John put up some Christmas decorations.

约翰布置了一些圣诞装饰。

decrease /de·'crease; dɪ'kriːs/ *v.*

(**decreasing, decreased, decreased**)

get fewer; get less 减少

The number of people who watch football is decreasing.

看足球的观众日渐减少。

opp. 反义词：increase 增加

deep [1] /deep; di:p/ *adj.*
how far down; going a long way down 深；深的
The hole was a metre deep.
这个洞有一米深。
The river was very deep.
那条河很深。
opp. 反义词：shallow 浅的

deep [2] /deep; di:p/ *adv.*
far down or in 深入
The MTR goes deep under the ground.
地下铁路深入地底。
deep-fried 油炸
Sam likes deep-fried chicken.
萨姆爱吃炸鸡。

deer /deer; dɪə/ *n.*
(two **deer**)
wild animal with horns and long, thin legs 鹿
There were some deer in the forest.
森林里有一些鹿。

defeat /de·'feat; dɪ'fi:t/ *v.*
beat in battle 打败；击败
The army was defeated.
那支军队被打败了。

defend /de·'fend; dɪ'fend/ *v.*
try to save or protect by fighting 保卫；防卫
The army defended the city.
军队保卫那座城市。

definite /'de·fin·ite; 'defɪnət/ *adj.*
(**more definite, most definite**)
sure; clear; that you know 明确的；肯定的
Tom's answer was definite.
汤姆的回答是明确的。
definitely *adv.* 明确地；肯定地
Tom will definitely come tomorrow.
明天汤姆肯定会来。

degree /de·'gree; dɪ'gri:/ *n.*
measurement of heat or an angle 度数
The temperature was 40 degrees.
当时的温度是四十度。

delicious /de·'li·cious; dɪ'lɪʃəs/ *adj.*
(**more delicious, most delicious**)
very good to eat; with a very nice taste 好吃的；美味的
They had a delicious lunch in the restaurant.
他们在餐厅吃了一顿美味的午饭。

deliver /de·'liv·er; dɪ'lɪvə/ *v.*
take something to a special place 递送
A postman delivers the mail.
邮递员递送邮件。
delivery *n.* 递送
There are two deliveries a day.
每天送两次信。

democracy /de·'mo·cra·cy; dɪ'mɒkrəsɪ/ *n.*
(**no plural**)
way of ruling a country in which all the people elect a government to represent them 民主制；民主政治
Democracy means government by all the people.
民主制即是由人民共同管理的制度。
democratic *adj.* 民主的
They live in a democratic country.
他们生活在一个民主国家里。

dense /dense; dens/ *adj.*
(**denser, densest**)
thick; having a lot of people or things 稠密的
There was dense traffic in the city.
市内交通十分繁忙。

dentist /'den·tist; 'dentɪst/ *n.*
someone who looks after your teeth 牙医
The dentist examined David's teeth.
牙医检查戴维的牙齿。

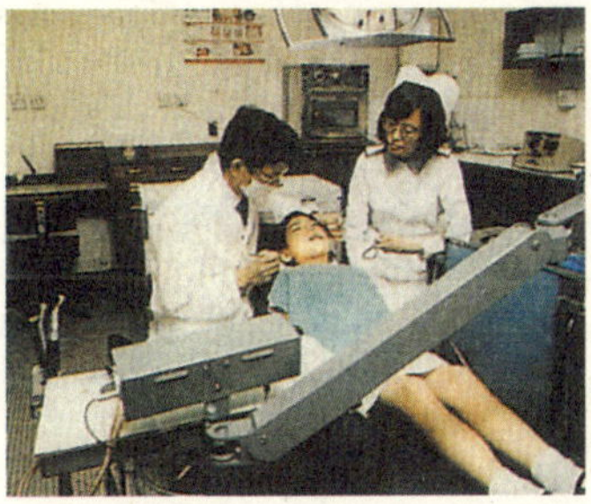

depart /de·'part; dɪ'pɑ:t/ *v.*
go away 离开；出发；(交通工具)开出
The flight departs at six o'clock.
这次班机六时起飞。

department /de·'part·ment; dɪ'pɑ:tmənt/ *n.*
part of a school, shop, etc.
(学院中的)系;(机构中的)部门
Miss Li teaches in the English Department at the college.
李小姐在学院里的英语系任教。
department store *n.* 百货公司
Anna bought some shoes in a department store.
安娜在百货公司买了几双鞋。

depend /de·'pend; dɪ'pend/ *v.*
1 to be decided by 由…来决定
It depends on the weather what we do on Sunday.
星期天我们干什么，要看天气来决定。
2 trust 依靠；信赖
You can depend on Peter.
你可信赖彼得。

depth /depth; depθ/ *n.*
how deep something is; how far down from the top to the bottom 深度
He measured the depth of the pool.
他测量这池塘的深度。

describe /de·'scribe; dɪ'skraɪb/ *v.*
(**describing, described, described**)
say what someone or something is like 描述；形容
Anna described the robber to the policeman.
安娜向警察形容那抢劫者的外貌。
description *n.* 描述；描写
Anna gave a description of the robber to the policeman.
安娜就那抢劫者的外貌向警察提供了描述。

desert /'des·ert; 'dezət/ *n.*
big, empty piece of land with a lot of sand and few plants 沙漠
Very few people can live in a desert.
很少人能在沙漠中生活。

deserve /de·'serve; dɪ'zɜ:v/ *v.*
(**deserving, deserved, deserved**)
be good or bad enough to have something 应得；值得
Baoling deserved her prize.
宝玲得奖是应该的。

design[1] /de·'sign; dɪ'zaɪn/ *n.*
pattern or shape 图案；花样
Susan's dress had a nice design on it.
苏珊连衣裙上的图案很好看。

design[2] /de·'sign; dɪ'zaɪn/ *v.*
do a drawing to show how to make something 设计
An architect designs buildings.
建筑师设计建筑物。

desk /desk; desk/ *n.*
sort of table where you sit to work 书桌；办公桌
There are 30 desks in our classroom.
我们的教室里有30张书桌。

dessert /des·'sert; dɪ'zɜ:t/ *n.*
sweet food that you eat at the end of a meal 饭后吃的水果或甜品
We had ice-cream for dessert.
我们饭后吃冰淇淋做甜品。

destination /des·ti·'na·tion; destɪ'neɪʃn/ *n.*
place you are going to 目的地
His destination is Beijing.
他的目的地是北京。

destroy /de·'stroy; dɪ'strɔɪ/ *v.*
break something completely 破坏；摧毁
The typhoon destroyed many buildings.
台风摧毁了许多房屋。

detective /de·'tec·tive; dɪ'tektɪv/ *n.*
special policeman 侦探

The detective was looking for the thieves.
侦探在追寻那些小偷。

detergent /de·'ter·gent; dɪ'tɜːdʒənt/ *n.*
stuff for washing clothes, dishes, etc. 清洁剂；洗衣粉；去污粉
We use detergent to wash our clothes.
我们用洗衣粉来洗衣服。

devil /'de·vil; 'devl/ *n.*
bad spirit 魔鬼；恶魔
Sam doesn't believe in devils.
萨姆不信有魔鬼。

dew /dew; djuː/ *n.*
(**no plural**)
drops of water that appear on grass at night 露水
In the morning the grass was covered with dew.
早晨的草地上满是露水。

diagonal /di·'ag·o·nal; daɪ'ægənl/ *adj.*
going across the middle from corner to corner 对角的
Mary drew a diagonal line across the square.
玛丽在正方形上画了一条对角线。

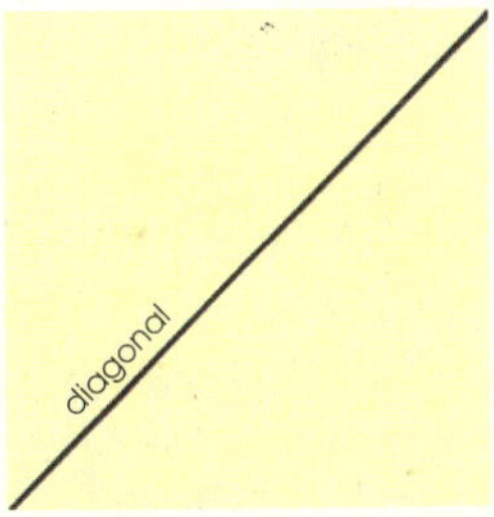

dial /'di·al; 'daɪəl/ *v.*
(**dialling, dialled, dialled**)
make a number on a telephone 拨号码打电话
David dialled the wrong number.
戴维拨错了电话号码。

diameter /di·'am·e·ter; daɪ'æmɪtə/ *n.*
distance across a circle 直径
What is the diameter of the circle?
这个圆的直径是多少?

diamond /'di·a·mond; 'daɪəmənd/ *n.*
1 sort of jewel 钻石
Miss Li has a ring with a large diamond.
李小姐有只镶了一颗大钻石的戒指。

2 shape of '◆' 菱形
He drew a diamond on the paper.
他在纸上画了个菱形。

diary /'di·a·ry; 'daɪərɪ/ *n.*
(two **diaries**)
book where you write what you have done or will do 日记
Mary marked her friends' birthdays in her diary.
玛丽把朋友的生日都记在日记里。

dice /dice; daɪs/ *n.*
(two **dice**)
cube of wood or plastic which you throw when playing games 骰子
The boys were playing a game with dice.
那些男孩子在玩掷骰子游戏。

dictation /dic·'ta·tion; dɪk'teɪʃn/ *n.*
words that you say for someone to write down 听写；默书(方言)
Sam made a lot of mistakes in the dictation.
萨姆听写时犯了很多错误。

dictionary /'dic·tion·a·ry; 'dɪkʃənrɪ/ *n.*
(two **dictionaries**)
book that tells you what words mean 字典；词典
This is an English-Chinese dictionary.
这是一本英汉词典。

did /did; dɪd/ *v.*
p.t. of **do** do 的过去式
Did you see Tom at school?
你在学校见过汤姆吗?
opp. 反义词: did not, didn't
没有; 不

didn't /ˈdid·n't; ˈdɪdnt/ *v.*
did not 即 did not
Peter didn't do his homework.
彼得没有做家庭作业。

die /die; daɪ/ *v.*
(**dying, died, died**)
come to the end of life 死
If you don't water the flowers, they will die.
如果你不浇水，花就会枯死。
opp. 反义词: live, be born 生存; 活着

diet /ˈdi·et; ˈdaɪət/ *n.*
special meals you eat to lose weight or when you are ill
节食或生病时可以进食的某些食品
Susan was getting fat, so she went on a diet.
苏珊发胖了，因此她实行节食。

difference /ˈdif·fer·ence; ˈdɪfrəns/ *n.*
the way things are unlike 不同之处; 差别
What's the difference between a fish and a dog?
鱼和狗有什么不同?

different /ˈdif·fer·ent; ˈdɪfrənt/ *adj.*
(**more different, most different**)
not like another person or thing 不同的
There are many different kinds of butterflies in Hong Kong.
香港有许多不同种类的蝴蝶。
opp. 反义词: same 相同的

difficult /ˈdif·fi·cult; ˈdɪfɪkəlt/ *adj.*
(**more difficult, most difficult**)
not easy to do or understand
困难的
Susan finds maths very difficult.
苏珊觉得数学非常难。
syn. 同义词: hard
opp. 反义词: easy 容易的

difficulty /ˈdif·fi·cul·ty; ˈdɪfɪkəltɪ/ *n.*
(some **difficulties**)
being difficult; hard to do
困难
Susan has difficulty with her maths.
苏珊学习数学有困难。
syn. 同义词: trouble

dig /dig; dɪg/ *v.*
(**digging, dug, dug**)
cut into the earth 掘
The workmen dug a hole in the road.
那些工人在路上掘了一个洞。

dilute /di·ˈlute; daɪˈlju:t/ *v.*
(**diluting, diluted, diluted**)
make a liquid less strong by adding water 冲淡
Mrs Chen diluted the orange squash with water.
陈太太用水把橙汁冲淡。

dining-room /ˈdi·ning·room; ˈdaɪnɪŋru:m/ *n.*
room where you eat 饭厅
The children went to the dining-room for lunch.
孩子们进饭厅吃午饭。

dinner /ˈdin·ner; ˈdɪnə/ *n.*
main meal of the day 一天的主餐(午饭或晚饭)
Baoling has her dinner at seven o'clock.
宝玲七时吃晚饭。
dinner time *n.* 晚饭时间
Mr Chen comes home at dinner time.
陈先生在吃饭时间回家。
Usage note: In some parts of Britain, *dinner* means the *midday meal — Peter has his dinner at one o'clock.*
用法: 在英国某些地方，dinner 指午饭，例如 Peter has his dinner at one o'clock。

dip /dip; dɪp/ *v.*
(dipping, dipped, dipped)
put something into a liquid
蘸；把物件浸入液体中
Jenny dipped her toes in the swimming pool.
詹妮把脚趾浸入泳池的水中。

direct [1] /di·'rect; dɪ'rekt/ *adj.*
(more direct, most direct)
without stopping 直接的
There is a direct flight from Hong Kong to London.
从香港到伦敦有直航班机。
directly *adv.* 直接地
The flight does directly to London.
这班机直飞伦敦。

direct [2] /di·'rect; dɪ'rekt/ *v.*
tell or show someone how to do something or go somewhere 指示；指导
The policeman was directing the traffic.
警察在指挥交通。

direction /di·'rec·tion; dɪ'rekʃn/ *n.*
where you are going to or looking 方向
Look in both directions before you cross the road.
过马路前，先看左、右两方。

dirt /dirt; dɜ:t/ *n.*
(no plural)
unclean things 污物；脏东西
You have some dirt on your clothes.
你衣服上有些脏东西。

dirty /'dirt·y; 'dɜ:tɪ/ *adj.*
(dirtier, dirtiest)
not clean 肮脏的
Tom's shirt was dirty.
汤姆的衬衣很脏。
opp. 反义词：clean 清洁的；干净的

dirty

disagree /dis·a·'gree; dɪsə'gri:/ *v.*
(disagreeing, disagreed, disagreed)
not to have the same feelings as someone 不同意
The children disagreed about the answer.
孩子们不同意这答案。
opp. 反义词：agree 同意

disappear /dis·ap·'pear; dɪsə'pɪə/ *v.*
go away and not be seen
消失；不见了
The aeroplane disappeared into the clouds.
飞机在云层中消失了。
opp. 反义词：appear 出现

disappointed
/dis·ap·'point·ed; dɪsə'pɔɪntɪd/ *adj.*
(more disappointed, most disappointed)
sad because what you wanted did not happen
失望的
Mary was disappointed when she got her examination marks.
玛丽拿到考试成绩单时感到很失望。
opp. 反义词：satisfied 满意的
disoppointing *adj.* 令人失望的
Mary's examination marks were disappointing.
玛丽的考试成绩令人失望。
disappointment *n.* 失望
Mary's examination results were a big disappointment.
玛丽的考试成绩令人大大失望。

disc /disc; dɪsk/ *n.*
1 plastic circle used with a computer 磁盘
Tom put the disc in his computer.
汤姆把磁盘放进电脑中。
2 plastic circle with music and songs 唱片
Laura played a disc on her record-player.
劳拉用唱机放唱片。

disco /'dis·co; 'dɪskəʊ/ *n.*
place where you listen to pop music and dance 迪斯科；播放流行音乐的跳舞场所；的士高（方言）
David goes to a disco every Saturday night.
戴维每个星期六晚上都去迪斯科舞厅。

discount /'dis·count; 'dɪskaʊnt/ *n.*
money taken off the price of something 折扣
There was 20% discount on the dress.
那件连衣裙的价钱打了个八折。
Usage note: Note the difference between English (25% off) and Chinese (75%).
用法：注意汉英说法有不同。英语说扣去的百分比(25% off 即扣去 25%)，汉语说扣剩的百分比(25% off 即扣剩 75%，即七五折)。

discover /dis·'cov·er; dɪs'kʌvə/ *v.*
find or learn something for the first time 发现；发觉
The children discovered some nice shells on the beach.
孩子们在海滩上发现了一些漂亮的贝壳。

discovery /dis·'cov·er·y; dɪ'skʌvərɪ/ *n.*
(two **discoveries**)
finding or learning 发现；发觉
The discovery of the robber did not take long.
抢劫者的行踪很快就被发现了。

discuss /dis·'cuss; dɪ'skʌs/ *v.*
talk about 讨论；谈论
The boys were discussing the football match.
那些男孩子在谈论这场足球比赛。

disease /di·'sease; dɪ'zi:z/ *n.*
illness 疾病
A doctor cures diseases.
医生会治病。

disguise /dis·'guise; dɪs'gaɪz/ *v.*
(**disguising, disguised, disguised**)
make yourself look different so that people will not know who you are 假扮
Sam disguised himself as a robber.
萨姆装扮成盗贼。

dish /dish; dɪʃ/ *n.*
(two **dishes**)
1 plate or bowl for food 碟子；盘子
Xiaofang put the rice in a dish.
小芳把饭盛在碟子里。

2 part of a meal 一道菜
Baoling's favourite dish is roast chicken.
宝玲最爱吃的菜是烤鸡。

dishonest /dis·'hon·est; dɪs'ɒnɪst/ *adj.*
(**more dishonest, most dishonest**)
saying what is not true or cheating 不诚实的；欺骗人的
Lying is dishonest.
说谎是不诚实的行为。
opp. 反义词：honest 诚实的

dislike /dis·'like; dɪs'laɪk/ *v.*
(**disliking, disliked, disliked**)
not like someone or something 不喜欢
I dislike wet weather.
我不喜欢潮湿的天气。
opp. 反义词：like 喜欢

dismiss /dis·'miss; dɪs'mɪs/ *v.*
send away 解散(队伍)；开除
The teacher dismissed the class.
老师让学生下课。

disobey /dis·o·'bey; dɪsə'beɪ/ *v.*
not do what someone tells you to do 不服从；不听话
Tom never disobeys his father.
汤姆从来没有不听父亲的话。
opp. 反义词：obey 服从；听话
disobedient *adj.* 不服从的；不听话的
Tom is sometimes disobedient at school.
汤姆在学校有时不听话。

display /dis·'play; dɪ'spleɪ/ *n.*
showing something so that many people can see it 展览；陈列
There was a fireworks display in the harbour at Chinese New Year.
过农历新年的时候，海港有烟火表演。

distance /'dis·tance; 'dɪstəns/ *n.*
how far it is 距离
What is the distance from Hong Kong to Beijing?
香港与北京距离多远?
distant *adj.* 很远的
Macao is not very distant from Hong Kong.
澳门离香港并不远。

district /'dis·trict; 'dɪstrɪkt/ *n.*
part of a country, town or city 区域
Baoling lives in Central district.
宝玲住在中区。

disturb /dis·'turb; dɪ'stɜ:b/ *v.*
stop someone working, thinking or resting 扰乱；骚扰；打扰
Loud radios on the beach disturb people.
在沙滩上，收音机的声音太大会干扰别人。

ditch /ditch; dɪtʃ/ *n.*
(two **ditches**)
long hole to take water away from land 沟渠
The ditch was full of water.
沟渠里满是水。

dive [1] /dive; daɪv/ *v.*
(**diving, dived, dived**)
jump into water, arms first
跳水
Tom dived into the swimming pool.
汤姆跳入游泳池里。
diver *n.* 跳水的人
Tom is a good diver.
汤姆是个优秀的跳水员。

dive [2] /dive; daɪv/ *n.*
going into water with your arms and head first 跳水
Peter made a good dive.
彼得作了一个很漂亮的跳水动作。

dives

divide /di·'vide; dɪ'vaɪd/ *v.*
(**dividing, divided, divided**)
1 find out how many times one number will go into another （数学）除
Ten divided by two is five.
十除以二等于五。
2 share 分开
Peter and Mary divided the sweets.
彼得和玛丽分了那些糖果。
division *n.* （数学）除法
David is good at division.
戴维擅长除法。

divide

do /do; du:/ *v.*
(**doing, did, done**)
1 work on something 做
Can you do this exercise?
你能做这练习吗？
2 have a job 职业
What does your father do for a living?
你父亲的职业是什么？
3 word you use with not 与 not 连用
Tom likes potatoes but I do not.
汤姆爱吃马铃薯，我却不爱吃。
4 word you use to ask a question 用在疑问句开头
Do you like potatoes?
你爱吃马铃薯吗？
5 word you use in place of another word 用来代替另一词语
I can't swim as well as you do.
我游泳游得没你好。
do something up 把…整理好
Do your shoes up, Tom.
汤姆，把鞋穿好。
do without 没有
John can't do without rice.
约翰不可以没有米饭吃。
How do you do? 你好

dock /dock; dɒk/ *n.*
place in a port where ships are loaded or unloaded 船坞
There are many ships in the dock.
许多船停泊在船坞里。

doctor /'doc·tor; 'dɒktə/ *n.*
someone who makes sick people well 医生
When you are ill you go to see a doctor.
你生病时会去找医生。

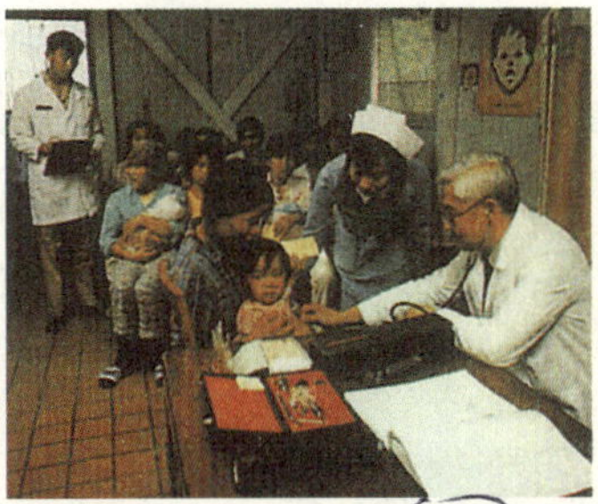

does /does; dʌz/ *v.*
3rd person singular present tense of **do** do 的第三人称单数现在式
Does Mary go to your school?
玛丽也在你那所学校上学吗？
opp. 反义词：does not, doesn't 不

doesn't /'does·n't; 'dʌznt/ *v.*
does not 即 does not
Mr Chen doesn't like loud music.
陈先生不喜欢吵闹的音乐。

dog /dog; dɒg/ *n.*
kind of animal that lives with people 狗
Mr Chen takes his dog for a walk every day.
陈先生每天都带他的狗去散步。

doing /ˈdo·ing; ˈduːɪŋ/ *v.*
pres.p. of **do** do 的现在分词
What are you doing?
你在干什么?

doll /doll; dɒl/ *n.*
toy like a very small person
玩偶; 洋娃娃
Peter bought a doll for his baby sister.
彼得买了一个洋娃娃给年幼的小妹妹。

dollar ($) /ˈdol·lar; ˈdɒlə/ *n.*
money used in some countries or regions 元(某些国家或地区的货币)
The dress cost a hundred dollars.
这件连衣裙是花了一百港元买的。

Hong Kong one dollar

dolphin /ˈdol·phin; ˈdɒlfɪn/ *n.*
sea animal 海豚
Some dolphins followed the ship.
有些海豚跟着船只。

done /done; dʌn/ *v.*
p.p. of **do** do 的过去分词
What have you done today?
你今天做过什么事?

donkey /ˈdon·key; ˈdɒŋkɪ/ *n.*
animal like a small horse with long ears 驴子
Susan had a ride on a donkey.
苏珊骑过驴子。

don't /don't; dəunt/ *v.*
do not 即 do not
Please don't smoke.
请勿吸烟。

door /door; dɔː/ *n.*
wooden thing that closes the entrance to a room or building, etc. 门
Mary closed the door.
玛丽关上了门。
next door 邻居; 隔壁
Tom lives next door to David.
汤姆住在戴维隔壁。
doorbell *n.* 门铃
Tom rang the doorbell.
汤姆按响门铃。
doorway *n.* 门口
David stood in the doorway.
戴维站在门口。

dot /dot; dɒt/ *n.*
small round mark 小圆点
The letter 'i' has a dot.
i 这个字母有一个小圆点。

double [1] /ˈdoub·le; ˈdʌbl/ *n.*
(no plural)
two times as much 两倍
Double the number of tourists has arrived.
到来的游客数目是平日的两倍。

double [2] /ˈdoub·le; ˈdʌbl/ *v.*
(doubling, doubled, doubled)
make or become two times as much 加倍
The price of apples doubled from $2 to $4 each.
苹果价格涨了一倍，从每个两港元加至四港元。

dough /dough; dəu/ *n.*
(no plural)
mixture of flour, water, etc. for making bread (做面包、点心的)生面团
Anna mixed some dough to make bread.
安娜和了些生面团做面包。

down /down; daun/ *adv. prep.*
from a higher to a lower place 下面; 往下
Peter walked down the hill.
彼得从山上走下来。
opp. 反义词: up 上面; 在上

lie down 躺下
Sam lay down and went to sleep.
萨姆躺下来睡着了。

sit down 坐下
The teacher told the children to sit down.
老师叫孩子们坐下来。

downstairs /down·'stairs; daʊn'steəz/ *adv.*
to or in a lower part of the building 楼下
My friend lives downstairs.
我的朋友住在楼下。
opp. 反义词：upstairs 楼上

downwards /'down·wards; 'daʊnwədz/ *adv.*
from a higher to a lower place 向下
The arrow pointed downwards.
箭头记号指向下面。
opp. 反义词：upwards 向上

dozen /'doz·en; 'dʌzn/ *n.*
(two **dozen** or **dozens**)
twelve 一打（十二个）
Mrs Lin bought a dozen eggs.
林太太买了一打鸡蛋。

drag /drag; dræg/ *v.*
(dragging, dragged, dragged)
pull something heavy 拖；用力拉
Peter dragged the heary case into the room.
彼得把那沉重的箱子拖入房间。

dragon /'drag·on; 'drægən/ *n.*
big, dangerous animal which breathes fire in fairy stories 龙
Baoling read a story about dragons.
宝玲阅读了一个关于龙的故事。

dragon boat *n.* 龙舟
The children watched the dragon boat races.
孩子们看龙舟竞赛。

dragon dance *n.* 舞龙
There are lots of dragon dances at Chinese New Year.
农历新年有许多舞龙表演。

drain /drain; dreɪn/ *n.*
pipe that takes away dirty water 下水道；排水沟
Mary poured the dirty water down the drain.
玛丽把污水倒进排水沟里。

drama /'dra·ma; 'drɑːmə/ *n.*
play for the theatre or television 戏；戏剧
I saw a good drama on television last night.
昨晚，我在电视上看了一出好戏。

drank /drank; dræŋk/ *v.*
p.t. of **drink** drink 的过去式
Mary drank a glass of water.
玛丽喝了一杯水。

draw /draw; drɔː/ *v.*
(drawing, drew, drawn)
1 make a picture with a pen or pencil （用钢笔或铅笔）画；绘
Susan drew a picture.
苏珊画了一幅画。

draw

2 end a game with the same score on both sides （比赛中）不分胜负；平手
The teams drew 2:2.
两队以二比二打成平手。

drawer /drawer; drɔː/ *n.*
sliding box in a table, desk, etc. 抽屉
Peter keeps his shirts in a drawer.
彼得把衬衣都放在抽屉里。

drawer

drawing /'draw·ing; 'drɔːɪŋ/ *n.*
picture someone has drawn 图画
Susan did a drawing of a ship.
苏珊画了一艘船。

dream[1] /dream; driːm/ *n.*
what you see or think in your sleep 梦
Tom had a bad dream last night.
汤姆昨晚做了个恶梦。

dream [2] /dream; driːm/ *v.*
(**dreaming, dreamt, dreamt**)
have pictures in your mind when you are asleep 做梦
Tom dreamt he was an astronaut.
汤姆梦见自己是个宇航员。

dress [1] /dress; dres/ *n.*
(two **dresses**)
piece of clothing a girl or a woman wears 连衣裙
Susan has a lot of dresses.
苏珊有许多连衣裙。

dress [2] /dress; dres/ *v.*
put clothes on 穿衣服
Peter dressed quickly and went downstairs.
彼得很快穿好衣服就下楼去了。
opp. 反义词: undress 脱衣服

drew /drew; druː/ *v.*
p.t. of **draw** draw 的过去式
Mary drew a picture.
玛丽画了一幅画。

dried [1] /dried; draɪd/ *v.*
p.t. of **dry** dry 的过去式
Peter dried his hands.
彼得把手擦干。

dried [2] /dried; draɪd/ *adj.*
not wet; with all the water taken out 干了的
Mrs Lin bought some dried fish.
林太太买了些干鱼。

drill /drill; drɪl/ *n.*
1 tool for making holes 钻
Mr Lin made a hole in the wall with his drill.
林先生用钻子在墙上钻了个洞。
2 making someone practise something by doing it again and again 操练；反复练习
The teacher made the children do a pronunciation drill.
老师要孩子们做发音练习。

drink [1] /drink; drɪŋk/ *n.*
something you drink 饮料
Tea is David's favourite drink.
戴维最喜欢的饮料是茶。

drink [2] /drink; drɪŋk/ *v.*
(**drinking, drank, drunk**)
take liquid through your mouth 喝；饮
David drank some tea.
戴维喝了些茶。

drip /drip; drɪp/ *v.*
(**dripping, dripped, dripped**)
fall in drops 滴落；滴下
Water was dripping from the tap.
水龙头在滴水。

drive [1] /drive; draɪv/ *v.*
(**driving, drove, driven**)
make a car or bus move 驾车
Mr Tan drives his car to work.
谭先生驾车上班。

drive [2] /drive; draɪv/ *n.*
journey in a car or bus 驾车；乘车
Mr Tan went for a drive in his car.
谭先生驾车出外一游。

driver /ˈdriv·er; ˈdraɪvə/ *n.*
someone who drives 司机；驾驶员
Mr Tan is a good driver.
谭先生是个好司机。
bus-driver *n.* 公共汽车司机；巴士司机(方言)
Mr Wang is a bus-driver.
王先生是公共汽车司机。
taxi-driver *n.* 出租汽车司机；的士司机(方言)
Mr Lin is a taxi-driver.
林先生是出租汽车司机。

drop [1] /drop; drɒp/ *n.*
1 very small spot of liquid 滴
The window was covered with drops of rain.
窗上满是雨点。

2 fall 下跌；下降
There was a big drop in the temperature.
温度大降。

drop [2] /drop; drɒp/ *v.*
(dropping, dropped, dropped)
let something fall 掉下
Tom dropped the vase and broke it.
汤姆摔破了花瓶。

drove /drove; drəʊv/ *v.*
p.t. of **drive** drive 的过去式
Mr Wang drove his bus to town.
王先生把公共汽车开进城里。

drown /drown; draʊn/ *v.*
die in water because one cannot breathe 淹死；溺死
If you swim when there is a red flag at the beach, you might drown.
如在海滩挂起红旗时游泳，会有遇溺的可能。

drum /drum; drʌm/ *n.*
musical instrument that you hit 鼓
David can play the drums.
戴维会打鼓。
drummer *n.* 打鼓的人；鼓手
David is a good drummer.
戴维打鼓打得很好。

drunk /drunk; drʌŋk/ *v.*
p.p. of **drink** drink 的过去分词
The boys have drunk the lemonade.
那些男孩子把柠檬水喝了。

dry [1] /dry; draɪ/ *adj.*
(drier, driest)
not wet 干的
Tom put on some dry clothes.
汤姆穿上些干衣服。
opp. 反义词：wet 湿的

dry [2] /dry; draɪ/ *v.*
(drying, dried, dried)
make something dry; take the water out of something 弄干
David dried his hands.
戴维把手弄干。
hair-dryer *n.* 吹风机
Susan has a hair-dryer.
苏珊有一个吹风机。

duck /duck; dʌk/ *n.*
bird which swims 鸭子
There were a lot of ducks in the pond.
池塘里有许多鸭子。
duckling *n.* 小鸭子
There were six ducklings with the duck.
六只小鸭子和那只大鸭子在一起。

ducks

dug /dug; dʌg/ *v.*
p.t. of **dig** dig 的过去式
The workmen dug a hole in the road.
那些工人在路上挖了个洞。

dull /dull; dʌl/ *adj.*
1 not interesting; boring 枯燥的；无趣味的
This book is dull.
这本书很枯燥。
2 not bright or clear 阴暗的
It was a dull, cloudy day.
这是阴暗而多云的一天。

dumb /dumb; dʌm/ *adj.*
not able to speak 哑的
The man was deaf and dumb.
那人又聋又哑。

dumpling /ˈdum·pling; ˈdʌmplɪŋ/ *n.*
small, round piece of dough with meat or vegetables that you steam or boil 面团；饺子
Tom likes dumplings in soup.
汤姆爱吃汤饺。

during /ˈdur·ing; ˈdjʊərɪŋ/ *prep.*
at that time 在那一段时间里
It rained during the night.
夜里下起雨来。

dust [1] /dust; dʌst/ *n.*
(no plural)
dry dirt like powder 尘土；灰尘
The car was covered with dust.
汽车上盖满灰尘。

dust [2] /dust; dʌst/ *v.*
wipe dust off something 拭去灰尘
Mary dusted the furniture.
玛丽拭去家具上的灰尘。

dusty *adj.* 满是灰尘的
The furniture was dusty.
家具上满是灰尘。

dustbin /ˈdust·bin; ˈdʌstbɪn/ *n.*
container for rubbish 垃圾箱
Put your rubbish in a dustbin.
把垃圾放入垃圾箱。

duster /ˈdust·er; ˈdʌstə/ *n.*
cloth for wiping away dust 擦布；抹布
Anna cleaned the blackboard with a duster.
安娜用抹布把黑板擦干净。

duty /ˈdu·ty; ˈdju:tɪ/ *n.*
(two **duties**)
what you must do 责任
Miss Li was on duty at school.
李小姐在学校值班。

dwarf /dwarf; dwɔ:f/ *n.*
(two **dwarfs** or **dwarves**)
very small person 矮小的人；侏儒
Tom saw some dwarfs at the circus.
汤姆在马戏团见到一些侏儒。

dying /ˈdy·ing; ˈdaɪɪŋ/ *v.*
pres.p. of **die** die 的现在分词
The flowers are dying.
花儿快死了。

each /each; i:tʃ/ *pron. adj. adv.*
every person or thing 每一
Tom and Peter each have a bicycle.
汤姆和彼得每人有一辆自行车。
each other 互相；彼此
Tom and Peter help each other at school.
汤姆和彼得在学校里互相帮助。
Usage note: Use *each* before nouns you can count — *Each child had a present.* The verb after *each* is always singular — *Each of the presents was different.*
用法： each 用于可数名词前面，例如 Each child had a present。each 后面的动词一定用单数，例如 Each of the presents was different。

eager /ˈea·ger; ˈi:gə/ *adj.*
(**more eager, most eager**)
wanting to do something very much 十分希望；渴望
The patient was eager to go for a walk.
那个病人十分希望到街上走走。

eagle /ˈea·gle; ˈi:gl/ *n.*
sort of big bird 鹰
The eagle caught a rabbit.
那只鹰抓住了一只兔子。

ear /ear; ɪə/ *n.*
part of the head you hear with 耳朵
A donkey has long ears.
驴子有长长的耳朵。

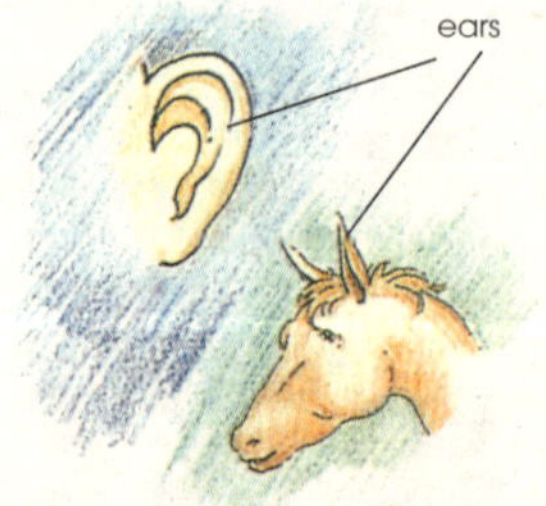

early /ˈear·ly; ˈɜ:lɪ/ *adj. adv.*
(**earlier, earliest**)
coming before the right time （较规定时间）早；提早

Peter always arrives at school early.
彼得总是提早到学校。
opp. 反义词：late 迟

earn /earn; ɜ:n/ *v.*
get the money for the work you do 赚钱
Mr Wang does not earn much money.
王先生赚钱不多。

earring /ˈear·ring; ˈɪərɪŋ/ *n.*
pretty ring that you wear in your ear 耳环
Mrs Lin has a pair of diamond earrings.
林太太有一对钻石耳环。

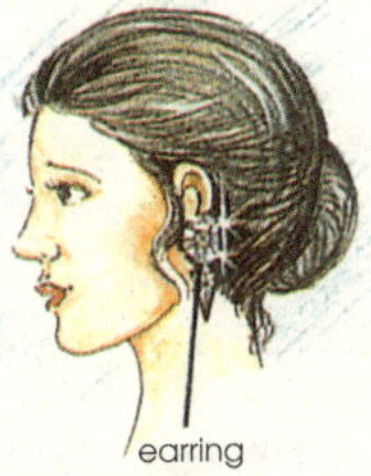

earth /earth; ɜ:θ/ *n.*
(no plural)
1 world 地球
The earth is round.
地球是圆的。

2 soil 泥土
Mr Tan put some earth in his plant-pots.
谭先生在花盆里放了些泥土。
Usage note: Sometimes you can also use *ground*, *floor* and *soil* in the same way as *earth* — *The plane fell to the earth. The earth* (also *Earth*) is the name for our planet. It can also mean *land*.
用法：有时可以用 ground, floor 和 soil 来代替 earth，例如 The plane fell to the earth。The earth（或 Earth）是地球的英文名称。earth 也可解作 land。

earthquake /ˈearth·quake; ˈɜ:θkweɪk/ *n.*
ground shaking 地震
The earthquake destroyed the buildings.
地震摧毁了建筑物。

east /east; i:st/ *n. adj. adv.*
where the sun comes up in the morning 东方；东面的；向东
Japan is east of China.
日本在中国的东面。
Peter lives in East Kowloon.
彼得住在九龙东部。
The boat is sailing east.
船向着东面航行。
opp. 反义词：west 西方；西面的；向西
eastern *adj.* 东方的
Some people think that eastern religions are mysterious.
有些人觉得东方的宗教很神秘。

Easter /ˈEast·er; ˈi:stə/ *n.*
Christian festival in spring 复活节
Children eat chocolate eggs at Easter.
复活节时，孩子们都吃巧克力蛋。

easy /ˈeas·y; ˈi:zɪ/ *adj.*
(easier, easiest)
not difficult; simple 容易的；简单的
The questions were easy.
那些问题很容易。
opp. 反义词：hard, difficult 困难的

easily *adv.* 轻易地
David won the race easily.
戴维轻易地赢了这场比赛。

eat /eat; i:t/ *v.*
(eating, ate, eaten)
take food into your mouth 吃
Mary ate her breakfast.
玛丽吃了早餐。

edge /edge; edʒ/ *n.*
side, top or bottom end of something 边
Peter was standing at the edge of the swimming pool.
彼得正站在游泳池边。

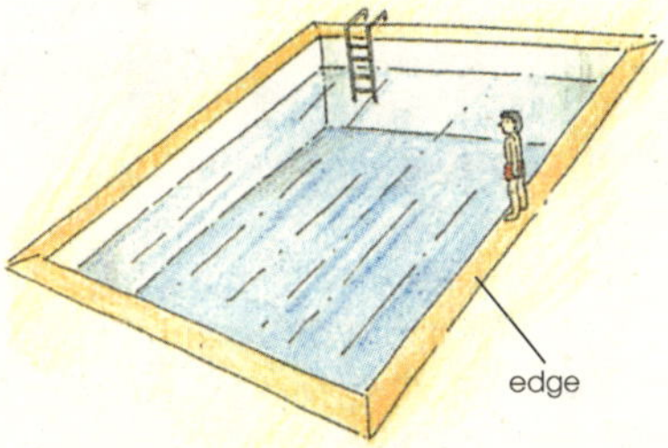

educate /ˈed·u·cate; ˈedʒʊkeɪt/ *v.*
(educating, educated, educated)
teach someone 教育
Peter was educated in Hong Kong.
彼得在香港受教育。
education *n.* 教育
Peter had a good education.
彼得受过良好教育。

effort /'ef·fort; 'efət/ *n.*
trying hard 努力；尽力
Tom made a great effort to win the race.
汤姆很努力，想要赢这场比赛。

egg /egg; eg/ *n.*
round thing with a shell which comes from a bird 蛋
David always has a boiled egg for breakfast.
戴维的早餐通常是一个熟鸡蛋。

eggs

eight (8) /eight; eɪt/ *n. adj.*
number 8 八
Laura is eight years old.
劳拉八岁。
eighth (8th) *n. adj.* 第八
It was Laura's eighth birthday yesterday.
昨天是劳拉的八岁生日。

eighteen (18) /eight·'een; eɪ'ti:n/ *n. adj.*
number 18 十八
Eighteen children went to Sam's birthday party.
共有十八个小孩子参加了萨姆的生日聚会。
eighteenth (18th) *n. adj.*
第十八
David was eighteenth in the examination.
戴维的考试成绩是第十八名。

eighty (80) /'eigh·ty; 'eɪtɪ/ *n. adj.*
number 80 八十
The house is eighty years old.
这所房子有八十年了。

eightieth (80th) *n. adj.*
第八十
It is Mrs Chen's eightieth birthday tomorrow.
明天是陈太太的八十岁生日。

either /'ei·ther; 'aɪðə/ *conj.*
this or that （两者之中）任选一个
You can sit in either desk.
你可选择两张书桌中的一张来坐。
either...or …或…
You can have either rice or noodles.
你可以吃饭或吃面条。

elastic /e·'las·tic; ɪ'læstɪk/ *n. adj.*
(no plural)
(more elastic, most elastic)
stuff that gets longer when you pull it and then goes back to its normal size 橡皮筋；弹性的
John's socks fell down because the elastic was worn out.
约翰的袜子掉下来了，因为袜子的橡皮筋用旧了。
Mary fastened her hair with an elastic band.
玛丽用橡皮圈束头发。

elbow /'el·bow; 'elbəʊ/ *n.*
place where the arm bends 肘
David hurt his elbow when playing tennis.
戴维打网球时弄伤了肘部。

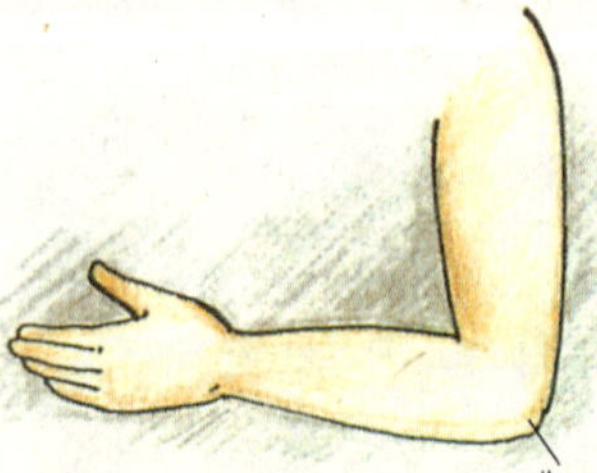

elder /'el·der; 'eldə/ *adj.*
older one of two people 年纪较大的
Tom has an elder sister who is a nurse.
汤姆有一个当护士的姐姐。
Usage note: *Elder* is only used to describe members of a family.
用法： elder 只用来指年长的家庭成员。

elderly /'el·der·ly; 'eldəlɪ/ *adj.*
old 年纪大的
Sam helped the elderly woman to carry her bag.
萨姆帮助老太太拿包。
Usage note: *Elderly* is more polite than *old*.
用法： 用 elderly 比用 old 礼貌些。

eldest /'el·dest; 'eldɪst/ *adj.*
oldest 年纪最大的
Peter is the eldest child in his family.
彼得是家里最大的孩子。

elect /e·'lect; ɪ'lekt/ *v.*
choose 选举；选择
The people elected a new president.
人民选举出一位新总统。

electric /e·'lec·tric; ɪ'lektrɪk/ *adj.*
by electricity 电的；用电的；发电的
Mr Tan has an electric cooker.
谭先生有个电饭锅。

electrical *adj.* （关于）电的
Mr Feng sells electrical goods.
冯先生卖电器。
electricity *n.* 电
The flat has electricity and gas.
这套公寓有电和煤气供应。

electronic /e·lec·'tron·ic; ɪlek'trɒnɪk/ *adj.*
making computers, radios, etc., work 电子的
David has an electronic calculator.
戴维有个电子计算器。

elephant /'el·e·phant; 'elɪfənt/ *n.*
big, wild animal with a long nose 象
Anna saw an elephant at the zoo.
安娜在动物园里看见一头大象。

eleven (11) /e·'lev·en; ɪ'levn/ *n. adj.*
number 11 十一
There are eleven players in a football team.
一支足球队共有十一个球员。
eleventh (11th) *n. adj.*
第十一
Sam was eleventh in the race.
萨姆在比赛中取得第十一名。

else /else; els/ *adv.*
other; more; extra 其他；别的
Would you like anything else?
你还要些什么别的吗?

embarrassed /em·'bar·rass·ed; ɪm'bærəst/ *adj.*
(**more embarrassed, most embarrassed**)
feeling shy 难为情；尴尬
Mary was too embarrassed to sing at the concert.
玛丽怕难为情，不愿在音乐会上唱歌。

emergency /e·'mer·gen·cy; ɪ'mɜːdʒənsɪ/ *n.*
(two **emergencies**)
dangerous happening when something has to be done quickly 紧急事件；紧急情况
The doctor was called to an emergency.
医生被请来诊治急症。

emigrate /'em·i·grate; 'emɪgreɪt/ *v.*
(**emigrating, emigrated, emigrated**)
leave your own country to live in another country 移民；移居外国
The Wang family emigrated to Canada.
王家移民加拿大。

emperor /'em·per·or; 'empərə/ *n.*
man who rules a big country 皇帝
The emperor lived in a beautiful palace.
那皇帝住在漂亮的皇宫里。
empire *n.* 帝国
That country was an empire.
那个国家过去是个帝国。

emperor

empty [1] /'emp·ty; 'emptɪ/ *adj.*
with nothing or nobody inside 空的
The classroom was empty.
教室是空的。
opp. 反义词：full 满的

empty [2] /'emp·ty; 'emptɪ/ *v.*
(**emptying, emptied, emptied**)
take everything out of something 使…变空；全部取出
Tom emptied his glass.
汤姆喝干了一杯。
opp. 反义词：fill 使…变满；装满

encourage /en·'cou·rage; ɪn'kʌrɪdʒ/ *v.*
(**encouraging, encouraged, encouraged**)
try to get someone to do something 鼓励
The teacher encouraged the children to work harder.
老师鼓励孩子们加倍努力。

encyclopaedia /en·cy·clo·'pae·di·a; ɪnsaɪklə'piːdɪə/ *n.*
set of books which tell you about all subjects 百科全书
Janet looked in an encyclopaedia to find out about pandas.
珍妮特翻查百科全书，要找关于熊猫的资料。

end [1] /end; end/ *n.*
furthest part; last part 末端；尽头；末尾部分
Sam sat at the end of the row.
萨姆坐在那排椅子的末端。
Anna came to the end of the book.
安娜读到那本书的末尾部分。
opp. 反义词：beginning, start 开头；开端

end [2] /end; end/ *v.*
finish; stop 完结
The match ended at five o'clock.
比赛于五时结束。
opp. 反义词：begin, start 开始
in the end 最后；终于
In the end, Tom found his pen.
汤姆终于找到了他的笔。

enemy /ˈen·e·my; ˈenəmɪ/ *n.*
(two **enemies**)
someone who wishes to hurt another person or country 敌人
The two countries were enemies.
这两国是敌对的。
opp. 反义词：friend 朋友

energy /ˈen·er·gy; ˈenədʒɪ/ *n.*
(**no plural**)
power to work; strength 精力；力量；能量
A runner needs a lot of energy.
赛跑运动员需要很多能量。

engine /ˈen·gine; ˈendʒɪn/ *n.*
1 machine that makes something move 发动机；引擎
The car had a good engine.
这辆车子的发动机性能良好。

2 machine that pulls a train 火车头
The engine was pulling twenty coaches.
这个火车头正拖动着二十个车厢。

engineer /en·gin·ˈeer; endʒɪˈnɪə/ *n.*
someone who designs and makes machines 工程师
Mr Lin is an engineer.
林先生是位工程师。
engineering *n.* 工程学
Tony is studying engineering.
托尼现正攻读工程学。

England /ˈEng·land; ˈɪŋglənd/ *n.*
part of Britain 英格兰
John lives in England.
约翰住在英格兰。

English [1] /ˈEng·lish; ˈɪŋglɪʃ/ *n.*
1 (**plural**) people from England 英格兰人
The English like football.
英格兰人喜欢足球运动。
2 (**no plural**) language 英语
Peter speaks English.
彼得会说英语。

English [2] /ˈEng·lish; ˈɪŋglɪʃ/ *adj.*
person or thing from England 英格兰的
John is English.
约翰是英格兰人。

enjoy /en·ˈjoy; ɪnˈdʒɔɪ/ *v.*
like something very much 享受；非常喜欢
Baoling enjoys swimming.
宝玲非常喜欢游泳。
enjoy yourself 玩得愉快
Enjoy yourself at the party.
在聚会中愉快地玩吧。
enjoyment *n.* 享受；乐趣；兴致
The noisy children spoiled her enjoyment of the film.
吵闹的孩子们破坏了她看电影的兴致。

enjoyable /en·ˈjoy·a·ble; ɪnˈdʒɔɪəbl/ *adj.*
giving joy or pleasure 令人愉快的；令人快乐的
Swimming is very enjoyable.
游泳令人非常畅快。

enormous /e·ˈnor·mous; ˈnɔːməs/ *adj.*
very big 巨大的
The elephant had enormous tusks.
大象有(一对)巨大的长牙。

enough [1] /e·ˈnough; ɪˈnʌf/ *adj.*
having as much or as many as you need 足够
Tom did not have enough money to buy the radio.
汤姆没有足够的钱买那个收音机。

enough [2] /e·ˈnough; ɪˈnʌf/ *adv.*
as great or as much as is needed 足够
Janet is not old enough to go to school.
珍妮特年纪太小，还不能上学。

enter /ˈen·ter; ˈentə/ *v.*
1 go into a place 进入
The teacher entered the room.
老师走进房间。

2 become a member 加入；参加
Peter entered the school when he was seven.
彼得七岁入学。
opp. 反义词：leave 离开

entertain /en·ter·ˈtain; entəˈteɪn/ *v.*
do something to interest people or make them laugh
引起兴趣；提供娱乐
The choir entertained the parents.
合唱团为家长们表演。

entertainment *n.* 娱乐；表演；游艺节目
There was a lot of entertainment in the park.
公园里有许多游艺节目。

entire /en·ˈtire; ɪnˈtaɪə/ *adj.*
whole; with all its parts 整个的；全部的
Peter ate the entire cake.
彼得吃掉了整个蛋糕。

entirely *adv.* 全部；整个
The cake was entirely eaten.
整个蛋糕都被吃掉了。

entrance /ˈen·trance; ˈentrəns/ *n.*
way into a place 入口
There was a crowd at the entrance.
入口处聚集了一群人。
opp. 反义词：exit 出口

entrance examination *n.*
入学考试
Xiaofang passed the entrance examination and entered the school.
小芳通过入学考试，进了那所学校。

entry /ˈen·try; ˈentrɪ/ *n.*
(two **entries**)
going in 进入
There was no entry into the street.
不准进入这条街道。

envelope /ˈen·ve·lope; ˈenvələʊp/ *n.*
container for a letter 信封
Mary wrote the address on the envelope.
玛丽把地址写在信封上。

envelopes

environment /en·ˈvir·on·ment; ɪnˈvaɪərənmənt/ *n.*
(**no plural**)
world around us 环境
Rubbish spoils the environment.
垃圾有损环境。

equal [1] /ˈe·qual; ˈiːkwəl/ *adj.*
same 相等的
The children had equal shares of cake.
孩子们各分得一块分量相等的蛋糕。
opp. 反义词：unequal 不相等的

equally *adv.* 相等地
Anna and Tom divided the sweets equally.
安娜和汤姆平分了糖果。

equal [2] /'e·qual; 'i:kwəl/ *v.*
(**equalling, equalled, equalled**)
be the same as 等于
Five plus five equals ten (5+5=10).
五加五等于十。

equator /e·'qua·tor; ɪ'kweɪtə/ *n.*
imaginary line round the middle of the earth 赤道
Singapore is near the equator.
新加坡接近赤道。

equipment /e·'quip·ment; ɪ'kwɪpmənt/ *n.*
(**no plural**)
things you need to do something 设备
The school had good equipment.
这所学校设备很好。

eraser /e·'ras·er; ɪ'reɪzə/ *n.*
thing you use to rub out mistakes on paper 橡皮；擦胶（方言）
Sam used an eraser to rub out his mistakes.
萨姆用橡皮把写错的地方擦去。
syn. 同义词：rubber

escalator /'es·ca·la·tor; 'eskəleɪtə/ *n.*
stairs that move and take you up or down 自动扶梯
Peter took the escalator to the second floor.
彼得乘自动扶梯上了二楼。

escape /es·'cape; ɪ'skeɪp/ *v.*
(**escaping, escaped, escaped**)
get free 逃脱
A lion escaped from the zoo.
一只狮子从动物园里逃了出来。

especially /es·'pe·cial·ly; ɪ'speʃəlɪ/ *adv.*
(**more especially, most especially**)
more than others 特别地
Mary likes fruit, especially apples.
玛丽爱吃水果，特别是苹果。

essay /'es·say; 'eseɪ/ *n.*
piece of written work 文章；论文
Susan writes interesting essays.
苏珊会写有趣的文章。

etc. /et·'cet·er·a; ɪt'setərə/
and other things 等等
Apples, oranges, etc., are fruit.
苹果、橙等都是水果。

Europe /'Eu·rope; 'jʊərəp/ *n.*
one of the seven continents of the world 欧洲
France is in Europe.
法国位于欧洲。

European *adj.* 欧洲的
France is a European country.
法国是个欧洲国家。

even /'e·ven; 'i:vn/ *adj.*
numbers that can be divided by two with nothing left （数目）可被2除尽的；偶数的
2, 4 and 6 are even numbers.
2, 4和6都是偶数。
opp. 反义词：odd 奇数的

evening /'eve·ning; 'i:vnɪŋ/ *n.*
time between late afternoon and bedtime 晚间（约下午六时至睡觉之间的一段时间）
Anna watches television every evening.
每天晚上安娜都看电视。
opp. 反义词：morning 早上

event /e·'vent; ɪ'vent/ *n.*
something that happens 事件
The dragon boat race is an important event in Hong Kong.
龙舟竞渡是香港的盛事。

ever /'ev·er; 'evə/ *adv.*
at any time 任何时候
Have you ever been to China?
你以前到过中国吗？

every /'eve·ry; 'evrɪ/ *adj.*
each person or thing 每一
Mrs Lin goes to the market every day.
林太太每天都去市场。

everybody, everyone /'eve·ry·bo·dy, 'eve·ry·one; 'evrɪbɒdɪ, 'evrɪwʌn/ *pron.*
each person; all people 每个人；各人
Everybody watches television.
每个人都看电视。

everything /'eve·ry·thing; evrɪθɪŋ/ *pron.*
each thing; all things 每件东西；各种东西
Mary cleaned everything in the kitchen.
马丽把厨房里的每件东西都洗刷干净。

everywhere /'eve·ry·where; evrɪweə/ *adv.*
at, in, or to all places 各个地方；到处
There was rubbish everywhere.
到处都是垃圾。

evil /'e·vil; 'i:vl/ *adj.*
(**more evil, most evil**)
very bad; wicked 罪恶的；邪恶的
The police caught the evil men.
警方逮捕了坏人。

exact /ex·'act; ɪg'zækt/ *adj.*
correct and complete; not more or less than 准确的；刚好的；不多不少的
You need the exact change for the tram.
乘电车要准备数值刚好的零钱缴付车费。
exactly *adv.* 准确地
He answered the question exactly.
他准确地回答了问题。

exam /ex·'am; ɪg'zæm/ *n.*
short for **examination**
examination 的缩写形式
We have two exams in a school term.
我们一个学期考试两次。

examination /ex·am·i·'na·tion; ɪgzæmɪ'neɪʃn/ *n.*
1 test of your work 考试
Anna passed her examinations.
安娜考试及格。
2 looking at someone or something carefully 仔细察看；检查
Tom went to the hospital for an examination.
汤姆到医院作体格检查。

examine /ex·'am·ine; ɪg'zæmɪn/ *v.*
(**examining, examined, examined**)
look at someone or something carefully 仔细察看；检查
The doctor examined the sick man.
医生检查那个病人。

example /ex·'am·ple; ɪg'zɑ:mpl/ *n.*
one thing that shows what others are like 例子
The exercise started with examples.
这个练习的开头有些例句。
for example 举例来说
I like ball games — football and basketball, for example.
我喜欢球类活动，例如足球和篮球。

excellent /'ex·cel·lent; 'eksələnt/ *adj.*
very good 极好的；优异的
Susan's examination marks were excellent.
苏珊考试成绩优异。

except /ex·'cept; ɪk'sept/ *prep.*
but not 除了…之外
Mr Tan works every day except Sunday.
谭先生除了星期日之外，天天上班。

exchange /ex·'change; ɪks'tʃeɪndʒ/ *v.*
(**exchanging, exchanged, exchanged**)
give one thing and get another for it 交换
Peter exchanged toys with David.
彼得和戴维交换玩具。

excited /ex·'cit·ed; ɪk'saɪtɪd/ *adj.*
(**more excited, most excited**)
with strong feelings 兴奋；激动
The audience was very excited.
观众非常兴奋。
opp. 反义词: bored 厌烦
excite *v.* 使兴奋；刺激
Don't excite the dog.
别招惹那只狗。
excitement *n.* 兴奋；刺激
There was a lot of excitement at the circus.
马戏表演有许多惊险刺激的场面。

exciting /ex·'cit·ing; ɪk'saɪtɪŋ/ *adj.*
making you feel excited; giving strong feelings 使人兴奋的；刺激的
The film was exciting.
这部电影非常刺激。
opp. 反义词: boring 沉闷的

exclaim /ex·'claim; ɪk'skleɪm/ *v.*
say something loudly 呼喊；惊叫
'What?' he exclaimed.
"什么?"他惊叫道。

exclamation mark /ex·clam·'a·tion mark; ekskləmeɪʃn mɑ:k/ *n.*
sign (!) you put at the end of a sentence to show loud or strong words 感叹号

excuse [1] /ex·'cuse; ɪk'skju:s/ *n.*
what you say or write to show why you have done something wrong 借口；解释
Peter had no excuse for being late.
彼得找不到迟到的借口。

excuse [2] /ex·'cuse; ɪk'skju:z/ *v.*
(**excusing, excused, excused**)
forgive someone 原谅
Please excuse me. I must leave now.
对不起，我现在得走了。

exercise [1] /'ex·er·cise; 'eksəsaɪz/ *n.*
1 (**no plural**) moving your body to keep it strong and well 运动
You should take plenty of exercise.
你应该多运动。
2 way of working that helps you to learn 练习
Sam finished the English exercise.
萨姆做完了英语练习。

exercise book *n.* 练习簿
Sam has filled his English exercise book.
萨姆已经用完了他的英语练习簿。

exercise books

exercise [2] /'ex·er·cise; 'eksəsaɪz/ *v.*
(**exercising, exercised, exercised**)
move your body to keep it strong and well 做运动；锻炼
Mrs Chen exercises in the park every morning.
陈太太每天早上在公园做运动。

exhibition /ex·hi·'bi·tion; eksɪ'bɪʃn/ *n.*
showing something so that lots of people can see it 展览
The school had an exhibition of paintings.
学校举行画展。

exist /ex·'ist; ɪg'zɪst/ *v.*
live; be real 生存；存在
Monsters do not exist.
怪兽并不存在。

exit /'ex·it; 'eksɪt/ *n.*
way out of a place 出口
This building has two exits.
这座建筑物有两个出口。
opp. 反义词：entrance 入口

expect /ex·'pect; ɪk'spekt/ *v.*
think that something will happen 预期；预料
I expect it will rain tomorrow.
我预料明天会下雨。

expensive /ex·'pen·sive; ɪk'spensɪv/ *adj.*
(**more expensive, most expensive**)
costing a lot of money 昂贵的
Mr Tan bought an expensive watch.
谭先生买了一只很昂贵的手表。
opp. 反义词：cheap 便宜的

experiment /ex·'per·i·ment; ɪk'sperɪmənt/ *n.*
test that you do to see if something is true 试验；实验
The teacher did an experiment in the science class.
老师在科学课上做了一个实验。

explain /ex·'plain; ɪk'spleɪn/ *v.*
say or show what something means 解释；讲解
The teacher explained how to do the exercise.
老师讲解这个练习该怎么做。
explanation *n.* 解释
The explanation was very clear.
这个解释非常清楚。

explode /ex·'plode; ɪk'spləʊd/ *v.*
(**exploding, exploded, exploded**)
burst open suddenly and dangerously, with a loud noise 爆炸
The firework exploded with a bang.
烟火啪的一声炸响了。
explosion *n.* 爆炸
There was a loud explosion.
那里传来一声爆炸巨响。

explore /ex·'plore; ɪk'splɔː/ *v.*
(**exploring, explored, explored**)
go all over a place to find out about it 探索；到处仔细察看
The tourists explored the old city.
那些游客在这古城里到处仔细察看。
explorer *n.* 探险家
The explorer found an old city.
那位探险家找到了一个古城(遗址)。

expression /ex·'pres·sion; ɪk'spreʃn/ *n.*
1 word or phrase 话；词句；措辞
There are lots of English expressions in this dictionary.
这本词典里有许多英语词句。
2 look on someone's face 面部表情
Baoling always has a happy expression.
宝玲脸上常常露出高兴的表情。

expressions

extra /'ex·tra; 'ekstrə/ *adj.*
more than usual 额外的
John had extra homework to do.
约翰有额外的家庭作业要做。

eye /eye; aɪ/ *n.*
part of the head that sees 眼睛
Susan has blue eyes.
苏珊有一双蓝眼睛。
eyebrows *n.* 眉毛
Mary has thick eyebrows.
玛丽的眉毛很浓密。
eyelash *n.* 眼睫毛
Anna has long eyelashes.
安娜的眼睫毛很长。
eyesight *n.* 视力
Tom has good eyesight.
汤姆的视力良好。

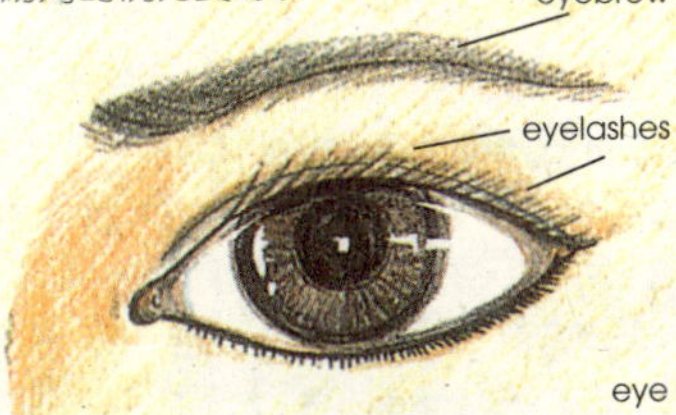

fable /'fa·ble; 'feɪbl/ *n.*
story, usually about animals, which teaches you something 寓言故事
The children are reading a book of fables.
孩子们正在阅读寓言故事书。

face[1] /face; feɪs/ *n.*
front part of the head 脸；面孔
Susan has a pretty face.
苏珊有一副漂亮的面孔。

face[2] /face; feɪs/ *v.*
(**facing, faced, faced**)
have the front towards someone or something 面对；向着
Our building faces the sea.
我们的房子向着大海。

fact /fact; fækt/ *n.*
something that is true or real 事实
It is a fact that the earth is round.
地球是圆的，这是事实。

factory /'fac·to·ry; 'fæktərɪ/ *n.*
(two **factories**)
place where people make things 工厂
Mr Mai works in a factory.
麦先生在工厂工作。

fail /fail; feɪl/ *v.*
try to do something but not be able to do it 失败；（考试）不及格
Sam failed his science exam.
萨姆的科学考试不及格。
opp. 反义词：pass, succeed 及格；成功

faint [1] /faint; feɪnt/ *adj.*
(**fainter, faintest**)
not strong or clear 微弱的；模糊的
We heard a faint noise.
我们听到微弱的声音。

faint [2] /faint; feɪnt/ *v.*
fall down suddenly because you are ill 晕倒
It was so hot that Anna fainted.
天气太热，安娜晕倒了。

fair /fair; feə/ *adj.*
(**fairer, fairest**)
1 behaving in the same way to all people 公平的
All the children got fair shares of the sweets.
每个小孩都分到同等分量的糖果。
opp. 反义词：unfair 不公平的
2 with a light colour 浅色的
Anna has fair skin.
安娜的皮肤白皙。
opp. 反义词：dark 深色的

fairly /'fair·ly; 'feəlɪ/ *adv.*
a little; quite 相当；还算
The film was fairly interesting.
这部电影相当有趣。

fairy /'fair·y; 'feərɪ/ *n.*
(two **fairies**)
little magic person with wings 小神仙；小仙人
Anna likes stories about fairies.
安娜喜欢神话故事。
fairy tale *n.* 神话；童话
The teacher read a fairy tale to the children.
老师给孩子们讲了一个童话。

fall /fall; fɔ:l/ *v.*
(**falling, fell, fallen**)
go down quickly 跌落；跌倒
Tom fell off his bicycle.
汤姆骑自行车跌倒了。
opp. 反义词：rise 升起；起来

fall

fall asleep 睡着
Sam fell asleep in class.
萨姆上课时睡着了。

false /false; fɔ:ls/ *adj.*
not true or not real 错误的；假的
Is this sentence true or false?
这个句子是正确的(或"是")还是错误的(或"非")?

false

false teeth *n.* 假牙
Tom's grandfather has false teeth.
汤姆的爷爷镶了假牙。

familiar /fa·'mil·i·ar; fə'mɪlɪə/ *adj.*
(**more familiar, most familiar**)
that you know well 熟悉的
The tune was familiar.
这调子很熟悉。

family /'fam·i·ly; 'fæməlɪ/ *n.*
(two **families**)
father, mother and their children 家庭
There are five people in my family.
我家共有五人。

family

famous /ˈfa·mous; ˈfeɪməs/ *adj.*
(more famous, most famous)
that many people know about 著名的
He is a famous singer.
他是著名的歌唱家。

fan /fan; fæn/ *n.*
thing that moves the air so that you feel cool 扇；电风扇
I am hot. May I switch on the fan?
我热得很。开电风扇好吗？

fans

far /far; fɑ:/ *adj.*
(farther or **further, farthest** or **furthest)**
long way 远的
Beijing is far from Hong Kong.
北京离香港很远。
opp. 反义词：near 近的

as far as 在…范围内
As far as I know, Peter has not got a bicycle.
就我所知，彼得没有自行车。
how far 有多远
How far is it to Beijing?
这儿离北京有多远？

fare /fare; feə/ *n.*
money you pay to travel on a bus, etc. 车费；船费
What is the fare to Shatin?
往沙田的车费是多少？

farm /farm; fɑ:m/ *n.*
place where you grow crops and keep animals 农场
Mr Yu keeps ducks on his farm.
余先生在农场里养鸭子。

farmer /ˈfarm·er; ˈfɑ:mə/ *n.*
person who works on a farm 农民；农夫
Mr Yu is a farmer.
余先生是个农民。

farmers

farther /ˈfar·ther; ˈfɑ:ðə/ *adj.*
longer way 远些；比较远的
Beijing is farther than Shanghai from Hong Kong.
北京比上海离香港远些。

farthest *adj.* 最远的
Which is farthest from Hong Kong: Beijing, Shanghai or Guangzhou?
北京、上海和广州，哪儿离香港最远？
Usage note: *Further* is used more often now — *Tom can swim farther than Peter. Tom can swim further than Peter.*
用法： further较常用，例如 Tom can swim farther than Peter 多写为 Tom can swim further than Peter。

fashion /ˈfash·ion; ˈfæʃn/ *n.*
popular way of dressing 流行服饰
Long skirts are the latest fashion.
长裙子是最新的流行服饰。

fast [1] /fast; fɑ:st/ *adj.*
(faster, fastest)
quick 快的
Mr Liu has a fast car.
刘先生有一辆速度很快的车子。
opp. 反义词：slow 慢的

fast [2] /fast; fɑ:st/ *adv.*
quickly 快
David can run fast.
戴维跑得很快。
opp. 反义词: slowly 慢
fast asleep 熟睡
The baby was fast asleep.
这婴儿睡熟了。

fasten /'fast·en; 'fɑ:sn/ *v.*
close tightly; do up 关牢; 缚紧
Tom fastened his shoes.
汤姆系紧鞋带。

fat [1] /fat; fæt/ *adj.*
(fatter, fattest)
with a lot of flesh 肥胖的
He is fat because he eats too much.
他胖是因为吃得太多。
opp. 反义词: thin 瘦的

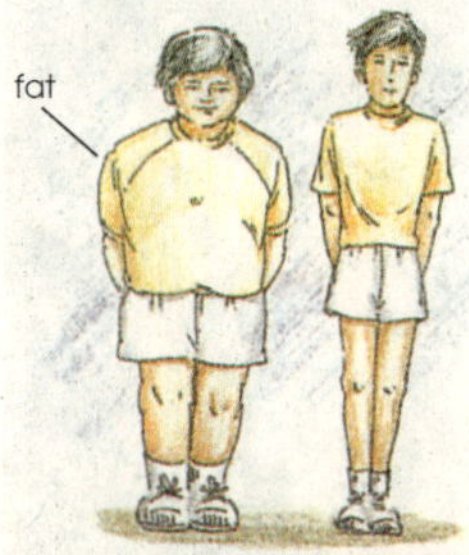

fat [2] /fat; fæt/ *n.*
1 **(no plural)** oily part of meat 脂肪; 肥肉
Don't eat too much fat.
不要吃太多肥肉。
2 oily food like butter or margarine 食用的动物油或植物油
Vegetable fats are healthier than animal fats.
植物油比动物油更有益于我们的健康。

father /'fa·ther; 'fɑ:ðə/ *n.*
man who has a child 父亲
Tom always obeys his father.
汤姆总是听父亲的话。

fault /fault; fɔ:lt/ *n.*
something not correct 错误; 毛病; 缺点
There are many faults in his work.
他的作业中有许多错误。
syn. 同义词: mistake

favourite /'fa·vour·ite; 'feɪvərɪt/ *adj. n.*
that you like best 最喜爱的(人或物)
Ice-cream is my favourite dessert.
冰淇淋是我最喜爱的甜品。
Chocolate is my favourite.
我最喜欢吃巧克力。

fear /fear; fɪə/ *n.*
what you feel when you are afraid 恐惧; 害怕
She has a great fear of snakes.
她非常怕蛇。

feast /feast; fi:st/ *n.*
very good meal that you eat at a special time 宴会
We had a feast at the wedding.
我们参加了一个婚宴。

feather /'feath·er; 'feðə/ *n.*
what grows on a bird's body 羽毛
The hen had white feathers.
这只母鸡的羽毛是白色的。

February /'Feb·ru·a·ry; 'februərɪ/ *n.*
second month of the year 二月
There is not much rain in February.
二月雨水不多。

fee /fee; fi:/ *n.*
money you pay for special work 费用
School fees are expensive.
学费很贵。

feed /feed; fi:d/ *v.*
(feeding, fed, fed)
give food to a person or animal 喂
Mary feeds her cat twice a day.
玛丽每天喂两次猫。

feel /feel; fi:l/ *v.*
(feeling, felt, felt)
1 touch something 触摸
Baoling felt the cloth.
宝玲触摸那块布。
2 know something inside yourself 感觉; 觉得
Tom feels cold.
汤姆感到冷。

feeling /'fee·ling; 'fi:lɪŋ/ *n.*
something that you feel 感觉; 预感
I have a feeling that Mary will be late.
我有预感玛丽将会迟到。

feet /feet; fiːt/ *n.*
(**plural**)
more than one **foot** foot 的复数
The child had no shoes on his feet.
那小孩脚上没穿鞋。

fell /fell; fel/ *v.*
p.t. of **fall** fall 的过去式
Sam fell and hurt himself.
萨姆摔下来，受了伤。

felt /felt; felt/ *v.*
p.t. of **feel** feel 的过去式
Tom felt tired.
汤姆感到很累。

felt-pen, felt-tip
/felt·'pen, felt·'tip; felt'pen, felt'tɪp/ *n.*
pen that has a soft point
毡头笔
Mary coloured a picture with felt-pens.
玛丽用毡头笔给一幅画着色。

fence /fence; fens/ *n.*
line of wood or metal poles
栅栏
There is a fence round the park.
公园四周有栅栏围住。

ferry /'fer·ry; 'ferɪ/ *n.*
(two **ferries**)
boat that takes people or things over a river, harbour, etc. 渡轮
Peter took the ferry across the harbour.
彼得乘渡轮横渡海港。

ferries

festival /'fes·ti·val; 'festəvl/ *n.*
time when people come together for singing, dancing, etc. 节日
There are many festivals in Hong Kong.
香港有许多节日。

fetch /fetch; fetʃ/ *v.*
go and get someone or something 拿来；接来
Would you fetch my shoes, please?
请你把我的鞋子拿来好吗？

fever /'fe·ver; 'fiːvə/ *n.*
illness that makes you feel very hot or cold 发烧；发热
Sam was ill with a fever.
萨姆发烧病倒了。

few /few; fjuː/ *adj.*
(**fewer, fewest**)
not many 不多的；很少的
Few people like snakes.
很少人喜欢蛇。
a few 有几个
A few people like snakes.
有些人喜欢蛇。
Usage note: Use *few* with nouns you can count — *David has a few sweets.* Use *some* with nouns you cannot count — *David has some bread.*
用法：few 用来形容可数的事物，例如 David has a few sweets。some 形容不可数的事物，例如 David has some bread。

field /field; fiːld/ *n.*
1 piece of land on a farm
田地；田野
The farmer grew vegetables in the field.
农民在田里种菜。

2 piece of land where you play games 场地
The school has a sports field.
学校里有一个运动场。

fierce /fierce; fɪəs/ *adj.*
(**fiercer, fiercest**)
angry; making people afraid 凶恶的
They have a fierce dog.
他们有一只凶恶的狗。

fifteen (15) /fit·'teen; fɪf'ti:n/ *n. adj.*
number 15 十五
There were fifteen girls in the class.
班上有十五个女学生。
fifteenth (15th) *n. adj.* 第十五
It was Jenny's fifteenth birthday yesterday.
昨天是詹妮的十五岁生日。

fifth (5th) /fifth; fɪfθ/ *n. adj.*
next after the fourth 第五
David was fifth in the race.
戴维在比赛中得了第五名。

fifty (50) /'fif·ty; 'fɪftɪ/ *n. adj.*
number 50 五十
Mr Chen is fifty years old.
陈先生五十岁。
fiftieth (50th) *n. adj.* 第五十
His fiftieth birthday was last week.
上星期，他度过了五十岁生日。

fight [1] /fight; faɪt/ *v.*
(**fighting, fought, fought**)
try to hurt another person, animal or country 打架；打仗
The two countries fought each other.
那两个国家互相打仗。

fight [2] /fight; faɪt/ *n.*
time when people or animals try to hurt one another 打架；打斗；交战
The two dogs had a fight.
那两只狗打架。

fight

figure /'fig·ure; 'fɪgə/ *n.*
sign that shows a number 数字
1, 2, 3, etc., are figures.
1, 2, 3 等都是数字。

fill /fill; fɪl/ *v.*
put more and more inside something until it can hold no more （把容器）装满
Mrs Lin filled the glasses with lemonade.
林太太把玻璃杯装满柠檬水。
fill in 填写
Please fill in this form.
请填写这份表格。

film /film; fɪlm/ *n.*
1 special plastic to make photographs 胶卷；软片；菲林（方言）
Sam put a film in his camera.
萨姆把胶卷装入照相机里。

films

2 moving picture that you can see at a cinema or on television 影片
There are some good films on television.
电视里会播放一些好影片。

final /'fi·nal; 'faɪnl/ *adj.*
last 最后的
The final lesson of the day was English.
今天的最后一节课是英语课。

finally /'fi·nal·ly; 'faɪnəlɪ/ *adv.*
at last 最后；终于
The bus finally arrived.
公共汽车终于来了。

find /find; faɪnd/ *v.*
(**finding, found, found**)
come to something by chance; come to something you are looking for 无意中发现；找到
Sam found ten dollars in the street.
萨姆在街上捡到十港元钱。
syn. 同义词: discover
opp. 反义词: lose 失去
find out 找出；查出
Can you find out where Tom lives?
你能查出汤姆住在哪里吗?

fine /fine; faɪn/ *adj.*
(**finer, finest**)
1 very good or beautiful 很好；很美丽
I feel fine.
我很好。
2 not raining; clear 天气晴朗
It's fine today.
今天天气晴朗。

finger /'fin·ger; 'fɪŋgə/ *n.*
one of the parts of the hand 手指
People wear rings on their fingers.
人们把戒指戴在手指上。
finger-nail *n.* 指甲
The woman has long finger-nails.
那女人的指甲很长。

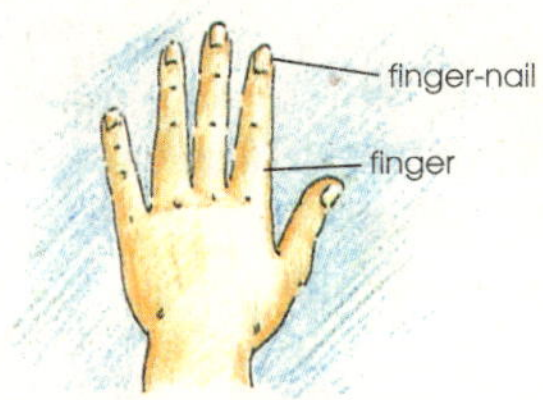

fingerprint *n.* 指纹
The police found the burglar's fingerprints on the window.
警方在窗户上发现了窃贼的指纹。

finish [1] /ˈfin·ish; ˈfɪnɪʃ/ *v.*
1 come to the end; stop doing something 完成
Mary finished her homework.
玛丽做完了家庭作业。
syn. 同义词：complete
2 come to an end; stop happening 完毕；结束
School finished at four o'clock.
学校四时放学。
opp. 反义词：start 开始

finish [2] /ˈfin·ish; ˈfɪnɪʃ/ *n.*
(two **finishes**)
last part; end 终结；结束
The children waited near the finish of the race.
孩子们在靠近赛跑的终点等候。

fire [1] /ˈfire; ˈfaɪə/ *n.*
1 things burning 火；火警；火灾
There was a fire in the airport.
机场发生火警。

2 something that heats a room 火炉；暖气炉
Peter switched on the electric fire.
彼得开了电暖炉。
catch fire 烧着；着火
The hut caught fire.
茅屋着火了。
fireboat *n.* 消防艇；救火船
The fireboat went to the burning ship.
消防艇向那艘燃烧着的船开去。
fire-brigade *n.* 消防队
Send for the fire-brigade.
去叫消防队来。
fire-engine *n.* 救火车
The fire-engine arrived at the fire.
救火车来到了火场。
fire extinguisher *n.* 灭火筒；灭火器
There's a fire extinguisher on the wall.
墙上挂着个灭火筒。
fireman *n.* 消防队员
Mr Lin is a fireman.
林先生是个消防队员。
fire station *n.* 消防局
Mr Lin works at the fire station.
林先生在消防局工作。
firework *n.* 烟火；烟花(方言)
We have fireworks at Chinese New Year.
农历新年时，我们有烟火表演。

fire [2] /ˈfire; ˈfaɪə/ *v.*
(**firing, fired, fired**)
shoot with a gun 放(枪、炮)；射击
They fire a gun every day at noon.
他们每天中午鸣炮。

first (1st) /first; fɜːst/ *n. adj. adv.*
before all others 第一
January is the first month of the year.
一月是一年的第一个月份。
at first 最初；起先
At first, Sam did not understand the question.
最初，萨姆不明白那个问题。
first aid *n.* 急救
Mary gave the injured girl first aid.
玛丽对受伤的女孩子进行急救。
first of all 首先
First of all, have a shower.
首先，要洗个淋浴。

fish [1] /fish; fɪʃ/ *n.*
(two **fish**)
animal that lives in water 鱼
Henry caught a fish in the pond.
亨利在池塘里捉到一条鱼。
Usage note: *Fish* as a noun you can count has two plurals — *Peter caught seven fish. David is studying the fishes of the China Sea.*
用法：fish 的复数，一般用 fish，例如 Peter caught seven fish。如指不同品种的鱼，复数则用 fishes，例如 David is studying the fishes of the China Sea。

fish [2] /fish; fɪʃ/ *v.*
try to catch fish 捕鱼；钓鱼
Henry was fishing in the pond.
亨利在池塘边钓鱼。
fishing *n.* 捕鱼；钓鱼
Henry likes fishing.
亨利喜欢钓鱼。

fisherman /ˈfisher·man; ˈfɪʃəmən/ *n.*
(two **fishermen**)
man who lives by fishing 渔民
Mr Liang is a fisherman.
梁先生是个渔民。

fist /fist; fɪst/ *n.*
hand that is closed 拳头
David hit the ball with his fist.
戴维用拳头打球。

fit [1] /fit; fɪt/ *adj.*
(**fitter, fittest**)
1 with a strong, healthy body 强健的；健康的
Football players should be very fit.
足球运动员应该非常强健。
2 good enough 合适；适宜
The fish was not fit to eat.
这条鱼不适宜食用。

fit [2] /fit; fɪt/ *v.*
(**fitting, fitted, fitted**)
to be the right size 合适
Do these shoes fit you?
这些鞋子合适吗？

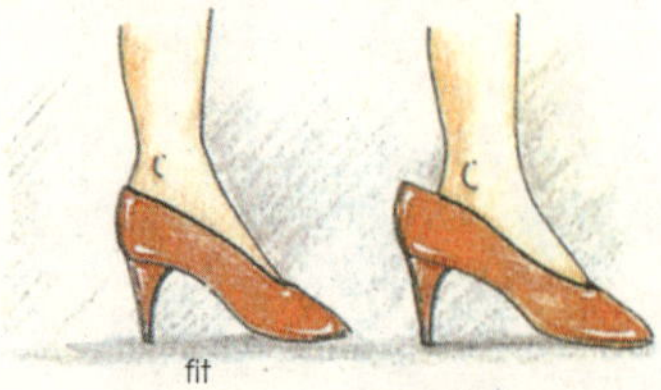
fit

five (5) /five; faɪv/ *n. adj.*
number 5 五
Peter ate five oranges.
彼得吃了五个橙子。
fifth (5th) *n. adj.* 第五
Yesterday was Peter's fifth birthday.
昨天是彼得的五岁生日。

fix /fix; fɪks/ *v.*
1 put something in place so that it will not move 使固定；缚紧；钉牢
Anna fixed a hook on the wall.
安娜把一个钩子钉在墙上。
2 mend something 修理
David fixed his broken radio.
戴维修理他那个坏了的收音机。

flag /flag; flæg/ *n.*
piece of cloth with a special pattern to show a country or group 旗；旗帜
The French flag is blue, white and red.
法国国旗是蓝、白、红三色的。

French flag

flame /flame; fleɪm/ *n.*
bright part of a fire 火焰
Smoke and flames came from the burning hut.
烟和火焰从烧着了的茅屋里冒出。

flash [1] /flash; flæʃ/ *n.*
(two **flashes**)
sudden, bright light 闪光
There was a flash of lightning.
有一道闪电。

flash [2] /flash; flæʃ/ *v.*
send or give out a sudden, bright light 发出闪光
Lightning flashed in the sky.
天空中有一道闪电。

flat [1] /flat; flæt/ *n.*
home that is part of a bigger building （公寓的）单元房
There are ten flats in the building.
这所房子有十套单元房。

flat [2] /flat; flæt/ *adj.*
(**flatter, flattest**)
with no lumps or hills 平的；平坦的
The land is very flat. There are no hills or mountains.
这个地区很平坦，没有丘陵和山脉。

flavour /ˈfla·vour; ˈfleɪvə/ *n.*
taste 味；味道
What flavour ice-cream do you like?
你喜欢哪种味道的冰淇淋？

flesh /flesh; fleʃ/ *n.*
(**no plural**)
soft part of the body 肉
There was a lot of flesh on the chicken.
那只鸡有很多肉。

flew /flew; fluː/ *v.*
p.t. of **fly** fly 的过去式
An aeroplane flew over the town.
一架飞机飞过那个镇的上空。

flight /flight; flaɪt/ *n.*
journey by plane (乘飞机)飞行
They had a comfortable flight to London.
他们乘飞机往伦敦的旅途很舒适。

float /float; fləʊt/ *v.*
stay on top of the water 浮
A lot of rubbish was floating in the harbour.
港内漂浮着许多垃圾。
opp. 反义词：sink 沉

flock /flock; flɒk/ *n.*
group of birds or animals (飞禽、牲畜等的)群
A flock of birds flew over the town.
一群鸟飞过那个城镇。

flood [1] /flood; flʌd/ *v.*
to cover with water 淹没
Heavy rain flooded the fields.
大雨把田地都淹没了。

flood [2] /flood; flʌd/ *n.*
lot of water that covers the land 洪水；水灾；泛滥
There are sometimes floods in Hong Kong during a typhoon.
台风来时，香港有时会发生水灾。

floor /floor; flɔ:/ *n.*
1 part of the room you walk on 地板
There was a carpet on the floor.
地板上铺了地毯。
opp. 反义词：ceiling 天花板

2 part of a building (一幢房子的)一层
We live on the second floor.
我们住在二楼。

Usage note: Note the difference between English (the *first floor* is the floor above the *ground floor*) and Chinese (the *first floor* is the *bottom floor*).
用法：注意英语说 first floor 是指底层以上的楼层，汉语的一楼指底层。

florist /'flo·rist; 'flɒrɪst/ *n.*
someone who sells flowers 经营花店者
Mary bought some flowers at the florist.
玛丽在花店里买了一些花。

flour /'flour; 'flaʊə/ *n.*
(**no plural**)
powder used to make bread, noodles, etc. 面粉
Anna mixed the flour and water in a bowl.
安娜把碗里的水和面粉混合起来。

flow /flow; fləʊ/ *v.*
move like water 流
The river flows into a lake.
那条河流入湖里。

flower /'flow·er; 'flaʊə/ *n.*
part of a plant which holds the seeds 花
Anna bought her mother a bunch of flowers.
安娜买了一束花给母亲。

flown /flown; fləʊn/ *v.*
p.p. of **fly** fly 的过去分词
The bird has flown into a tree.
那鸟儿已经飞到树上去了。

flu /flu; flu:/ *n.*
(**no plural**)
bad fever 流行性感冒
Peter caught flu and had to stay in bed.
彼得染上了流行性感冒，必须卧床。

flute /flute; flu:t/ *n.*
musical instrument that you blow 长笛
John can play the flute.
约翰会吹长笛。

fly [1] /fly; flaɪ/ *n.*
(two **flies**)
small insect with wings
苍蝇
Flies spread diseases.
苍蝇传播疾病。

fly [2] /fly; flaɪ/ *v.*
(**flying, flew, flown**)
1 move through the air with wings; go on an aeroplane
飞；乘飞机
Mr Mai flew to London yesterday.
麦先生昨天乘飞机去伦敦。
The birds were flying in the sky.
鸟儿在天空中飞翔。

2 make something move through the air 放上天空
Sam flew his kite in the park.
萨姆在公园里放风筝。

flying saucer
/'fly·ing 'sau·cer; 'flaɪɪŋ 'sɔːsə/ *n.*
round flying machine from space 飞碟
I have never seen a flying saucer.
我从来没有见过飞碟。

flying saucer

flyover /'fly·o·ver; 'flaɪəʊvə/ *n.*
bridge that carries a road over other roads 立交桥
There are a lot of flyovers in Hong Kong.
香港有许多立交桥。

focus /'fo·cus; 'fəʊkəs/ *n.*
(two **focuses**)
part of a camera, etc., that makes a picture clear 焦点
The photographs were not in focus.
这些相片的焦点没有对准。

fog /fog; fɒg/ *n.*
thick mist in the air 雾
We get fogs in winter.
冬天时常有雾。
foggy *adj.* 有雾的
It was foggy yesterday.
昨天有雾。

fold /fold; fəʊld/ *v.*
bend something over so that one part is on top of the other 折叠
Tom folded the letter and put it in an envelope.
汤姆把信折好放入信封里。

follow /'fol·low; 'fɒləʊ/ *v.*
1 come or go after someone or something 跟随
The dog followed Peter home.
那只狗跟着彼得回家。
opp. 反义词：lead 带领

follow

2 do the same as 跟着（做）
Sam followed Peter and bought a dictionary.
萨姆跟从彼得买了一本字典。
as follows 如下
The number eight is written as follows: 8.
八这个数字的另一写法如下：8。
the following 以下
Learn the following words.
学习以下各词。

fond /fond; fɒnd/ *adj.*
(**fonder, fondest**)
liking something a lot 很喜欢

Peter is fond of reading.
皮得很喜欢阅读。
Usage note: *Fond is always followed by of — David is fond of sweets.*
用法：fond 通常与 of 连用，例如 David is fond of sweets。

food /food; fu:d/ *n.*
(**no plural**)
things people and animals eat 食物；食品
The food is good in this restaurant.
这家餐厅的食品很好吃。

fool /fool; fu:l/ *n.*
very silly person 傻瓜；笨人
Only a fool runs into the road.
只有傻瓜才会在马路上乱闯。

foolish /'fool·ish; 'fu:lɪʃ/ *adj.*
(**more foolish, most foolish**)
not right, good or clever 愚蠢的；不明智的
It's foolish to run into the road.
在马路上乱闯是不明智的。
syn. 同义词：stupid
opp. 反义词：wise, sensible 聪明的；明智的

foolishly *adv.* 愚蠢地；傻傻地
Sam behaved foolishly in school.
萨姆在学校里表现得很傻气。

foot /foot; fʊt/ *n.*
(two **feet**)
1 part of the leg you stand on 脚
Mary has no shoes on her feet.
玛丽脚上没穿鞋。

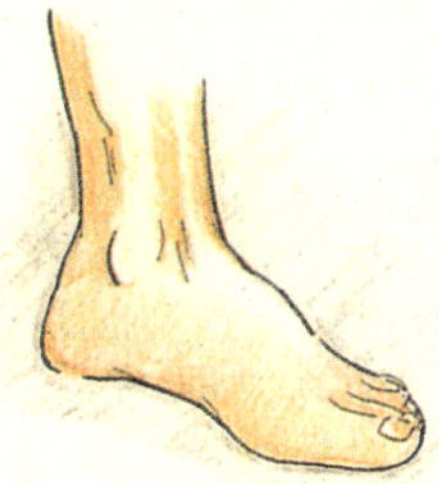

2 measure of length 英尺
The boat was 20 feet long.
这艘船有 20 英尺长。
3 bottom 底部
There was a restaurant at the foot of the hill.
山脚有一家餐厅。

footbridge *n.* 人行桥
There was a footbridge across the road.
有一座横过马路的人行桥。

footpath *n.* 小径
There are many footpaths in the park.
公园里有许多小径。

footstep *n.* 脚步声；脚印
Tom heard footsteps on the stairs.
汤姆听到楼梯上传来脚步声。

from head to foot 从头到脚
Tom was covered in mud from head to foot.
汤姆从头到脚都是泥。

on foot 步行
Peter goes to school on foot.
彼得步行上学。

football /'foot·ball; 'fʊtbɔ:l/ *n.*
(**no plural**)
game with two teams who kick a ball 足球
David plays football.
戴维踢足球。

for /for; fə/ *prep.*
1 word that shows who will get or have something 给（某人）
Mary bought a present for Tom.
玛丽买了一件礼物送给汤姆。
2 word that shows why you are doing something 为了
Bring your exercise book for me to mark.
把你的练习簿带来让我评分。
3 because of something 由于；因为
Peter won a prize for painting.
彼得的画得了奖。
4 word that shows how much you must pay 表示付出的代价
Anna bought a dress for $100.
安娜花一百港元买了一件连衣裙。
5 word that shows how far or how long 表示经过的时间或距离
I have been waiting for an hour.
我等了一个小时。
6 word that points to a person or thing you are talking about 指所谈及的人或物
These swings are for children to play on.
这些秋千是给小孩子玩的。

forbid /for·'bid; fə'bɪd/ *v.* (**forbidding, forbade, forbidden**)
say that someone must not do something 禁止
Cycling is forbidden in the park.
公园内禁止骑自行车。

force /force; fɔ:s/ *v.* (**forcing, forced, forced**)
make someone do something 强迫
Mr Chen forced Peter to do his homework.
陈先生强迫彼得做家庭作业。

forecast /'fore·cast; 'fɔ:kɑ:st/ *n.*
saying what will happen 预告
The weather forecast says it will rain.
天气预报说会下雨。

forehead /'fore·head; 'fɒrɪd/ *n.*
top part of your face 前额
Mary shows her forehead.
玛丽露出前额。

foreign /'for·eign; 'fɒrən/ *adj.*
from another country 外国的
Mr Mai likes to visit foreign countries.
麦先生喜欢到外国旅行。

foreigner *n.* 外国人
There are many foreigners in Hong Kong.
香港有许多外国人。

forest /'for·est; 'fɒrɪst/ *n.*
big piece of land with many trees 森林
There were wild animals in the forest.
森林里有野兽。

forever /for·'e·ver; fə'revə/ *adv.*
always; for your whole life 永远
David would like to be on holiday forever.
戴维希望永远放假。

forget /for·'get; fə'get/ *v.* (**forgetting, forgot, forgotten**)
let something go out of your mind 忘记
Peter forgot to do his homework.
彼得忘记了做家庭作业。
opp. 反义词: remember 记得

forgive /for·'give; fə'gɪv/ *v.* (**forgiving, forgave, forgiven**)
say or show that you are not angry with someone 原谅
Mrs Lin forgave Sam for breaking the window.
萨姆打破了玻璃窗，林太太原谅了他。
syn. 同义词: excuse, pardon

fork /fork; fɔ:k/ *n.*
something for lifting food to your mouth 叉子
Peter does not like eating with a knife and fork.
彼得不喜欢用刀叉进食。

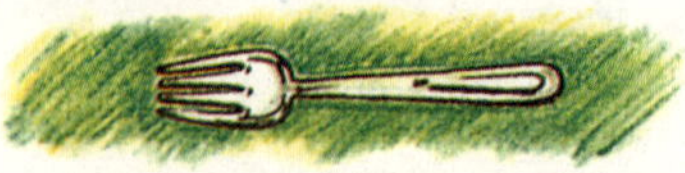

form [1] /form; fɔ:m/ *n.*
1 one of the ways you say or write a word （语法上的）形式
Did is a form of do.
Did是do的一种形式。
2 printed paper with spaces to be filled in 表格
Peter filled in the form.
彼得填好了表格。
3 class in a school 年级
Anna is in Form 2.
安娜读二年级。

form [2] /form; fɔ:m/ *v.*
make 组成；形成
The children formed lines.
孩子们站成几行。

fort /fort; fɔ:t/ *n.*
castle 堡垒
There was a fort on the hill.
山上有个堡垒。

fortnight /'fort·night; 'fɔ:tnaɪt/ *n.*
two weeks 两星期
Mr Tan went to Canada for a fortnight.
谭先生到加拿大去了两星期。

fortune /'for·tune; 'fɔ:tʃu:n/ *n.* (**no plural**)
luck; what happens in your life 运气；命运
David had the good fortune to win a prize.
戴维运气好，得了奖。

fortune-teller /'for·tune·tell·er; 'fɔ:tʃu:ntelə/ *n.*
someone who says what will happen to you 算命的人
The fortune-teller told Mrs Chen that she would have a long life.
算命先生对陈太太说她会长寿。

forty (40) /'for·ty; 'fɔ:tɪ/ *n. adj.*
number 40 四十
There are forty children in the class.
班上共有四十个学生。
fortieth (40th) *n. adj.* 第四十
Susan came fortieth in the examination.
苏珊的考试成绩排第四十名。

forward, forwards /'for·ward, 'for·wards; 'fɔ:wəd, 'fɔ:wədz/ *adv.*
to the front 向前
Come forward, Peter.
彼得，走上前来。

fought /fought; fɔ:t/ *v.*
p.t. of **fight** fight 的过去式
Mr Lin fought in the war.
林先生打过仗。

found /found; faund/ *v.*
p.t. of **find** find 的过去式
Mary found her book under the desk.
玛丽在书桌底下找到她的书。

fountain /'foun·tain; 'fauntɪn/ *n.*
water going into the air 喷泉；喷水池
There is a fountain in the park.
公园里有个喷水池。

fountain pen *n.* 自来水笔
Susan writes with a fountain pen.
苏珊用自来水笔写字。

four (4) /four; fɔ:/ *n. adj.*
number 4 四
Peter went to the beach with four friends.
彼得和四个朋友一起到海滩去。
fourth (4th) *n. adj.* 第四
April is the fourth month of the year.
April 是一年的第四个月。

fourteen (14) /four·'teen; fɔ:'ti:n/ *n. adj.*
number 14 十四
Mary's elder brother is fourteen years old.
玛丽的哥哥十四岁。
fourteenth (14th) *n. adj.* 第十四
It was his fourteenth birthday yesterday.
昨天是他的十四岁生日。

fox /fox; fɒks/ *n.*
(two **foxes**)
wild animal like a dog 狐狸
The hunters were chasing a fox.
猎人们正在追赶一只狐狸。

fraction /'frac·tion; 'frækʃn/ *n.*
part of a number （数学的）分数
Sam is learning fractions.
萨姆正在学分数。

frame /frame; freɪm/ *n.*
wood or metal edge for a picture, with glass in front 画框
The teacher put the best pictures in frames.
老师给最好的画装框。

free /free; fri:/ *adj.*
(**freer, freest**)
1 able to do what you want 自由的
Wild animals should be free.
野生动物应该自由自在地生活。
2 that costs nothing 免费的
The concert was free.
那个音乐会是免费的。
set free 释放
He opened the cage and set the bird free.
他打开笼子，把鸟放走了。
freedom *n.* 自由
It is better if wild animals live in freedom.
野生动物如能自由自在地生活会比较好些。

freeze /freeze; fri:z/ *v.*
(**freezing, froze, frozen**)
change into ice 结冰
It was so cold that the pond froze.
天气非常冷，池塘都结了冰。
freezer *n.* （冰箱内的）冷冻格
Put the ice-cream in the freezer.
把冰淇淋放到冷冻格里吧。

fresh /fresh; freʃ/ *adj.*
(**fresher, freshest**)
that was made or grown a short time ago 新鲜的
Mrs Lin bought some fresh eggs.
林太太买了些新鲜鸡蛋。

Friday /'Fri·day; 'fraɪdɪ/ *n.*
day of the week 星期五
I went to the cinema last Friday.
上星期五我去看电影。

fridge /fridge; frɪdʒ/ *n.*
short for **refrigerator**
refrigerator 的缩写形式
We keep fresh food in a fridge.
我们把新鲜食物放在冰箱里保存。

fried /fried; fraɪd/ *v.*
p.t. of **fry** fry 的过去式
Tom fried some eggs for breakfast.
汤姆煎了些鸡蛋做早餐。

friend /friend; frend/ *n.*
someone you know well and like 朋友
Peter and David are good friends.
彼得和戴维是好朋友。
make friends 成为朋友
The children soon made friends.
孩子们很快就成为朋友了。

friendly /ˈfriend·ly; ˈfrendlɪ/ *adj.*
(friendlier, friendliest)
be like a friend 友善的
The people are very friendly.
那些人都很友善。
opp. 反义词: unfriendly 不友善的
friendship *n.* 友谊
Their friendship lasted all their lives.
他们的友谊是终生的。

frighten /ˈfright·en; ˈfraɪtn/ *v.*
make someone afraid 使人害怕
Susan was frightened by the snake.
苏珊很害怕那条蛇。
syn. 同义词: scare
frightened *adj.* 受惊的; 吓怕了的
The little girl was very frightened.
那小女孩被吓坏了。
frightening *adj.* 可怕的
The storm was very frightening.
那场风暴非常可怕。

frog /frog; frɒg/ *n.*
small jumping animal 青蛙
There were some frogs in the pond.
池塘里有些青蛙。

from /from; frəm/ *prep.*
1 word that shows where someone or something starts 从…(地方)来
John came from Canada.
约翰从加拿大来。
2 word that shows when someone or something starts 从…(时候)开始
Mr Tan works from eight o'clock to five o'clock.
谭先生的工作时间是从八时到五时。
3 word that shows how far away something is 距离(多远)
Mary lives two kilometres from the school.
玛丽的家距离学校两公里远。
4 word that shows who gave or sent something 由…(某人)送来
Anna got a birthday card from Janet.
安娜收到珍妮特送来的生日贺卡。
5 word that shows the place where you get something 从…(地方)取得
We got food from the market.
我们从市场买来食物。

front [1] /front; frʌnt/ *n.*
(no plural)
1 part that comes before the others 前面
The front of the train was full.
火车的前面部分已满座。
2 part that looks forward 正面
The front of the house faces east.
房子的正面朝东。
opp. 反义词: back 后面; 背面
in front of 在…的前面
The car stopped in front of the post office.
汽车停在邮局前面。
front door *n.* 前门
The postman knocked at the front door.
邮递员敲前门。

front [2] /front; frʌnt/ *adj.*
placed before others 前面的
Sam sits in the front row.
萨姆坐在前排。

frown /frown; fraʊn/ *n.*
angry or worried look 皱眉头
The teacher had a frown on her face.
老师皱着眉头。

frown

frozen /ˈfro·zen; ˈfrəʊzn/ *adj.*
be changed into ice 结冰
The lake was frozen.
湖结冰了。

fruit /fruit; fru:t/ *n.*
(no plural)
part of a plant which holds seeds and which you can eat 水果
Apples, oranges, etc., are fruit.
苹果、橙子等都是水果。

fry /fry; fraɪ/ *v.*
(frying, fried, fried)
cook food in very hot oil 油煎；油炸
Anna is frying chicken legs.
安娜在炸鸡腿。
frying-pan *n.* 煎锅
Anna cooked the fish in a frying-pan.
安娜用煎锅烧鱼。

full /full; fʊl/ *adj.*
(fuller, fullest)
holding as much as it can 满的
The glass was full.
玻璃杯满了。
opp. 反义词：empty 空的

full

full stop /fullˈstop; fʊlˈstɒp/ *n.*
sign (.) to show the end of a sentence 句号

fun /fun; fʌn/ *n.*
(no plural)
what you like doing, seeing or hearing 乐事；有趣的人或事物
Parties are good fun.
朋友聚会是件乐事。
for fun 开玩笑；闹着玩
We dressed up for fun.
我们穿上别人的衣服来取乐。
have fun 玩得开心
We had fun at the party.
我们在那次聚会上玩得很开心。

funeral /ˈfu·ne·ral; ˈfju:nərəl/ *n.*
special meeting of people when someone dies 葬礼
There were a lot of people at the funeral.
参加葬礼的人很多。

funnel /ˈfun·nel; ˈfʌnl/ *n.*
thing for getting liquids into bottles 漏斗
Mrs Chen used a funnel to fill the bottles with water.
陈太太用漏斗把瓶子注满了水。

funny /ˈfun·ny; ˈfʌnɪ/ *adj.*
(funnier, funniest)
making you smile or laugh 好笑的；好玩的
The film was very funny.
这部电影很好笑。

fur /fur; fɜ:/ *n.*
(no plural)
soft, thick hair on some animals （动物身上的）软毛
The cat's fur was very long.
那猫的毛很长。

furniture /ˈfur·ni·ture; ˈfɜ:nɪtʃə/ *n.*
(no plural)
tables, chairs, beds, etc. 家具（桌、椅、床等等）
Mary dusted the furniture.
玛丽抹去家具上的灰尘。

further /'fur·ther; 'fɜːðə/ *adj.*
longer way 远些
Which is further from Hong Kong, Shanghai or Beijing?
上海和北京，哪儿离香港远些？
furthest *adj.* 最远的
Sam sat furthest away from the teacher.
萨姆坐在离老师最远的位置。

fussy /'fuss·y; 'fʌsɪ/ *adj.*
(fussier, fussiest)
choosing carefully 挑剔
Susan is fussy about what she eats.
苏珊对吃的东西十分挑剔。

future /'fu·ture; 'fjuːtʃə/ *n.*
(no plural)
time that is coming 将来；未来
We do not know what will happen in the future.
我们不知道将来会发生什么事情。

Gg

gale /gale; geɪl/ *n.*
very strong wind 强风；大风
The wind got stronger. It became a gale.
风愈刮愈大，变成了一股强风。

gallop /'gal·lop; 'gæləp/ *v.*
run very fast （马等）飞跑
The horses galloped round the field.
那些马绕着场地飞跑。

gallop

gamble /'gam·ble; 'gæmbl/ *v.*
(gambling, gambled, gambled)
try to win money 赌博
Peter often goes to Macao to gamble.
彼得常去澳门赌博。

game /game; geɪm/ *n.*
play with rules 游戏；运动
We played a game of football on the beach.
我们在沙滩上踢了一场足球。

gang /gang; gæŋ/ *n.*
group of people who usually do bad things 一帮人；一伙人
The police arrested the gang.
警方拘捕了那一帮人。

gap /gap; gæp/ *n.*
hole where there is usually something 缺口；裂缝
The children went through a gap in the fence.
孩子们穿过了栅栏的缺口。

garage /'ga·rage; 'gærɑːʒ/ *n.*
1 place where you keep a car 车房
He keeps his car in his garage.
他把车子停在自己的车房里。
2 place where pleople sell petrol or mend cars 路边加油站
He stopped the car at a garage to buy petrol.
他把车子停在加油站买汽油。

garden /'gar·den; 'gɑːdn/ *n.*
piece of land near a house for flowers and grass 花园
There are some beautiful flowers in the garden.
花园里有一些美丽的花朵。

gardener *n.* 园丁
The gardener was planting some flowers.
园丁正在种花。

garlic /'gar·lic; 'gɑːlɪk/ *n.*
(no plural)
plant with a strong taste and smell used in cooking 蒜
Susan does not like the smell of garlic.
苏珊不喜欢蒜的气味。

gas [1] /gas; gæs/ *n.*
(two **gases**)
something like air; not solid or liquid 气体
Air is a mixture of gases.
空气中混合了多种气体。

gas [2] /gas; gæs/ *n.*
(no plural)
something like air which burns to give heat 易燃气体（如煤气和天然气）
Be careful when you use a gas water-heater.
用燃气热水器时要小心。

gate /gate; geɪt/ *n.*
door in a wall or fence outside a building 大门；闸门
They close the park gates at six o'clock.
他们六时就关上公园的大门。

gather /ˈgath·er; ˈgæðə/ *v.*
1 come together 聚集；集合
A crowd of people gathered in the street.
街上聚集了一群人。
2 bring things together; collect 收集；采集
She gathered a bunch of flowers from the garden.
她在花园里采了一束花。

gave /gave; geɪv/ *v.*
p.t. of **give** give 的过去式
Baoling gave a present to her father.
宝玲送给爸爸一份礼物。

geese /geese; gi:s/ *n.*
(plural)
more than one **goose** goose 的复数
Geese lay very big eggs.
鹅下的蛋很大。

general [1] /ˈgen·er·al; ˈdʒenrəl/ *n.*
important person in an army 将军
He was a famous general in the war.
他是战时著名的将军。

General Xu Haidong

general [2] /ˈgen·er·al; ˈdʒenrəl/ *adj.*
not for one special thing, person or use 普遍的；一般的
We will have a general knowledge test on Monday.
星期一，我们会有一个常识测验。

generally /ˈgen·er·al·ly; ˈdʒenrəlɪ/ *adv.*
usually 通常；一般
She generally goes shopping on Saturdays.
她通常在星期六去买东西。

generous /ˈgen·er·ous; ˈdʒenərəs/ *adj.*
(more generous, most generous)
liking to give things to people 慷慨的；大方的
He is very generous. He gives a lot of money to poor people.
他很慷慨，送给穷人很多钱。
opp. 反义词：mean 吝啬

gentle /ˈgen·tle; ˈdʒentl/ *adj.*
(gentler, gentlest)
1 kind and soft 轻轻的；温和的
Be gentle when you pick up the baby.
抱起婴儿时，动作要轻。
2 not strong 柔和的
A gentle wind was blowing.
那时正吹着柔和的风。
opp. 反义词：rough 粗鲁的；猛烈的

gently *adv.*
in a kind and soft way 轻轻地；温和地
She gently lifted the baby out of her cot.
她轻轻地把婴儿从床上抱起来。

gentleman /ˈgen·tle·man; ˈdʒentlmən/ *n.*
(two **gentlemen**)
1 good, kind man 有教养的男人；君子；绅士
He always behaves like a gentleman.
他常常表现得像个君子。
2 any man 男人
There were a lot of ladies in the audience but not many gentlemen.
听众中有许多妇女，但男人却不多。

geography /ge·ˈog·ra·phy; dʒɪˈɒgrəfɪ/ *n.*
(no plural)
learning about the world 地理
Most children study geography at school.
大多数小孩在学校里都学习地理。

germ /germ; dʒɜ:m/ *n.*
very small living thing which makes you ill 细菌
We put bandages on cuts to keep out germs.
我们用绷带包扎伤口，以防细菌侵人。

get /get; get/ *v.*
(getting, got, got)
1 take, buy, fetch or receive something 得到；买得；收到
Mary got a bicycle for her birthday.
玛丽生日时收到的礼物是一辆自行车。
2 become 变得
It gets very hot in summer.
夏天天气变得很热。

get along, get on 进展；生活；与人相处
Tom is getting along very well at school.
汤姆在学校里一切进展顺利。

got away 逃脱
The policeman chased the robber but he got away.
警察追捕那个劫匪，不过他还是逃脱了。

get into 进入
Sam got into the car.
萨姆上了车。

get off 下车；下来
The people got off the bus.
乘客走下公共汽车。

get on 上车
The children got on the bus.
孩子们上了公共汽车。

get on with 继续；(与人)相处
Stop talking and get on with your work.
不要说话，继续工作吧。

get out of 离开
The man got out of the small boat.
那人走出小艇。

get ready 准备好
Mary had breakfast and got ready for school.
玛丽吃了早餐，准备上学。

get up 起床
Sam gets up at seven o'clock every morning.
萨姆每天早上七时起床。

Usage note: We *get on* and *get off* big things like aeroplanes, buses, ferries, ships, trains and trams. *John got off the tram in Causeway Bay.* We also *get on* and *get off* bicycles and horses. *The cowboy got on his horse and rode away.* We *get into* and *get out of* smaller things like boats, cars and taxis. *Mary got out of the taxi.*

用法： get on 和 get off 指出入较大的交通工具，如飞机、公共汽车、渡轮、船只、火车或电车等，如 John got off the tram in Causeway Bay。get on 亦可指骑上自行车或马匹，而 get off 亦可指从自行车上或马匹上下来，如 The cowboy got on his horse and rode away。get into 和 get out of 指出入较小的交通工具，如小船、小汽车或出租汽车等，如 Mary got out of the taxi。

ghost /ghost; gəust/ *n.*
spirit of a dead person that a living person thinks he sees 鬼
Tom thought he saw a ghost in the empty house.
汤姆相信他在那所空房子里看见了鬼。

giant [1] /ˈgi·ant; ˈdʒaɪənt/ *n.*
very big, tall man 巨人
The giant was three metres tall.
那个巨人有三米高。

giant

giant [2] /ˈgi·ant; ˈdʒaɪənt/ *adj.*
bigger than usual 巨大的；巨型的
The film was about giant insects.
这是部关于巨型昆虫的影片。

gift /gift; gɪft/ *n.*
something that you give to someone 礼物
Tom's bicycle was a birthday gift.
那辆自行车是汤姆的生日礼物。

ginger /ˈgin·ger; ˈdʒɪndʒə/ *n.*
(no plural)
root with a strong taste used in cooking 姜
Mrs Chen cooked the crab with ginger and onions.
陈太太烧螃蟹放些姜和洋葱。

giraffe /gi·ˈraffe; dʒɪˈrɑːf/ *n.*
big, wild animal with a very long neck 长颈鹿
The giraffe is the tallest animal in the zoo.
长颈鹿是动物园里最高的动物。

giraffes

girl /girl; gɜːl/ *n.*
female child; young woman
女孩子；少女
There are twenty girls and twenty boys in the class.
班上有二十个女孩子和二十个男孩子。

give /give; gɪv/ *v.*
(giving, gave, given)
1 let someone have something 给；送给
John gave Mary a book for her birthday.
约翰送给玛丽一本书作为生日礼物。
opp. 反义词：take, receive 取得；收到

2 make something 产生
Cows give milk.
母牛产奶。

give away 送
Mrs Chen gave away her old furniture.
陈太太把她的旧家具送给别人。

give back 归还
Peter gave back his library book.
彼得把他从图书馆借来的书归还了。

give in 投降；屈服
If you don't give in you will find the answer.
如果你不屈服，你会找到答案的。

give out 分发；分派
Peter gave out the exercise books.
彼得分发练习簿。

give up 放弃
I give up. I don't know the answer.
我放弃了，我不知道答案。

glad /glad; glæd/ *adj.*
(gladder, gladdest)
happy; pleased 高兴的
Mary was glad to see her friends.
玛丽见到她的朋友，感到很高兴。

gladly *adv.* 高兴地；乐意地
He heard the good news gladly.
他高兴地听到那个好消息。

glass [1] /glass; glɑːs/ *n.*
(two **glasses**)
glass thing you drink from
玻璃杯
Tom drank a glass of orange juice.
汤姆喝了一杯橙汁。

glass [2] /glass; glɑːs/ *n.*
(no plural)
hard stuff you can see through 玻璃
Windows are made of glass.
窗子是玻璃做的。

glasses /'glass·es; 'glɑːsɪz/ *n.*
(plural)
pieces of glass worn over the eyes to see better 眼镜
If you can't see very well you may need glasses.
如果你看东西不大清楚，或许需要配戴眼镜。

two pairs of glasses

globe /globe; gləub/ *n.*
1 world 地球
The ship sailed round the globe.
这艘船环球航行。
2 model of the world 地球仪
We look at a globe in our geography lesson.
我们上地理课时看地球仪。

glove /glove; glʌv/ *n.*
what you wear over your hand 手套
It was cold so Mary wore her gloves.
天气寒冷，因此玛丽戴了手套。

gloves

glow /glow; gləʊ/ *v.*
shine not very brightly 发光
A candle glowed in the window.
一支蜡烛在窗口发出亮光。

glue [1] /glue; glu:/ *n.*
(**no plural**)
stuff used for sticking things 胶；胶水
Tom used paper and glue to make a kite.
汤姆用纸和胶水做了一只风筝。

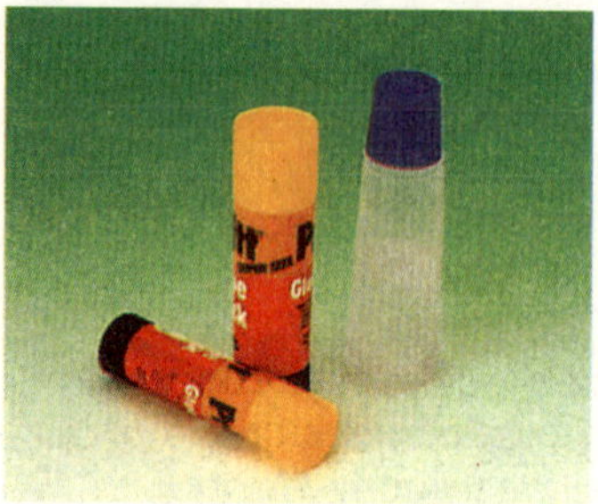

glue [2] /glue; glu:/ *v.*
(**gluing, glued, glued**)
stick things together 黏贴
Mary glued the pictures in her exercise book.
玛丽把那些图片贴在练习簿上。

go /go; gəʊ/ *v.*
(**going, went, gone**)
1 move there 去
Mary went to school.
玛丽上学了。
opp. 反义词：come 来
2 become 变成
The sky has gone black.
天(变)黑了。
3 work 运作；动
The car won't go.
车子开不动。
4 go out to do something 出外(活动，做事)
Mrs Chen went shopping.
陈太太出外购物。

go away 离去
We were glad when the typhoon went away.
台风离去了，我们都很高兴。
go back 回去
Mary is going back to Canada next year.
玛丽明年回加拿大去。
go off 爆炸；发射
The fireworks went off.
烟火发射出去了。
go on 发生；进行
What's going on?
发生了什么事?
go out 出去
Mrs Chen goes out every evening.
陈太太每天晚上都出去。
go round 足够分配
Mrs Chen always makes enough rice to go round.
陈太太做的饭总够大家吃。
going to 将要做
Susan is going to cook dinner tonight.
苏珊今晚将要做晚饭。

goal /goal; gəʊl/ *n.*
1 place where the ball must go to win a point in a game (球场上的)球门
Peter ran towards the goal.
彼得向球门跑去。
2 point that a team scores when the ball goes into a goal 得分
Our team won by three goals to one.
我们的球队以三比一获胜。
goalkeeper *n.* (球赛中的)守门员
David kicked the ball but the goalkeeper caught it.
戴维射门，但是球给守门员接住了。
goal-post *n.* 球门柱
The ball hit the goal-post and bounced back.
球碰着球门柱，弹了回来。

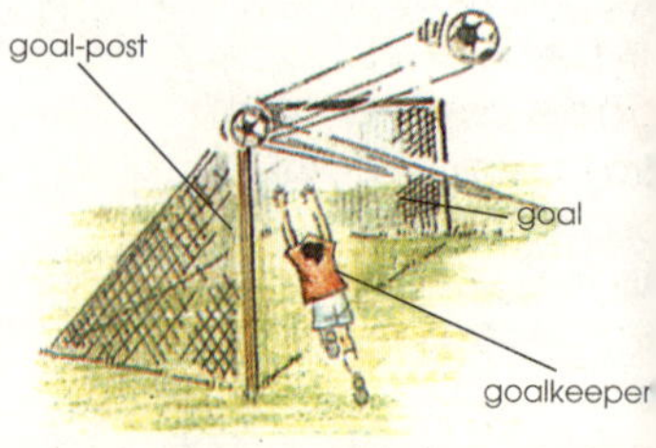

goat /goat; gəʊt/ *n.*
farm animal with long hair and horns 山羊
The farmer keeps goats and sheep.
这个农民饲养山羊和绵羊。

goats

God /God; gɒd/ *n.*
the being that people believe has power over people and the world 上帝；神
Many people believe in God.
很多人信上帝。

goddess /'god·dess; 'gɒdɪs/ *n.*
(two **goddesses**)
female god 女神
There are many goddesses in this story.
这个故事中有许多女神。

godown /'go·down; 'gəʊdaʊn/ *n.*
big building where things are stored 仓库；货仓

he truck took the apples to
a godown.
货车把苹果运到仓库去。

goes /goes; gəuz/ *v.*
3rd person singular present tense
of **go** go 的第三人称单数现在式
Mary goes to secondary school.
玛丽上中学。

going /ˈgo·ing; ˈgəuɪŋ/ *v.*
pres.p. of **go** go 的现在分词
We are going to the cinema.
我们正要到电影院去。

gold /gold; gəuld/ *n.*
(**no plural**)
shining yellow metal 金；黄金
Gold is very expensive.
黄金很贵重。
golden *adj.* 金色的
The girl had golden hair.
这个女孩子有一头金发。

goldfish /ˈgold·fish; ˈgəuldfɪʃ/ *n.*
(two **goldfish**)
fish with coloured body 金鱼
Mary has two goldfish in a bowl.
玛丽在碗里养了两条金鱼。

gone /gone; gɒn/ *v.*
p.p. of **go** go 的过去分词
Sam has gone to the cinema.
萨姆去电影院了。

good /good; gud/ *adj.*
(**better, best**)
1 right; does what you want; what you like 好的；令人满意的
Tom has a good watch.
汤姆有一只好手表。
2 kind; doing what is right 和善的；乖的
Mary is a good girl.
玛丽是个乖女孩。
3 able to do something well 好的；胜任的
Peter is a good swimmer.
彼得是个游泳好手。
opp. 反义词：bad 坏的；差的

good afternoon /good af·ter·ˈnoon; gud ɑːftəˈnuːn/ *int.*
words to greet someone in the afternoon（下午见面时的问候语）你好！午安！
Good afternoon. Did you have a nice lunch?
你好！午饭吃得好吗？

goodbye /good·ˈbye; gudˈbaɪ/ *int.*
what you say when someone goes away（道别时用语）再见
David said goodbye to his friends and went home.
戴维跟朋友们说再见，然后回家去了。

good evening /good ˈev·en·ing; gud ˈiːvnɪŋ/ *int.*
words to greet someone in the evening（晚上见面时的问候语）你好！
Good evening. Would you like to have dinner?
你好！要吃晚饭吗？

good morning /good ˈmor·ning; gud ˈmɔːnɪŋ/ *int.*
words to greet someone in the morning（早上见面时的问候语）你好！早安！
Good morning. Did you sleep well?
你好！晚上睡得好吗？

goodness /ˈgood·ness; ˈgudnɪs/ *n.*
(**no plural**)
what is good in something or someone 精华；优点
If you cook vegetables too long they lose their goodness.
蔬菜如果煮得太久，就会失掉(营养)精华。

good night /good ˈnight; gud ˈnaɪt/ *int.*
words that you say to people before they go to bed（临睡前与人分别时的用语）再见；晚安
Good night. Sleep well.
再见，好好地睡吧。

goods /goods; gudz/ *n.*
(**plural**)
things that you sell or buy 货物；商品
They took the goods to a godown.
他们把货物搬到仓库去。

goose /goose; gu:s/ *n.*
(two **geese**)
large water bird 鹅
In the story, the goose laid golden eggs.
故事里的那只鹅会下金蛋。

geese

gorilla /go·ril·la; gəˈrɪlə/ *n.*
big monkey 大猩猩
The gorilla was very strong.
那只大猩猩很强壮。

got /got; gɒt/ *v.*
p.t. of **get** get 的过去式
Peter got a kite for his birthday.
彼得生日时收到的礼物是只风筝。

government /ˈgov·ern·ment; ˈgʌvənmənt/ *n.*
people who are in charge of a country 政府
The government is building a new airport.
政府正在兴建一个新机场。
govern *v.* 统治；管理
Who governs the country?
谁管理这个国家？

governor /ˈgov·er·nor; ˈgʌvənə/ *n.*
person who governs a place
州长；总督；主管人员
He is the Governor of California.
他是加利福尼亚州州长。

grab /grab; græb/ *v.*
(**grabbing, grabbed, grabbed**)
take something roughly and quickly 抢；攫取；快速抓住
David grabbed an apple from the tree.
戴维从树上快速地摘下一个苹果。

grain /grain; greɪn/ *n.*
1 **(no plural)** seed of a food-plant 谷物
The farmer was harvesting his grain.
那个农民在收割谷物。

2 tiny piece of something 颗粒
Mary dropped some grains of rice on the floor.
玛丽掉了几颗米粒在地上。

gram (g) /gram; græm/ *n.*
measure of weight 克（重量单位）
Mary bought two hundred grams of sweets.
玛丽买了二百克糖果。

grammar /ˈgram·mar; ˈgræmə/ *n.*
(no plural)
rules that tell you how to put words together when you write or speak 语法；文法
Baoling knows a lot of English words but her grammar is bad.
宝玲懂许多英语单词，不过她的语法很差。

grand /grand; grænd/ *adj.*
very big and fine 宏大壮观的
They live in a grand house with a swimming pool.
他们住在一所有游泳池的豪华大宅里。

grandchild /ˈgrand·child; ˈgræntʃaɪld/ *n.*
(two **grandchildren**)
child of one's son or daughter
孙子；孙女；外孙；外孙女
Mrs Chen has ten grandchildren.
陈太太有十个(外)孙子女。

granddaughter /ˈgrand·daugh·ter; ˈgrændɔ:tə/ *n.*
daughter of one's son or daughter 孙女；外孙女
Mary is Mrs Smith's granddaughter.
玛丽是史密斯太太的(外)孙女。

Grandma, grandmother /ˈGrand·ma, ˈgrand·mo·ther; ˈgrænmɑ:, ˈgrænmʌðə/ *n.*
mother of one's father or mother 祖母；外祖母
Mary's grandma is very old.
玛丽的(外)祖母很老了。

Grandpa, grandfather /ˈGrand·pa, ˈgrand·fa·ther; ˈgrænpɑ:, ˈgrænfɑ:ðə/ *n.*
father of one's mother or father 祖父；外祖父
Tom's grandpa is eighty years old.
汤姆的(外)祖父八十岁。

grandparent /ˈgrand·pa·rent; ˈgrænpeərənt/ *n.*
father or mother of one's father or mother 祖父母；外祖父母

My grandparents are over seventy.
我的(外)祖父母都七十多岁了。

grandson /ˈgrand·son; ˈgrænsʌn/ *n.*
son of one's son or daughter 孙子；外孙
Mrs Chen has six grandsons and four granddaughters.
陈太太有六个(外)孙子和四个(外)孙女。

grape /grape; greɪp/ *n.*
small green or black fruit 葡萄
Susan bought a bunch of grapes at the market.
苏珊在市场上买了一串葡萄。

grapes

graph /graph; grɑːf/ *n.*
line or picture that shows how something changes 图表
He drew a graph of the ages of the children.
他画了一张图表来显示孩子们的年龄。

grass /grass; grɑːs/ *n.*
(no plural)
plant with thin green leaves which animals eat 草
The school has a grass playing field.
学校里有一个草地游戏场。

grasshopper
/ˈgrass·hop·per; ˈgrɑːshɒpə/ *n.*
small jumping insect 蚱蜢
Peter catches grasshoppers with a net.
彼得用网来捉蚱蜢。

grateful /ˈgrate·ful; ˈgreɪtfl/ *adj.*
(more grateful, most grateful)
feeling that you want to thank someone 感激的
Tom was grateful for his present.
汤姆感激人家送他礼物。
gratefully *adv.* 感激地
Tom accepted the present gratefully.
汤姆感激地接受了礼物。

grave /grave; greɪv/ *n.*
place in the ground where you put a dead person 坟墓
The family visited the grave.
那家人去了墓地。

great /great; greɪt/ *adj.*
1 big; much 大的；很多的
Tom takes great care of his books.
汤姆十分爱护他的书籍。
2 important; very good 伟大的
He was a great man.
他是个伟大的人。
great!, that's great!
真好！
We are going to the beach! That's great!
我们要到沙滩去！真好！

Great Britain /Great ˈBrit·ain; greɪt ˈbrɪtən/ *n.*
country in Europe 大不列颠；英国
Sixty million people live in Great Britain.
六千万人居住在英国。

greedy /ˈgreed·y; ˈgriːdɪ/ *adj.*
(greedier, greediest)
wanting too much 贪心的；贪吃的
The greedy boy ate all the cakes.
那贪吃的男孩把蛋糕全吃光了。
greedily *adv.* 贪婪地
Sam ate the ice-cream greedily.
萨姆狼吞虎咽地吃冰淇淋。

green /green; gri:n/ *adj.*
with the colour of grass 绿色的；青色的
Green vegetables are good for us.
吃绿色蔬菜对我们很有益处。

greet /greet; gri:t/ *v.*
say or do something when you see someone 打招呼
Mary greeted her friends.
玛丽向朋友们打招呼。
greeting *n.* 打招呼
'Hello' is a greeting.
Hello 是打招呼的话。

grew /grew; gru:/ *v.*
p.t. of **grow** grow 的过去式
Beautiful flowers grew in the park.
公园里种了美丽的花朵。

grey /grey; greɪ/ *adj.*
colour between black and white 灰色的
We have a grey cat.
我们有一只灰色的猫。

groan /groan; grəʊn/ *v.*
make a low sound because you are sad or hurt 发出痛苦的声音
The injured man is groaning.
那个受伤的人在呻吟着。

grocer /ˈgro·cer; ˈgrəʊsə/ *n.*
shopkeeper who sells food 杂货店商人
Tom bought some biscuits from the grocer's shop.
汤姆在杂货店买了些饼干。

ground /ground; graʊnd/ *n.*
(no plural)
soil; earth 地面；地上；土地
When it rains the ground is muddy.
下雨时遍地泥泞。

group /group; gru:p/ *n.*
number of people or things (一)群
The teacher took a group of children to the zoo.
老师带领一群小孩去动物园。

grow /grow; grəʊ/ *v.*
(growing, grew, grown)
1 become bigger, taller, longer, etc. 成长；长大；增长
The tree grew very tall.
那棵树长得很高。
2 keep plants and take care of them 种植
Mrs Chen grows flowers in pots.
陈太太在花盆里种花。

growl /growl; graʊl/ *v.*
make a low, angry sound 低沉地吼叫
The dog growled at Peter.
那狗向着彼得低沉地吼叫。

grown-up /ˈgrown·up; ˈgrəʊnʌp/ *n.*
adult; person who is not a child 成年人
There were only two grown-ups at the party.
这个聚会只有两个成年人参加。

grumble /ˈgrum·ble; ˈgrʌmbl/ *v.*
(grumbling, grumbled, grumbled)
say angrily that you do not like something 抱怨；发牢骚
Mr Chen was always grumbling about the noise his children made.
陈先生老是抱怨孩子们太吵。

guard [1] /guard; gɑ:d/ *n.*
someone who keeps a person or place safe
保安人员；卫兵
There was a guard in the bank.
银行里有一个保安人员。

guard [2] /guard; gɑ:d/ *v.*
keep a person or place safe
看守；保卫
The dog was guarding the house.
那只狗看守着房子。

guess [1] /guess; ges/ *v.*
give an answer when you are not sure 猜测

Sam guessed how many apples were in the bag.
萨姆猜袋里有多少苹果。

guess [2] /guess; ges/ *n.*
(two **guesses**)
answer that you give when you are not sure 猜测
My guess is that there are five apples in the bag.
据我的猜测，袋里共有五个苹果。

guest /guest; gest/ *n.*
someone you invite to your home or to a party 宾客；客人
There were a hundred guests at the wedding.
有一百个宾客参加这个婚礼。

guide [1] /guide; gaɪd/ *n.*
1 someone who shows you where to go 导游
The guide showed us round the temple.
导游带我们参观那座庙宇。
2 member of a special club for girls 女童子军
Susan is a girl guide.
苏珊是个女童子军。

guide [2] /guide; gaɪd/ *v.*
(**guiding, guided, guided**)
show someone where to go 带领；引导
The girl guided the tourists round the temple.
那女孩子带领游客参观那座庙宇。

guilty /'guilt·y; 'gɪltɪ/ *adj.*
(**guiltier, guiltiest**)
having done wrong 有罪的；犯罪的
The man was guilty of robbery.
这个人犯了抢劫罪。
opp. 反义词：innocent 无罪的

guitar /gui·'tar; gɪ'tɑ:/ *n.*
musical instrument with strings 吉他
Mary is learning to play the guitar.
玛丽正在学弹吉他。

gum [1] /gum; gʌm/ *n.*
1 (**no plural**) stuff that sticks things together; glue 树胶；胶水
Peter used gum to make the kite.
彼得做风筝时要用胶水。
2 (**no plural**) stuff that you chew 口香糖；香口胶(方言)
Baoling likes to chew gum.
宝玲爱嚼口香糖。
3 part of your mouth where your teeth are 齿龈；牙肉(方言)
When you brush your teeth you should clean your gums too.
刷牙的时候，也应该刷一刷齿龈。

gum [2] /gum; gʌm/ *v.*
(**gumming, gummed, gummed**)
stick things together 用胶水黏合
David gummed some pictures into his book.
戴维用胶水把一些图片粘在他的书本上。

gun /gun; gʌn/ *n.*
thing that shoots 枪
Hong Kong policemen carry guns.
香港警察都佩枪。

gutter /'gut·ter; 'gʌtə/ *n.*
long hole at the side of the road to take rain away (路旁的)排水沟
When it rains, the gutters are full of water.
下雨时，路旁的排水沟里满是水。

gymnasium /gym·'na·si·um; dʒɪm'neɪzɪəm/ *n.*
room or building where you do exercise, sports, etc. 体育馆
David is playing basketball in the gymnasium.
戴维正在体育馆里打篮球。

gymnastics /gym·'nas·tics; dʒɪm'næstɪks/ *n.*
(**plural**)
doing exercises with your body 体操
The children do gymnastics twice a week.
孩子们每周做两次体操。

Hh

ha! ha! /ha ha; hɑ: hɑ:/ *int.*
sound you make when you laugh 哈哈!(笑声)
'Ha! Ha!' laughed Sam.
"哈哈!"萨姆大笑起来。

habit /ˈhab·it; ˈhæbɪt/ *n.*
what a person usually does 习惯
Sam has a habit of being late for school.
萨姆有上学迟到的习惯。

had /had; hæd/ *v.*
p.t. of **have** have 的过去式
Tom had breakfast early.
汤姆很早就吃了早餐。
opp. 反义词: had not, hadn't 没有

hadn't /ˈhad·n't; ˈhædnt/ *v.*
had not 即 had not
Mary hadn't eaten her breakfast.
玛丽还没有吃早餐。

hail /hail; heɪl/ *n.*
(**no plural**)
drops of rain that are frozen 冰雹
Hail was bouncing off the window.
冰雹打到窗上，反弹开来。

hair /hair; heə/ *n.*
what grows on your head 头发
Baoling has long, black hair.
宝玲的头发又黑又长。

hairbrush *n.* 发刷
Mary uses a hairbrush to tidy her hair.
玛丽用发刷来梳理头发。

haircut *n.* 理发
Peter's hair is too long. He needs a haircut.
彼得头发太长，要理个发了。

hairdresser *n.* 理发师；美容师
Mrs Chen goes to the hairdresser's every week.
陈太太每周都去理发店。

hairdryer *n.* 吹风机
Susan uses a hairdryer to dry her hair.
苏珊用吹风机来吹干头发。

hairstyle *n.* 发型
Anna has a short hairstyle.
安娜蓄短发。

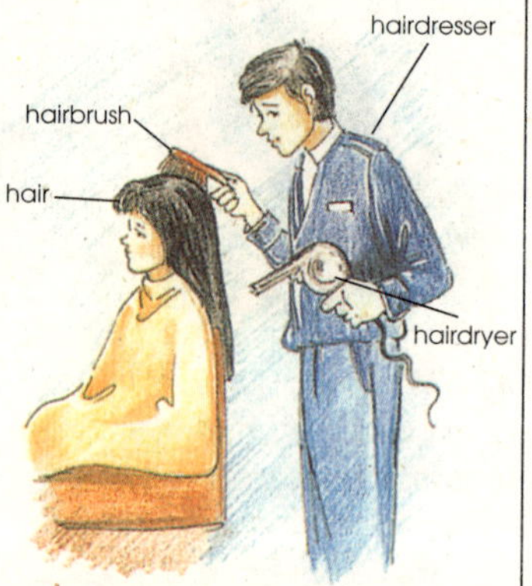

half /half; hɑ:f/ *n.*
(two **halves**)
one of two equal parts of something 一半
Mary gave Susan half of her sweets.
玛丽把她的糖果分给苏珊一半。

in half 两半
Tom cut the apple in half.
汤姆把苹果切成两半。

half past (时间)…时半
Sam gets up at half past six.
萨姆六时半起床。

halfway *adv.* 中途；半路
Halfway up the hill, the children stopped for a rest.
上山走了一半路，孩子们都停下来休息。

hall /hall; hɔ:l/ *n.*
1 big room or building for meetings 会堂；礼堂
They have concerts in the hall.
他们在礼堂开音乐会。

2 room in a house with doors to other rooms (住宅的)门厅
Mary took off her shoes in the hall.
玛丽在门厅里把鞋子脱掉。

ham /ham; hæm/ *n.*
(**no plural**)
meat from a pig's leg 火腿
David likes ham sandwiches.
戴维爱吃火腿三明治。

hamburger /ˈham·bur·ger; hæmbɜ:gə/ *n.*
round sandwich with chopped meat in it 汉堡包
Most children like hamburgers.
大多数孩子都喜欢吃汉堡包。

hammer /ˈham·mer; ˈhæmə/ *n.*
tool for hitting nails 锤子
Sam used a hammer to put a nail in the wall.
萨姆用锤子把钉子敲进墙里。

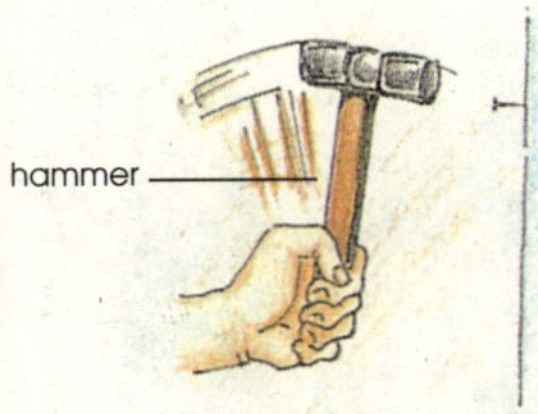

hand [1] /hand; hænd/ *n.*
part of the body at the end of the arm 手
David had dirty hands.
戴维的手很脏。

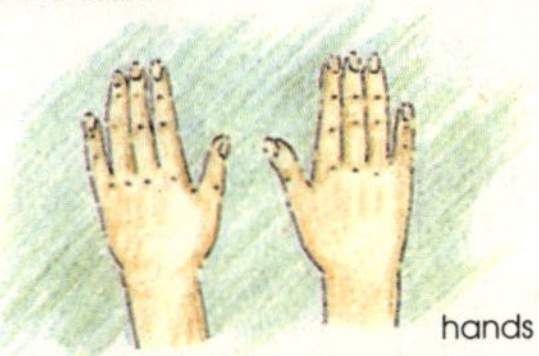

by hand 专人送的；亲手
The letter was delivered by hand.
那封信是专人送来的。

hand [2] /hand; hænd/ *v.*
give something to someone 交给；递给
David handed Sam a hammer.
戴维把锤子递给萨姆。

hand in 交
The children handed in their books.
孩子们把课本交给老师。

hand in hand 手拉着手
The little girls walked hand in hand.
小女孩们手拉着手往前走。

on my right hand 在我右边
On my right hand, there is a house.
在我右边有一所房子。

shake hand with 和…握手
Mr Qian shook hands with his friend.
钱先生和朋友握手。

handbag /ˈhand·bag; ˈhændbæg/ *n.*
woman's bag that holds small things （女用）手提包
Mrs Chen put some money in her handbag.
陈太太在她的手提包里放了些钱。

handcuffs /ˈhand·cuffs; ˈhændkʌfs/ *n.*
(plural)
pair of metal rings used to hold robbers 手铐
The policeman put handcuffs on the robber.
警察给盗贼戴上手铐。

handicapped /ˈhand·i·capped; ˈhændɪkæpt/ *adj.*
not able to live normally because of illness 残疾的
Baoling helped the handicapped child to get on the bus.
宝玲帮助残疾儿童上公共汽车。

handkerchief /ˈhand·ker·chief; ˈhæŋkətʃɪf/ *n.*
square piece of cloth you use to clean your nose, face, etc. 手帕；手巾
Paper handkerchiefs are the best.
纸手帕最好用。

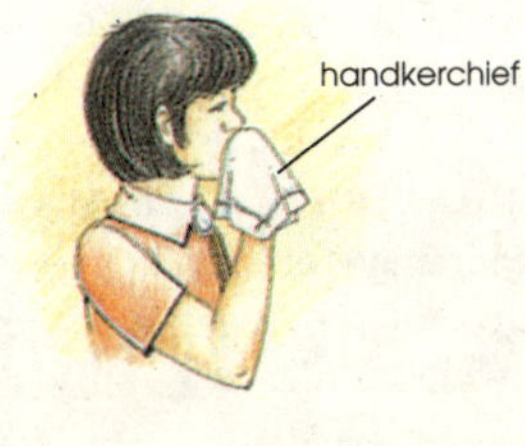

handle [1] /'han·dle; 'hændl/ *n.*
part of a thing that you hold 把手；柄
The handle of the brush was broken.
刷子的柄断了。

handle [2] /'han·dle; 'hændl/ *v.*
(handling, handled, handled)
touch, feel or move with the hands 触摸；拿起；搬动
Mr Chen handled the old vase carefully.
陈先生小心翼翼地拿起这只古董花瓶。

handlebar /'hand·le·bar; 'hændlbɑ:/ *n.*
part of a bicycle or motorcycle you hold when you are riding （自行车或摩托车的）把手
Sam took his hands off the handlebar of his bicycle and crashed into a tree.
萨姆放开了自行车的把手，便一下子撞到一棵树上。

handsome /'hand·some; 'hænsəm/ *adj.*
(more handsome, most handsome)
that you like to look at 漂亮的；英俊的
The singer is a very handsome man.
这个歌手长得很英俊。
Usage note: We usually use *beautiful* and *pretty* to describe women and children, and *handsome* to describe men.
用法： beautiful 及 pretty 通常用来形容女子及小孩；handsome 则用来形容男子。

handwriting /'hand·writ·ing; 'hændraɪtɪŋ/ *n.*
(no plural)
way you write 笔迹；书法
Sam's handwriting is very bad.
萨姆的字写得十分难看。

hang /hang; hæŋ/ *v.*
(hanging, hung, hung)
put something on a line or hook 挂；吊
Mrs Chen was hanging the washing on the line.
陈太太把洗好的衣服晾在绳子上。
hang up 挂起来
Don't throw your coat on the floor. Hang it up.
不要把外衣丢在地上，把它挂起来吧。

hanger /'han·ger; 'hæŋə/ *n.*
something for hanging clothes 衣架
Sam put his jacket on a hanger.
萨姆把他的短上衣挂在衣架上。

happen /'hap·pen; 'hæpən/ *v.*
take place 发生
The accident happened at one o'clock.
意外事故发生在一时正。
Usage note: Use *happen* for something that was not planned — *The accident happened yesterday.* If something is planned, use *take place* — *The concert took place yesterday.*
用法： 未经计划的事情发生了，我们用 happen，例如 The accident happened yesterday。经计划好的事情发生时，则用 take place，例如 The concert took place yesterday。

happy /'hap·py; 'hæpɪ/ *adj.*
(happier, happiest)
glad; pleased 快乐的；愉快的；高兴的；满足的
Tom was very happy with his presents.
汤姆对他收到的礼物很满意。
opp. 反义词：unhappy, sad 不快乐的；悲哀的；难过的
happily *adv.* 快乐地
The children ran happily home.
孩子们快乐地跑回家。
happiness *n.* 愉快；幸福
The rain did not spoil his happiness.
下雨并没有破坏他愉快的心情。

harbour /'har·bour; 'hɑ:bə/ *n.*
place where ships can go and stay 港口；海港
The harbour was full of ships.
港口里有很多船只。

hard [1] /hard; hɑ:d/ *adj.*
1 difficult 困难的
This sum is hard.
这道算术题很难。
opp. 反义词：easy 容易的
2 not soft 硬的
My pillow is hard.
我的枕头太硬。
opp. 反义词：soft 软的

hard [2] /hard; hɑ:d/ *adv.*
strongly 用功；努力
Mr Chen works hard.
陈先生努力工作。

hare /hare; heə/ *n.*
small wild animal with long ears 野兔
The dogs chased the hare across the field.
那些狗在田野上追逐那只野兔。

harm [1] /harm; hɑ:m/ *n.*
(no plural)
damage; injury 伤害；损伤
The fall did not do Tom any harm.
汤姆摔了一跤，一点没有受伤。

harm [2] /harm; hɑ:m/ *v.*
hurt someone or something 伤害；损害
The dog is friendly. He won't harm you.
这只狗很友善，不会伤害你。
harmful *adj.* 有害的
Broken bottles on the beach are harmful.
海滩上的破瓶会弄伤人。
harmless *adj.* 无害的
Most snakes are harmless.
大部分的蛇都是无害的。

harmonica /har·'mon·i·ca; hɑ:'mɒnɪkə/ *n.*
musical instrument played with the mouth 口琴
Tom plays the harmonica.
汤姆会吹口琴。

harvest /'har·vest; 'hɑ:vɪst/ *n.*
time when you cut or pick crops 收成；收获
The rice harvest was very good.
稻米收成很好。

has /has; hæz/ *v.*
3rd person singular present tense of **have** have 的第三人称单数现在式
Mr Chen has a new car.
陈先生有一辆新汽车。
opp. 反义词：has not, hasn't 没有

hasn't /'has·n't; 'hæznt/ *v.*
has not 即 has not
Mr Lin hasn't got a car.
林先生没有汽车。

hat /hat; hæt/ *n.*
something you wear on your head 帽子
When it is sunny, Mary wears a hat.
阳光普照的时候，玛丽会戴上帽子。

hate /hate; heɪt/ *v.*
(hating, hated, hated)
dislike; feel something is very bad 憎恶；憎恨；讨厌
I hate snakes.
我讨厌蛇。
opp. 反义词：love 喜爱

have /have; hæv/ *v.*
(having, had, had)
1 own or keep something or someone 有
Tom has a bicycle.
汤姆有一辆自行车。
2 word you use with another word to show the past 用来表示完成时态
Susan has lost her book.
苏珊丢失了她的书。
3 word that shows something is happening to someone or something 发生；遭受
Mr Chen had an accident.
陈先生发生了意外。
opp. 反义词：have not, haven't 没有
have something on 穿着；戴着
Susan has a blue dress on.
苏珊穿了一件蓝色的连衣裙。
have to, have got to 必须
We have to go to school.
我们必须上学。
Usage note: We use *have got* more often than *have* to show that someone owns something — *I have got seven goldfish.*
用法：表示某人拥有某些东西，我们可以用 have 或者 have got，两者中，have got 较为常用，例如 I have got seven goldfish。

haven't /'have·n't, 'hævnt/ *v.*
have not 即 have not
I haven't finished the book.
我还没有看完这本书。

hawker /'hawk·er; 'hɔ:kə/ *n.*
someone who sells things in the street 小贩
The hawker was selling vegetables.
那个小贩在卖蔬菜。

(40)

he /he; hiː/ *pron.*
(**they**)
word that shows a man or a boy 他
Is he your father?
他是你父亲吗？

head /head; hed/ *n.*
part of the body above the neck 头
You wear a hat on your head.
你头上戴了一顶帽子。

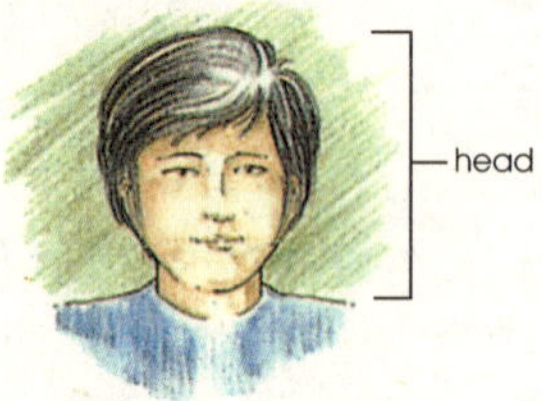

headache /ˈhead·ache; ˈhedeɪk/ *n.*
pain in your head 头痛
The noise gave Mrs Chen a headache.
噪音使陈太太头痛。

heading /ˈhead·ing; ˈhedɪŋ/ *n.*
words at the top of a piece of writing 标题；题目
Tom underlined the heading of his composition.
汤姆在他的作文题目下画上一条线。

headmaster /head·ˈma·ster; hedˈmɑːstə/ *n.*
man in charge of a school 校长
Mr Tan is the headmaster of a big school.
谭先生是一所很大的学校的校长。

headmistress /head·ˈmis·tress; hedˈmɪstrɪs/ *n.*
(two **headmistresses**)
woman in charge of a school 女校长
Mrs Li is the headmistress of the school.
李太太是这所学校的校长。

heal /heal; hiːl/ *v.*
get better; make better 治愈；痊愈
The cut on Peter's hand healed quickly.
彼得手上的伤口很快便痊愈了。

health /health; helθ/ *n.*
(**no plural**)
how your body is 健康
Eat plenty of fruit for good health.
要身体好，就要多吃水果。

healthy /ˈhealth·y; ˈhelθɪ/ *adj.*
(**healthier, healthiest**)
1 well; not ill 健康的；健壮的
The children are very healthy.
孩子们都很健康。
2 good for you 有益的
Fruit and vegetables are healthy foods.
水果和蔬菜都是有益身体的食物。
opp. 反义词：unhealthy 不健康的

heap /heap; hiːp/ *n.*
pile of things, one on top of the other (一)堆
There was a heap of stones on the beach.
海滩上有一堆石头。

hear /hear; hɪə/ *v.*
(**hearing, heard, heard**)
learn about something with your ears 听见；听到
She heard the baby crying.
她听到那个婴儿的哭声。

heart /heart; hɑːt/ *n.*
part inside your body that makes your blood move 心；心脏
Running makes your heart beat faster.
跑步使你心跳加速。
by heart 熟记；能背出
Mary learnt the poem by heart.
玛丽背得出这首诗。

heat [1] /heat; hiːt/ *n.*
(**no plural**)
feeling that comes from hot things 热；热力
We can feel the heat of the sun.
我们可以感觉到太阳的热力。

heat [2] /heat; hiːt/ *v.*
make something hot 加热
Mary heated some water to make tea.
玛丽烧了些开水来泡茶。
opp. 反义词：cool 冷却

heater /ˈheat·er; ˈhiːtə/ *n.*
thing that makes things warm 暖气设备；火炉；热水器
Be careful with gas heaters.
小心使用燃气热水器。

heavy /ˈheav·y; ˈhevɪ/ *adj.*
(**heavier, heaviest**)
1 not easy to lift or move 重的；沉重的
Tom could not lift the heavy suitcase.
汤姆抬不起那个沉重的行李箱。

2 a lot at the same time
大量的
The traffic was very heavy.
交通非常繁忙。
opp. 反义词：light 轻的；稀少的
heavily *adv.* 重重地；大量地
The rain fell heavily.
雨下得很大。

he'd /he'd; hi:d/
1 he had 即 he had
I thought he'd seen the film.
我想他看过那部电影了。
2 he would 即 he would
He'd like an ice-cream.
他想吃一客冰淇淋。

hedge /hedge; hedʒ/ *n.*
row of plants or bushes at the edge of a field or garden 树篱
There was a hedge round the garden.
花园四周种了一道树篱。

heel /heel; hi:l/ *n.*
back part of your foot or shoe 脚跟;(鞋的)后跟
The heel came off Mrs Chen's shoe.
陈太太的鞋后跟脱落了。

height /height; haɪt/ *n.*
distance from the bottom to the top 高度
What is the height of that mountain?
那座山的高度是多少?

held /held; held/ *v.*
p.t. of **hold** hold 的过去式
Susan held her mother's hand.
苏珊拉着她妈妈的手。

helicopter /'hel·i·cop·ter; 'helɪkɒptə/ *n.*
sort of aeroplane 直升机
The helicopter rescued the sailors from the sinking ship.
直升机把水手从正在下沉的船上救起。

he'll /he'll; hi:l/
he will 即 he will
He'll paly football tomorrow.
他明天要踢足球。

hello, hallo /hel·'lo, hal·'lo; hə'ləʊ, hə'ləʊ/ *int.*
friendly greeting (打招呼用语)喂!
Tom said hello to Peter.
汤姆向彼得打了个招呼。

helmet /'hel·met; 'helmɪt/ *n.*
hard hat that keeps your head safe 头盔
Motorcyclists should always wear a helmet.
骑摩托车的人应该戴头盔。

help [1] /help; help/ *v.*
do something for someone
帮助；帮忙
Peter helps his father in the shop.
彼得在店里帮他父亲工作。

help [2] /help; help/ *n.*
(no plural)
doing something for someone 帮助；帮忙
Do you need any help?
你需要帮忙吗?

helpful /'help·ful; 'helpfl/ *adj.*
(more helpful, most helpful)
useful; wanting to help 有用的；能帮忙的
Susan is always helpful in the house.
苏珊在家里很能帮得上忙。

hen /hen; hen/ *n.*
bird that you keep to eat and for eggs 母鸡
The farmer has a lot of hens.
那农民养了许多母鸡。

her /her; hɜ:/ *pron. adj.*
1 **(them)** word that shows a woman or girl 她
Where is Mary? I can't see her.
玛丽在哪里?我看不见她。
2 **(their)** of a woman or girl
她的
This is her coat.
这是她的外衣。

herd /herd; hɜ:d/ *n.*
group of animals (一)群
There was a herd of cows in the field.
田野里有一群牛。

here /here; hɪə/ *adv.*
in this place; to this place 在这里；到这里
Come here, Tom.
汤姆，到这里来。
here's, here is 这是…
Here's your book, Mary.
玛丽，这是你要的书。

hero /'he·ro; 'hɪərəʊ/ *n.*
(two **heroes**)
very brave man; chief man in a story, play, etc. 英雄；主角
He was the hero of the film.
他是影片中的主角。

heroine /'he·ro·ine; 'herəʊɪn/ *n.*
very brave woman; chief woman in a story, play, etc.
女英雄；女主角
She was the heroine of the story.
她是故事中的女主角。

hers /hers; hɜːz/ *pron.*
(**theirs**)
thing that belongs to a woman or girl 她的
This is Mary's book. It's hers.
这是玛丽的书，这书是她的。

herself /her·'self; hɜː'self/ *pron*
(**themselves**)
word for the woman or girl you have just talked about
她自己；她本人
Susan fell and hurt herself.
苏珊跌倒了，弄伤了自己。

he's /he's; hiːz/
1 he is 即 he is
He's my brother.
他是我的兄弟。
2 he has 即 he has
He's worked all day.
他工作了一整天。

hide /hide; haɪd/ *v.*
(**hiding, hid, hidden**)
1 be in a place where no one can see you 躲藏
Peter hid under the bed.
彼得躲在床底下。
2 put something in a secret place 收藏
Sam hid his money behind a picture.
萨姆把他的钱藏在一幅画后面。

hide-and-seek *n.* 捉迷藏
The children were playing hide-and-seek.
孩子们在玩捉迷藏。

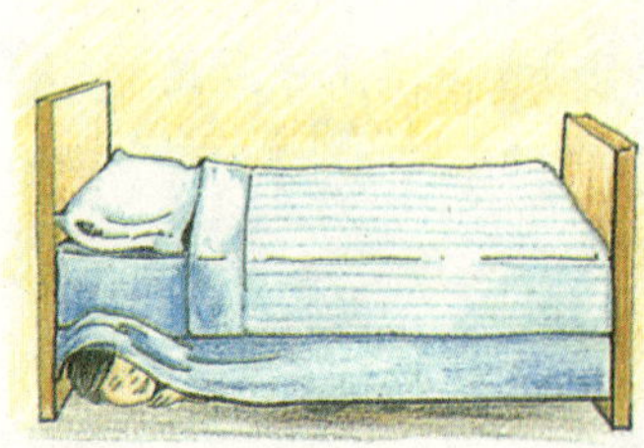

high /high; haɪ/ *adj.*
1 distance from bottom to top; going up a long way
高；高的
The mountain is a thousand metres high.
这座山有一千米高。
The Bank of China is very high.
中国银行大厦很高。
2 great 高的
In summer, the temperature is high.
夏天时气温很高。
opp. 反义词：low 低的

highway /'high·way; 'haɪweɪ/ *n.*
main road 公路；大道
There were a lot of cars on the highway.
公路上汽车很多。

hijack /'hi·jack; 'haɪdʒæk/ *v.*
force the pilot of a plane to take you somewhere 劫机
The man hijacked the plane.
那人劫持了飞机。
hijacker *n.* 劫机者
The police arrested the hijacker.
警方拘捕了劫机者。

hike /hike; haɪk/ *v.*
(**hiking, hiked, hiked**)
walk in the countryside 徒步旅行；远足
Tom hiked across the country park.
汤姆去郊野公园远足旅行。

hill /hill; hɪl/ *n.*
high piece of ground 小山；小丘
There are many hills on the island.
这岛上有许多小山。
hilly *adj.* 多山的
The island is very hilly.
这个岛山地非常多。

him /him; hɪm/ *pron.*
(**them**)
word that shows a man or boy 他
I'm looking for Peter. Have you seen him?
我在找彼得，你看见过他吗？

himself /him·'self; hɪm'self/ *pron.*
(**themselves**)
word for the man or boy you have just talked about 他自己；他本人
Peter is teaching himself to play the guitar.
彼得自学弹吉他。
by himself 独自；单独
Peter made the kite by himself.
彼得独自做了这只风筝。

hip /hip; hɪp/ *n.*
part where your legs join your body 臀部
The old lady fell and broke her hip.
那老太太跌倒了，伤了臀部。

hire /ˈhire; ˈhaɪə/ *v.*
(**hiring, hired, hired**)
pay to use something for a time 雇用；租用
Mr Chen hired the car for the day.
那天陈先生租了一辆汽车。

his /his; hɪz/ *adj. pron.*
1 (**their**) of a man or boy
他的
Have you seen Peter? This is his ball.
你见到彼得吗？这是他的球。
2 (**theirs**) that belongs to a man or boy 他的
This ball is his.
这球是他的。

hiss /hiss; hɪs/ *v.*
make the sound of 'sss' 发出嘶嘶声
The goose hissed at the children.
那只鹅对孩子们发出嘶嘶声。

history /ˈhis·to·ry; ˈhɪstrɪ/ *n.*
(**no plural**)
things that happened in the past 历史
In history we learn about the past.
历史告诉我们过去的事情。

hit /hit; hɪt/ *v.*
(**hitting, hit, hit**)
knock someone or something
打；击
The ball hit Sam on the head.
那球正好打中萨姆的头部。

Usage note: You can use *strike* in the same way as *hit* — *Tom hit Peter. Tom struck Peter.* You can *hit* or *strike* something by accident or on purpose — *The car hit a lamp-post. David hit the nail with a hammer.*
用法：strike 和 hit 用法相同，例如 Tom hit Peter 可以写成 Tom struck Peter。hit 或 strike 的动作可以是有意或者是无意的，例如 The car hit a lamp-post 及 David hit the nail with a hammer。

hobby /ˈhob·by; ˈhɒbɪ/ *n.*
(two **hobbies**)
what you like to do when you are not working 嗜好
David's hobby is stamp-collecting.
戴维的嗜好是集邮。

hockey /ˈhock·ey; ˈhɒkɪ/ *n.*
(**no plural**)
game where the players hit a ball with sticks 曲棍球
Anna plays hockey at school.
安娜在学校打曲棍球。

hold /hold; həuld/ *v.*
(**holding, held, held**)
1 have something in your hand 拿着；握着
Mary was holding a bunch of flowers.
玛丽拿着一束花。

2 have something inside
装；盛
The jug holds a litre of water.
这只壶可以装一升水。
hold on 请等一等
I'll bring Mr Chen to the phone. Please hold on.
请等一下，我去叫陈先生来听电话。
hold up 延误；高举
Rain held up the tennis match.
下雨延误了网球赛。
Please hold up your hands.
请你们举手。

hole /hole; həul/ *n.*
opening or space in something 洞；孔
Tom has a hole in his sock.
汤姆的袜子上有一个洞。

holiday /ˈhol·i·day; ˈhɒlədeɪ/ *n.*
rest from school or work 假期；假日
The family went to Canada for a holiday.
他们全家去加拿大度假。
syn. 同义词：vacation
Usage note: A day when you do not work is a *holiday* — *Sunday is a holiday in many countries.* Going away for a longer rest is a *holiday* or a *vacation* — *I am going on holiday next week. I am going on vacation next week.*
用法：holiday 指不用工作的一天，例如 Sunday is a holiday in many countries。如果指较长的假期，可以用 holiday 或 vacation，例如 I am going on holiday next week 及 I am going on vacation next week。

hollow /ˈhol·low; ˈhɒləʊ/ *adj.*
(**more hollow, most hollow**)
empty; with nothing inside 空的
Bamboo is hollow.
竹子是空心的。
opp. 反义词：solid 实心的

holy /ˈho·ly; ˈhəʊlɪ/ *adj.*
(**holier, holiest**)
of a god 神圣的
A church is a holy place.
教堂是神圣的地方。

home /home; həʊm/ *n.*
place where you live 家
Divid's home is in Hong Kong.
戴维的家在香港。
homeless *adj.* 无家可归的
The old man was homeless.
那个老人无家可归。
homesick *adj.* 想家的
Xiaofang felt homesick when she went to Canada.
小芳去了加拿大后很想家。

homework /ˈhome·work; ˈhəʊmwɜːk/ *n.*
(**no plural**)
work you do at home 家庭作业
Baoling finished her homework and then watched TV.
宝玲做完家庭作业后才看电视。

honest /ˈhon·est; ˈɒnɪst/ *adj.*
(**more honest, most honest**)
saying what is true; not cheating 诚实的；老实的
Mr Li is an honest man.
李先生是个老实的人。
opp. 反义词：dishonest 不诚实的
honestly *adv.* 诚实地
The boy behaved honestly.
这男孩很诚实。

honesty /ˈhon·es·ty; ˈɒnəstɪ/ *n.*
(**no plural**)
saying what is true; not cheating 诚实；老实
Mr Wang is well known for his honesty.
王先生以诚实出名。

honey /ˈhon·ey; ˈhʌnɪ/ *n.*
(**no plural**)
sweet food that bees make 蜂蜜
Mary made a hot drink with honey and lemon.
玛丽用蜂蜜和柠檬做了一道热饮。

Hong Kong /Hong ˈKong; hɒŋˈkɒŋ/ *n.*
place on the South China coast 香港
Xiaofang comes from Hong Kong.
小芳是从香港来的。

HK Cultural Centre

hoof /hoof; huːf/ *n.*
(two **hooves**)
hard foot of some animals （马、牛等的）蹄
We heard the noise of a horse's hooves.
我们听到了马蹄声。

hook /hook; hʊk/ *n.*
bent piece of metal or plastic 钩
Mary hung her coat on a hook.
玛丽把外衣挂在钩上。

hop /hop; hɒp/ *v.*
(**hopping, hopped, hopped**)
jump on one leg 单足跳
The children were hopping about.
孩子们单足到处跳。

hop

hope [1] /hope; həup/ *n.*
wishing for something 希望；期望
His hope is to go to study in Canada.
他的希望是去加拿大读书。

hope [2] /hope; həup/ *v.*
(hoping, hoped, hoped)
wish for something 希望；期望
Peter hopes to study in Canada.
彼得希望去加拿大读书。

horizon /hor·'i·zon; hə'raɪzn/ *n.*
line between the sky and sea or land 地平线；海平线
A ship appeared on the horizon.
一艘船出现在海平线上。

horizontal /hor·i·'zon·tal; hɒrɪ'zɒntl/ *adj.*
going straight from side to side 水平的；横的
Sam drew a horizontal line.
萨姆画了一道横线。

horn /horn; hɔ:n/ *n.*
hard, sharp thing on an animal's head 角
The cow has long horns.
这只母牛有长长的角。

horrible /'hor·ri·ble; 'hɒrəbl/ *adj.*
(more horrible, most horrible)
very bad 可怕的；糟极了的
The food was horrible.
食物糟极了。

horror /'hor·ror; 'hɒrə/ *n.*
(no plural)
great fear 恐怖；恐惧
She looked at the rat with horror.
她看着那只老鼠，感到非常恐惧。

horse /horse; hɔ:s/ *n.*
large animal used for riding or pulling carts 马
The cowboy was riding a horse.
那个牛仔骑着马。

hose, hosepipe /hose, 'hose·pipe; həuz, 'həuzpaɪp/ *n.*
sort of long, soft pipe 软管
Mr Chen used a hosepipe to put out the fire.
陈先生用一条消防软管把火扑灭。

hospital /'hos·pi·tal; 'hɒspɪtl/ *n.*
place where doctors and nurses look after sick people 医院
David was in hospital with a broken leg.
戴维断了一条腿，住进医院里了。

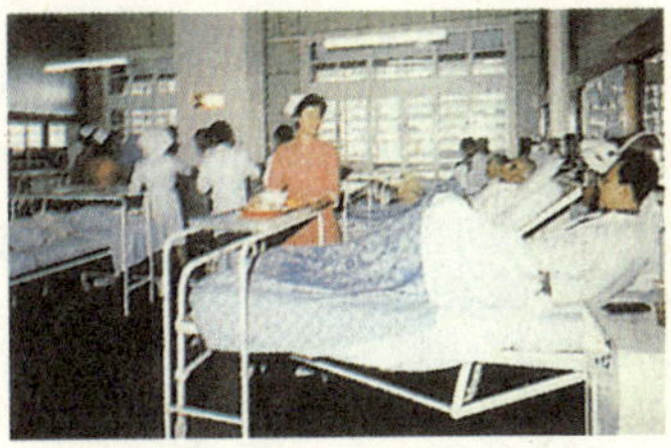

hot /hot; hɒt/ *adj.*
(hotter, hottest)
1 very warm 热的
The wok was very hot.
那炒菜锅很热。
opp. 反义词：cold 冷的
2 that tastes very strong 辣的
The sauce is very hot.
这种酱汁很辣。

hot dog /hot 'dog; hɒt 'dɒg/ *n.*
bread with a sausage in it 热狗
Peter likes hot dogs.
彼得喜欢吃热狗。

hotel /ho·'tel; həu'tel/ *n.*
building where you pay to sleep and eat 旅馆；酒店
When the Chen family go to Canada, they stay in a hotel.
陈家一家人在加拿大时住在旅馆里。

hour /'hour; 'auə/ *n.*
sixty minutes 小时
It takes an hour to get to the island.
去那个岛要一小时。
hourly *adv.* 每小时
The ferries leave hourly.
渡轮每小时开一班。

house /house; haus/ *n.*
building where you can live
房子；房屋
The family moved from a flat to a house.
那家人从公寓搬到一所房子去。

housewife *n.* 家庭主妇
Mrs Chen is a housewife.
陈太太是家庭主妇。
housework *n.* 家务
Mr Chen does the housework.
陈先生做家务。

housing estate /'hou·sing es·'tate; 'hauzɪŋ ɪ'steɪt/ *n.*
place where there are many houses or flats together
住宅区
John lives on a housing estate.
约翰住在一个住宅区内。
Usage note: The preposition we use is always *on* — *They live on a big housing estate.*
用法：与 estate 连用的介词是 on, 例如 They live on a big housing estate.

hovercraft /'ho·ver·craft; 'hɒvəkrɑ:ft/ *n.*
(two **hovercraft**)
special boat that moves across water on a cushion of air 气垫船
David took the hovercraft to the island.
戴维乘坐气垫船去那个岛。

how /how; hau/ *adv.*
in what way 怎样；如何
Peter knows how to play the guitar.
彼得懂得怎样弹吉他。
how about...? …怎么样？
How about going to the cinema?
去看电影怎么样？
how are you? 你好吗？
how do you do? 你好（与人初次见面时说的问候语）。
how much, many, often, big, etc. 多少；多久；多大
How much is that dress?
那件连衣裙多少钱？
how's, how is …身体怎样？
How's your father? Is he well?
你父亲好吗？身体健康吗？

however /how·'ev·er; hau'evə/ *adv.*
but 可是；不过
I'd like a new bicycle. However, I haven't enough money.
我希望有一辆新的自行车，不过我的钱不够。

howl [1] /howl; haul/ *n.*
high sound made by some animals （狼、狗等的）吼叫
The dog gave a howl.
那只狗吼叫。

howl [2] /howl; haul/ *v.*
make a high sound （狼、狗等）吼叫
The dog is howling.
那只狗在吼叫。

huge /huge; hju:dʒ/ *adj.*
very big 非常大的
China is a huge country.
中国是个非常大的国家。

hum /hum; hʌm/ *v.*
(**humming, hummed, hummed**)
sing without words 哼
Sam was humming a song.
萨姆哼着一首歌。

human /'hu·man; 'hju:mən/ *n.*
man, woman or child 人类
Humans are more intelligent than other animals.
人类比其他动物聪明。

humid /'hu·mid; 'hju:mɪd/ *adj.*
(**more humid, most humid**)
damp 潮湿的
Hong Kong has a humid climate.
香港气候潮湿。
opp. 反义词：dry 干燥的

humidity *n.* 湿气；湿度
Hong Kong has high humidity in summer.
香港夏天湿度很高。

hundred (100)
/ˈhun·dred; ˈhʌndrəd/ *n. adj.*
number 100 一百
There are a hundred years in a century.
一个世纪有一百年。

hundredth (100th) *n. adj.*
第一百
The company celebrated its hundredth year.
这家公司庆祝成立一百周年。

hung /hung; hʌŋ/ *v.*
p.t. of **hang** hang 的过去式
Mary hung her coat on a hook.
玛丽把外衣挂在钩上。

hunger /ˈhun·ger; ˈhʌŋgə/ *n.*
(**no plural**)
need for food 饥饿
Many children die of hunger every year.
每年都有很多小孩子饿死。

hungry /ˈhun·gry; ˈhʌŋgrɪ/ *adj.*
(**hungrier, hungriest**)
wanting food 饿的
I'm hungry. Is dinner ready?
我肚子饿了，饭菜做好了没有？

hungrily *adv.* 饥饿地
Peter ate his dinner hungrily.
彼得狼吞虎咽地吃了饭。

hunt /hunt; hʌnt/ *v.*
chase wild animals 打猎
The men were hunting rabbits.
那些人在猎兔。

hunter /ˈhunt·er; ˈhʌntə/ *n.*
someone who kills wild animals 猎人
The hunter chased the rabbits.
猎人追赶兔子。

hurrah!, hurray!
/hur·ˈrah, hur·ˈray; hʊˈrɑː, hʊˈreɪ/ *int.*
word you say or cheer when you are happy about something 欢呼声
When Tom won the race, his friends shouted, 'hurray!'
汤姆赢了比赛，他的朋友们为他欢呼。

hurry [1] /ˈhur·ry; ˈhʌrɪ/ *n.*
(**no plural**)
doing something quickly 匆忙
There is no hurry. We have plenty of time.
别忙，时间多着呢。

in a hurry 匆忙
The children were in a hurry.
孩子们都很匆忙。

hurry [2] /ˈhur·ry; ˈhʌrɪ/ *v.*
(**hurrying, hurried, hurried**)
move or do something quickly 赶快；匆忙
The children hurried to school.
孩子们匆匆忙忙地赶去学校。

hurry up 赶快
Hurry up or you will be late.
赶快走吧，你要迟到了。

hurt /hurt; hɜːt/ *v.*
(**hurting, hurt, hurt**)
1 make someone feel pain 伤害
Baoling fell and hurt her knee.
宝玲摔了一跤，伤了膝盖。
2 feel pain 疼痛
Baoling's knee hurts.
宝玲的膝盖很痛。

husband /ˈhus·band; ˈhʌzbənd/ *n.*
man who has a wife 丈夫
Mrs Chen's husband is a pilot.
陈太太的丈夫是飞行员。

hut /hut; hʌt/ *n.*
small building of wood or stone 小屋
The refugees were living in huts.
难民住在一些小屋里。

huts

hydrofoil /'hy·dro·foil; 'haɪdrəfɔɪl/ *n.*
special fast boat 水翼船
Peter went to Macao by hydrofoil.
彼得乘坐水翼船去澳门。

hymn /hymn; hɪm/ *n.*
song that praises God
赞美诗；圣歌
They were singing hymns in the church.
他们在教堂唱赞美诗。

hyphen /'hy·phen; 'haɪfn/ *n.*
small line (-) that joins two words or parts of words 连字号
'Finger-nail' is written with a hyphen.
Finger-nail 这个词中有一个连字号。

I /I; aɪ/ *pron.*
word for myself 我
I like ice-cream.
我喜欢吃冰淇淋。

ice /ice; aɪs/ *n.*
(no plural)
water that has become hard because it is very cold 冰
Tom put some ice in his drink.
汤姆在饮料里放了一些冰块。

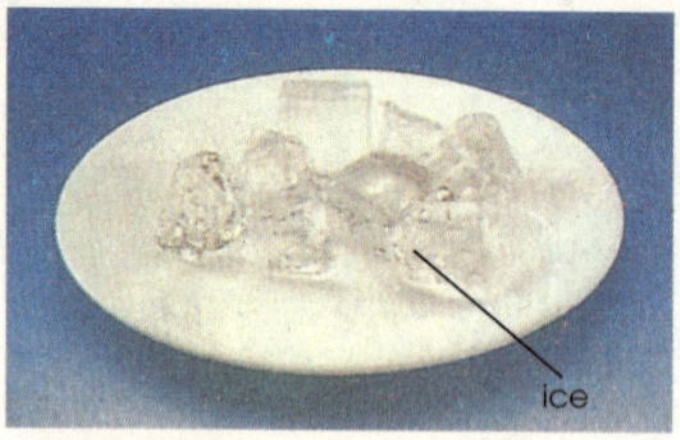

ice-cream /ice·'cream; aɪs'kri:m/ *n.*
kind of very cold, sweet food
冰淇淋；雪糕(方言)
It was hot, so Tom bought an ice-cream.
天气很热，因此汤姆买了一个冰淇淋。

I'd /I'd; aɪd/
1 I had 即 I had
I'd hoped to see David.
我本来希望见到戴维的。
2 I would 即 I would
I'd like an ice-cream please.
请你给我一个冰淇淋。

idea /i·'de·a; aɪ'dɪə/ *n.*
new thought; plan 意见；主意
I have an idea. Let's go to the beach.
我有一个主意，我们去海滩玩吧。

identity card (ID card) /i·'den·ti·ty card; aɪ'dentətɪ kɑ:d/ *n.*
card with a photograph which says who you are
身份证
We always carry our identity cards.
我们总是带着身份证。

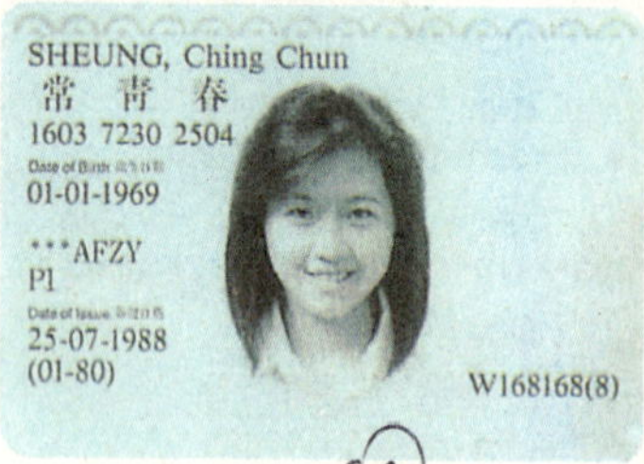

if /if; ɪf/ *conj.*
1 when 当…的时候
If it rains, I will take an umbrella.
下雨的时候，我会带雨伞。
2 word to show what is possible 如果
If you work hard you will pass your exams.
如果你用功，你考试就会及格。
3 word to show a question
(提问时用)是否
Do you know if Tom is at home?
你知道汤姆是否在家吗？

ignore /ig·'nore; ɪg'nɔ:/ *v.*
(ignoring, ignored, ignored)
know about someone or something but not do anything 不理会；忽视
Tom ignored the noise and did his work.
汤姆不理会那些声音，埋头工作。

ill /ill; ɪl/ *adj.*
(worse, worst)
sick; not healthy 生病的；健康不佳的

When Mary was ill, she stayed in bed.
玛丽生病时就卧床休息。
opp. 反义词：well 健康正常的；没有生病的

I'll /I'll; aɪl/
I will 即 I will
I'll see you tomorrow.
明天再见。

illegal /il·'le·gal; ɪ'li:gl/ *adj.*
not allowed by law 不合法的；非法的
Many illegal immigrants come to Hong Kong.
许多非法入境者来到香港。
opp. 反义词：legal 合法的

illness /'ill·ness; 'ɪlnɪs/ *n.*
something that makes people sick 疾病
Mary's illness soon got better.
玛丽的病不久就好些了。
syn. 同义词：disease

I'm /I'm; aɪm/
I am 即 I am
I'm eight years old.
我今年八岁。

imagine /i·'ma·gine; ɪ'mædʒɪn/ *v.*
(imagining, imagined, imagined)
have a picture of something in your mind 想像；幻想
The boy imagined he was a pilot.
那男孩幻想自己是飞行员。

imagination *n.* 幻想；想像力
Baoling used her imagination to write a story.
宝玲运用想像力写了一个故事。

immediately
/im·'me·di·ate·ly; ɪ'mi:dɪətlɪ/ *adv.*
now 立即；立刻
Wash your dirty hands immediately.
你的手太脏，立刻去洗一洗。

immigrate /'im·mi·grate; 'ɪmɪgreɪt/ *v.*
(immigrating, immigrated, immigrated)
come to live in another country from your own 移居
The family immigrated to Hong Kong from Vietnam.
那家人是从越南移居到香港的。

immigrant *n.* 移民
Many immigrants come to Hong Kong.
许多移民来香港。

impatient /im·'pa·tient; ɪm'peɪʃnt/ *adj.*
(more impatient, most impatient)
not wanting to wait for something 不耐烦的
When the singer did not come, the audience became impatient.
演唱者没有来，听众等得不耐烦了。
opp. 反义词：patient 耐心的

impatiently *adv.* 不耐烦地
The audience waited impatiently.
听众不耐烦地等着。

impolite /im·po·'lite; ɪmpə'laɪt/ *adj.*
(more impolite, most impolite)
not polite; rude 不礼貌的；无礼的
We should never be impolite.
我们绝不能无礼。
opp. 反义词：polite 有礼貌的

import /im·'port; ɪm'pɔ:t/ *v.*
buy something from another country （货物）输入；进口
Hong Kong imports a lot of food.
香港进口很多食品。
opp. 反义词：export 出口

important /im·'por·tant; ɪm'pɔ:tnt/ *adj.*
(more important, most important)
1 what you must do, have or think about 重要的
Keeping ourselves clean is very important.
保持身体清洁是十分重要的。
2 powerful; special （指人）重要的；显要的
The governor is an important man.
州长是个重要的人物。

impossible
/im·'pos·si·ble; ɪm'pɒsəbl/ *adj.*
that cannot happen; that you cannot do 不可能的
It is impossible for elephants to fly.
大象是不可能飞的。
opp. 反义词：possible 可能的

improve /im·'prove; ɪm'pru:v/ *v.*
(**improving, improved, improved**)
1 become better 进步
Mary's work is improving.
玛丽的功课有进步。
2 make something better 改良；改进
Tom improved his handwriting.
汤姆的字写得好一点了。
improvement *n.* 进步；改良
Tom's work showed a lot of improvement.
汤姆的功课有很大的进步。

in [1] /in; ɪn/ *adv.*
1 at home or work 在家；在工作的地方
Is Peter in?
彼得在家吗？
2 not outside 里面
Please come in.
请进来。
opp. 反义词：out 出去了；不在

in [2] /in; ɪn/ *prep.*
1 word that shows where 在…地方
David lives in Hong Kong.
戴维住在香港。
2 word that shows when 在…时候
Xiaofang was born in 1980.
小芳在1980年出生。
in front of 在前面
The car is in front of the building.
汽车停在大厦前面。

in pain 感到疼痛
The doctor asked the man if he was in pain.
医生问那人是不是很痛。

inch /inch; ɪntʃ/ *n.*
(two **inches**)
measure of height or length 英寸
There are about forty inches in a metre.
一米大约有四十英寸。

include /in·'clude; ɪn'klu:d/ *v.*
(**including, included, included**)
have someone or something as part of the total amount 包括；包含
The football team included two girls.
那支足球队中有两个女孩子。

incorrect /in·cor·'rect; ɪŋkə'rekt/ *adj.*
(**more incorrect, most incorrect**)
not correct; wrong 不正确的；错的
Your answer is incorrect.
你的答案是错误的。
opp. 反义词：correct 正确的

increase /in·'crease; ɪn'kri:s/ *v.*
(**increasing, increased, increased**)
become or make something bigger or more 增加；加多
The price of ice-cream has increased.
冰淇淋已经涨价了。

Mrs Chen increased Peter's pocket money.
陈太太多给了彼得一些零用钱。
opp. 反义词：decrease 减少

indeed /in·'deed; ɪn'di:d/ *adv.*
word that makes other words stronger （加强语气）的确；实在
A giraffe is very tall indeed.
长颈鹿的确很高。

independent /in·de·'pend·ent; ɪndɪ'pendənt/ *adj.*
(**more independent, most independent**)
able to look after yourself 独立的
Sam is an independent boy.
萨姆是个性格独立的孩子。

index /'in·dex; 'ɪndeks/ *n.*
(two **indexes**)
list at the back of the book to tell you where things are 索引
There was an index at the back of the book.
这本书的后面有一个索引。

India /'In·dia; 'ɪndɪə/ *n.*
country 印度
David went to India for a holiday.
戴维去印度度假。
Indian *adj. n.* 印度的；印度人
Mr Chen likes Indian tea.
陈先生喜欢喝印度茶。
Mr Chen's mother is an Indian.
陈先生的妈妈是印度人。

indoors /in·'doors; ɪn'dɔ:z/ *adv.*
in or into a building 室内；户内
When it rains, Mary stays indoors.
下雨的时候，玛丽就留在户内。
opp. 反义词：outdoors 户外

indoors

industry /'in·dus·try; 'ɪndəstrɪ/ *n.*
(two **industries**)
work done in factories 工业
There are many industries in Hong Kong.
香港有多种工业。
industrial *adj.* 工业的
Hong Kong is an industrial city.
香港是个工业城市。

infant /'in·fant; 'ɪnfənt/ *n.*
small child 幼儿；婴儿
The mothers took their infants to the park.
母亲们带幼儿去公园玩。

information /in·for·'ma·tion; ɪnfə'meɪʃn/ *n.*
(**no plural**)
words that tell you about something 消息；资料
Tom got some information about holidays in China.
汤姆取得一些去中国度假的资料。

inhabitant /in·'ha·bi·tant; ɪn'hæbɪtənt/ *n.*
someone who lives in a place 居民
Hong Kong has more than six million inhabitants.
香港有六百多万居民。

initials /i·'ni·tials; ɪ'nɪʃlz/ *n.* (**plural**)
first letters of a person's name 姓名起首的字母
Peter Chen's initials are PC.
Peter Chen 这个名字的首字母是 PC。

injection /in·'jec·tion; ɪn'dʒekʃn/ *n.*
medicine that you get through the skin with a needle 注射
Sam does not like having injections.
萨姆不喜欢打针。

injure /'in·jure; 'ɪndʒə/ *v.*
(**injuring, injured, injured**)
hurt someone or something
伤害；损害
Tom fell and injured his hand.
汤姆跌了一跤，伤了手。
injury *n.* 伤害
The injury was not bad.
伤势并不重。

ink /ink; ɪŋk/ *n.*
(**no plural**)
liquid for writing and printing
墨水；墨汁
Mr Chen uses ink to write Chinese characters.
陈先生用墨水写汉字。

innocent /'in·no·cent; 'ɪnəsnt/ *adj.*
not guilty; not having done wrong 无罪的
The judge said the man was innocent.
法官说这个人没有罪。

insect /'in·sect; 'ɪnsekt/ *n.*
very small animal with six legs 昆虫
Mosquitoes are dangerous insects.
蚊子是危险的昆虫。

insects

inside /in·'side; ɪn'saɪd/ *n.* *prep.* *adv.*
part nearest the middle; in a building or other place 内部；在里面
The inside of the house was very beautiful.
房子的内部很漂亮。
We were inside the house.
我们在房子里。
It was raining so we went inside.
下雨了，所以我们走进房子里。

inspector /in·ˈspec·tor; ɪnˈspektə/ *n.*
1 police officer 督察
The inspector gave orders to his men.
督察对他的下属下命令。

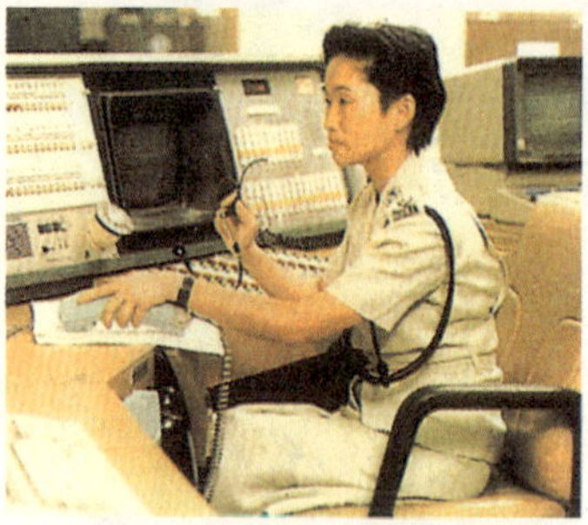

2 someone who visits schools, factories, etc. to see that everything is all right 检查员；督学
The inspector went to visit the factory.
检查员去那家工厂检查。
inspect *v.* 检查；视察
The principal inspected the classrooms.
校长去各教室视察。

instant /ˈin·stant; ˈɪnstənt/ *adj.*
ready after a short time 立即的
Mary ate some instant noodles.
玛丽吃了一些方便面。

instead /in·ˈstead; ɪnˈsted/ *adv.*
in place of; rather than 代替；更换
Tom did not want cake so he had fruit instead.
汤姆不想吃蛋糕，因此改吃水果。
instead of 代替
Tom had fruit instead of cake.
汤姆吃了水果而没有吃蛋糕。

instructions /in·ˈstruc·tions; ɪnˈstrʌkʃnz/ *n.* **(plural)**
words that tell you what to do 指示；命令；说明
Before you take the medicine, read the instructions carefully.
在吃药之前，先仔细看看使用说明。

instrument /ˈin·stru·ment; ˈɪnstrumənt/ *n.*
thing for making music; tool for doing a special job 乐器；工具；仪器
Can you play a musical instrument?
你会玩乐器吗？

instruments

intelligent /in·ˈtel·li·gent; ɪnˈtelɪdʒənt/ *adj.*
(more intelligent, most intelligent)
clever 聪明的；有智慧的
Tom's dog is very intelligent.
汤姆的狗很聪明。
opp. 反义词：foolish, stupid 愚蠢的

intend /in·ˈtend; ɪnˈtend/ *v.*
think or say that you will do something 打算；计划
What do you intend to do tomorrow?
明天你打算干什么？

interest [1] /ˈin·terest; ˈɪntrəst/ *n.*
1 something you like 兴趣；嗜好；爱好
Mary's main interest is reading.
玛丽主要的兴趣是读书。
syn. 同义词：hobby
2 **(no plural)** money paid to you by a bank （银行存款的）利息
If you save money in a bank it earns interest.
如果你在银行储蓄，便可以获取利息。

interest [2] /ˈin·terest; ˈɪntrəst/ *v.*
liking something and wanting to know more about it 令人感兴趣
This book will interest you.
你会对这本书感兴趣。
interested *adj.* 感兴趣的
David is very interested in science.
戴维对科学十分感兴趣。
interesting *adj.*
what you like 有趣味的
Is that book interesting?
那本书有趣吗？

international /in·ter·ˈna·tion·al; ɪntəˈnæʃnəl/ *adj.*
between countries 国际的
English is an international language.
英语是国际语言。

interrupt /in·ter·ˈrupt; ɪntəˈrʌpt/ *v.*
speak while another person is speaking 打断；打扰
It's rude to interrupt when someone is speaking.
打断别人讲话是没有礼貌的。

terruption *n.* 中断；打断；打扰
When he was teaching, he did not like interruptions.
讲课的时候不喜欢别人打扰。

terview /ˈin·ter·view; ntəvju:/ *n.*
neeting when you try to find out more about someone by alking to them and asking uestions 会见；接见；面试
eter had an interview with he principal.
获得会见过校长。

nto /ˈin·to; ˈɪntə/ *prep.*
word that shows where
到…里面
David went into the classroom.
戴维进了教室。

word that shows something is changing 变成
Anna broke the chocolate into pieces.
安娜把巧克力分成小块。
word you use in arithmetic
（算术）除
Three into twelve is four (12÷3=4).
三除十二等于四。

introduce /in·tro·ˈduce; ɪntrəˈdju:s/ *v.*
(introducing, introduced, introduced)
bring people together and tell them each other's names
介绍
Mary introduced her friends to her mother.
玛丽给妈妈介绍她的朋友们。

invade /in·ˈvade; ɪnˈveɪd/ *v.*
(invading, invaded, invaded)
go into another country and attack it 侵入；侵略
During the war, the country was invaded.
大战时，这个国家受到侵略。

invent /in·ˈvent; ɪnˈvent/ *v.*
to think of and make something new 发明
Marconi invented radio.
马可尼发明了无线电。
invention *n.* 发明
Radio was a wonderful invention.
无线电是一项奇妙的发明。
inventor *n.* 发明者；发明家
Marconi was an inventor.
马可尼是个发明家。

investigate /in·ˈves·ti·gate; ɪnˈvestɪgeɪt/ *v.*
(investigating, investigated, investigated)
find out about 调查；审查
The detective investigated the robbery.
那个侦探调查这起抢劫案件。

invisible /in·ˈvis·i·ble; ɪnˈvɪzəbl/ *adj.*
something you cannot see
看不见的
The insect's colour made it invisible.
这种昆虫的颜色使人看不见它。
opp. 反义词：visible 看得见的

invite /in·ˈvite; ɪnˈvaɪt/ *v.*
(inviting, invited, invited)
ask someone to come somewhere or do something
邀请
Sam invited all his friends to his birthday party.
萨姆邀请他所有的朋友来参加他的生日聚会。
invitation *n.* 邀请；请帖
Sam sent invitations to all his friends.
萨姆向他所有的朋友发出请帖。

iron [1] /ˈi·ron; ˈaɪən/ *n.*
1 **(no plural)** sort of metal 铁
The bridge was made of iron.
这座桥是铁造的。
2 hot metal thing you use to make clothes smooth 熨斗
Anna switched on the iron.
安娜插上电熨斗。

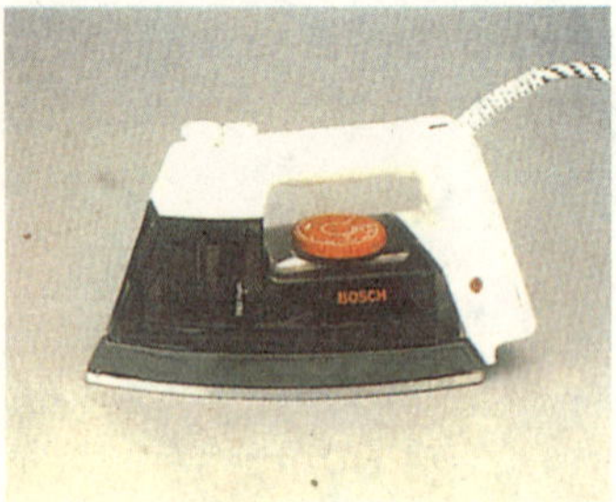

iron [2] /ˈi·ron; ˈaɪən/ *v.*
use an iron 熨平
Anna ironed her dress.
安娜熨平她的连衣裙。

irregular /ir·ˈreg·u·lar; ɪˈregjʊlə/ *adj.*
(more irregular, most irregular)
not following the usual rules 不规则的
'Be' is an irregular verb.
Be 是一个不规则动词。
opp. 反义词：regular 有规则的

is /is; ɪz/ *v.*
3rd person singular present tense of **be** be 的第三人称单数现在式
Anna is a girl guide.
安娜是个女童子军。
opp. 反义词：is not, isn't 不是

isn't /ˈis·n't; ˈɪznt/ *v.*
is not 即 is not
David isn't at home.
戴维不在家。

island /ˈis·land; ˈaɪlənd/ *n.*
piece of land with water all around it 岛；岛屿
Lantau is an island.
大屿山是一个岛。

it /it; ɪt/ *pron.*
1 **(they)** word for a thing or animal 它
Our dog is beautiful. Have you seen it?
我们的狗长得很好看，你见过它没有?
2 word that points to words that follow 用来指后面的一组词
It is a beautiful day.
天气很好。

itch /itch; ɪtʃ/ *v.*
feeling that makes you want to scratch 发痒
Mosquito bites itch.
蚊子叮过的地方会发痒。

its /its; ɪts/ *adj.*
of it; that belongs to it 它的
The dog is scratching its head.
那只狗在抓自己的头。

it's /it's; ɪts/
it is 即 it is
It's six o'clock.
六时了。

itself /it·ˈself; ɪtˈself/ *pron.*
(themselves)
word for the same thing or animal you have just talked about 它自己
The dog is scratching itself.
那只狗在给自己抓痒。

I've /I've; aɪv/
I have 即 I have
I've finished my ice-cream.
我已经把冰淇淋吃完了。

ivory /ˈi·vo·ry; ˈaɪvərɪ/ *n.*
(no plural)
hard, white stuff that comes from elephants 象牙
People killed elephants to get ivory in the years before.
从前人们猎杀大象以取得象牙。

jacket /ˈjack·et; ˈdʒækɪt/ *n.*
short coat with sleeves 短上衣；短外套
When it's cold, Tom wears a jacket.
天气冷的时候，汤姆便穿上短外套。

ade /jade; dʒeɪd/ *n.*
no plural)
ard green stone for
ewellery, etc. 玉；翡翠
3aoling has a jade bracelet.
玲有一只玉镯子。

ail /jail; dʒeɪl/ *n.*
prison 监牢
They sent the robber to jail.
也们把盗贼送进监牢。

am /jam; dʒæm/ *n.*
no plural)
sweet food made with fruit
and sugar 果酱
Peter likes bread and jam.
彼得喜欢吃面包涂果酱。

jam

January /ˈJan·u·a·ry; ˈdʒænjuərɪ/ *n.*
first month of the year 一月
In Hong Kong, it's cold in January.
香港的一月份很冷。

Japan /Ja·ˈpan; dʒəˈpæn/ *n.*
country in Asia 日本
Our car was made in Japan.
我们的汽车是日本制造的。
Japanese *adj. n.* 日本的；日本人
We have a Japanese car.
我们有一辆日本制造的汽车。

jar /jar; dʒɑː/ *n.*
pot that holds food 阔口瓶
Susan bought a jar of honey.
苏珊买了一瓶蜂蜜。

jars

jaw /jaw; dʒɔː/ *n.*
part of the mouth 颚
Our jaws move when we eat.
我们吃东西时颚会动。

jealous /ˈjeal·ous; ˈdʒeləs/ *adj.*
(**more jealous, most jealous**)
feeling sad and angry because you want what another person has 妒忌
You should not be jealous of your friends.
你不应该妒忌你的朋友们。

jeans /jeans; dʒiːnz/ *n.*
(**plural**)
trousers made of strong blue material 牛仔裤；斜纹布裤
The children can't wear jeans to school.
小孩子不准穿牛仔裤上学。

jelly /ˈjel·ly; ˈdʒelɪ/ *n.*
(two **jellies**)
soft, sweet food made with fruit, water and sugar 果冻；啫喱（方言）
Sam likes jelly.
萨姆爱吃果冻。

jersey /ˈjer·sey; ˈdʒɜːzɪ/ *n.*
piece of woollen clothing you wear on the top part of your body 毛织上衣
Peter wears a jersey when it's cold.
天气冷的时候，彼得就穿上毛织上衣。

jet /jet; dʒet/ *n.*
aeroplane that flies when its engines send out hot gas
喷气式飞机
Most aeroplanes are jets now.
现在大多数飞机都是喷气式飞机了。

jewel /ˈjew·el; ˈdʒuːəl/ *n.*
valuable stone 宝石；宝石饰物
The woman was wearing a lot of jewels.
那个女人戴了许多珠宝。
jeweller *n.* 宝石商；珠宝商
Mr Tan is a jeweller.
谭先生是个珠宝商。
jewellery *n.* 珠宝首饰
Mr Tan sells jewellery.
谭先生卖珠宝首饰。

jewels

job /job; dʒɒb/ *n.*
1 piece of work 一件工作
Cleaning a house is not an easy job.
清扫房子不是一件容易的工作。
2 work you do for money
职业；工作
Mrs Lin got a job in a factory.
林太太在一家工厂找到一份工作。

jockey /ˈjock·ey; ˈdʒɒkɪ/ *n.*
someone who rides horses in races 骑师
That jockey won the race.
那位骑师在赛事中获胜。

join /join; dʒɔɪn/ *v.*
1 fix or stick things together
连接；接合
Mary joined the two pieces of cloth.
玛丽把两块布缝起来。
2 become a member of a club or group 参加；加入
Anna joined the girl guides.
安娜参加了女童子军。
3 go and do something with someone 与…一起
Peter joined the boys for a game of football.
彼得与那些男孩子一起踢足球。
join in 参加；伴随
Peter joined in the game.
彼得参加了比赛。
join up 联合起来；连接起来
Join up the dots to make a picture.
把各点连接起来就是一幅图画。

joke /joke; dʒəuk/ *n.*
something done or said to make people laugh 玩笑；笑话
The children laughed at Sam's jokes.
萨姆讲笑话，使孩子们大笑。

joss-stick /ˈjoss·stick; ˈdʒɒstɪk/ *n.*
special stick you burn for its smell 香
Mrs Chen burnt some joss-sticks at the temple.
陈太太在庙里烧香。

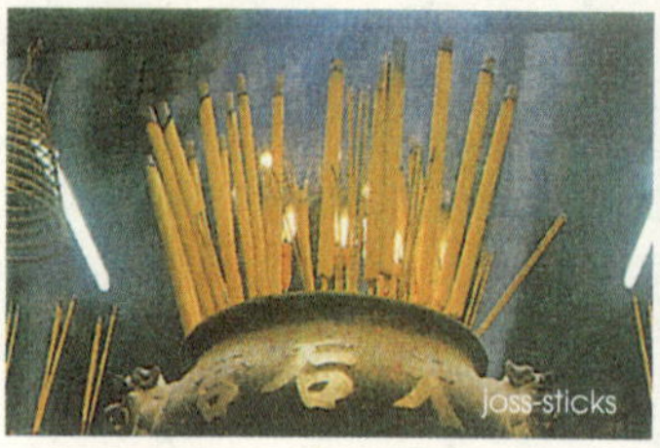
joss-sticks

journey /ˈjour·ney; ˈdʒɜːnɪ/ *n.*
going from one place to another 旅行；旅程；路程
He made a long journey across China.
他做了一次横跨中国的长途旅行。
Usage note: *A journey* can be a long or short distance — *How long is your journey to school? He went on a journey to the North Pole.*
用法：journey 可以指长途或短途的旅程，例如 How long is your journey to school? 和 He went on a journey to the North Pole.

joy /joy; dʒɔɪ/ *n.*
(no plural)
happiness 快乐；高兴
They heard the good news with great joy.
他们听到这个好消息，十分高兴。

judge /judge; dʒʌdʒ/ *n.*
person in a court who decides how to punish a person who has done wrong
法官
The judge sent the robber to prison.
法官判盗贼入狱。

udges

udo /'ju·do; 'dʒu:dəu/ *n.*
no plural)
port where you hold and try
o throw the other person
柔道
Judo is Tom's favourite sport.
柔道是汤姆喜爱的运动。

ug /jug; dʒʌg/ *n.*
pot with a handle for holding
and pouring liquids 壶
Mrs Chen put a jug of
orange juice on the table.
陈太太把一壶橙汁放在桌子上。

juice /juice; dʒu:s/ *n.*
(**no plural**)
liquid in fruit and vegetables
果汁；菜汁
Children like orange juice.
小孩子喜欢喝橙汁。
juicy *adj.* 多汁的
The oranges were very juicy.
这些橙有很多汁。

July /Ju·'ly; dʒu:'laɪ/ *n.*
seventh month of the year
七月
In Hong Kong, it is hot in July.
香港的七月份很热。

jumbo jet /jum·bo 'jet; dʒʌmbəu 'dʒet/ *n.*
very large jet plane 大型喷气式客机
Peter went to London on a jumbo jet.
彼得乘坐大型喷气式客机去伦敦。

jump /jump; dʒʌmp/ *v.*
move up so that your feet leave the ground 跳
Tom jumped over the wall.
汤姆跳过那堵墙。

June /June; dʒu:n/ *n.*
sixth month of the year 六月
June is usually a nice month in Hong Kong.
在香港，六月份的天气通常很好。

jungle /'jun·gle; 'dʒʌŋgl/ *n.*
thick forest in hot countries
森林；丛林
There were snakes in the jungle.
丛林里有蛇。

junior /'jun·ior; 'dʒu:nɪə/ *adj.*
for younger people 较年幼的
The children go to a junior school.
小孩子上小学。

junk /junk; dʒʌŋk/ *n.*
Chinese boat with sails
中国帆船
A junk sailed across the harbour.
一艘中国帆船驶过海港。

just /just; dʒʌst/ *adv.*
1 exactly 刚好；正好
A bicycle was just what Sam wanted.
自行车正好是萨姆所需要的。
2 very recently 刚刚；刚才
The bus has just left.
公共汽车刚刚开走。
3 now 现在
The bus is just coming.
公共汽车现在来了。
4 only 只是
Mary just wanted to buy some sweets.
玛丽只想买些糖果。
just as 正在…的时候
Sam arrived just as the bus was leaving.
萨姆到达的时候，公共汽车正要开走。
just now 刚才；刚刚
The bus left just now.
公共汽车刚刚开走。

Kk

kangaroo /kan·ga·'roo; kæŋgə'ruː/ *n.*
large animal from Australia
袋鼠
There are kangaroos in Australia.
澳洲有袋鼠。

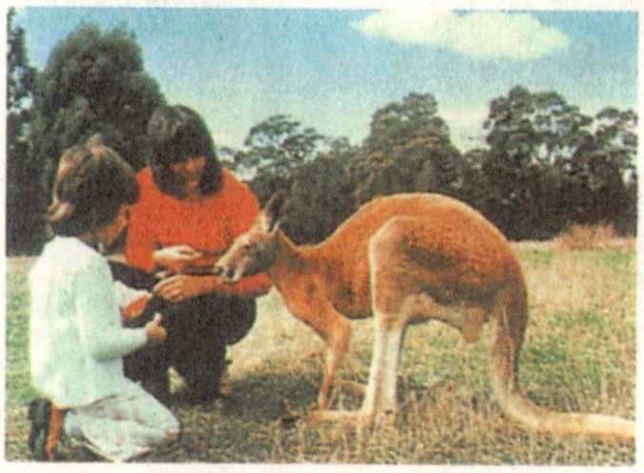

kart /kart; kɑːt/ *n.*
small racing car 小型赛车
There are kart races in Hong Kong every year.
香港每年都举行小型赛车竞赛。

keen /keen; kiːn/ *adj.*
wanting to do something
渴望；热心
Peter is keen to be a doctor.
彼得渴望成为医生。

keen on 对…有兴趣；喜欢
David is keen on science.
戴维对科学有兴趣。

keep /keep; kiːp/ *v.*
(**keeping, kept, kept**)
1 have something in a place
保存；保管
Mr Chen keeps his money in a bank.
陈先生把他的钱存在银行。
2 not change; not stop 继续；不断
Mr Chen kept working until eight o'clock.
陈先生一直工作到八时。
3 make someone or something stay the same
保持
Mary keeps her room tidy.
玛丽保持她的房间整齐清洁。

keep away 远离；避开
Keep away from fierce dogs.
不要走近凶猛的狗。

kettle /'ket·tle; 'ketl/ *n.*
metal pot with a handle on top, for boiling water (烧水用的)水壶
Susan boiled a kettle of water to make tea.
苏珊烧了一壶开水来泡茶。

key /key; kiː/ *n.*
thing that opens and closes a lock 钥匙
Tom lost his key and could not open the door.
汤姆的钥匙不见了，没法开门。

keyhole *n.* 钥匙孔
Tom looked through the keyhole.
汤姆从钥匙孔往里面看。

key-ring *n.* 钥匙圈
Mary put her keys in a key-ring.
玛丽把她的钥匙都串在一个钥匙圈上。

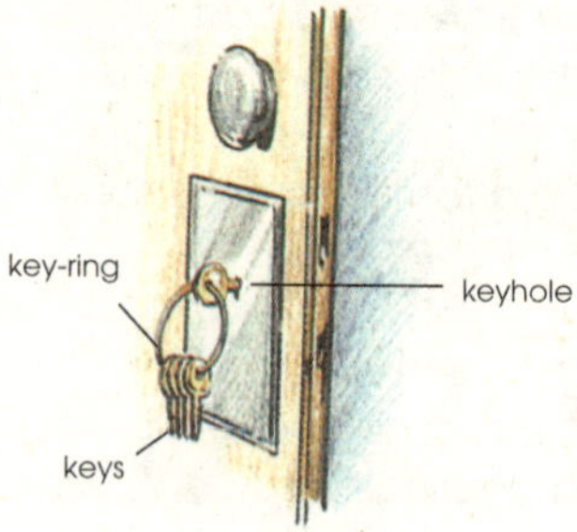

kick [1] /kick; kɪk/ *v.*
hit with your foot 踢
Sam kicked the ball.
萨姆踢那球。

kick [2] /kick; kɪk/ *n.*
hitting with your foot 踢
Sam gave the ball a kick.
萨姆把球踢了一脚。

kid /kid; kɪd/ *n.*
young goat 小山羊
The goat had a small kid.
那只山羊有一只小山羊。

kidnap /'kid·nap; 'kɪdnæp/ *v.*
(**kidnapping, kidnapped, kidnapped**)
take and hide someone so that his family and friends will

give money to get him back 绑架；绑票
They kidnapped the rich man.
他们绑架了那个有钱人。
kidnapper *n.* 绑架者
The police arrested the kidnappers.
警察拘捕了绑架者。

kill /kill; kɪl/ *v.*
make a person, animal or plant die 杀死；宰杀
The dog killed the rat.
那只狗咬死了老鼠。

kilogram (kg) /ˈki·lo·gram; ˈkɪləgræm/ *n.*
measure of weight 千克；公斤
Susan bought a kilogram of rice.
苏珊买了一公斤米。

kilometre (km) /ˈki·lo·me·tre; ˈkɪləmi:tə/ *n*
measure of distance 千米；公里
It is two kilometres to Susan's school.
这里离苏珊的学校有两千米。

kind [1] /kind; kaɪnd/ *adj.*
good to other people 亲切的；慈爱的；和蔼的
She is a kind woman.
她是个亲切和蔼的女人。
opp. 反义词：unkind, cruel 不和善的；残忍的
kindly *adv.* 亲切地；和善地
She always behaved kindly.
她一贯对人和善亲切。
kindness *n.* 亲切；和蔼；仁慈
Everyone knew about her kindness.
人人都知道她亲切和蔼。

kind [2] /kind; kaɪnd/ *n.*
sort 种类
What kind of ice-cream do you like?
你喜欢哪一种冰淇淋？
Usage note: We usually have a singular noun after *kind* -- *What kind of tree is that?*
用法：kind之后的名词通常用单数，例如 What kind of tree is that?

kindergarten
/ˈkin·der·gar·ten; ˈkɪndəgɑ:tn/ *n.*
school for very young children 幼儿园
Little children go to the kindergarten.
年纪小的小孩上幼儿园。

king /king; kɪŋ/ *n.*
man who rules a country 国王
The king ruled the country for fifty years.
那个国王统治了国家五十年。
kingdom *n.* 王国
Great Britain is a kingdom.
英国是一个王国。

kiss [1] /kiss; kɪs/ *v.*
touch someone with your lips 吻；亲吻
Mrs Chen kissed her baby.
陈太太亲吻她的婴儿。

kiss [2] /kiss; kɪs/ *n.*
(two **kisses**)
touching someone with your lips 吻；亲吻
Mrs Chen gave her baby a kiss.
陈太太亲吻她的婴儿。

kitchen /ˈkitch·en; ˈkɪtʃɪn/ *n.*
room where you cook food 厨房
Mrs Chen was making lunch in the kitchen.
陈太太在厨房里准备午饭。

kite /kite; kaɪt/ *n.*
paper toy that flies in the wind 风筝
Sam flew his kite in the park.
萨姆在公园里放风筝。

kitten /ˈkit·ten; ˈkɪtn/ *n.*
young cat 小猫
The cat had three kittens.
那只猫有三只小猫。

knee /knee; ni:/ *n.*
place where the leg bends
膝部；膝盖
Susan fell and hurt her knee.
苏珊跌了一跤，伤了膝盖。

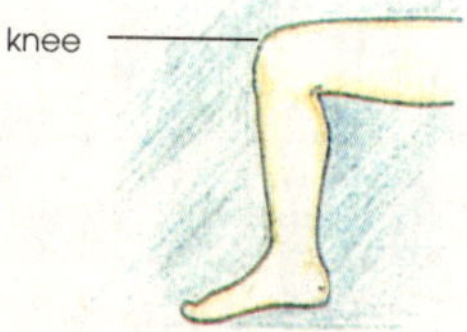

kneel /kneel; ni:l/ *v.*
(**kneeling, knelt, knelt**)
go down on your knees 跪下
Mary knelt down and cleaned the kitchen floor.
玛丽跪下来擦厨房的地板。

knew /knew; nju:/ *v.*
p.t. of **know** know 的过去式
Baoling knew all the answers in the test.
宝玲知道怎样回答测验卷里所有的题目。

knife /knife; naɪf/ *n.*
(two **knives**)
tool for cutting 刀
Tom used his knife to cut up the melon.
汤姆用他的刀把瓜切开。

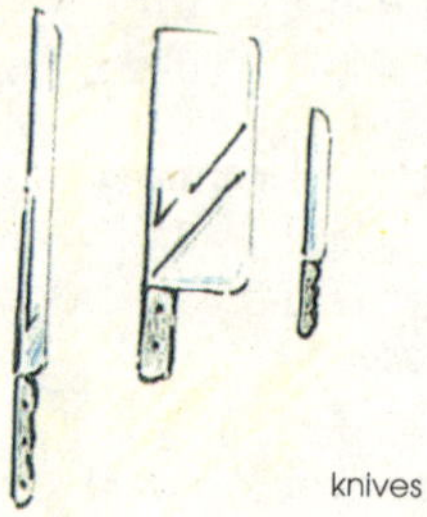

knit /knit; nɪt/ *v.*
(**knitting, knitted, knitted**)
use long needles and wool to make clothes 编织
Anna knitted a pullover for her mother.
安娜给她妈妈织了一件套头毛衣。

knob /knob; nɒb/ *n.*
round handle on a door or drawer （门或抽屉的）圆形把手
The knob came off the kitchen door.
厨房门上的圆形把手脱落了。

knock [1] /knock; nɒk *n.*
hitting something 敲；打；击
Mary heard a knock at the door.
玛丽听见敲门的声音。

knock [2] /knock; nɒk/ *v.*
1 hit something 碰；撞
Tom knocked a glass over.
汤姆碰翻了一只玻璃杯。
2 hit a door so that someone will hear you and open it
敲门
Susan knocked at Mary's door.
苏珊敲玛丽的房门。

knock down 撞倒
The man was knocked down by a car.
那人给一辆汽车撞倒了。

knot /knot; nɒt/ *n.*
place where you have tied string or rope 绳结
There was a knot in Tom's shoelace.
汤姆的鞋带打了个结。

know /know; nəʊ/ *v.*
(**knowing, knew, known**)
1 have something in your mind 知道；晓得；懂得
Do you know where Tibet is?
你知道西藏在哪里吗？
2 have met someone before 认识（某人）
Do you know Peter Chen?
你认识陈彼得吗？

knowledge /ˈknow·ledge; ˈnɒlɪdʒ/ *n.*
(**no plural**)
things you know 知识；认识
Peter's knowledge about Hong Kong is good.
彼得懂得不少关于香港的知识。

knuckle /ˈknuc·kle; ˈnʌkl/ *n.*
parts of fingers that bend （手指的）关节
Sam hurt his knuckles when he knocked too hard on the door.
萨姆敲门用力过猛，伤了手指的关节。

Kowloon /Kow·ˈloon; kaʊˈluːn/ *n.*
part of Hong Kong 九龙
Sam lives in Kowloon.
萨姆住在九龙。

label /ˈla·bel; ˈleɪbl/ *n.*
small piece of paper that you put on something to give information about it 标签
Mary tied a label to her suitcase.
玛丽在她的衣箱上系了一个标签。

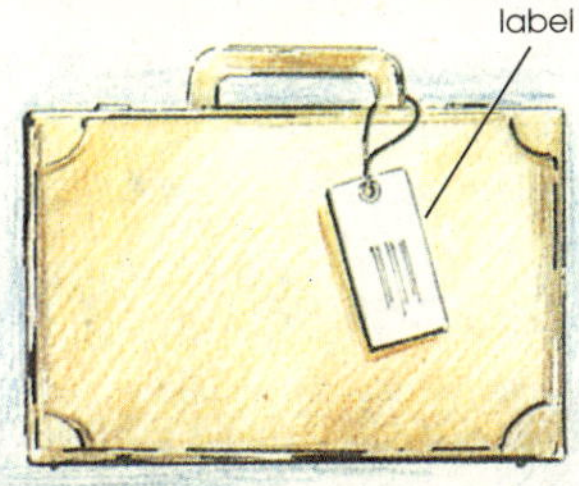

laboratory /la·ˈbor·a·to·ry; ləˈbɒrətrɪ/ *n.*
(two **laboratories**)
place where scientists work 实验室
Ten scientists work in the laboratory.
有十个科学家在这个实验室工作。

lace[1] /lace; leɪs/ *n.*
string that fastens a shoe 鞋带；带
Tom's shoe fell off when the lace broke.
汤姆的鞋带断了，鞋也就掉了。

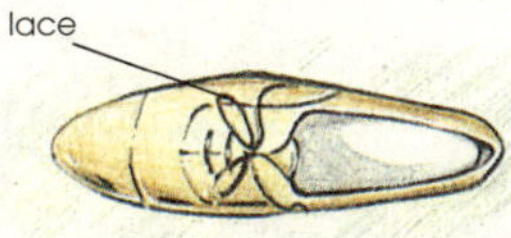

lace[2] /lace; leɪs/ *v.*
(**lacing, laced, laced**)
fasten with laces 用带系紧
Tom laced his shoes.
汤姆系紧鞋带。

ladder /ˈlad·der; ˈlædə/ *n.*
two poles with steps for climbing 梯子
Mary climbed up the ladder.
玛丽爬上梯子。

lady /ˈla·dy; ˈleɪdɪ/ *n.*
(two **ladies**)
woman 女士
The lady came out of the shop.
那位女士从商店里走出来。

laid /laid; leɪd/ *v.*
p.t. of **lay** lay 的过去式
The hen laid an egg.
那母鸡生了一个蛋。

lain /lain; leɪn/ *v.*
p.p. of **lie** lie 的过去分词
She has lain down.
她已经躺下了。

lake /lake; leɪk/ *n.*
big piece of water with land round it 湖
There were trees round the lake.
湖畔有树。

lamb /lamb; læm/ *n.*
young sheep 小羊；羔羊
There were some lambs in the field.
田野上有些小羊。

lamp /lamp; læmp/ *n.*
thing that gives light 灯
Tom switched on the lamp.
汤姆开了灯。

lamp-post *n.* 灯柱
The car crashed into a lamp-post.
那汽车撞到灯柱上。

lampshade *n.* 灯罩
The lamp has a green lampshade.
这盏灯有个绿色的灯罩。

land [1] /land; lænd/ *n.*
1 (**no plural**) ground 土地；地
Land is expensive in Hong Kong.
香港的土地昂贵。
2 country 国家
China is a huge land.
中国是个非常大的国家。

land [2] /land; lænd/ *v.*
go down onto the ground from the air 着陆；降落
The plane landed at the airport.
飞机在机场降落。
opp. 反义词：take off 起飞

landslide /ˈland·slide; ˈlændslaɪd/ *n.*
earth and rocks that fall from a hill 泥石崩塌；山崩
There were landslides after the heavy rain.
大雨后发生了泥石崩塌。

lane /lane; leɪn/ *n.*
1 part of a wide road 车道
The road has six lanes.
这条马路有六个车道。
2 narrow road 小径
The farmer walked down the lane.
那农民沿着小径走。

language /ˈlan·guage; ˈlæŋgwɪdʒ/ *n.*
how people talk 语言；语文
Tom finds the Chinese language difficult.
汤姆觉得汉语很难学。

lantern /ˈlan·tern; ˈlæntən/ *n.*
thing that gives light 灯笼
We see lots of lanterns during the Lantern Festival.
元宵节时，我们看见许多灯笼。

lanterns

lap /lap; læp/ *n.*
top part of your legs when you are sitting （人坐着时）大腿部分
The baby was sitting on Mrs Chen's lap.
那婴儿坐在陈太太的大腿上。

large /large; lɑːdʒ/ *adj.*
(**larger, largest**)
big 大的
The large bird caught a fish.
那只大鸟抓了一条鱼。
opp. 反义词：small 小的

laser /'la·ser; 'leɪzə/ *n.*
machine that makes a special beam of light 激光(器)
A laser beam can cut metal.
激光可以切割金属。

last [1] /last; lɑːst/ *adj.*
1 at the end; after all the others 最后的
Mary is the last one in the row.
玛丽排在队末。
opp. 反义词: first 第一个; 最前的

2 coming just before this one 最近的; 上一次的
David played football last Saturday.
上星期六戴维踢足球。
opp. 反义词: next 下一次的

at last 终于; 最后
At last, he finished the exercise.
他终于做完了练习。

last [2] /last; lɑːst/ *adv.*
1 after all the others 最后的
Tom came last in the test.
汤姆的测验成绩最差，排名最后。
opp. 反义词: first 第一; 最前
2 time before this 上一次
When did you last see Peter?
你上一次是什么时候见到彼得的?
opp. 反义词: next 下一次

last [3] /last; lɑːst/ *v.*
go on 持续; 延续
How long does the film last?
这部电影片长多久?

late [1] /late; leɪt/ *adj.*
(later, latest)
coming after the right time 迟的
David was late for school.
戴维上学迟到。
opp. 反义词: early 早的

late [2] /late; leɪt/ *adv.*
1 not early 很晚
Mr Chen goes to bed late.
陈先生很晚才睡觉。
2 after the right time 迟了; 晚了
Baoling arrived too late.
宝玲来得太迟了。
opp. 反义词: early 早

lately /'late·ly; 'leɪtlɪ/ *adv.*
recently; not a long time ago 近来; 近期
Have you seen Baoling lately?
你近来见过宝玲吗?

later /'la·ter; 'leɪtə/ *adj.*
1 coming after the right time 更迟的
Baoling was late for school, but Mary was later.
宝玲上学迟到，但是玛丽更迟。
2 at a time which comes after 以后的
Let's do our homework now. We can watch TV later.
我们现在做家庭作业吧，做完以后再看电视。

latest /'la·test; 'leɪtɪst/ *adj.*
1 last 最迟的
Anna was the latest to arrive.
安娜是最迟来到的一个。
2 newest 最新式的
Sam has the latest automatic camera.
萨姆有一架最新式的自动照相机。

laugh /laugh; lɑːf/ *v.*
make a loud happy sound 笑
The children laughed at the clown.
孩子们看到那小丑而发笑。

laughter *n.* 笑声
We could hear the children's laughter.
我们可以听到孩子们的笑声。

launch /launch; lɔːntʃ/ *v.*
put a boat or a ship in the water; put a rocket in space
使(轮船)下水; 发射(火箭)
They launched the new ship.
他们让新船下水。

laundry /'laun·dry; 'lɔːndrɪ/ *n.*
(no plural)
clothes, etc. that are being washed 所洗的衣服
Mrs Wang does her laundry once a week.
王太太每星期洗衣服一次。

lavatory /'lav·a·to·ry; 'lævətrɪ/ *n.*
(two **lavatories**)
toilet 洗手间；厕所
Where's the lavatory, please?
请问洗手间在哪里？

law /law; lɔ:/ *n.*
rules for the people of a country 法律
We have traffic laws to stop accidents.
我们有交通法规来防止事故。
break the law 犯法
If you break the law, you will be punished.
如果你犯法，就会受到惩罚。

lawn /lawn; lɔ:n/ *n.*
piece of ground with short grass in a garden 草地
The children were playing on the lawn.
孩子们在草地上玩。

lawyer /'law·yer; 'lɔ:jə/ *n.*
someone who has studied the laws of your country and helps you with them 律师
Mr Li is a lawyer.
李先生是个律师。

lay /lay; leɪ/ *v.*
(**laying, laid, laid**)
1 put something on top of another thing 铺
she laid the cloth on the table.
她把布铺在桌子上。
2 make an egg 生蛋
The goose laid an egg.
那只鹅生了一个蛋。
3 p.t. of **lie** lie 的过去式
Peter lay on the beach.
彼得躺在海滩上。

layer /'lay·er; 'leɪə/ *n.*
flat piece of something, with other flat pieces on top and underneath 层
The cake had three layers.
那个蛋糕有三层。

lazy /'la·zy; 'leɪzɪ/ *adj.*
(**lazier, laziest**)
not wanting to work 懒惰的
Sometimes, the children are lazy.
孩子们有时候会懒惰。

lead /lead; li:d/ *v.*
(**leading, led, led**)
take a person or animal somewhere by going in front 带领；领导；率领
The firemen led the people to safety.
消防员带领人们到安全的地方。
opp. 反义词：follow 跟随

leader /'lead·er; 'li:də/ *n.*
chief person 领导人；领袖
He is the country's leader.
他是这个国家的领导人。

leaf /leaf; li:f/ *n.*
(two **leaves**)
one of the green parts of a plant or tree 树叶
The leaves were falling off the trees.
树叶从树上纷纷落下。

leak /leak; li:k/ *n.*
small hole that lets liquid or gas escape 漏水或漏气的洞隙
There was a leak in the glass.
那玻璃杯有裂缝。

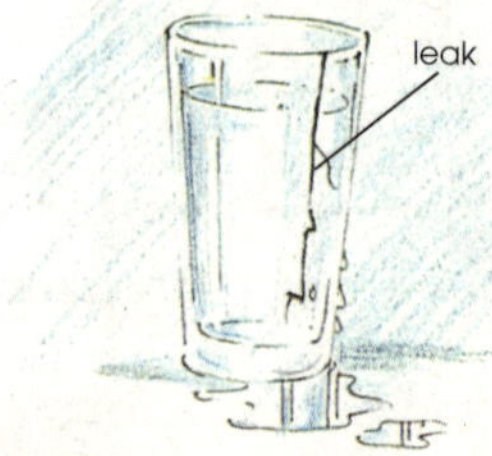

lean /lean; li:n/ *v.*
(**leaning, leant, leant**)
1 bend yourself or itself 倾斜；弯着身子
Don't lean out of the window.
不要把身子伸出窗外。
2 put something against another thing 把（一物）靠在（另一物）上

He leant the ladder against the tree.
他把梯子靠在树上。

leap /leap; li:p/ *v.*
(**leaping, leapt, leapt**)
jump 跳
The man leapt over the wall.
那人跳过了那堵墙。

learn /learn; lɜ:n/ *v.*
(**learning, learnt, learnt**)
begin to know something or how to do something 学习
We are learning English.
我们在学习英语。

least /least; li:st/ *adj.*
smallest amount 最少的
Tom has the least money.
汤姆的钱最少。
at least 至少
He saw at least fifty ships in the harbour.
他看见港内至少有五十艘船。

leather /ˈleath·er; ˈleðə/ *n.*
(**no plural**)
animal skin for making things 皮革
The bag was made of leather.
那袋子是皮革做的。

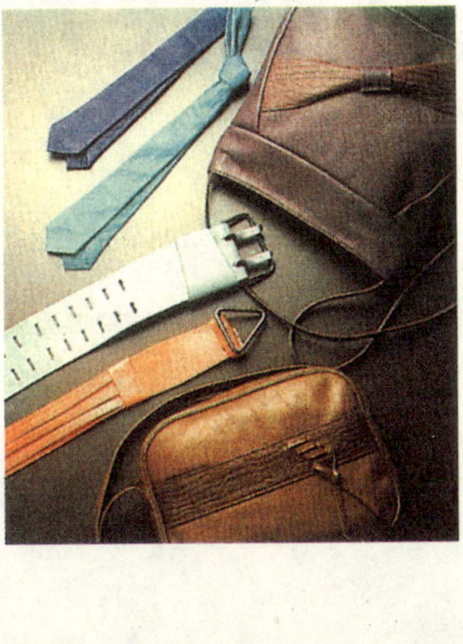

leave /leave; li:v/ *v.*
(**leaving, left, left**)
1 go away from a person, thing or place 离开
They left Hong Kong last week.
他们上星期离开香港。
2 let a person or thing stay where it was or as it was 让；留
Don't leave the door open.
不要让门开着。
leave alone 不要动；不要理
Please leave my things alone.
请不要动我的东西。
leave behind 留下；忘记携带
Susan left her umbrella behind.
苏珊把她的雨伞留下了。
leave out 不包括；省去
Tom was unhappy when he was left out of the football team.
足球队没有让汤姆加入，他很不高兴。

led /led; led/ *v.*
p.t. of **lead** lead 的过去式
The farmer led the horse to the field.
那个农民把马带到田野里去。

left [1] /left; left/ *v.*
p.t. of **leave** leave 的过去式
David left school last year.
戴维去年离开学校。

left [2] /left; left/ *n. adj.*
opposite of right 左
In Hong Kong, cars drive on the left.
在香港，汽车靠左开。
I write with my left hand.
我用左手写字。
opp. 反义词：right 右

leg /leg; leg/ *n.*
part of the body that walks 腿
Mary has long legs.
玛丽的腿很长。

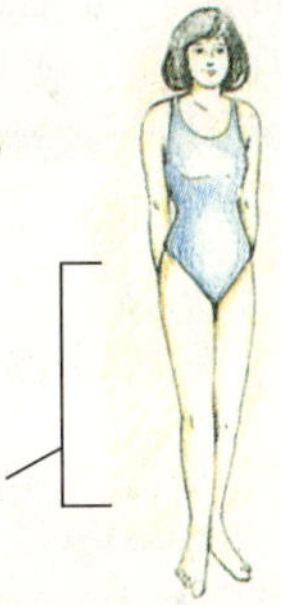

legal /ˈle·gal; ˈli:gl/ *adj.*
allowed by law 合法的
Horse – racing is legal in Hong Kong.
在香港赛马是合法的。
opp. 反义词：illegal 非法的

lemon /ˈlem·on; ˈlemən/ *n.*
yellow fruit that is not sweet 柠檬
Mary likes a slice of lemon in her tea.
玛丽喜欢在茶里放一片柠檬。

lemons

lemonade /lem·on·ˈade; leməˈneɪd/ *n.*
drink made from lemons, sugar and water 柠檬水
Would you like some lemonade?
你要点柠檬水吗?

lend /lend; lend/ *v.*
(**lending, lent, lent**)
give something to someone for a time 借(给别人)
Tom lent his bicycle to Peter.
汤姆把他的自行车借给彼得。
opp. 反义词：borrow (向别人)借

length /length; leŋθ/ *n.*
(no plural)
how far from one end to the other 长度
Do you know the length of the Lion Rock Tunnel?
你知道狮子山隧道的长度吗？

lens /lens; lenz/ *n.*
(two **lenses**)
part of a camera that light goes through 镜头；镜片
Mrs Wang bought a new lens for her camera.
王太太给她的照相机买了个新镜头。

lent /lent; lent/ *v.*
p.t. of **lend** lend 的过去式
Mary lent Susan a pen.
玛丽借了一枝笔给苏珊。

leopard /ˈleop·ard; ˈlepəd/ *n.*
wild animal with spots on its fur 豹
There were leopards in the jungle.
丛林里有豹。

less /less; les/ *adj. adv. n.*
not as much 较少
I have less money than Sam.
我的钱比萨姆少。
In Hong Kong, it rains less in winter.
香港的冬天较少下雨。
The more you talk, the less you hear.
你说得越多，听到的就越少。
opp. 反义词：more 较多
Usage note: Use *fewer* instead of *less* with plural nouns —
There is less noise in the school.
There are fewer children in the school.
用法：复数名词前用 fewer, 不用 less, 例如 There is less noise in the school 及 There are fewer children in the school。

lesson /ˈles·son; ˈlesn/ *n.*
time when you learn something with a teacher 课；一节课
Sam likes science lessons.
萨姆喜欢科学课。

let /let; let/ *v.*
(letting, let, let)
say that someone can have or do something 让；允许
Mrs Chen did not let her children play in the street.
陈太太不让她的孩子们在街上玩。
let go 放开手
Sam let go of the kite and it flew into the air.
萨姆放开风筝，风筝便飞上天空了。
let's, let us 让我们
Let's go to the beach.
让我们到海滩去吧。

letter /ˈlet·ter; ˈletə/ *n.*
1 one of the signs in writing 字母
There are twenty-six letters in the English alphabet.
英语字母表里共有二十六个字母。
2 some writing that one person sends to another 信
Mary wrote a letter to her friend in Canada.
玛丽写信给一个在加拿大的朋友。
capital letter *n.* 大写字母
'A' and 'B' are capital letters.
A 和 B 都是大写字母。
letter-box *n.* 邮箱
Mary posted the letter in a letter-box.
玛丽把信投入邮箱。

small letter *n.* 小写字母
'a' and 'b' are small letters.
a 和 b 都是小写字母。

lettuce /ˈlet·tuce; ˈletɪs/ *n.*
plant with big green leaves that you can eat 莴苣；生菜(方言)
Mary ate a bacon, lettuce and tomato sandwich.
玛丽吃了一客夹熏咸肉、生菜和番茄的三明治。

library /ˈli·bra·ry; ˈlaɪbrərɪ/ *n.*
(two **libraries**)
room or building for books 图书馆
Sam borrowed some books from the library.
萨姆在图书馆借了一些书。

lick /lick; lɪk/ *v.*
touch something with the tongue 舔
Susan licked her ice-cream.
苏珊舔着冰淇淋。

lid /lid; lɪd/ *n.*
cover for a box, pot or other container 盖子

Mrs Chen lifted the lid of the teapot and poured some water in the pot.
陈太太揭开茶壶的盖子，倒了些开水进去。

lie [1] /lie; laɪ/ *n.*
something that is not true
谎言；假话
Susan never tells lies.
苏珊从来不说谎。
opp. 反义词：truth 真话；事实

lie [2] /lie; laɪ/ *v.*
1 (**lying, lay, lain**) rest on a bed, etc. 躺下
The children were lying on the beach.
孩子们躺在海滩上。

2 (**lying, lied, lied**) say something that is not true
说谎
Susan never lies.
苏珊从来不说谎。

life /life; laɪf/ *n.*
(two **lives**)
time from the day you are born to the day you die 生命；一生
He has had a long life.
他的寿命很长。
opp. 反义词：death 死亡

lifeboat *n.* 救生艇
The lifeboat rescued the sailors from the sinking ship.
救生艇从正在下沉的船上救出船员。

lifeguard *n.* 救生员
In the summer, there are lifeguards on Hong Kong beaches.
在夏天，香港的海滩都有救生员。

lift [1] /lift; lɪft/ *v.*
take a person or thing and move it up 提起；举起；抬起
Tom could not lift the heavy suitcase.
汤姆提不起那个沉重的衣箱。

lift [2] /lift; lɪft/ *n.*
machine that takes people and things up and down in a high building 电梯
Susan took the lift to the tenth floor.
苏珊乘电梯到十楼。

light [1] /light; laɪt/ *n.*
1 (**no plural**) what makes us able to see 光
The sun gives us light.
太阳带给我们光。
2 electric thing that makes a place bright so we can see 电灯
Mary switched on the light.
玛丽开了电灯。

light [2] /light; laɪt/ *v.*
(**lighting, lit, lit**)
make something start to burn
点燃；生火
Don't light fires in country parks.
不要在郊野公园生火。

light [3] /light; laɪt/ *adj.*
(**lighter, lightest**)
1 easy to lift or move 轻的
Mary's suitcase was small and light.
玛丽的衣箱又小又轻。
opp. 反义词：heavy 重的
2 with a pale colour 浅色的
Susan has a light blue dress.
苏珊有一件浅蓝色的连衣裙。
opp. 反义词：dark 深色的

lighthouse /ˈlight·house; ˈlaɪthaʊs/ *n.*
light that warns ships that they are near land 灯塔
There is a lighthouse on Waglan Island.
横澜岛上有个灯塔。

lightning /ˈlight·ning; ˈlaɪtnɪŋ/ *n.*
(no plural)
sudden, bright light in the sky in a storm 闪电
There was a flash of lightning.
有一道闪电。

photographed by Roux Aime, JACANA

like [1] /like; laɪk/ *v.*
(liking, liked, liked)
think that a person or thing is good 喜欢
Peter likes ice-cream.
彼得喜欢吃冰淇淋。
opp. 反义词: dislike, hate 不喜欢
would like 想要
Would you like some tea?
你想要茶吗?
opp. 反义词: dislike 不喜欢

like [2] /like; laɪk/ *prep.*
in the same way as 和…一样
I wish I could swim like you.
我希望能游得和你一样好。

like [3] /like; laɪk/ *adj.*
(more like, most like)
same as another 像的; 相似的
Your pen is like mine.
你的笔和我的笔很相似。
opp. 反义词: unlike 不像的; 不相似的

line /line; laɪn/ *n.*
1 mark like this — 线
Sam can't draw a straight line.
萨姆不会画直线。
2 piece of rope, string or wire 线; 绳
Mrs Chen hung her washing on a line.
陈太太把洗净的衣服晾在绳子上。
3 row of people or things 一排; 一行
The children stood in lines.
孩子们分行站好。
4 what a train or tram moves on (火车或电车的)路轨
Don't walk along the railway line.
不要在铁路路轨上走。
line up 排队
The children lined up in the yard.
孩子们在院子里排队。

lines

lion /ˈli·on; ˈlaɪən/ *n.*
big wild animal 狮子
David saw a lion at the zoo.
戴维在动物园见到一头狮子。

lions

lip /lip; lɪp/ *n.*
one of the front parts of your mouth 唇
When you speak your lips move.
讲话时嘴唇就动。
lipstick *n.* 口红; 唇膏(方言)
The girls can't wear lipstick at school.
女孩子在学校不准涂口红。

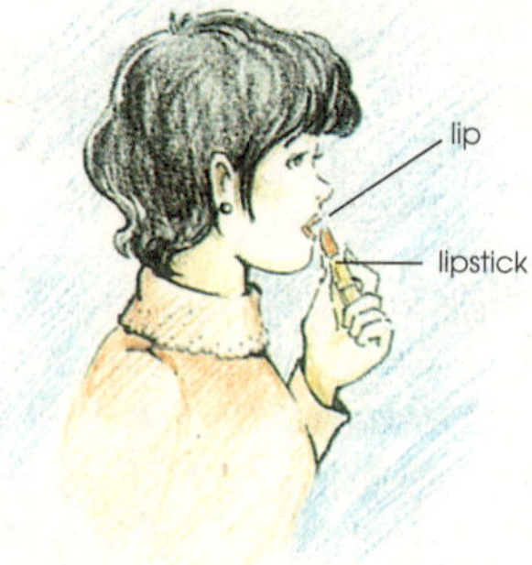

liquid /ˈli·quid; ˈlɪkwɪd/ *n.*
anything that moves like water 液体; 流质
Milk is a liquid.
牛奶是液体。

list /list; lɪst/ *n.*
a lot of names or things that you have written with each thing under another 名单; 表
The teacher made a list of the children's names.
老师把孩子们的名字列成一张名单。

listen /ˈlis·ten; ˈlɪsn/ *v.*
try to hear sounds 听
David was listening to the radio.
戴维在听收音机广播。

lit /lit; lɪt/ *v.*
p.t. of **light** light 的过去式
We lit a fire and had a barbecue.
我们生了个火来烧烤。

itre (l) /ˈli·tre; ˈliːtə/ *n.*
neasure of liquid 升
David bought a litre of milk.
戴维买了一升牛奶。

itter /ˈlit·ter; ˈlɪtə/ *n.*
(**no plural**)
rubbish 垃圾
Don't leave litter on the beach.
不要在海滩上留下垃圾。
itter-bin *n.* 垃圾箱
Please put your rubbish in the litter-bin.
请把垃圾丢在垃圾箱内。

ittle /ˈlit·tle; ˈlɪtl/ *adj.*
(**littler, littlest**)
1 small 矮小
Sarah is a little girl.
莎拉是个小女孩。
2 younger 较年幼的
Anna has a little sister.
安娜有个妹妹。
opp. 反义词: big 大的; 较年长的

a little 一点
Peter only has a little money.
彼得只有一点钱。

live [1] /live; laɪv/ *adj.*
alive; living 活着的
There was a live mouse in the house.
房子里有一只活老鼠。
opp. 反义词: dead 死去的

live [2] /live; lɪv/ *v.*
(**living, lived, lived**)
1 be alive 生存; 活着
The old man lived until he was a hundred.
那老人一直活到一百岁。
opp. 反义词: die 死亡
2 have your home 居住
Mary lives in Kowloon.
玛丽住在九龙。
living-room *n.* 起居室; 客厅
Our TV is in the living-room.
我家的电视机放在客厅。

living /ˈli·ving; ˈlɪvɪŋ/ *adj.*
alive 生存的; 活着的
There are millions of living things in the sea.
海里有数以百万计的生物。
opp. 反义词: dead 死去的

lizard /ˈliz·ard; ˈlɪzəd/ *n.*
animal with a skin like a snake and four legs 蜥蜴; 四脚蛇
A lizard ran across the wall.
一条蜥蜴爬过那堵墙。

load [1] /load; ləud/ *n.*
something that is carried 载着的货物
The truck had a heavy load.
那辆货车满载着货物。

load [2] /load; ləud/ *v.*
put things onto a truck, etc. 装货
They loaded the furniture onto a truck.
他们把家具装上货车。

loaf /loaf; ləuf/ *n.*
(two **loaves**)
big piece of bread 一条面包
Susan bought a loaf of bread.
苏珊买了一条面包。

lobster /ˈlob·ster; ˈlɒbstə/ *n.*
sea animal with big claws 龙虾
The fisherman was catching lobsters.
渔民正在捕龙虾。

local /'lo·cal; 'ləukl/ *adj.*
near a place; near where you live 当地的；本地的
The local schools are very good.
当地的学校都很好。

lock [1] /lock; lɒk/ *n.*
thing that keeps a door, a lid, etc. closed 锁
Sam put the key in the lock.
萨姆把钥匙插入锁中。

lock [2] /lock; lɒk/ *v.*
close with a key 锁上
Sam locked the door.
萨姆锁上了门。
opp. 反义词：unlock 把锁打开

log /log; lɒg/ *n.*
piece of a tree 一段木头
Sam put a log on the fire.
萨姆把一段木头放进炉火里。

lonely /'lone·ly; 'ləunlɪ/ *adj.*
(lonelier, loneliest)
sad because you are alone; far from other people 寂寞的；孤独的；偏僻的
The lighthouse is in a lonely place.
那灯塔建在偏僻的地方。

long [1] /long; lɒŋ/ *adj.*
(longer, longest)
1 how far from one end to the other 长
The tunnel is a kilometre long.
隧道有一千米长。
2 far from one end to the other 长的
Susan has long hair.
苏珊有长长的头发。

3 going on for a lot of time 长时间的；很久的
It was a long match.
这场比赛进行了很久。
opp. 反义词：short 短的

long [2] /long; lɒŋ/ *adv.*
going on for a lot of time
很久
Have you been waiting long?
你等了很久吗？
as long as 只要；条件是
You can borrow my bicycle as long as you don't break it.
你可以借用我的自行车，条件是你不可撞坏它。
no longer 不再
She no longer lives in Hong Kong.
她不再住在香港了。

long jump /long jump; lɒŋ dʒʌmp/ *n.*
competition in which people try to jump the farthest 跳远
Peter is good at the long jump.
彼得擅长跳远。

look /look; luk/ *v.*
1 try to see; keep your eyes on someone or something 看
Mrs Li is looking at dresses.
李太太在看连衣裙。
2 seem 看来
Mrs Li looks happy.
李太太看来很愉快。
look after 照顾
Susan looks after her little brother.
苏珊照顾她的小弟弟。
look for 寻找
Mrs Li is looking for a new dress.
李太太在找一件新连衣裙。
look forward to 盼望；期待
We look forward to holidays.
我们盼望假日的来临。
look like 像；看来像是
Mary looks like her mother.
玛丽长得像她妈妈。
look out 小心
Look out! A car is coming.
小心！一辆汽车正驶过来。
look up 查(字典等的资料)
He looked up the word in a dictionary.
他查词典找那个词。

loose /loose; lu:s/ *adj.*
(looser, loosest)
not tied or fitting very closely
松的；阔大的
This dress is too loose.
这件连衣裙太宽松了。
opp. 反义词：tight 紧的；窄的
loosely *adv.* 宽松地
She tied the bandage loosely.
她把绷带裹得很松。
loosen *v.* 松开；解开
He tried to loosen the knot.
他试着把结解开。
Usage note: Note the difference between *loose* meaning *not tight* and *loose*

meaning *not tied up* — *Mary was wearing a loose dress. The dog was loose in the garden.*
用法：注意loose有两个意思，第一个指宽松，例如 Mary was wearing a loose dress; 第二个指没有拴好，例如 The dog was loose in the garden。

lorry /ˈlor·ry; ˈlɒrɪ/ *n.*
(two **lorries**)
vehicle that carries heavy loads 货车
The lorry had a load of sand.
那货车装载沙子。

lose /lose; lu:z/ *v.*
(**losing, lost, lost**)
1 not being able to find something 遗失；失去
Susan lost her purse.
苏珊遗失了钱包。
opp. 反义词：find 找到
2 not win a game 输
The school football team lost 2:0.
学校足球队以零比二输了。
opp. 反义词：win 赢

lost /lost; lɒst/ *adj.*
not sure where you are 迷路的
Mary took the lost child to the police.
玛丽带那迷路的小孩到警署去。
get lost 迷路
Sam got lost in Kowloon.
萨姆在九龙迷了路。

lot /lot; lɒt/ *n.*
much; many 很多
Hong Kong uses a lot of water.
香港用水很多。
There were a lot of people on the ferry.
渡轮上人很多。
lots of 很多
Mrs Li has lots of money.
李太太有很多钱。
Usage note: *A lot* is usually followed by *of* — *I have a lot of books.*
用法：a lot 通常与 of 连用，例如 I have a lot of books。

loud /loud; laʊd/ *adj.*
(**louder, loudest**)
with a lot of noise 声音很大的；很响的
He heard a loud bang.
他听到一声巨响。
opp. 反义词：quiet 寂静的

loudly *adv.* 大声地；响亮地
The children were singing loudly.
孩子们大声地唱着歌。

loudspeaker /loud·ˈspeak·er; laʊdˈspi:kə/ *n.*
thing for making sounds louder 扬声器
The radio has two loudspeakers.
这台收音机有两个扬声器。

lounge /lounge; laʊndʒ/ *n.*
room in a house where you sit 休息室
They were watching TV in the lounge.
他们正在休息室看电视。

love [1] /love; lʌv/ *n.*
strong liking of a person or thing 爱；爱好
Mary has a great love of ice-cream.
玛丽非常爱吃冰淇淋。

love [2] /love; lʌv/ *v.*
(**loving, loved, loved**)
like someone or something very much 爱；喜爱
Mary loves ice-cream.
玛丽爱吃冰淇淋。
opp. 反义词：hate 憎恨；很不喜欢

lovely /ˈlove·ly; ˈlʌvlɪ/ *adj.*
(**lovelier, loveliest**)
beautiful; pretty 可爱的；美丽的
She's a lovely child.
她是个可爱的孩子。
opp. 反义词：ugly 丑陋的

low /low; ləʊ/ *adj.*
(**lower, lowest**)
not going up a long way; not tall 低的；矮的
The buildings round the airport are low.
机场附近都是矮房子。
opp. 反义词：high 高的

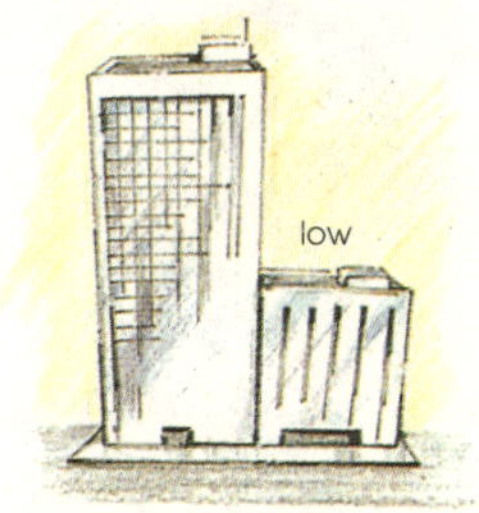

lower *adj.* 较低的
The lower deck of the ferry is cheaper.
渡轮下层的船费便宜些。

luck /luck; lʌk/ *n.*
(no plural)
what happens to someone or something 运气；幸运
She wished her friend good luck in the exam.
她祝朋友好运，考试成功。

lucky /'luck·y; 'lʌkɪ/ *adj.*
(luckier, luckiest)
1 having good luck 幸运的；运气好的
Sam was lucky. He won a prize.
萨姆很幸运，得了奖。
2 bringing good luck 带来好运的
Baoling's lucky number is eight.
宝玲的幸运数字是八。
opp. 反义词：unlucky 不幸的；带来恶运的
luckily *adv.* 幸而；幸运地
Luckily, the falling stone missed Tom.
那块掉下来的石头幸而没有打中汤姆。
lucky money *n.* 红包钱；利是钱（方言）
Peter got lots of lucky money at New Year.
彼得过新年时得到许多红包钱。

luggage /'lug·gage; 'lʌgɪdʒ/ *n.*
bags and suitcases that you carry on a journey 行李
Mr Chen put his luggage in the taxi.
陈先生把行李放入出租汽车里。

luggage

lump /lump; lʌmp/ *n.*
small, hard piece of something 一块；一团
Sarah puts two lumps of sugar in her coffee.
萨拉在咖啡里放进两块方糖。

lunch /lunch; lʌntʃ/ *n.*
(two **lunches**)
meal you eat in the middle of the day 午餐
Sam had some noodles for lunch.
萨姆午餐吃了些面条。
lunch-box *n.* 午餐饭盒
Baoling takes a lunch-box to school.
宝玲带午餐饭盒去学校。
lunchtime *n.* 午餐时间
Peter and David play chess at lunchtime.
彼得和戴维在午餐时间下棋。

lung /lung; lʌŋ/ *n.*
part inside the body that holds the air you breathe 肺
Smoking is bad for your lungs.
吸烟对肺有害。

lychee /'ly·chee; 'laɪtʃi:/ *n.*
small, brown fruit 荔枝
Lychees are Peter's favourite fruit.
荔枝是彼得最爱吃的水果。

lychees

lying /'ly·ing; 'laɪɪŋ/ *v.*
pres.p. of **lie** lie 的现在分词
The children were lying on the beach.
孩子们躺在海滩上。

Mm

machine /ma·'chine; mə'ʃi:n/ *n.*
thing with many parts that move together to do work 机器
We have machines to do many different jobs.
我们用机器来做许多不同的工作。

machines

nad /mad; mæd/ *adj.* (madder, maddest)

silly 疯狂的；愚蠢的
You are mad to go out in a typhoon.
刮台风时你还外出，你疯啦。

2 angry 愤怒的
David was mad when his bicycle was stolen.
戴维的自行车给人偷了，他很愤怒。

nadam /ˈmad·am; ˈmædəm/ *n.*
itle for a lady that you espect 夫人；女士（对妇女的尊称）
Can I help you, madam?
夫人，我能帮助你吗？

nade /made; meɪd/ *v.*
ɔ.t. of **make** make 的过去式
Mary made a cake.
玛丽做了一个蛋糕。

nagazine /mag·a·ˈzine; nægəˈziːn/ *n.*
ɔook with a paper cover that comes every week, month, etc. 杂志；期刊
Susan likes reading magazines.
苏珊喜欢看杂志。

magic [1] /ˈmag·ic; ˈmædʒɪk/ *n.*
(no plural)
strange, wonderful power; clever tricks to surprise people 魔法；巫术；魔术
Mr Li does magic.
李先生会变魔术。

magic [2] /ˈmag·ic; ˈmædʒɪk/ *adj.*
having magic 魔法的；魔术的
Mr Li has a magic wand.
李先生有一根魔杖。

magician /ma·ˈgi·cian; məˈdʒɪʃn/ *n.*
someone who does magic 术士；魔术师
Mr Li is a magician.
李先生是魔术师。

magnet /ˈmag·net; ˈmægnɪt/ *n.*
piece of iron that pulls other pieces of iron towards it 磁铁
Anna picked up the pins with a magnet.
安娜用磁铁捡起一些大头针。

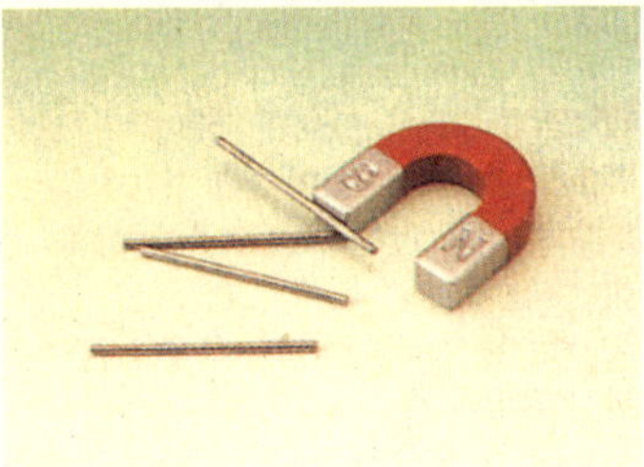

magnify /ˈmag·ni·fy; ˈmægnɪfaɪ/ *v.*
(magnifying, magnified, magnified)
make something look bigger 放大
The lens magnified the writing.
那镜片把字迹放大了。

magnifying glass *n.* 放大镜
The old man uses a magnifying glass to read the newspaper.
那个老人用放大镜来看报纸。

mahjong /mah·ˈjong; mɑːˈdʒɒŋ/ *n.*
(no plural)
game where four people play with small tiles 麻将牌
Mr Chen likes playing mahjong.
陈先生喜欢玩麻将。

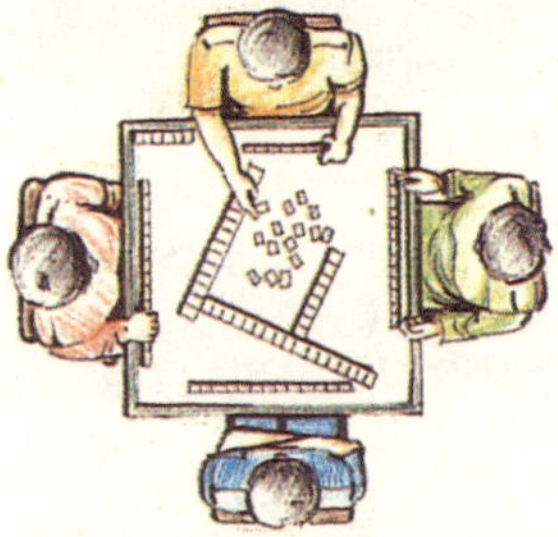

maid /maid; meɪd/ *n.*
woman who works in the house for money 女仆；保姆
The Chen family have a maid.
陈家有一个保姆。

mail /mail; meɪl/ *n.*
(no plural)
letters or parcels 邮件
The postman delivered the mail.
邮递员递送邮件。

main /main; meɪn/ *adj.*
chief; most important 主要的
Guangzhou is one of China's main ports.
广州是中国的主要港口之一。

mainland /'main·land; 'meɪnlænd/ *n.*
(**no plural**)
chief part of a country, not its islands 大陆
David had a holiday on the mainland of China.
戴维在中国大陆度假。

mainly /'main·ly; 'meɪnlɪ/ *adv.*
mostly; usually 主要地；大部分
The population of Hong Kong is mainly Chinese.
香港人口大部分是中国人。

majesty /'ma·jes·ty; 'mædʒəstɪ/ *n.*
title for a royal person 陛下
Her Majesty the Queen will visit the country.
女王陛下将会访问该国。

major /'ma·jor; 'meɪdʒə/ *adj.*
important 重要的
Hong Kong is a major port.
香港是个重要港口。

make /make; meɪk/ *v.*
(**making, made, made**)
1 put parts together so that you have a new thing
制造；做
Sam made a cage for his rabbit.
萨姆给他的兔子做了个笼子。
2 cause a sound, smell, feeling, etc. 发出；引起；使得
The children were making a noise.
孩子们发出吵闹的声音。
3 say or do something so that someone will do what you want 要；使
Mrs Chen made Peter get up for school.
陈太太要彼得起床上学去。
4 equal in mathematics(数学)等于
Two and two make four.
二加二等于四。

made of 用…做
The table is made of wood.
这桌子是木头做的。

make friends 交朋友
The children made friends with their new classmate.
孩子们和新同学交朋友。

make something up 编造；捏造
Susan made up a good story.
苏珊编造了一个很好的故事。

make sure 确定；肯定
Please make sure that the door is locked.
请确定门已上锁。

make-up /'make·up; 'meɪkʌp/ *n.*
(**no plural**)
special powder and paint for the skin 化妆品
The girls can't wear make-up to school.
女孩子上学不能化妆。

male /male; meɪl/ *adj. n.*
boy or man; animal that cannot have baby animals
男性；雄性
A male ox is called a bull.
雄性的牛称为公牛。
There were more males than females in the room.
房间里的男人比女人多。
opp. 反义词：female 女性；雌性

mammal /'mam·mal; 'mæml/ *n.*
animal that has babies and feeds them on milk 哺乳动物
Whales are mammals.
鲸鱼是哺乳动物。

man /man; mæn/ *n.*
(two **men**)
male person who is not a child 男人
The men were working on the building.
那些男人正在盖房子。
Usage note: The word *Man* with a capital 'm' can also mean *all men and women* — *Man is more intelligent than animals.*
用法： 如Man用大写M，可指全人类，例如Man is more intelligent than animals。

manage /'man·age; 'mænɪdʒ/ *v.*
(**managing, managed, managed**)
be able to do something difficult 成功；努力办到
Tom managed to finish the homework.
汤姆努力做完家庭作业。

manager /'man·a·ger; 'mænɪdʒə/ *n.*
someone in charge of a business 经理
The hotel has a good manager.
这家酒店有一个好经理。

mango /'man·go; 'mæŋgəʊ/ *n.*
(two **mangoes**)
fruit with a big stone inside
芒果

Sam likes mangoes.
萨姆喜欢吃芒果。

mangoes

manners /'man·ners; 'mænəz/ *n.*
way you behave with other people 礼貌
It is bad manners to talk with your mouth full.
满嘴食物来说话是没有礼貌的。

many [1] /'man·y; 'menɪ/ *adj.*
a lot of 很多的
There are many people in the street.
街上的人很多。

many [2] /'man·y; 'menɪ/ *pron.*
many persons or things 很多（人或物）
I've got some sweets but I haven't got many.
我有些糖果，但不多。
opp. 反义词: few 很少
Usage note: Use *many* with nouns you can count — *There are many children in the school.*
用法：many 用在可数名词前面，例如 There are many children in the school。

map /map; mæp/ *n.*
flat drawing of the world, a country or a town 地图
The children drew a map.
孩子们画了一张地图。

map

marble /'mar·ble; 'mɑ:bl/ *n.*
1 **(no plural)** hard stone for buildings, statues, etc. 大理石
The statue was made of marble.
这雕像是用大理石做的。
2 small glass ball of game （小孩玩的）玻璃弹珠
Anna likes to play with marbles.
安娜喜欢玩弹珠。

March [1] /March; mɑ:tʃ/ *n.*
third month of the year 三月
It often rains in March.
三月份常常下雨。

march [2] /march; mɑ:tʃ/ *v.*
walk like soldiers 齐步前进；行军
The soldiers marched through the town.
士兵齐步前进，穿过这个城镇。

margarine /mar·gar·'ine; mɑ:dʒə'ri:n/ *n.*
(no plural)
soft, oil food you put on bread or use in cooking 人造黄油；人造牛油（方言）
Peter put some margarine and jam on his bread.
彼得在面包上抹人造黄油和果酱。

margin /'mar·gin; 'mɑ:dʒɪn/ *n.*
empty space at the edge of a page 页边空白
Leave a margin at the left of the page in your exercise book.
在练习本每页的左边留空白。

mark [1] /mark; mɑ:k/ *n.*
1 spot or scratch in the wrong place 污点；污渍；痕迹
Mary had a black mark on her dress.
玛丽的连衣裙上有一处黑色的污渍。
2 score to show how good your school work is 成绩；分数
Peter always gets good marks in maths.
彼得数学常得高分。

mark [2] /mark; mɑ:k/ *v.*
put marks on school work to show how good it is 评分
The teacher was marking exercise books.
老师在批阅练习簿。

market /'mar·ket; 'mɑ:kɪt/ *n.*
place where people go to buy and sell things 市场
Mrs Chen goes to the market every morning.
陈太太每天早上去市场。

married /ˈmar·ried; ˈmærɪd/ *adj.*
having a husband or wife 已婚的
Mr Chen is married.
陈先生已婚。
opp. 反义词：single 未婚的；单身的

marry /ˈmar·ry; ˈmærɪ/ *v.*
(marrying, married, married)
take someone as a husband or wife 结婚
Mr Chen married in a church.
陈先生在教堂结婚。
get married 结婚
Mr Chen got married last year.
陈先生去年结了婚。

marvellous /ˈmar·vel·lous; ˈmɑːvələs/ *adj.*
(more marvellous, most marvellous)
very good 非常好的
The Wangs have a marvellous flat.
王家有一套非常好的公寓房。

mask /mask; mɑːsk/ *n.*
cover for the face 面罩；面具
The actor wore a mask.
那个演员戴了面具。

mast /mast; mɑːst/ *n.*
tall, straight piece of wood or metal on a boat, which holds the sails, etc. （船的）桅杆
The boat has a tall mast.
那船的桅杆很高。

master /ˈmas·ter; ˈmɑːstə/ *n.*
man who is in charge; teacher 主管人；教师
The master came into the classroom.
教师走进教室。

mat /mat; mæt/ *n.*
cover for the floor （放在地上的）席；垫
Peter wiped his feet on the mat.
彼得在垫上把鞋底擦干净。

match [1] /match; mætʃ/ *n.*
(two **matches**)
1 small stick that can make fire 火柴
Don't play with matches.
不要玩火柴。

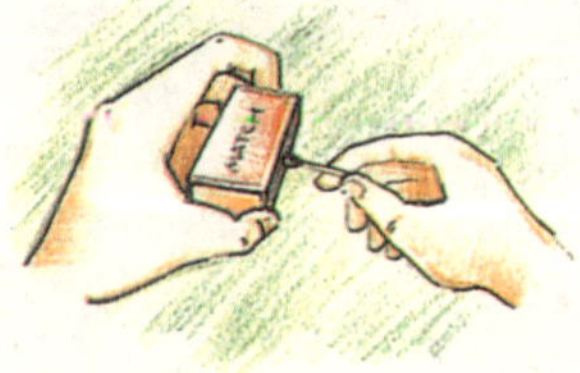

2 game 比赛
We went to the football match.
我们去看足球比赛

match [2] /match; mætʃ/ *v.*
same as, in some way 相配
Mary's blouse matches her skirt.
玛丽的短上衣跟裙子很相配。

material /ma·ˈte·ri·al; məˈtɪərɪəl/ *n.*
1 cloth 布料
Baoling bought some material to make a dress.
宝玲买了些布料来做连衣裙。
2 what you use to make things 材料
Stone is a very hard material.
石头是很硬的材料。

mathematics, maths /math·e·ˈmat·ics, maths; mæθəˈmætɪks, mæθs/ *n.*
(no plural)
learning about numbers, sizes and shapes 数学
David is good at maths.
戴维的数学很好。

matter [1] /ˈmat·ter; ˈmætə/ *n.*
thing you talk about or do 事情
School work is an important matter.
学业是重要的事情。
what's the matter? 什么事?
What's the matter with Tom?
汤姆有什么困难?

matter [2] /ˈmat·ter; ˈmætə/ *v.*
be important 重要；要紧
It doesn't matter if you are late.
你就是迟到也不要紧。

mattress /ˈmat·tress; ˈmætrɪs/ *n.*
(two **mattresses**)
soft part of a bed under you 床垫

Peter has a soft mattress on his bed.
彼得的床上有一张软垫。

May [1] /May; meɪ/ *n.*
fifth month of the year 五月
May is usually a warm month.
五月通常是个暖和的月份。

may [2] /may; meɪ/ *v.*
(might)
1 can; be allowed to do something 可以；得到许可
You may go out now.
你现在可以走了。
2 word that shows what perhaps will happen 可能
We may go to Canada next year.
明年我们可能会去加拿大。

maybe /'may·be; 'meɪbi:/ *adv.*
perhaps; it is possible 也许
Maybe we'll go to Shanghai next year.
也许我们明年会去上海。

me /me; mi:/ *pron.*
word for myself 我
My father gave me a bicycle for my birthday.
我生日时，爸爸送给我一辆自行车。

meal /meal; mi:l/ *n.*
food that you eat at one time 一顿饭；一餐
We had a good meal in the restaurant.
我们在饭店里吃了一顿很好的饭。

mean /mean; mi:n/ *v.*
(meaning,meant,meant)
1 say something in different words 有…的意思；指
What does this word mean?
这个词是什么意思?
2 show something 表示
Dark clouds mean that it is going to rain.
乌云表示将要下雨。
3 plan to do something 打算
I mean to go to Canada next year.
我打算明年去加拿大。

meaning /'mean·ing; 'mi:nɪŋ/ *n.*
what something is in other words 意思；意义
What is the meaning of this word?
这个词是什么意思?

measles /'mea·sles; 'mi:zlz/ *n.*
(no plural)
disease 麻疹
Peter was ill with measles.
彼得患了麻疹。

measure /'meas·ure; 'meʒə/ *v.*
(measuring, measured, measured)
find out how big something is 度量
Mr Wang measured the room.
王先生度量那个房间的大小。
measurements *n.* 大小；尺寸
Mr Wang took the measurements of the room.
王先生度量那个房间的大小。

meat /meat; mi:t/ *n.*
(no plural)
flesh of an animal which we eat 肉
Beef is Peter's favourite meat.
牛肉是彼得最爱吃的肉类。

mechanic /me·'chan·ic; mɪ'kænɪk/ *n.*
someone who works with machines 技工
The mechanic repaired the car.
那个技工修理汽车。

medal /'med·al; 'medl/ *n.*
piece of metal like a coin, given as a prize 奖章；勋章
The fireman won a medal for rescuing the children.
那位消防员因救出一些小孩而获得奖章。

medicine /'med·i·cine; 'medsn/ *n.*
tablets or special drinks that make you better when you are ill 药物
If you don't take your medicine you won't get better.
如果你不吃药，你的病就不会好。

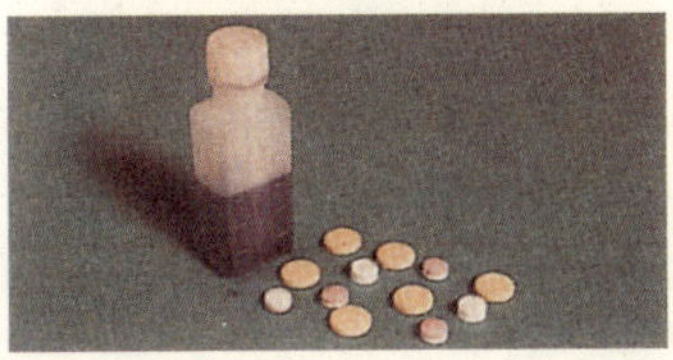

medium /ˈme·dium; ˈmi:dɪəm/ *adj.*
not big and not small 中等的
Susan is of medium height.
苏珊中等身材。

meet /meet; mi:t/ *v.*
(**meeting, met, met**)
come to another person; come together 遇见
Peter met David in the park.
彼得在公园里遇见戴维。

meeting /ˈmeet·ing; ˈmi:tɪŋ/ *n.*
time when people come together 会议；会面
There was a parents' meeting at the school.
学校举行家长会议。

melon /ˈmel·on; ˈmelən/ *n.*
big, round fruit 瓜
David cut the melon into slices.
戴维把瓜切成一片片。

melons

melt /melt; melt/ *v.*
1 become liquid because it is warmer 融化
The ice melted in the sun.
冰在太阳下融化了。
2 make into a liquid by heating it 加热(使某物)融化
Susan melted the butter in a pan.
苏珊在煎锅内把黄油融解。
opp. 反义词：freeze 冻结

member /ˈmem·ber; ˈmembə/ *n.*
someone in a group or team 成员；会员
Peter is a member of the school orchestra.
彼得是学校乐队的成员。

memory /ˈmem·o·ry; ˈmemərɪ/ *n.*
(two **memories**)
1 person's power to remember things 记忆力
Sam is good at history because he has a good memory.
萨姆的历史成绩很好，因为他记忆力强。
2 things you remember 回忆
Mary has happy memories of her holiday in China.
那次在中国度过的假期给玛丽留下愉快的回忆。

men /men; men/ *n.*
more than one man man 的复数
There are eleven men in a football team.
一支足球队共有十一个人。

mend /mend; mend/ *v.*
make something good again 修补
Sam mended his kite.
萨姆修补他的风筝。
syn. 同义词：repair, fix
opp. 反义词：break 破坏

menu /ˈmen·u; ˈmenju:/ *n.*
list of food in a café, restaurant, etc. 菜单
Could I have a menu, please?
请给我菜单好吗？

merchant /ˈmer·chant; ˈmɜ:tʃənt/ *n.*
someone who buys and sells things 商人
Mr Li is a rice merchant.
李先生是个米商。

mermaid /ˈmer·maid; ˈmɜ:meɪd/ *n.*
person in stories who is half woman and half fish (传说中的)美人鱼

The sailor told stories about mermaids.
那个水手讲美人鱼的故事。

merry /ˈmer·ry; ˈmerɪ/ *adj.*
(merrier, merriest)
very happy 欢乐的；愉快的
Peter wished everyone 'Merry Christmas'.
彼得祝贺每一个人"圣诞快乐"。

merry-go-round
/ˈmer·ry·go·round; ˈmerɪgəuraund/ *n.*
big, round machine where you can ride at a fair （游乐场的）旋转木马
The children were riding on the merry-go-round.
孩子们正在玩旋转木马。
syn. 同义词：roundabout

mess /mess; mes/ *n.*
(no plural)
many untidy, dirty things in the wrong place 混乱；肮脏
There was a mess in the classroom.
教室里乱七八糟。
messy *adj.* 混乱的；肮脏的
Sam's desk is very messy.
萨姆的书桌很乱。

message /ˈmes·sage; ˈmesɪdʒ/ *n.*
words that you send to someone 消息；讯息
The spaceship sent a message back to earth.
太空船向地球传递讯息。

messenger /ˈmes·sen·ger; ˈmesɪndʒə/ *n.*
someone who brings a message or package 送信人
The messenger delivered the parcel.
送信人递送包裹。

met /met; met/ *v.*
p.t. of **meet** meet 的过去式
Peter met David in front of the school.
彼得在学校前面遇见戴维。

metal /ˈmet·al; ˈmetl/ *n.*
iron, silver, gold, etc. 金属
Gold is a valuable metal.
金是贵重金属。

method /ˈmeth·od; ˈmeθəd/ *n.*
way of doing something 方法
Peter learnt a new method of doing the sums.
彼得学会了一个做算术题的新方法。

metre (m) /ˈme·tre; ˈmiːtə/ *n.*
measure of length 米
Sam lives fifty metres from his school.
萨姆住的地方离学校有五十米。

mice /mice; maɪs/ *n.*
more than one mouse
mouse 的复数
There were some mice in the house.
房子里有些老鼠。

microphone
/ˈmi·cro·phone; ˈmaɪkrəfəun/ *n.*
thing that makes sounds louder 话筒；麦克风
The singer used a microphone.
那个歌星使用话筒。

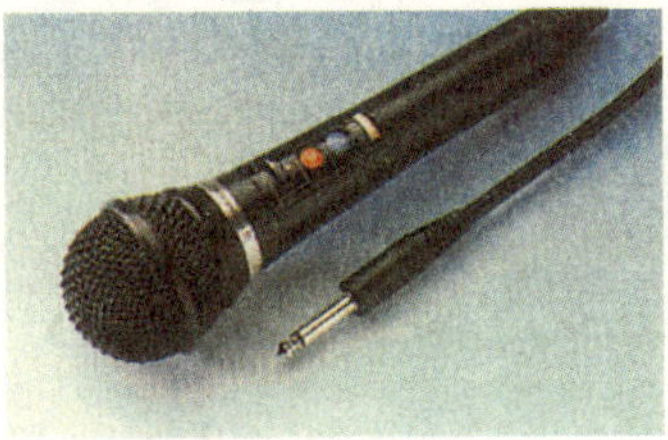

microscope
/ˈmi·cro·scope; ˈmaɪkrəskəup/ *n.*
thing that makes very small things look bigger 显微镜
The scientist looked through the microscope.
那科学家透过显微镜来观察。

microwave oven
/ˈmi·cro·wave ˈoven; ˈmaɪkrəweɪv ˈʌvn/ *n.*
electric oven that heats things very quickly 微波炉
Mrs Qian has a microwave oven.
钱太太有一台微波炉。

Mid-Autumn Festival
/Mid·ˈAu·tumn ˈFes·ti·val; mɪdˈɔːtəm ˈfestɪvl/ *n.*
Chinese festival 中秋节
We eat mooncakes during the Mid-Autumn Festival.
中秋节时我们吃月饼。

midday /mid·'day; mɪd'deɪ/ *n.*
(**no plural**)
12 o'clock in the day 中午
Peter has his lunch at midday.
彼得中午吃午饭。
syn. 同义词: noon

middle [1] /'mid·dle; 'mɪdl/ *n.*
(**no plural**)
centre 中间
There is a big stone in the middle of a mango.
芒果中间有一颗大核。

middle [2] /'mid·dle; 'mɪdl/ *adj.*
coming after the beginning and before the end 中间的
Baoling has a ring on her middle finger.
宝玲的中指上戴了一枚戒指。

middle

midnight /'mid·night; 'mɪdnaɪt/ *n.*
(**no plural**)
12 o'clock at night 午夜
Mr Chen goes to bed at midnight.
陈先生午夜才睡觉。

might /might; maɪt/ *v.*
p.t. of **may** may 的过去式
Take your umbrella. It might rain.
出门带雨伞，也许会下雨。

mighty /'migh·ty; 'maɪtɪ/ *adj.*
(**mightier, mightiest**)
very strong; powerful 强大的
It is a mighty country.
这是个强大的国家。

mile /mile; maɪl/ *n.*
measure of distance 英里
The river is a hundred miles long.
这条河长一百英里。

milk /milk; mɪlk/ *n.*
(**no plural**)
white liquid we get from cows 牛奶
David drank a glass of milk.
戴维喝了一杯牛奶。

millilitre (ml)
/'mil·li·li·tre; 'mɪlɪli:tə/ *n.*
measure of liquid 毫升
There are a thousand millilitres in a litre.
一升有一千毫升。

millimetre (mm)
/'mil·li·me·tre; 'mɪlɪmi:tə/ *n.*
measure of length 毫米
There are a thousand millimetres in a metre.
一米有一千毫米。

million (1 000 000)
/'mil·lion; 'mɪljən/ *n. adj.*
number 1 000 000 一百万
Sixty million people live in Britain.
英国有六千万人。

millionth (1 000 000th)
n. adj. 第一百万
The millionth car was given to the customer.
第一百万辆汽车送给了顾客。

millionaire /mil·li·on·'aire; mɪljə'neə/ *n.*
person with a million dollars or more 百万富翁
There are many millionaires in Hong Kong.
香港有很多百万富翁。

mind [1] /mind; maɪnd/ *v.*
1 take care of someone or something 照顾；看管
Anna minds the baby when her mother is out.
安娜的母亲不在家时，安娜就照顾婴儿。
2 have a feeling against something 介意；在乎
Open the window if you want to -- I don't mind.
如你想打开窗子，请随便 —— 我不介意。

do you mind? 你介意吗?
Do you mind if I open the window?
如果我打开窗子，你介意吗?

never mind 不要紧
Never mind the rain. You have an umbrella.
下雨不要紧，你有雨伞。

mind [2] /mind; maɪnd/ *n.*
part of you that thinks 思想；脑筋；头脑
Peter has a very quick mind.
彼得思维敏捷。

make up your mind 决心；决定
Make up your mind. Do you want rice or noodles?
你决定吧。你要吃饭还是要吃面条?

mine [1] /mine; maɪn/ *pron.*
thing that belongs to me 我的

This book is mine.
这本书是我的。

mine [2] /mine; maɪn/ *n.*
big hole in the ground where people find coal, metals, etc. 矿
Mr Chen works in a coal mine.
陈先生在煤矿工作。
miner *n.* 矿工
Mr Chen is a miner.
陈先生是个矿工。

miners

minibus /ˈmin·i·bus; ˈmɪnɪbʌs/ *n.*
(two **minibuses**)
small bus for a few people only 小型公共汽车；小巴(方言)
Sam took a minibus to the railway station.
萨姆乘小型公共汽车去火车站。

minus /ˈmi·nus; ˈmaɪnəs/ *prep.*
take away; sign (–) in arithmetic for subtracting numbers 减
Three minus two is one (3 – 2 = 1).
三减二等于一。

minute /ˈmin·ute; ˈmɪnɪt/ *n.*
measure of time 分钟
There are sixty minutes in an hour.
一小时有六十分钟。
in a minute 立刻；马上
I'll be ready in a minute.
我马上就准备好。
wait a minute 等一会
Wait a minute. You have taken my pen.
等一会，你拿走我的笔啦。

mirror /ˈmir·ror; ˈmɪrə/ *n.*
piece of glass where you can see yourself 镜子
Anna combed her hair in the mirror.
安娜对着镜子梳头。

mirror

mischief /ˈmis·chief; ˈmɪstʃɪf/ *n.*
(**no plural**)
trouble 胡闹；恶作剧
Tom is always up to mischief.
汤姆总是在胡闹。
mischievous *adj.* 顽皮的；淘气的
Tom is a mischievous boy.
汤姆是个顽皮的男孩。

Miss [1] /Miss; mɪs/
title for a girl or woman who is not married 小姐
Miss Li is our teacher.
李小姐是我们的老师。

miss [2] /miss; mɪs/ *v.*
1 not hit, catch, or see what is coming to you 未打中；未捉到；错过
Tom missed the bus.
汤姆没赶上公共汽车。
2 feel sad about someone who has gone away 想念；怀念
When Peter was in Canada, he missed his friends.
彼得在加拿大的时候，很想念他的朋友。

miss 2

missing /ˈmis·sing; ˈmɪsɪŋ/ *adj.*
that you cannot find 找不到的；失去的
Susan's book was missing from her bag.
苏珊袋子里的一本书不见了。

misspell /mis·ˈspell; mɪsˈspel/ *v.*
spell wrongly (英语单词)误拼；拼错
David misspells a lot of words.
戴维拼错许多单词。

mist /mist; mɪst/ *n.*
sort of thin cloud near the ground 雾
There was a mist over the mountains.
山上有雾。
misty *adj.* 有雾的
The mountains were misty.
山上有雾。

mistake /mis·ˈtake; mɪˈsteɪk/ *n.*
something that is not correct 错误
There were a lot of mistakes in Sam's homework.
萨姆的家庭作业有许多错误。
by mistake 错误地
Mary took the wrong umbrella by mistake.
玛丽拿错了别人的雨伞。

mistress /ˈmis·tress; ˈmɪstrɪs/ *n.*
(two **mistresses**)
woman who is in charge; female teacher 女主人；女教师
The mistress left the classroom.
那位女教师离开教室。

mix /mix; mɪks/ *v.*
put different things together 混在一起；混合
Peter mixed eggs and milk to make an omelette.
彼得把鸡蛋和牛奶混在一起，做煎蛋卷。
mix up 分不清；搞乱
David and Peter look alike. I always mix them up.
戴维和彼得模样相似，我常分不清楚。
mixture *n.* 混合物
Peter made an omelette with a mixture of eggs and milk.
彼得把鸡蛋和牛奶混在一起，做煎蛋卷。

model /ˈmod·el; ˈmɒdl/ *n.*
1 small copy of something 模型
Susan likes making models.
苏珊喜欢制造模型。

2 person who wears new clothes for people to look at 模特儿
Sarah wants to be a model.
萨拉想做模特儿。

modern /ˈmod·ern; ˈmɒdn/ *adj.*
(**more modern, most modern**)
of now; not old 现代的；时髦的
The Chens live in a modern house.
陈家住在一所现代化的房子里。
opp. 反义词：ancient, old-fashioned 古代的；过时的

moment /ˈmo·ment; ˈməʊmənt/ *n.*
very short time 一会儿；片刻
It only took a moment to mend the kite.
只花片刻时间便修好了风筝。
at the moment 现在；此刻
At the moment the teacher is busy.
老师现在忙得很。
in a moment 一会儿
I'll be ready in a moment.
我一会儿就准备好。
just a moment 等一等
Just a moment. There is some mud on your shirt.
等一等，你衬衫上有点泥污。
wait a moment 等一会儿
Wait a moment. I'll come with you.
请等一会儿，我跟你一起走。

monastery /ˈmon·as·tery; ˈmɒnəstrɪ/ *n.*
(two **monasteries**)
place where a group of men live and pray 修道院；寺院
There is a monastery on Lantau.
大屿山有一座修道院。

monastery

Monday /ˈMon·day; ˈmʌndɪ/ *n.*
day of the week 星期一
We go to school on Monday.
星期一我们都要上学。

money /ˈmon·ey; ˈmʌnɪ/ *n.*
(**no plural**)
coins and notes 钱
Sam hasn't got any money.
萨姆一点钱也没有。

monitor /ˈmon·i·tor; ˈmɒnɪtə/ *n.*
boy or girl with a special duty at school 班长
Susan is the class monitor.
苏珊是班长。

monk /monk; mʌŋk/ *n.*
holy man who lives and prays with a group of other men 修士；僧侣
There are twenty monks in the monastery.
修道院里有二十个修士。

monkey /ˈmon·key; ˈmʌŋkɪ/ *n.*
wild animal with a long tail 猴子

The children saw some monkeys at the zoo.
孩子们在动物园看见一些猴子。

monsoon /mon·'soon; mɒn'su:n/ *n.*
wind that changes direction in winter and summer 季风；季候风
The monsoon brought a lot of rain.
季风带来了大量雨水。

monster /'mon·ster; 'mɒnstə/ *n.*
big, ugly animal or person in stories 怪兽；妖怪
The film was about monsters.
这是一部关于妖怪的电影。

month /month; mʌnθ/ *n.*
one of the twelve parts of the year 月；月份
August is a hot month in Hong Kong.
香港的八月很热。
monthly *adj.* 每月的
Susan buys a monthly magazine.
苏珊购买月刊。

moon /moon; mu:n/ *n.*
big, round thing that shines in the sky at night 月亮
There was a full moon last night.
昨天晚上月圆。

moonlight *n.* 月光
He could see the houses in the moonlight.
在月光下，他可以看见那些房子。

mooncake /'moon·cake; 'mu:nkeɪk/ *n.*
cake eaten during the Mid-Autumn Festival 月饼
Baoling doesn't like mooncakes.
宝玲不喜欢吃月饼。

mooncakes

more /more; mɔ:/ *adj.*
bigger number or amount 多些
Could I have some more rice, please?
我可以再来点儿饭吗？
opp. 反义词：less, fewer 少些

morning /'morn·ing; 'mɔ:nɪŋ/ *n.*
early part of the day 早上
Mrs Chen goes to the market every morning.
陈太太每天早上去市场。
opp. 反义词：night, evening 晚上

mosque /mosque; mɒsk/ *n.*
building where people pray 清真寺
There is a big mosque in Kowloon.
九龙有一座很大的清真寺。

mosquito /mos·'qui·to; məs'ki:təʊ/ *n.*
(two **mosquitoes**)
flying insect that bites 蚊子
The mosquitoes kept Peter awake.
蚊子叮得彼得睡不着。

most /most; məʊst/ *adj. adv.*
1 biggest amount; nearly all 大多数的；大部分的
Most children like ice-cream.
大多数孩子都爱吃冰淇淋。
2 more than all others 最多
Peter likes chocolate ice-cream most.
彼得最爱吃巧克力冰淇淋。
opp. 反义词：least 最少

moth /moth; mɒθ/ *n.*
insect that flies at night 蛾
Moths were flying round the lamp.
蛾绕着灯飞舞。

mother /'moth·er; 'mʌðə/ *n.*
woman who has a child 母亲
Peter's mother is a good cook.
彼得的母亲很会做菜。

motor /'mo·tor; 'məʊtə/ *n.*
machine or engine that makes something move
发动机
The truck has a big motor.
货车的发动机很大。

motor bike, motor cycle *n.*
摩托车
Sam likes motor bikes.
萨姆喜欢摩托车。

motor boat *n.* 汽艇；快艇
The motor boat was pulling a water-skier.
那艘快艇正拖着一个滑水者。

motor cyclist *n.* 骑摩托车的人
The motor cyclist fell off his machine.
那个骑摩托车的人从车上掉了下来。

mountain /'moun·tain; 'maʊntɪn/ *n.*
very high piece of ground 山
Tai Mo Shan is the highest mountain in Hong Kong.
大帽山是香港最高的山。

mouse /mouse; maʊs/ *n.*
(two **mice**)
small wild animal with a long tail 老鼠
Mrs Wang saw a mouse in the kitchen.
王太太在厨房看见一只老鼠。

moustache /mous·'tache; mə'stɑːʃ/ *n.*
hair above a man's mouth
（唇上的）胡子
Mr Tan has a moustache.
谭先生唇上蓄胡子。

mouth /mouth; maʊθ/ *n.*
1 part of the head that speaks and eats 口；嘴
Sam put a sweet in his mouth.
萨姆把糖放进嘴里。

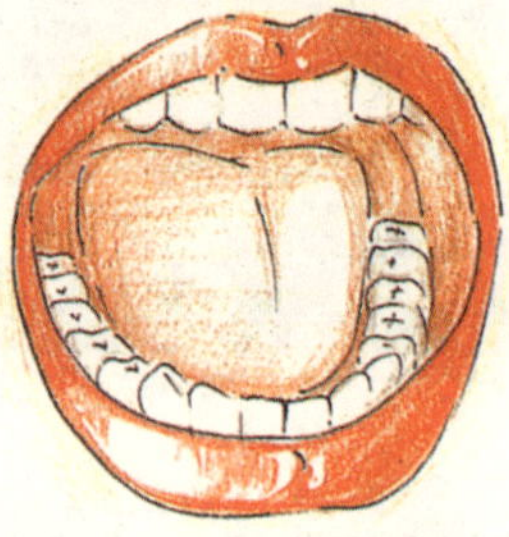

2 part of a river near the sea
河口
The ship sailed into the mouth of the Zhujiang River.
船驶入珠江口。

mouthful *n.* 一口（的分量）
David took a mouthful of water.
戴维喝了一口水。

move /move; muːv/ *v.*
(**moving, moved, moved**)
1 change your house 搬家
The Wang family have moved to Lantau.
王家已经搬到大屿山去了。
2 put something in another place 移开；搬动
Would you move your books off the table, please?
请从桌子上拿走你的书好吗？
3 go to another place 改变位置；移动
Sam moved to the front of the class.
萨姆坐到班上的前排来。

movement *n.* 移动；运动
The smallest movement will frighten the birds away.
极轻微的动作也会把鸟儿吓走。

novie /'mov·ie; 'mu:vɪ/ *n.*
lm 影片
here was a good movie on
V last night.
日晚电视放映了一部很好的影片。

Ar /'Mis·ter; 'mɪstə/
itle for a man 先生
Ar Qian is a fisherman.
钱先生是个渔民。

Mrs /'Mrs; 'mɪsɪz/
itle for a married woman
太太；夫人
Ars Qian works in a factory.
钱太太在一家工厂工作。

Ms /Ms; mɪz/
itle for a woman 女士
Ms Wang is a secretary.
王女士是个秘书。

nuch /much; mʌtʃ/ *adj. adv.*
a lot 很多
Did you buy much rice?
你买了很多米吗？
They have a much bigger
lat than us.
他们住的公寓房比我们的大得多。
how much 多少；多少钱
How much rice did you buy?
你买了多少米？
How much is the watch?
这表值多少钱？
hank you very much 谢谢你
Thank you very much for your
etter.
多谢你的来信。
oo much 太多
Don't give the baby too
much milk.
不要给婴孩吃太多牛奶。
Jsage note: Use *much* with
singular nouns — *There is not*
much orange juice.
用法：much 用在不可数名词前面，例
如 There is not much orange
juice.

mud /mud; mʌd/ *n.*
(no plural)
wet earth 软湿的泥土；泥泞
The rain changed the
ground to mud.
雨水使地上满是泥泞。
muddy *adj.* 泥泞的
After the rain, the ground was
muddy.
雨后地上满是泥泞。

multiply /'mul·ti·ply; 'mʌltɪplaɪ/ *v.*
(multiplying, multiplied, multiplied)
make a bigger number by
adding several times 乘
Two multiplied by three is six
(2 x 3 = 6).
二乘以三等于六。
multiplication *n.* 乘法
Peter knows his multiplication
tables.
彼得会用乘法表。
syn. 同义词：times

Mummy, Mum
/'Mum·my, Mum; 'mʌmɪ, mʌm/ *n.*
mother 妈妈
Could I have some sweets,
Mummy?
妈妈，我可以吃些糖吗？

murder [1] /'mur·der; 'mɜ:də/ *n.*
killing someone 谋杀
There was a murder
yesterday.
昨天发生了一宗谋杀案。

murder [2] /'mur·der; 'mɜ:də/ *v.*
kill someone 谋杀
The man was murdered.
那人被谋杀了。
murderer *n.* 凶手
The murderer was sent to
prison.
凶手被送进监狱。

muscle /'mus·cle; 'mʌsl/ *n.*
one of the soft parts in the
body which can move the
legs and arms, etc. 肌肉
Sam has strong muscles.
萨姆的肌肉很结实。

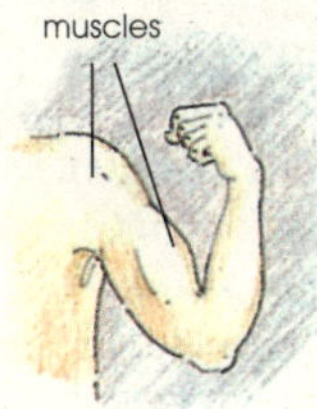

museum /mu·'se·um; mju:'zɪəm/ *n.*
building where we keep
beautiful, old or interesting
things so that people can
see them 博物馆
The teacher took her class to
a museum.
老师带全班学生去博物馆。

mushroom /'mush·room; 'mʌʃrum/ *n.*
plant with no leaves, that we
can eat 蘑菇
The farmer grows mushrooms.
农民培植蘑菇。

music /ˈmu·sic; ˈmjuːzɪk/ *n.*
(**no plural**)
sounds of singing or playing instruments 音乐
Susan was listening to music on the radio.
苏珊在听收音机播出的音乐。

musical *adj.* 音乐的
Drums, flutes and guitars are musical instruments.
鼓、长笛和吉他都是乐器。
musician *n.* 音乐家
Susan is a good musician.
苏珊是个优秀的音乐家。

must /must; mʌst/ *v.*
1 word that tells someone what to do 必须
You must cross the road here.
你必须在这里过马路。
2 certain to be 一定是
You must be tired after your long walk.
你走了这么远的路，一定很累了。
opp. 反义词：must not, mustn't
不可，一定不是
Usage note: Use *must* with another verb — *You must work harder.*
用法：must 要与另一动词连用，例如 You must work harder.

mustn't /ˈmust·n't; ˈmʌsnt/ *v.*
must not 即 must not
You mustn't make a noise.
你不可出声。

my /my; maɪ/ *adj.*
of me; that belongs to me
我的
Have you seen my book?
你见过我的书吗？

myself /my·ˈself; maɪˈself/ *pron.*
word for me when I talk about my own body and mind 自己
I fell down and hurt myself.
我跌倒了，弄伤了自己。
by myself 独自；自己做
I made the kite by myself.
这风筝是我自己做的。

mystery /ˈmy·ster·y; ˈmɪstərɪ/ *n.*
(two **mysteries**)
something strange that you cannot understand or explain
神秘事物；难解事物
The detective solved the mystery.
侦探解开了那个谜。
mysterious *adj.* 神秘的；难解的
Tom heard mysterious noises in the house.
汤姆听见房子里有些古怪的声音。

nail [1] /nail; neɪl/ *n.*
1 hard part at the end of your finger or toe 指甲
The lady had long nails.
那位女士有长长的指甲。
2 pointed piece of metal 钉子
Sam hung the picture on a nail.
萨姆把画挂在钉子上。

nail [2] /nail; neɪl/ *v.*
fix something with a nail
把…钉牢
He nailed a poster to the wall.
他把一张海报钉在墙上。

name [1] /name; neɪm/ *n.*
special words for a person or thing 名字；名称
What's your name?
你叫什么名字？

name [2] /name; neɪm/ *v.*
(**naming, named, named**)
give special words to a person or thing 取名；起名
Sam named his cat Tom.
萨姆给他的猫取了个名字，叫做汤姆。

narrow /ˈnar·row; ˈnærəʊ/ *adj.*
not wide; not far from one side to the other 狭窄的
The road was too narrow for the trucks to pass each other.
马路太窄了，来往货车不能并排通过。

ıasty /ˈnas·ty; ˈnɑːstɪ/ *adj.*
nastier, nastiest)
ɔad; that you do not like
讨厌的；有害的；严重的
Peter had a nasty cold.
彼得患了重感冒。

ıation /ˈna·tion; ˈneɪʃn/ *n.*
ɔig group of people who live
ı one country with one
government 国家
China is a huge nation.
中国是个非常大的国家。
ıational *adj.* 国家的
When is your national day?
哪一天是你们的国庆日?
ıationality *n.* 国籍
What is your nationality?
你的国籍是什么?

ıative /ˈna·tive; ˈneɪtɪv/ *n.*
someone born in a place
某地人；某国人
He is a native of China.
他是中国人。

ıature /ˈna·ture; ˈneɪtʃə/ *n.*
no plural)
everything in the world that is
ıot made by people 大自然
We study nature at school.
我们在学校学习大自然的事物。
ıatural *adj.* 自然的；大自然的
Susan likes films about the
natural world.
苏珊喜欢看关于自然界的电影。

naughty /ˈnaugh·ty; ˈnɔːtɪ/
adj.
(naughtier, naughtiest)
ɔad; making trouble 顽皮的；
淘气的
David is a naughty boy.
戴维是个顽皮的男孩。

navy /ˈna·vy; ˈneɪvɪ/ *n.*
(two **navies**)
warships of a country and
the people who work in them
海军
He is a sailor in the navy.
他在海军里当水兵。
naval *adj.* 海军的
There were some naval ships
in the harbour.
海港内有些海军舰艇。

naval ship

near [1] /near; nɪə/ *adj.*
close 近的
They are near relatives.
他们是近亲。

near [2] /near; nɪə/ *prep.*
close; not far 近
Sam lives near his school.
萨姆住在学校附近。
nearby *adv.* 附近
My friend lives nearby.
我的朋友住在附近。

nearly /ˈnear·ly; ˈnɪəlɪ/ *adv.*
almost 几乎
A car nearly knocked Sam
down.
一辆汽车差点儿把萨姆撞倒。

neat /neat; niːt/ *adj.*
tidy; with everything in the
right place 整齐的；整洁的
Mary's room is neat.
玛丽的房间很整洁。
opp. 反义词：untidy 零乱的
neatly *adv.* 整齐地；整洁地
David writes neatly.
戴维的字体端正。

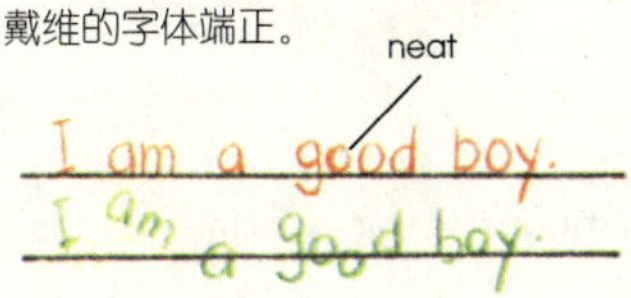

necessary /ˈnec·es·sa·ry; ˈnesəsərɪ/ *adj.*
(more necessary, most
necessary)
important; that you need
必需的；必要的
To travel abroad, a passport
is necessary.
到外国去，护照是必需的。
opp. 反义词：unnecessary 不需要的；
不必要的

neck /neck; nek/ *n.*
part of the body between
the shoulders and the head
颈；脖子
A giraffe has a very long
neck.
长颈鹿的颈很长。

necklace /ˈneck·lace; ˈneklɪs/ *n.*
pretty thing you wear round your neck 项链
Mrs Chen has a diamond necklace.
陈太太有一根钻石项链。

need[1] /need; ni:d/ *v.*
1 want something that is not there; must have 需要
Susan needs some new shoes.
苏珊需要一些新鞋。
2 must do something 必须；一定
Need I do the homework?
我必须做家庭作业吗？
need to 必须；一定
You need to work harder.
你必须加倍努力。
needn't, need not 不须
You needn't wash the dishes tonight.
今晚你不必洗碟子。

need[2] /need; ni:d/ *n.*
something you must have; something that is not there 需要
There is a need for more food in the country.
该国需要更多粮食。

needle /ˈnee·dle; ˈni:dl/ *n.*
long, thin piece of metal with a sharp point for sewing 针
Susan broke her needle.
苏珊把针弄断了。

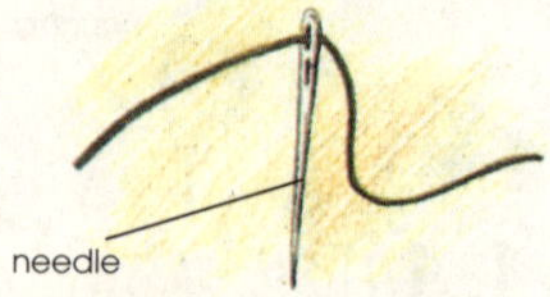

neighbour /ˈneigh·bour; ˈneɪbə/ *n.*
someone who lives near you 邻居
Our neighbours are very quiet.
我们的邻居都很安静。

neither /ˈnei·ther; ˈnaɪðə/ *adj.*
not this and not that 两者都不…
Neither pencil is sharp.
两支铅笔都不尖。
neither...nor 既不…也不…
I have neither pen nor pencil.
我既没有钢笔，也没有铅笔。

nephew /ˈneph·ew; ˈnevju:/ *n.*
son of your brother or sister 侄子；外甥
I haven't got any nephews.
我没有侄子或外甥。

nervous /ˈnerv·ous; ˈnɜ:vəs/ *adj.*
(more nervous, most nervous)
afraid; worried 紧张的；焦虑的
The children are nervous before a test.
孩子们测验前都很紧张。
nervously *adv.* 紧张地；焦虑地
She walked about nervously.
她紧张地走来走去。

nest /nest; nest/ *n.*
place where a bird lays its eggs 鸟巢
The bird built its nest in a tree.
鸟儿在树上筑巢。

net /net; net/ *n.*
strings or threads tied together to stop something going through 网
The fishermen caught a lot of fish in their net.
渔民们用鱼网捕了许多鱼。

netball /ˈnet·ball; ˈnetbɔ:l/ *n.*
(no plural)
game played with a ball and two nets 无挡板篮球
Susan plays netball at school.
苏珊在学校玩无挡板篮球。

never /ˈnev·er; ˈnevə/ *adv.*
not at any time 永远不
David is never late for school.
戴维上学从不迟到。
opp. 反义词：always 永远

new /new; nju:/ *adj.*
that someone has just made, bought or got 新的
Susan has a new dress.
苏珊有一件新连衣裙。
opp. 反义词：old 旧的

new

news /news; nju:z/ *n.*
(no plural)
words that tell people about things that have just happened 新闻；消息
We heard the news about the crash.
我们听到了那次交通事故的消息。

newspaper /'news·pa·per; nju:speɪpə/ *n.*
big sheets of printed paper, with news 报纸
David reads a newspaper every day.
戴维天天看报。

newspapers

New Territories /New 'Ter·ri·to·ries; nju: 'terɪtərɪz/ *n.*
part of Hong Kong 新界
Anna lives in the New Territories.
安娜住在新界。

new town /'new town; 'nju: taʊn/ *n.*
town which has just been built 新城镇
There are several new towns in the New Territories.
新界有几个新城镇。

next /next; nekst/ *adj.*
after this 下一个的
I'll see you next week.
我们下星期再见。
next door 隔壁
Peter's friend lives next door.
彼得的朋友住在隔壁。
next to 在…的旁边
Peter sits next to Tom.
彼得坐在汤姆的旁边。

nice /nice; naɪs/ *adj.*
(nicer, nicest)
good; that you like 好的；令人喜欢的
We had a nice dinner.
我们吃了一顿很好的晚饭。
opp. 反义词：nasty 坏的；令人不快的

nickname /'nick·name; 'nɪkneɪm/ *n.*
name given to someone that is not their real name 绰号；花名(方言)
John's nickname is Jack.
约翰的绰号是杰克。

niece /niece; ni:s/ *n.*
daughter of your brother or sister 侄女；甥女
I haven't got any nieces.
我没有侄女或甥女。

night /night; naɪt/ *n.*
time when it is dark
晚上
We sleep at night.
我们晚上睡觉。
opp. 反义词：day 白天
all night 整夜
They played mahjong all night.
他们整夜打麻将牌。
at night 晚上；夜间
Some people work at night.
有些人在夜间工作。
by night 晚上；夜间
They travelled to Canada by night.
他们晚上去加拿大。
good night 再见；晚安
Sam said good night to his mother.
萨姆向妈妈道晚安。
night-time 夜间
The streets are quiet at night-time.
夜间街上很宁静。
night-watchman 守夜人
Our building has a night-watchman.
我们的大厦有一个守夜人。

nightingale /'night·in·gale; 'naɪtɪŋgeɪl/ *n.*
bird that sings at night
夜莺
I heard a nightingale sing last night.
昨晚我听到夜莺的歌声。

nine (9) /nine; naɪn/ *n. adj.*
number 9 九
Susan has nine dresses.
苏珊有九件连衣裙。
ninth (9th) *n. adj.* 第九
Yesterday was Laura's ninth birthday.
昨天是劳拉的九岁生日。

nineteen (19) /nine·'teen; naɪn'ti:n/ *n. adj.*
number 19 十九
There are nineteen boys in the class.
班上有十九个男孩。
nineteenth (19th) *n. adj.*
第十九
It is John's nineteenth birthday.
这是约翰的十九岁生日。

ninety (90) /'nine·ty; 'naɪntɪ/ *n. adj.*
number 90 九十
The old man is ninety years old.
那老人九十岁了。
ninetieth (90th) *n. adj.* 第九十
He is in his ninetieth year.
他今年九十岁。

no [1] /no; nəʊ/ *adv.*
word to show that you do not agree 不
No, you can't go out.
不，你不能出去。
opp. 反义词：yes 是

no [2] /no; nəʊ/ *adj.*
not a; not one; not any
没有；无
Sam has no money.
萨姆没有钱。
no wonder 难怪
It's midnight. No wonder you are tired.
午夜了，难怪你累了。

nobody /'no·bo·dy; 'nəʊbədɪ/ *pron.*
no person 没有人
There's nobody at home.
没有人在家。
syn. 同义词：no one

nod /nod; nɒd/ *v.*
(nodding, nodded, nodded)
move your head downwards
点头
Sam nodded to his friends.
萨姆向朋友们点头。

noise /noise; nɔɪz/ *n.*
1 any sound 声音
Tom heard a noise in the house.
汤姆听见房子里有声音。
2 loud sound that you do not like 噪音；吵闹声
Stop making that noise!
别吵闹！

noisy /'nois·y; 'nɔɪzɪ/ *adj.*
(noisier, noisiest)
making a lot of sound 吵闹的
The children were very noisy.
孩子们很吵闹。
opp. 反义词：quiet 安静的
noisily *adv.* 吵闹地
The children were playing noisily.
孩子们在玩耍，吵得很。

none /none; nʌn/ *pron.*
not one; not any
没有；一个也没有
None of the children was late.
孩子们没有一个迟到。

nonsense /'non·sense; 'nɒnsns/ *n.*
(no plural)
silly words or ideas 废话；愚昧的想法
The boy was talking nonsense.
那男孩在胡说八道。

noodle /'noo·dle; 'nu:dl/ *n.*
long, narrow piece of food made with flour and water
面条
Peter ate a bowl of noodles for lunch.
彼得午饭吃了一碗面。

noodles

noon /noon; nu:n/ *n.*
(no plural)
12 o'clock in the day 中午
We have our lunch at noon.
我们中午吃饭。

no one /'no one; 'nəʊ wʌn/ *pron.*
no person 没有人
There was no one at home.
家里没有人。

normal /'nor·mal; 'nɔ:ml/ *adj.*
usual 平常的；正常的
On a normal day, Mr Chen works very hard.
陈先生平日非常努力工作。

north /north; nɔ:θ/ *n. adj. adv.*
word to show direction 北方；北面的；向北
They live in the north.
他们住在北方。
They went to the North Pole.
他们去北极。

They went north.
他们向北走。
opp. 反义词：south 南方；南面的；向南
northern *adj.* 北方的；北面的；向北的
They are a northern people.
他们是一个北方民族。

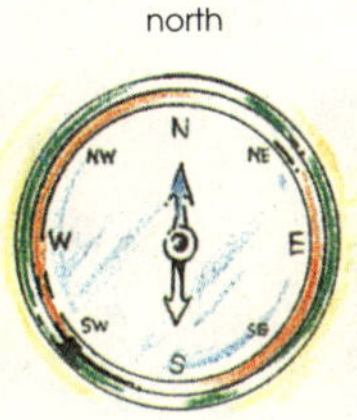

nose /nose; nəuz/ *n.*
part of the head that breathes and smells 鼻子
The man had a big nose.
那个男人有个大鼻子。

nostril /ˈnos·tril; ˈnɒstrəl/ *n.*
part of the nose 鼻孔
We breathe through our nostrils.
我们经鼻孔呼吸。

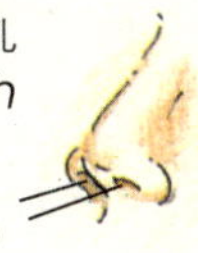

not /not; nɒt/ *adv.*
word that says 'no'; word that gives an opposite meaning to the word after it 不
David does not like milk.
戴维不爱喝牛奶。

note /note; nəut/ *n.*
1 short letter 便条；短信
Mrs Wang wrote a note to the teacher.
王太太写了张便条给老师。
2 words to help you to remember something 笔记
The reporter made notes about the speech.
记者听演讲时做笔记。
3 piece of paper money 钞票；纸币
Sam found a ten-dollar note.
萨姆找到一张十港元钞票。
4 sound in music; mark that shows a sound in music 单音；音符
Sam can't sing a note.
萨姆一个音都唱不出来。

notebook /ˈnote·book; ˈnəutbuk/ *n.*
small book where you write things that you want to remember 笔记簿
Peter wrote the sentences in his notebook.
彼得把句子抄在笔记簿上。

nothing /ˈnoth·ing; ˈnʌθɪŋ/ *n.*
(no plural)
not any thing 什么都没有
There was nothing in the box.
盒子里什么都没有。

notice [1] /ˈno·tice; ˈnəutɪs/ *n.*
piece of writing to tell people something 布告；告示
There was a 'No Parking' notice.
这里有"不准停车"的告示。
notice-board *n.* 布告板
The teacher put the list on the notice-board.
老师把名单张贴在布告板上。

notice [2] /ˈno·tice; ˈnəutɪs/ *v.*
(noticing, noticed, noticed)
see someone or something 注意到；看到
No one noticed when Tom arrived late.
没有人注意到汤姆迟到。

nought (0) /nought; nɔ:t/ *n. adj.*
number 0 零
Two minus two equals nought (2 – 2 = 0).
二减二等于零。
Usage note: The number 0 has several different names. We say *nought* for parts of numbers — *A million has six noughts.* We say the *letter '0'* for telephone numbers. We say *nil* for the score in a game — *The team lost three – nil.* We say *zero* for temperatures, but you can also use *zero* for all these examples.
用法： 0（零）这个数字有几种读法。说数目时读 nought，例如 A million has six noughts；说电话号码时读英文字母 0；说比赛积分时读 nil，例如 The team lost three – nil；说温度时读 zero。上述各情况下，亦可全读 zero。

noun /noun; naun/ *n.*
word that is the name of someone or something 名词
'Table' and 'chair' are nouns.
Table 和 chair 都是名词。

novel /'no·vel; 'nɒvl/ *n.*
long story in a book
小说
Mary reads novels.
玛丽常看小说。

November /No·'vem·ber; nə'vembə/ *n.*
eleventh month of the year
十一月
In Hong Kong the weather is good in November.
香港的十一月天气很好。

now /now; naʊ/ *adv.*
at this time 现在；目前
Mary now lives in Great Britain.
玛丽现在住在英国。

nowadays /'now·a·days; 'naʊədeɪz/ *adv.*
at this time 现今
Nowadays, lots of people use computers.
现今许多人都用电脑。

nowhere /'no·where; 'nəʊweə/ *adv.*
in no place 哪个地方都不在
Tom was nowhere in the house.
这房子里哪儿都找不到汤姆。

nuclear /'nu·cle·ar; 'nju:klɪə/ *adj.*
using a special sort of energy to make electricity 原子核的
There is a nuclear power station at Daya Bay.
大亚湾有一座核电站。

number /'num·ber; 'nʌmbə/ *n.*
word or figure that shows how many 数字
Two (2) and twenty (20) are numbers.
二和二十都是数字。

a large number of 大量的；许多的
There was a large number of people at the football match.
看那场足球比赛的人很多。

a number of 一些；若干
A number of people came into the room .
有一些人走进了房间。

numbers

number-plate /'num·ber·plate; 'nʌmbəpleɪt/ *n.*
piece of metal on a car, etc., which shows its number
号码牌；车牌
He bought a number-plate with three eights on it.
他买了"888"号车牌。

number-plate

numeral /'num·er·al; 'nju:mərəl/ *n.*
number 数字
2 and 3 are numerals.
二和三都是数字。

nurse /nurse; nɜ:s/ *n.*
someone who looks after sick people 护士
There are lots of nurses at the hospital.
医院里有许多护士。

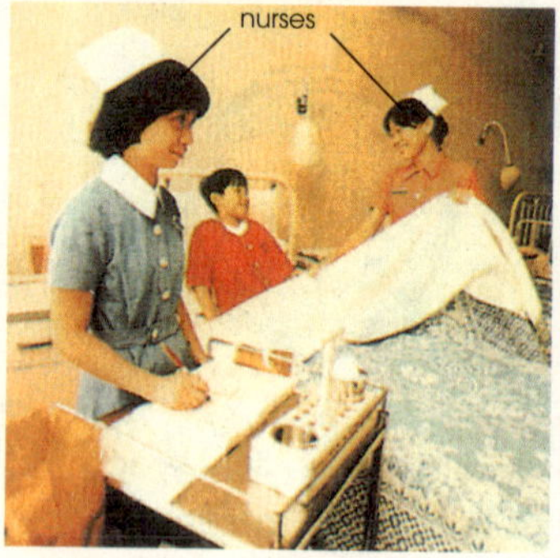

nursery /'nurs·er·y; 'nɜ:sərɪ/ *n.*
(two **nurseries**)
place where babies are looked after 托儿所
There are ten babies in the nursery.
托儿所里有十个婴儿。

nursery school *n.* 幼儿园
The little boy goes to nursery school.
那小男孩上幼儿园。

nut /nut; nʌt/ *n.*
hard fruit of a tree 坚果；果仁
Sam likes nuts.
萨姆喜欢吃果仁。

nuts

Oo

oar /oar; ɔː/ *n.*
long piece of wood for rowing a boat 船桨
Tom rowed the boat with the oars.
汤姆用桨划船。

oasis /o·'a·sis; əʊ'eɪsɪs/ *n.*
(two **oases**)
place in a desert which has water （沙漠中的）绿洲
They came to an oasis in the desert.
他们来到沙漠中的一个绿洲。

obedient /o·'be·di·ent; ə'biːdɪənt/ *adj.*
(**more obedient, most obedient**)
doing what someone tells you 服从的；听话的
The children are very obedient.
孩子们非常听话。
opp. 反义词：disobedient 不服从的；不听话的

obediently *adv.* 服从地
The children behaved obediently.
孩子们表现得很听话。

obey /o·'bey; ə'beɪ/ *v.*
do what someone tells you to do 服从；听话
The children always obey the teacher.
孩子们总是听老师的话。
opp. 反义词：disobey 不服从；不听话

object /'ob·ject; 'ɒbdʒɪkt/ *n.*
thing 物体；物件
The museum was full of interesting objects.
博物馆里摆满了有趣的展品。

obtain /ob·'tain; əb'teɪn/ *v.*
get or buy something 取得；买到
They obtained tickets for the concert.
他们买到了音乐会的票子。

obvious /'ob·vi·ous; 'ɒbvɪəs/ *adj.*
(**more obvious, most obvious**)
easy to see 明显的
The dirt on the dress was obvious.
这件连衣裙上的污迹很明显。

occupation
/oc·cu·'pa·tion; ɒkjʊ'peɪʃn/ *n.*
job; work that you do for money 职业
What is Mr Wang's occupation?
王先生的职业是什么？

ocean /'o·cean; 'əʊʃn/ *n.*
very big piece of water between continents 海洋
The Pacific Ocean is huge.
太平洋非常大。

o'clock /o·'clock; ə'klɒk/ *n.*
(**no plural**)
word that shows what the hour is 时；钟点
It's two o'clock.
现在是二时正。
Usage note: We use *o'clock* after whole hours -- *It is six o'clock. It's half past six.*
用法： o'clock 只用来表示整点，例如 It is six o'clock。表示分钟时，不能用 o'clock，例如六时半须写成 half past six。

October /Oc·'to·ber; ɒk'təʊbə/ *n.*
tenth month of the year 十月
In Hong Kong, October is usually a sunny month.
香港的十月通常天气晴朗。

octopus /'oc·to·pus; 'ɒktəpəs/ *n.*
(two **octopuses**)
sea animal with eight legs 章鱼；八爪鱼（方言）
Peter caught an octopus in his net.
彼得用网捉了一条章鱼。

odd /ɔd; ɒd/ *adj.*
not even 奇数的；单个的
One and three are odd numbers.
一和三都是奇数。

of /ɔf; əv/ *prep.*
1 word that shows who or what has or owns something 属于…的
It's a book of mine.
那本书是我的。
2 word that shows where a part is …的（表示部位）
The children sat in the back of the car.
孩子们坐在汽车的后座。
3 word that follows an amount …的（表示分量）
Susan bought a dozen of apples.
苏珊买了一打苹果。
4 word that shows what is inside a thing …的（表示包含）
Mary had a cup of tea.
玛丽喝了一杯茶。
5 about someone or something 关于
I've never heard of it.
我从来没有听说过这事。
of course 当然
Of course I'll come to your party.
当然，我会来参加你们的聚会。
a kind of 一种；一类
A rose is a kind of flower.
玫瑰是一种花。
a sort of 似乎是；一类
The children made a sort of tent on the beach.
孩子们在海滩上搭了个类似帐篷的东西。

off /ɔf; ɒf/ *prep. adv.*
1 from; down from 离开；脱掉
Tom fell off his bicycle.
汤姆从自行车上掉了下来。
2 not on; not working 中断；失灵；关掉
The lights were off when I came home.
我回到家时，电灯熄了。

3 away to another place 离开
The man ran off with the bag.
那人带着袋子逃了。
4 not at school or work 休假
We have a day off tomorrow.
明天我们休假一天。
5 showing distance 表示距离
The ship was a long way off.
那艘船开远了。

offer [1] /ˈɔf·fer; ˈɒfə/ *v.*
say that you are happy to give something 给予；提供
Peter offered Tom a sweet.
彼得给了汤姆一颗糖。

offer [2] /ˈɔf·fer; ˈɒfə/ *n.*
what you want to give 提供；提议
The teacher thanked Tom for his offer to help.
老师感谢汤姆自愿帮忙。

office /ˈɔf·fice; ˈɒfɪs/ *n.*
room where you work 办公室；办事处
There are a lot of offices in the building.
这座大厦里有许多办公室。

officer /ˈɔf·fi·cer; ˈɒfɪsə/ *n.*
1 leader in the army, navy or airforce （陆、海、空三军的）军官
Sam's brother is an officer in the army.
萨姆的哥哥是位陆军军官。
2 someone who does important work, especially for the government 官员
The police officers arrested the robber.
那警官拘捕了盗贼。

often /ˈɔf·ten; ˈɒfn/ *adv.*
many times 常常；经常
Peter often goes to the cinema.
彼得常常看电影。

oh /oh; əʊ/ *int.*
word that shows any strong feeling 啊！噢！
Oh! I've lost my purse.
啊！我的钱包不见了。
oh dear *int.* 啊哟！
Oh dear! It's raining.
啊哟，下雨了！

oil [1] /oil; ɔɪl/ *n.*
sort of thick liquid for cooking and machines 油
Mrs Wang cooks with vegetable oil.
王太太用植物油做菜。

oil-lamp *n.* 油灯
The children had an oil-lamp at the barbecue.
孩子们烧烤时带油灯。

oil tanker *n.* 油轮
The oil tanker sailed into the harbour.
油轮驶入海港内。

oily *adj.* 油腻的；沾满油的
Peter got his hands oily.
彼得的手沾满了油。

oil [2] /oil; ɔɪl/ *v.*
put oil on 加润滑油
Sam oiled his bicycle.
萨姆给他的自行车加润滑油。

ointment /'oint·ment; 'ɔɪntmənt/ *n.*
medicine that you put on the skin 药膏；油膏
The nurse put some ointment on the cut.
护士在伤口上涂了些药膏。

OK, okay /o·'kay; əʊ'keɪ/ *int.*
all right; yes 好
OK, you may borrow my pen.
好吧，你可以借用我的笔。

old /old; əʊld/ *adj.*
1 word that shows how long someone has been alive or how long something has been made （人）岁数；（物）有多久
Peter is nine years old.
彼得九岁。

2 having lived a long time; not young 年老的；年长的
Tom's grandfather is very old.
汤姆的祖父很老。
opp. 反义词：young 年轻的

3 that was made or bought a long time ago; not new 旧的；古老的
Mrs Wang's old car broke down.
王太太那辆旧车坏了。
opp. 反义词：new 新的

old-fashioned *adj.* 旧式的
Mrs Lin wears old-fashioned clothes.
林太太穿旧式衣服。

Usage note: You can use *old* to describe people, animals and things — *An old man. An old elephant. An old building.*
用法：old 可用来形容人、动物及物件，例如 an old man, an old elephant 或 an old building.

omelette /'om·e·lette; 'ɒmlɪt/ *n.*
food made with eggs
煎蛋卷
David made an omelette for his breakfast.
戴维做了一个煎蛋卷做早餐。

on [1] /on; ɒn/ *adv.*
1 moving further 继续；向前
Move on, please.
请往前走。

2 not off; working 开动着；操作中的
The TV is on.
电视机正开着。

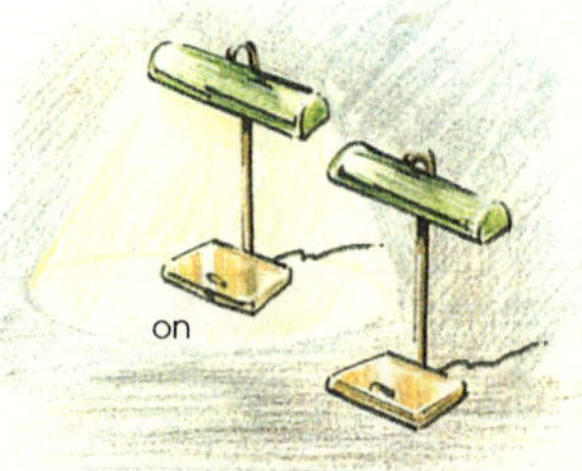

on [2] /on; ɒn/ *prep.*
1 word that shows where 在…上
Your lunch is on the table.
你的午饭放在桌子上。

2 word that shows when 在（某时间）
We are going to the beach on Sunday.
我们星期日要去海滩玩。

3 about something 关于
Mary is reading a book on ballet.
玛丽正在看一本关于芭蕾舞的书。

once /once; wʌns/ *adv.*
1 one time 一次
I've only been to Canada once.
我只到过加拿大一次。

2 some time in the past 曾经；从前
He once lived in Hong Kong but now he lives in Canada.
他从前住在香港，但现在住在加拿大。

all at once 突然
All at once the door opened.
门突然打开了。

at once 立刻；马上
Come here at once.
立刻到这里来。

once again, once more
再一次
The children sang the song once again.
孩子们把那首歌又唱了一遍。

once upon a time
从前(故事开端时用)
Once upon a time, there was a giant.
从前有一个巨人。

one [1] (1) /one; wʌn/ *n. adj.*
number 1 一
One and one make two.
一加一等于二。

one [2] /one; wʌn/ *art.*
a 一个
We went to Canada for one week.
我们在加拿大待了一个星期。

one [3] /one; wʌn/ *pron.*
word that you use in place of a person or thing 人或物的代用语
I've got some sweets. Would you like one?
我有些糖果，你要一块吗?

one another 互相；彼此
The children were playing with one another.
孩子们在一起玩耍。

one day 总有一天
One day, John will be a doctor.
总有一天，约翰会当上医生的。

onion /ˈon·ion; ˈʌnɪən/ *n.*
round vegetable with a strong smell and taste 洋葱
Mrs Chen was cooking beef with onions.
陈太太在煮洋葱牛肉。

only [1] /ˈon·ly; ˈəunlɪ/ *adj.*
not anyone else; not anything else 唯一的
Sam was the only boy at the party.
参加这个聚会的男孩只有萨姆一个。

only [2] /ˈon·ly; ˈəunlɪ/ *adv.*
nothing more; no more 只有
I only have ten dollars.
我只有十港元。

not only... but also... 不但…而且…
Mary not only sings but also plays the piano.
玛丽不但会唱歌，而且会弹钢琴。

onto /ˈon·to; ˈɒntu:/ *prep.*
on 在…上
Susan put the books onto the shelf.
苏珊把书放到架子上。

open [1] /ˈo·pen; ˈəupən/ *adj.*
1 not closed 开着的
The windows are open.
窗子都开着。
2 ready for business 开始营业
When are the shops open?
商店什么时候开始营业?
opp. 反义词: closed 关闭的

open [2] /ˈo·pen; ˈəupən/ *v.*
1 unfasten something; move something so that things or people can get in and out 开
Sam opened the door.
萨姆把门打开。
2 be ready for business 开始营业
The shops open at nine o'clock.
商店九时开始营业。
opp. 反义词: close, shut 关

opera /ˈop·e·ra; ˈɒprə/ *n.*
a play with songs 歌剧
Mary saw an opera in London.
玛丽在伦敦看了一场歌剧。

operation /op·er·ˈa·tion; ɒpəˈreɪʃn/ *n.*
doctor's work when he cuts your body to mend a part inside 手术
Mary had an operation on her leg.
玛丽的腿动过手术。

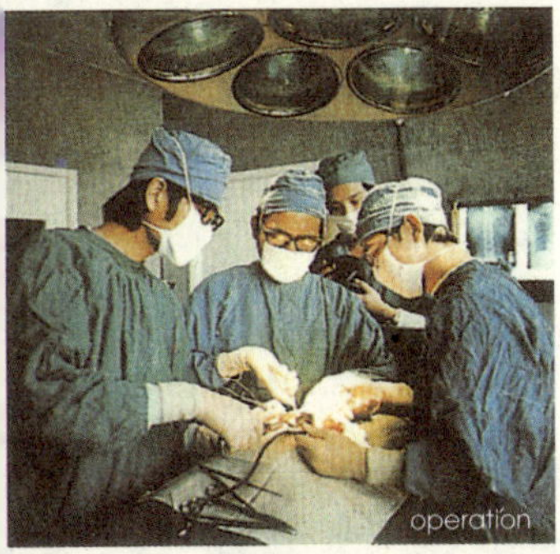
operation

opinion /o·'pin·i·on; ə'pɪnɪən/ *n.*
what you think about something 意见；主张
Mary asked Anna's opinion about the dress.
玛丽问安娜对那件连衣裙有什么意见。

opposite [1] /'op·po·site; 'ɒpəzɪt/ *adj.*
on the other side 对面的；另一边的
Peter saw Tom on the opposite side of the road.
彼得看见汤姆在马路的另一边。
opp. 反义词：same 相同的

opposite [2] /'op·po·site; 'ɒpəzɪt/ *n.*
different in every way
反义词
Big is the opposite of small.
大的反义词是小。
opp. 反义词：synonym 同义词

optician /op·'ti·cian; ɒp'tɪʃn/ *n.*
someone who looks after your eyes 眼镜店主
Mary went to the optician for a new pair of glasses.
玛丽到眼镜店配一副新眼镜。

or /or; ɔ:/ *conj.*
words that join the words for two different people or things
或；还是
Would you like coffee or tea?
你要咖啡还是茶？
or else 否则
Run or else you'll miss the bus.
赶快跑吧，否则你会赶不上公共汽车。

orange [1] /'or·ange; 'ɒrɪndʒ/ *n.*
round fruit with a yellow-red skin 橙；橘子；柑
Peter ate an orange.
彼得吃了一个橙子。

orange [2] /'or·ange; 'ɒrɪndʒ/ *adj.*
with a yellow-red colour 橙黄色的
Mrs Chen bought an orange dress.
陈太太买了一件橙黄色的连衣裙。

orchestra /'or·ches·tra; 'ɔ:kɪstrə/ *n.*
big group of people who play music together 乐队
John plays the piano in the orchestra.
约翰在乐队里弹钢琴。

order [1] /'or·der; 'ɔ:də/ *n.*
1 **(no plural)** way that you place things or people
次序
The children lined up in class order.
孩子们按班级的次序排列成行。
2 words that tell you to do something 命令
The officer was giving soldiers orders.
军官向士兵发出命令。
in order to 为了…
Susan left early in order to catch the ferry.
为了赶上渡轮，苏珊提早离开。
keep in order 维持秩序
The teacher keeps the children in order.
老师要孩子们守秩序。
put in order 放置整齐
The children put the library books in order.
孩子们把图书馆的书放置整齐。

order [2] /'or·der; 'ɔ:də/ *v.*
1 tell someone to do something 命令；吩咐
The doctor ordered Tom to stay in bed.
医生吩咐汤姆卧床休息。
2 ask to buy goods in a shop, tickets, etc. 订购
Mr Chen ordered a new car.
陈先生订购了一辆新车。

ordinary /'or·di·na·ry; 'ɔ:dənrɪ/ *adj.*
not special; usual 一般的；平常的
It was an ordinary day at school.
这天学校里一切如常。

organ /'or·gan; 'ɔ:gən/ *n.*
musical instrument 风琴
Mr Qian plays the organ.
钱先生弹奏风琴。

organize, organise /'or·gan·ize, 'or·gan·ise; 'ɔ:gənaɪz, 'ɔ:gənaɪz/ *v.*
(**organizing, organized, organized**)
put in order; arrange 组织；筹办
Mr Chen organized the concert.
陈先生筹办了那次音乐会。

orphan /'or·phan; 'ɔ:fn/ *n.*
someone whose mother and father are dead 孤儿
An orphan went to live with the Chen family.
有一个孤儿去陈家居住。

other [1] /'other; 'ʌðə/ *adj.*
not the same 另外的；其他的；别的
The ferry goes to the other side of the harbour.
渡轮开到海港的另一边。

other [2] /'other; 'ʌðə/ *pron.*
not the same one 另一
One pen is mine, the other is Tom's.
一支笔是我的，另外一支是汤姆的。

ought to /'ought to;'ɔ:t tu:/ *v.*
should; words that tell someone what is the right thing to do 应该
It's late. We ought to go home.
晚了，我们应该回家去。
opp. 反义词：ought not；oughtn't 不应该

ounce (oz) /ounce; aʊns/ *n.*
measure of weight 盎司
There are sixteen ounces in a pound.
一磅有十六盎司。

our /'our; 'aʊə/ *adj.*
of us 我们的
This is our flat.
这是我们居住的公寓房。

ours /'ours; 'aʊəz/ *pron.*
thing that belongs to us 我们的
This flat is ours.
这套公寓房是我们的。

ourselves /our·'selves; aʊə'selvz/ *pron.*
word for us when we talk about our own bodies and minds 我们自己
We helped ourselves to some food.
我们自己动手拿了些东西吃。
by ourselves 我们自己做
We made the kite by ourselves.
这个风筝是我们自己做的。

out /out; aʊt/ *adv.*
1 not at home or work; away 不在；出去了
I went to see John, but he was out.
我去找约翰，但是他出去了。
2 away from a place; from inside 离去；外出
Mrs Chen has gone out.
陈太太出去了。
opp. 反义词：in 在；在里面

3 not shining or burning; off 熄灭
The lights are out.
灯光熄灭了。
opp. 反义词：on 亮着
hold out 伸出
Sam held out his hand for a sweet.
萨姆伸手要糖吃。
pick out 挑选出
Susan picked out a new dress.
苏珊选了一件新连衣裙。
pull out 拉出；掏出
Mr Chen pulled out his wallet.
陈先生掏出钱包。
out of …之中；离开；利用
Peter scored nine out of ten in the test.
彼得在那次测验中十题答对了九题。
out of date 过时的
This newspaper is out of date.
这份报纸已过时。

out of order 坏了
The TV was out of order.
电视机坏了。

out of sight 看不见
The ship was out of sight.
那条船已看不见了。

outdoors /out·'doors; aʊt'dɔːz/ *adv.*
not in a building 户外；室外
The children are playing outdoors.
孩子们在户外玩耍。
opp. 反义词：indoors 户内；室内

outing /'out·ing; 'aʊtɪŋ/ *n.*
day in the country or outside 度假；远足；旅行
The children had an outing to the sea.
孩子们出海游玩。

outlying /'out·ly·ing; 'aʊtlaɪɪŋ/ *adj.*
not near 边远的
The ferries go to the outlying islands.
渡轮开往偏僻的岛屿。

outside [1] /out·'side; aʊt'saɪd/ *n. prep. adv.*
the part that is not inside; not in this place; not in a building 外面
The outside of the house was painted white.
房子的外面漆上白色。
There was a crowd outside the football ground.
足球场外面有人群聚集。
Please wait outside.
请在外面等候。
opp. 反义词：inside 里面

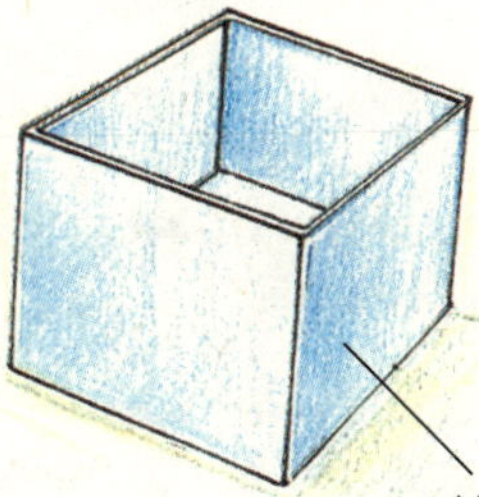

outside [2] /out·'side; aʊt'saɪd/ *adj.*
not inside 外面的
The outside walls of the school are white.
学校的外墙是白色的。
opp. 反义词：inside 里面的

oval /'o·val; 'əʊvl/ *n. adj.*
round, flat shape 椭圆形的
The sports field had an oval shape.
那运动场是椭圆形的。

oven /'ov·en; 'ʌvn/ *n.*
hot cupboard where you cook food 烤炉
Anna cooked a chicken in the oven.
安娜用烤炉烤鸡。

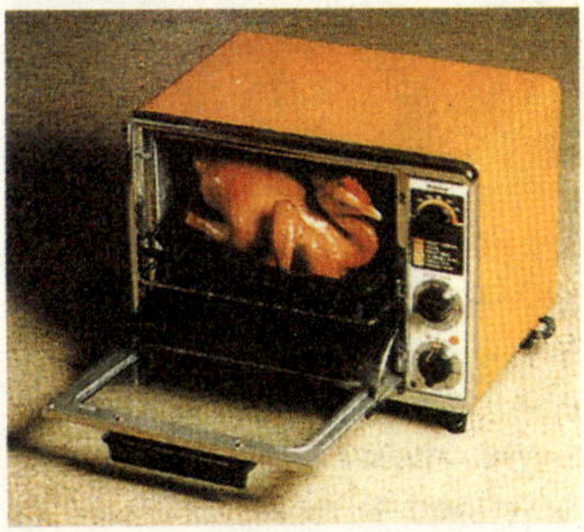

over [1] /'o·ver; 'əʊvə/ *adv.*
finished; ended 完成；结束
The match was over at five o'clock.
比赛于五时结束。

over here 这里
Come over here, please.
请到这里来。

over there 那里
Please put your books over there.
请把书放在那里。

over [2] /'o·ver; 'əʊvə/ *prep.*
1 from one side to the other; across 越过；横过
He walked over the bridge.
他走过了那座桥。

2 on something to cover it 盖在…上
She put a sheet over the baby.
她把被单盖在婴儿身上。
3 above someone or something 在…之上
The plane flew over the mountain.
飞机飞过那座山。
4 more than 多于
There are over six million people in Hong Kong.
香港有六百多万人。
opp. 反义词：under 在…之下；少于

overcoat /'o·ver·coat; 'əuvəkəut/ *n.*
long coat you wear when it is cold 大衣
It was cold so Susan wore an overcoat.
天气冷，因此苏珊穿上大衣。

overseas /o·ver·'seas; əuvə'si:z/ *adv.*
other countries 海外
Many Chinese people go overseas.
很多中国人到外国去。

owe /owe; əu/ *v.*
(owing, owed, owed)
have to give back money to someone 欠
John owes Peter ten dollars.
约翰欠彼得十港元。

owl /owl; aul/ *n.*
wild bird that comes out at night 猫头鹰
The owl caught a mouse.
那只猫头鹰抓了一只老鼠。

own [1] /own; əun/ *pron. adj.*
word that shows that something belongs to a person or thing 自己的
It's Mr Chen's own junk.
这是陈先生自己的帆船。

own [2] /own; əun/ *v.*
have something that is yours 拥有
Mr Chen owns a junk.
陈先生拥有一艘帆船。

owner /'own·er; 'əunə/ *n.*
someone who has something 拥有人；所有人
Mr Chen is the owner of the junk.
陈先生是这艘帆船的所有人。

ox /ox; ɒks/ *n.*
(two **oxen**)
male cow 牛
Oxen can pull carts.
牛可以拉车。

oyster /'oy·ster; 'ɔɪstə/ *n.*
sea animal with a shell 蚝；牡蛎
The fisherman found a pearl in the oyster.
渔民在蚝里发现一颗珍珠。

pack [1] /pack; pæk/ *n.*
bag or box of things 一包；一副
Mary bought a pack of cards.
玛丽买了一副纸牌。

pack [2] /pack; pæk/ *v.*
put clothes, etc., into bags for a journey 整理行装；包装(东西)
Mary packed her suitcase.
玛丽把衣服装进衣箱里。
opp. 反义词：unpack 打开行李，拆开包装

package /'pack·age; 'pækɪdʒ/ *n.*
something wrapped in paper; parcel 包裹
Tom received a package of magazines from Canada.
汤姆收到加拿大寄来的一包杂志。

packet /'pack·et; 'pækɪt/ *n.*
small paper container 小包

Sam bought a packet of biscuits.
萨姆买了一包饼干。

paddle /'pad·dle; 'pædl/ *v.*
(paddling, paddled, paddled)
move a canoe with a piece of wood 划船
John paddled his canoe across the harbour.
约翰划独木舟横渡海港。

page /page; peɪdʒ/ *n.*
piece of paper that is part of a book, newspaper, etc.
(书籍、报章等的)一页
There were sixty-four pages in the book.
这本书有六十四页。

paid /paid; peɪd/ *v.*
p.t. of **pay** pay 的过去式
Sam paid $20 for a ball.
萨姆花了二十港元买了一个球。

pain /pain; peɪn/ *n.*
what you feel when you are hurt 痛
John has a pain in his leg.
约翰的腿痛。
painful *adj.* 痛的
John's leg was painful.
约翰的腿很痛。

paint [1] /paint; peɪnt/ *n.*
coloured liquid that you put onto something with a brush
油漆；颜料
Sam bought a box of paints.
萨姆买了一盒颜料。
paintbrush *n.* 油漆刷；画笔
David bought some paintbrushes.
戴维买了一些画笔。

paint [2] /paint; peɪnt/ *v.*
1 put paint onto something with a brush 上漆；油漆
David painted his bicycle red.
戴维把他的自行车漆成红色。
2 make a picture with colours
(用颜料)画；绘画
The artist painted the harbour.
那位画家画这个海港。

painter /'paint·er; 'peɪntə/ *n.*
1 someone who paints houses, walls, etc. 油漆工人；油漆匠
The painters were working on the house.
油漆匠在漆房子。
2 someone who makes pictures with paint 画家
The painter finished his picture of the harbour.
那位画家完成了那幅海港的画。

painting /'paint·ing; 'peɪntɪŋ/ *n.*
picture that someone has painted 图画；油画；水彩画
Mr Chen bought a painting of Shanghai.
陈先生买了一幅描绘上海的画。

pair /pair; peə/ *n.*
two things or people together
一双；一对
Mary bought a pair of socks.
玛丽买了一双短袜。
Sam bought a pair of trousers.
萨姆买了一条裤子。

palace /'pal·ace; 'pælɪs/ *n.*
house of a king or other ruler
王宫；宫殿
The Queen of England lives in Buckingham Palace.
英国女王住在白金汉宫。

Palace Museum in Beijing

pale /pale; peɪl/ *adj.*
(paler, palest)
having little colour; with a light colour 苍白的；浅色的
You look pale today.
你今天的脸色很苍白。
Susan bought a pale blue dress.
苏珊买了一件浅蓝色的连衣裙。

palm /palm; pɑ:m/ *n.*
inside of the hand between the wrist and fingers 手掌
Sam had some coins in the palm of his hand.
萨姆的掌上有几个硬币。

palm tree /palm tree; pɑ:m tri:/ *n.*
sort of tree 棕榈树
There were some palm trees on the beach.
海滩上有些棕榈树。

pan /pan; pæn/ *n.*
dish for cooking 平底锅
Mary cooked some vegetables in a pan.
玛丽用平底锅煮了一些蔬菜。

pancake /ˈpan·cake; ˈpæŋkeɪk/ *n.*
very thin, round cake that you cook in a frying pan
薄煎饼
Mary likes pancakes for breakfast.
玛丽早餐喜欢吃薄煎饼。

panda /ˈpan·da; ˈpændə/ *n.*
big black and white animal that lives in China 熊猫
A panda is a rare animal.
熊猫是一种罕有的动物。

panic /ˈpan·ic; ˈpænɪk/ *n.*
great fear 惊慌；恐慌
There was no panic when the fire broke out.
房子着火时大家都没有惊慌失措。

panther /ˈpan·ther; ˈpænθə/ *n.*
big black animal 黑豹
The children saw a panther at the zoo.
孩子们在动物园里见到一只黑豹。

pants /pants; pænts/ *n.*
(plural)
piece of clothing that you wear on the bottom part of your body, under your other clothes 内裤
The children change their pants every day.
孩子们天天换内裤。

paper /ˈpa·per; ˈpeɪpə/ *n.*
1 **(no plural)** thin sheets for writing, drawing etc.
纸；纸张
Tom made a kite out of paper.
汤姆用纸做了一只风筝。
2 newspaper 报纸
Susan reads a paper every day.
苏珊天天看报纸。

parachute /ˈpar·a·chute; ˈpærəʃu:t/ *n.*
thing like an umbrella that stops you from falling too fast
降落伞
The pilot landed by parachute.
飞行员用降落伞着陆。

paragraph /ˈpar·a·graph; ˈpærəgrɑ:f/ *n.*
piece of writing that begins on a new line （文章的）一段
There were ten paragraphs in the essay.
这篇文章有十段。

parallel /ˈpar·al·lel; ˈpærəlel/ *adj.*
like lines which are always the same distance away
平行的
The lines are parallel.
这些线是平行的。

parcel /ˈpar·cel; ˈpɑ:sl/ *n.*
something you wrap in paper
包裹
Tom took the parcel to the post office.
汤姆把包裹拿到邮局去。

pardon /ˈpar·don; ˈpɑ:dn/ *v.*
forgive someone 原谅
Pardon me for being late.
请原谅我迟到。
I beg your pardon 对不起
I beg your pardon! I didn't see you.
对不起，我当时没看到你。
pardon? *int.* 对不起，请再说一遍
Pardon? I didn't hear you.
对不起，我听不到你说的话。

parent /ˈpar·ent; ˈpeərənt/ *n.*
father or mother 父亲；母亲
Sam's parents came to watch him play football.
萨姆的父母来看他踢足球。

park [1] /park; pɑːk/ *n.*
public garden in a town 公园
Mrs Chen took her children to the park.
陈太太带孩子们去公园。

country park *n.* 郊野公园
Hong Kong has some beautiful country parks.
香港有一些美丽的郊野公园。

park [2] /park; pɑːk/ *v.*
put a car, bus or lorry somewhere for a time 停车
Mr Wang parks his car near his office.
王先生把汽车停在他的办公室附近。

parrot /'par·rot; 'pærət/ *n.*
bird with coloured feathers 鹦鹉
Mr Chen has a green parrot in a cage.
陈先生在笼子里养了一只青绿色的鹦鹉。

part /part; pɑːt/ *n.*
some, but not all; a piece of something 部分
David watched TV for a part of the evening.
戴维晚上用部分的时间来看电视。
play a part in 扮演一个角色
Susan played a part in the school play.
苏珊在学校的戏剧表演中扮演一个角色。
take part in 参加
Peter took part in the Lion Dance.
彼得参加舞狮表演。

partner /'part·ner; 'pɑːtnə/ *n.*
another person that you play or dance with 伙伴；同伴；搭档
David was Tom's partner in the game.
在这次比赛中，戴维是汤姆的伙伴。

party /'par·ty; 'pɑːtɪ/ *n.*
(two **parties**)
1 time when friends come together to eat, drink, play games, or dance 聚会；茶会；舞会
Baoling had a birthday party.
宝玲开了个生日聚会。
2 group of people 一群人
The teacher took a school party to Ocean Park.
老师带领一群学生到海洋公园去。

pass /pass; pɑːs/ *v.*
1 walk or drive by someone or something 经过
The bus passes the school.
公共汽车经过学校。
2 go by （时间）过去
The school holidays passed quickly.
学校假期很快就过去了。
3 give something to someone 传递
Pass me the sugar, please.
请把糖递给我。
4 do well in a test 考试及格
Susan passed the exam.
苏珊考试及格。
opp. 反义词：fail 失败；不及格

passage /'pas·sage; 'pæsɪdʒ/ *n.*
1 long, narrow way inside a building 通道；走廊
We walked along the passage.
我们沿着走廊走。
2 piece of writing （文章的）一段
Peter read the passage.
彼得看了那一段文章。

passenger /'pas·sen·ger; 'pæsɪndʒə/ *n.*
someone who is travelling in a car, bus, ferry, etc. 乘客
The ferry had two hundred passengers.
渡轮上有两百名乘客。

passport /'pass·port; 'pɑːspɔːt/ *n.*
little book that says who you are and allows you to travel abroad 护照
You need a passport to travel abroad.
去外国旅行要有护照。

past [1] /past; pɑ:st/ *adj.*
that has gone 过去的；已过的
The past week has been very hot.
在过去的一周里一直很热。

past [2] /past; pɑ:st/ *n.*
(no plural)
time before now 过去；往时
In the past, only a few people lived in Hong Kong.
以前香港只有很少居民。
opp. 反义词：future 未来；将来

past [3] /past; pɑ:st/ *prep.*
1 by 经过
The bus went past me.
那辆公共汽车从我身旁经过。
2 later than something; after something 过了
It's past lunch-time.
已经过了午饭时间。

paste [1] /paste; peɪst/ *n.*
(no plural)
stuff that sticks things together 浆糊
Sam stuck the pictures in his book with paste.
森姆用浆糊把图片黏贴在书上。

paste [2] /paste; peɪst/ *v.*
(pasting, pasted, pasted)
fix something onto another thing with glue 黏贴
Sam pasted the pictures in his book.
森姆把图片黏贴在书上。

pastry /'pas·try; 'peɪstrɪ/ *n.*
(two **pastries**)
small cakes or pies 糕饼；馅饼
Xiaofang bought some pastries from a cake shop.
小芳在饼店买了一些馅饼。

patch /patch; pætʃ/ *n.*
(two **patches**)
piece of material you sew or stick over a hole in something （衣服上的）补钉；补片
Sam has patches on his jeans.
森姆的牛仔裤上有几处补钉。

patch

path /path; pɑ:θ/ *n.*
narrow way where people can walk 小径；小路
The children followed the path through the wood.
孩子们沿着小径穿过了树林。

patient [1] /'pa·tient; 'peɪʃnt/ *adj.*
(more patient, most patient)
happy to wait for something 有耐性的；忍耐的；容忍的
Be patient. Lunch will be ready soon.
耐心等一下，午饭很快便准备好啦。
opp. 反义词：impatient 不耐烦的
patience *n.* 耐心；耐性
The fisherman had a lot of patience.
那个渔民十分有耐性。
patiently *adv.* 耐心地
The people waited patiently for the bus.
人们耐心地等公共汽车。

patient [2] /'pa·tient; 'peɪʃnt/ *n.*
sick person in a hospital; customer of a doctor 病人
The doctor visited his patients.
医生巡查他的病人。

pattern /'pat·tern; 'pætn/ *n.*
shapes and colours on something 图案；花纹
Mary's dress had a nice pattern on it.
玛丽连衣裙上的花纹很好看。

pavement /'pave·ment; 'peɪvmənt/ *n.*
path for peple at the side of a road in a town 人行道
The pavements were full of people.
人行道上满是人。

pavement

paw /paw; pɔ:/ *n.*
foot of a cat, dog, etc. （猫、狗等的）脚爪
The dog lifted its paw.
那只狗举起脚爪。

paw

pay /pay; peɪ/ *v.*
(paying, paid, paid)
give money to get something
付给；付款
Mrs Wang paid for the dress.
王太太付钱买了那件连衣裙。
payment *n.* 支付的款额
The shop assistant took the payment.
店员收了钱。

pea /pea; piː/ *n.*
sort of very small, round vegetable 豌豆
Sarah put some peas in the soup.
萨拉放了些豌豆在汤里。

peace /peace; piːs/ *n.*
(no plural)
1 time when there is no fighting between countries 和平
Peace returned to Vietnam.
越南恢复了和平。
opp. 反义词：war 战争
2 time when it is quiet 安静；宁静
People go to the country parks for a little peace.
人们到郊野公园去享受一些宁静的时光。

peaceful /ˈpeace·ful; ˈpiːsfl/ *adj.*
(more peaceful, most peaceful)
quiet 安静的；宁静的
The countryside is very peaceful.
乡村非常宁静。
opp. 反义词：noisy 嘈吵的

peach /peach; piːtʃ/ *n.*
(two **peaches**)
round yellow-red fruit with a soft skin 桃子
John ate a peach.
约翰吃了一个桃子。

peacock /ˈpea·cock; ˈpiːkɒk/ *n.*
kind of bird 孔雀
The peacock has a beautiful tail.
孔雀的尾巴很美丽。

peak /peak; piːk/ *n.*
top of a hill or mountain 山顶；山峰
The climber reached the peak.
登山者到达了山顶。

peanut /ˈpea·nut; ˈpiːnʌt/ *n.*
small nut 花生
The children were eating peanuts.
孩子们在吃花生。

pear /pear; peə/ *n.*
green or yellow fruit 梨
Mrs Wang bought some pears at the market.
王太太在市场买了一些梨。

pearl /pearl; pɜːl/ *n.*
round, white jewel from an oyster 珍珠
Mrs Chen has a pearl necklace.
陈太太有一根珍珠项链。

peck /peck; pek/ *v.*
hit with a beak 啄
The bird pecked the apple.
鸟儿啄食那苹果。

pedal /ˈped·al; ˈpedl/ *n.*
part of a bicycle that you move with your foot 踏板
Tom's foot slipped off the pedal of his bicyle.
汤姆骑自行车时，一只脚滑离了踏板。

pedestrian /pe·ˈdes·tri·an; pɪˈdestrɪən/ *n.*
someone who is walking in a street 行人
The pavements were full of pedestrians.
人行道上满是行人。

peel [1] /peel; piːl/ *v.*
take the skin off a fruit or vegetable 去掉果皮
Sam peeled the pear.
萨姆把梨子的皮削掉。

peel[2] /peel; piːl/ *n.*
(**no plural**)
skin of a fruit or vegetable
果皮
Sam took the peel off the pear.
萨姆削掉梨子的皮。

peep /peep; piːp/ *v.*
look for a short time 偷看；窥视
Sam peeped at the answer to the sum.
萨姆偷看算术题的答案。

peg /peg; peg/ *n.*
piece of wood, metal or plastic on a door or wall, where you can hang things
（木、金属或塑料的）挂钉
Mary hung her coat on a peg.
玛丽把大衣挂在挂钉上。

pen /pen; pen/ *n.*
thing you use when you write with ink 笔；钢笔；圆珠笔
Baoling forgot to bring her pen.
宝玲忘记带笔。

pens

pencil /ˈpen·cil; ˈpensl/ *n.*
thing you use to write and draw 铅笔
Xiaofang drew a map with a pencil.
小芳用铅笔画了一张地图。

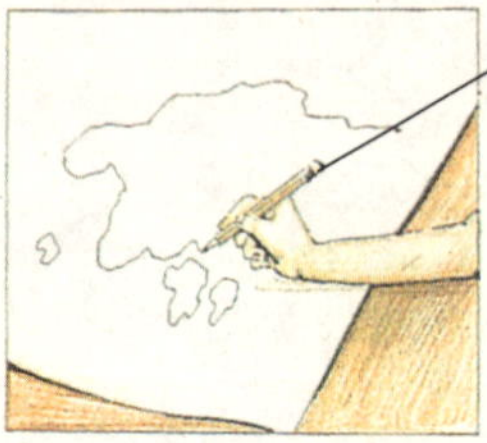
pencil

pencil-case *n.* 铅笔盒
Mary keeps her pens and pencils in a pencil-case.
玛丽把她的钢笔和铅笔都放在铅笔盒里。

pencil-sharpener *n.* 铅笔刀；铅笔刨
Tom sharpened his pencils with a pencil-sharpener.
汤姆用铅笔刀把铅笔削尖。

penguin /ˈpen·guin; ˈpeŋgwɪn/ *n.*
bird that can swim but cannot fly 企鹅
The zoo keeper gave some fish to the penguins.
动物园的管理员拿了些鱼给企鹅吃。

peninsula /pe·ˈnin·su·la; pəˈnɪnsjulə/ *n.*
narrow area of land with water on three sides 半岛
Malaysia is a peninsula.
马来西亚是个半岛。

people /ˈpeo·ple; ˈpiːpl/ *n.*
(**plural**)
1 men,women and children
人
There are more than six million people in Hong Kong.
香港有六百多万人。
2 anyone 任何人
People should not leave rubbish on the beach.
任何人都不应在海滩上丢垃圾。

Usage note: The most usual plural for *person* is *people — A lot of people visit Hong Kong.* The word *peoples* means nations or nationalities — *The English-speaking peoples of the world.*
用法：people 是 person 最常用的复数形式，例如A lot of people visit Hong Kong。Peoples 一词的意思是种族或民族，例如 The English-speaking peoples of the world。

pepper /ˈpep·per; ˈpepə/ *n.*
1 (**no plural**) hot powder that you put on food 胡椒粉
Tom likes pepper on his eggs.
汤姆喜欢在鸡蛋上撒些胡椒粉。
2 vegetable that tastes hot
辣椒
Mrs Chen cooked the prawns with peppers.
陈太太煮虾放些辣椒。

peppers

per /per; pə/ *prep.*
for each 每一
There are two sweets per child.
每个小孩有两粒糖。

per cent (%) /per·'cent; pə'sent/ *n.*
for each hundred 百分之…
Five per cent of the children were absent from school.
有百分之五的孩子没有上学。

perfect /'per·fect; 'pɜ:fɪkt/ *adj.*
(**more perfect, most perfect**)
with nothing wrong; very good 完美的；极佳的
The pearls were perfect.
那些珍珠毫无瑕疵。

perhaps /per·'haps; pə'hæps/ *adv.*
it is possble 也许；可能
Perhaps we'll go to Canada next year.
明年我们也许到加拿大去。
syn. 同义词：maybe

period /'pe·ri·od; 'pɪərɪəd/ *n.*
1 amount of time 一段时间
John was on holiday for a period of three weeks.
约翰休假三个星期。
2 lesson 一节课
We have four English periods a week.
我们一周上四节英语课。

permission /per·'mis·sion; pə'mɪʃn/ *n.*
(**no plural**)
allowing someone to do something 准许；允许
Tom got permission to leave the classroom.
汤姆得到允许离开教室。

person /'per·son; 'pɜ:sn/ *n.*
(two **people**)
man, woman, child 人
A doctor is a person who looks after sick people.
医生是照顾患者的人。

pest /pest; pest/ *n.*
harmful insects and animals 对人有害的昆虫和动物
Rats and cockroaches are pests.
老鼠和蟑螂都是对人有害的动物。

pet /pet; pet/ *n.*
animal that you like very much and keep in your home 宠物
Susan has two pets -- a dog and a cat.
苏珊有两只宠物——一只狗和一只猫。

petal /'pe·tal; 'petl/ *n.*
outside part of a flower 花瓣
The flowers were losing their petals.
那些花的花瓣逐渐脱落了。

petrol /'pet·rol; 'petrəl/ *n.*
(**no plural**)
sort of oil that makes car engines go 汽油
Mr Wang put some petrol in his car.
王先生给他的汽车加了些汽油。
petrol station *n.* 汽油站
Mr Wang went to the petrol station.
王先生去了汽油站。

phone [1] /phone; fəʊn/ *n.*
short for **telephone**
telephone 的缩写式
Mrs Chen answered the phone.
陈太太接了电话。

phone [2] /phone; fəʊn/ *v.*
(**phoning, phoned, phoned**)
short for **telephone**
telephone 的缩写式
Sam phoned his mother.
萨姆打电话给他母亲。

photograph, photo [1] /'pho·to·graph, 'pho·to; 'fəʊtəgrɑ:f, 'fəʊtəʊ/ *n.*
picture that you make with a camera 相片；照片
David has some old photographs of Hong Kong.
戴维有一些香港的旧照片。

photograph 2
/'pho·to·graph; 'fəutəgrɑ:f/ *v.*
take a photograph 拍照；摄影
David photographed the harbour.
戴维拍摄港口的景色。
photographer *n.* 摄影者；摄影师
David is a good photographer.
戴维是个优秀的摄影师。
photography *n.* 摄影；摄影术
David likes photography.
戴维喜欢摄影。

phrase /phrase; freɪz/ *n.*
a few words that go together 短语
Baoling writes English phrases in a notebook.
宝玲把英语短语写在笔记簿上。

physical education
/'phy·si·cal ed·u·'ca·tion; 'fɪzɪkl edʒʊ'keɪʃn/ *n.*
(**no plural**)
running and exercises 体育课
The children have physical education twice a week.
孩子们一周上两次体育课。

physics /'phy·sics; 'fɪzɪks/ *n.*
(**no plural**)
learning about heat, light, sound, etc. 物理
John is studying physics.
约翰在攻读物理学。

piano /pi·'an·o; pɪ'ænəʊ/ *n.*
big musical instrument 钢琴
Mary can play the piano.
玛丽会弹钢琴。

pick /pick; pɪk/ *v.*
1 take what you like best; choose 挑选
The captain picked Sam for the football team.
队长挑选了森姆入足球队。
2 take flower or fruit from plants or trees 采；摘
Don't pick flowers in the park.
不要摘公园里的花。
pick up 捡起；拾起
Pick up that empty can, please.
请把空罐捡起来。

picnic /'pic·nic; 'pɪknɪk/ *n.*
special party outside 野餐
The children had a picnic on the beach.
孩子们在海滩上野餐。

picture /'pic·ture; 'pɪktʃə/ *n.*
drawing, painting or photograph 图画；照片
David took some pictures of Hong Kong.
戴维拍了一些香港的照片。

pictures

pie /pie; paɪ/ *n.*
dish of meat or fruit with pastry 馅饼
Peter likes fruit pies.
彼得爱吃果子馅饼。

piece /piece; pi:s/ *n.*
part of something 一块；一片；一部分
Peter ate a piece of fruit pie.
彼得吃了一块果子馅饼。
in pieces 成为碎片
The vase was in pieces.
花瓶破成碎片。
Usage note: The word *piece* can be replaced by other words — *A slice of bread. A bar of soap.*
用法：piece 可用其他词代替，例如 a slice of bread 或 a bar of soap 等。

pier /pier; pɪə/ *n.*
wall from the land into the sea where you can get on and off boats 码头
We waited at the pier for the ferry.
我们在码头等渡轮。

pig /pig; pɪg/ *n.*
fat farm animal 猪
The farmer keeps pigs.
这农民养猪。

pigeon /ˈpi·geon; ˈpɪdʒɪn/ *n.*
sort of bird 鸽子
There were some pigeons sitting on the roof.
屋顶上停着些鸽子。

piglet /ˈpig·let; ˈpɪglɪt/ *n.*
young pig 小猪
The pig had six piglets.
那只猪有六只小猪。

pigtail /ˈpig·tail; ˈpɪgteɪl/ *n.*
hair woven together 辫子
Baoling has pigtails.
宝玲有辫子。

pile /pile; paɪl/ *n.*
many things together, one on top of the other 一堆；一叠
The teacher was marking a pile of exercise books.
老师正在批改一叠练习簿。

pill /pill; pɪl/ *n.*
small,hard piece of medicine 药丸
Susan had to take some pills because she was ill.
苏珊因为生病，所以要服食些药丸。

pillow /ˈpil·low; ˈpɪləʊ/ *n.*
soft thing in bed, where your head lies 枕头
Sam likes two pillows on his bed.
萨姆喜欢在床上放两个枕头。
pillowcase *n.* 枕套
Mary put clean pillowcases on the pillows.
玛丽给枕头套上干净的枕套。

pilot /ˈpi·lot; ˈpaɪlət/ *n.*
someone who makes an aeroplane fly 飞行员
The pilot landed the plane at Hong Kong International Airport.
飞行员使飞机在香港国际机场降落。

pin [1] /pin; pɪn/ *n.*
small, thin piece of metal with a sharp point 大头针；别针
Tom fixed the photo to the board with a pin.
汤姆用大头针把相片钉在板上。

pin [2] /pin; pɪn/ *v.*
(pinning, pinned, pinned)
stick something together with pins 钉住
Tom pinned the photo to the board.
汤姆把相片钉在板上。

pineapple /ˈpine·ap·ple; ˈpaɪnæpl/ *n.*
big fruit with a rough skin
菠萝；凤梨
Mary likes pineapples.
玛丽爱吃菠萝。

ping-pong /ˈping·pong; ˈpɪŋpɒŋ/ *n.*
(no plural)
game where players hit a small ball over a net on a big table 乒乓球
Peter and David were playing ping-pong.
彼得和戴维在打乒乓球。
syn. 同义词：table tennis

pink /pink; pɪŋk/ *adj.*
with a pale red colour
淡红色的；粉红色的
Mary bought her mother some pink flowers.
玛丽买了一些粉红色的花给妈妈。

pip /pip; pɪp/ *n.*
seed in a fruit 核；种子
The orange was full of pips.
这个橙有许多核。

pipe /pipe; paɪp/ *n.*
1 tube that carries water, oil or gas 管
The water pipe was leaking.
水管在漏水。
2 thing for smoking 烟斗
Mr Chen smokes a pipe.
陈先生抽烟斗。

pirate /ˈpi·rate; ˈpaɪərət/ *n.*
man who robs people at sea
海盗
The pirates attacked the ship.
海盗袭击了那艘船。

pity ¹ /ˈpi·ty; ˈpɪtɪ/ *n.*
(no plural)
sad feeling 同情；可怜
We feel pity for poor people.
我们都觉得穷人可怜。

it's a pity, what a pity 可惜
It's a pity you can't come to my birthday party.
你不能参加我的生日聚会，真可惜。

pity ² /ˈpi·ty; ˈpɪtɪ/ *v.*
(pitying, pitied, pitied)
feel sad for another person
同情；怜悯
I pity the refugees.
我同情那些难民。

pizza /ˈpiz·za; ˈpi:tsə/ *n.*
flat, round pastry with tomato, cheese, etc., on top
意大利薄饼；比萨饼
Sam had pizza for his lunch.
萨姆午餐吃比萨饼。

place ¹ /place; pleɪs/ *n.*
1 where something or someone is 地方
Put the drinks in a cool place.
把饮料放在阴凉的地方。
2 city, town, village, etc. 城市；镇；村
Hong Kong is a crowded place.
香港是个拥挤的城市。
3 where you usually are 常处的位置
Jenny changed places with Peter.
詹妮和彼得换了位置。

in place of 代替
Sam played in the team in place of Tom.
萨姆取代汤姆加入球队。
take place 发生；举行
The match took place last Saturday.
比赛在上星期六举行。

place ² /place; pleɪs/ *v.*
(placing, placed, placed)
put something somewhere
放置；安排
Tom placed his books on a shelf.
汤姆把书籍放在架子上。

plain /plain; pleɪn/ *adj.*
1 easy to see, hear or understand 明显的；清楚的；易了解的
It's plain that Peter can't do the work.
显然彼得干不了这件工作。
2 ordinary 简单的；平常的
Baoling prefers plain food.
宝玲比较喜欢简单的食物。
3 with no pattern 款式简单的；朴素的
Mary is wearing a plain white dress.
玛丽穿了一条款式简单的白色连衣裙。

plan ¹ /plan; plæn/ *n.*
thing that you have decided to do 计划
The bad weather spoiled our plan to have a barbecue.
恶劣的天气破坏了我们去烧烤的计划。

plan ² /plan; plæn/ *v.*
(planning, planned, planned)
think or say that you will do something 计划；打算
David plans to visit Canada next year.
戴维打算明年到加拿大旅行。

plane /plane; pleɪn/ *n.*
short for **aeroplane**
aeroplane 的缩写式
The plane landed at Hong Kong International Airport.
飞机在香港国际机场降落。

planet /ˈplan·et; ˈplænɪt/ *n.*
big, round world in space
行星
Jupiter is a planet.
木星是行星。

Jupiter

planetarium *n.* 天文馆
The class visited a planetarium.
那班学生去参观天文馆。

plant [1] /plant; plɑːnt/ *n.*
anything that grows from the ground 植物
There are lots of plants in the park.
公园里有很多植物。

plant

plant [2] /plant; plɑːnt/ *v.*
put seeds, etc., into the ground to grow 栽种；种植
The school planted a lot of trees.
学校里种了许多树。

plaster /ˈplas·ter; ˈplɑːstə/ *n.*
small bandage that sticks to the skin 橡皮膏；药用胶布（方言）
The nurse put a plaster on the cut.
护士在伤口上贴了一块橡皮膏。

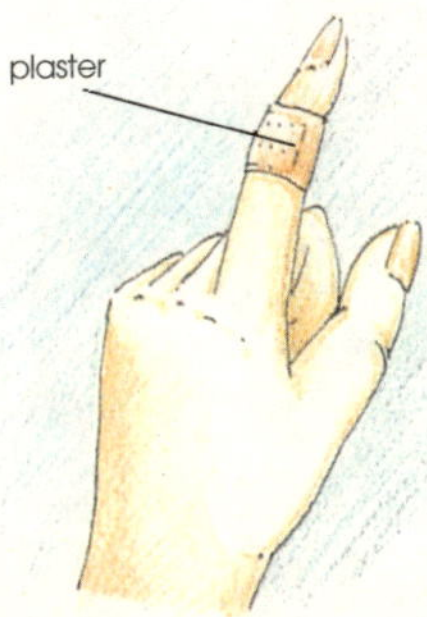

plastic [1] /ˈplas·tic; ˈplæstɪk/ *n.*
(no plural)
light, strong material made in a factory 塑料
The bags were made of plastic.
那些袋子都是用塑料做的。

plastic [2] /ˈplas·tic; ˈplæstɪk/ *adj.*
made of plastic 塑料的
There were a lot of plastic bags on the beach.
海滩上有许多塑料袋。

plasticine /ˈplas·ti·cine; ˈplæstɪsiːn/ *n.*
(no plural)
soft stuff that you can make models with 彩泥；橡皮泥
The children were making models with plasticine.
孩子们在用橡皮泥塑造模型。

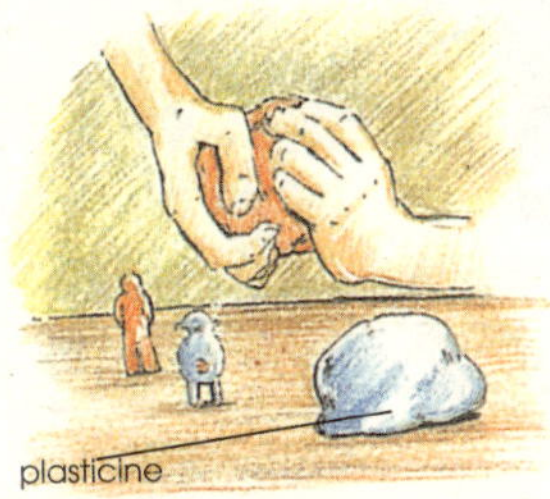

plate /plate; pleɪt/ *n.*
round, flat dish for food 碟子；盘子
Mrs Chen put some biscuits on a plate.
陈太太在碟子里放了一些饼干。

platform /ˈplat·form; ˈplætfɔːm/ *n.*
place in a station where you stand to wait for a train
月台
On the platform, please stand behind the yellow line.
请站在月台上黄线的后面。

play [1] /play; pleɪ/ *n.*
story that you see at the theatre, on TV, etc. 戏剧
There was a good play on TV.
电视里播放了一出好戏。
playtime *n.* 游戏时间
At playtime, the children go into the school yard.
到了游戏时间，孩子们都到学校操场上去。

play[2] /ˈplay; pleɪ/ *v.*
1 do things for fun 玩耍；游戏
The children were playing in the park.
孩子们在公园里玩耍。
2 be in game 参加游戏或比赛
The children were playing football.
孩子们在踢足球。
3 make music with a musical instrument 演奏
Mary plays the piano.
玛丽弹钢琴。

player /ˈplay·er; ˈpleɪə/ *n.*
1 someone who plays in a game 游戏者；队员
There are eleven players in a football team.
一支足球队有十一个队员。
2 someone who plays a musical instrument 演奏乐器者
Mary is a good piano player.
玛丽弹得一手好钢琴。

playground /ˈplay·ground; ˈpleɪgraʊnd/ *n.*
piece of ground where children can play 运动场；游乐场；操场
There is a big playground near Tom's school.
汤姆的学校附近有一个很大的游乐场。

pleasant /ˈpleas·ant; ˈpleznt/ *adj.*
(**more pleasant, most pleasant**)
good; that you like 愉快的；宜人的
In Hong Kong, the weather is pleasant in November.
香港十一月的天气很宜人。
syn. 同义词：nice
opp. 反义词：nasty, unpleasant 讨厌的；不愉快的

please /ˈplease; ˈpli:z/ *int.*
word you say when you ask politely 请
Please sit down.
请坐下。
yes, please 好的，谢谢
'Would you like a sweet?' 'Yes, please!'
"你要糖果吗？""好的，谢谢！"

pleased /pleased; pli:zd/ *adj.*
(**more pleased, most pleased**)
happy; feeling that something is good 欢喜的；愉快的
Mary is always pleased to see Susan.
玛丽见到苏珊时总是很愉快。

pleasure /ˈpleas·ure; ˈpleʒə/ *n.*
(**no plural**)
feeling when you are happy and pleased 高兴；愉快
It's a pleasure to see you.
很高兴见到你。

plenty /ˈplen·ty; ˈplentɪ/ *n.*
(**no plural**)
a large number; as much as you need 大量；许多；充足
We have plenty of rice in the cupboard.
我们的食橱里有许多米。

plough[1] /plough; plaʊ/ *n.*
machine that digs and turns over the earth before you plant 犁
The tractor was pulling a plough.
拖拉机拖着一个犁。

plough[2] /plough; plaʊ/ *v.*
dig and turn over the earth with a plough 犁地；耕田
The farmer ploughed the field.
农民耕田。

plug /plug; plʌg/ *n.*
1 something which stops liquid going out 塞子
Mary put the plug in the hole of the sink.
玛丽用塞子塞着洗涤槽的排水口。
2 metal and plastic thing on the end of a wire that carries electricity 插头
Sam put a new plug on the radio.
萨姆给收音机装上一个新的插头。

plum /plum; plʌm/ *n.*
sort of fruit 梅子；李子
Mrs Chen bought a kilo of plums in the market.
陈太太在市场买了一公斤李子。

plural /ˈplu·ral; ˈplʊərəl/ *n.*
form of a word that shows there is more than one 复数
The plural of child is children.
child 的复数是 children。

plus /plus; plʌs/ *conj.*
and; word in arithmetic for adding numbers 加；加上
Two plus two make four (2 + 2 = 4).
二加二等于四。

p.m. /p·'m.; piː'em/
after midday 下午
The film starts at 3 p.m.
电影下午三时开始放映。

pocket /'pock·et; 'pɒkɪt/ *n.*
sort of small bag in your clothes for carrying things
口袋；衣袋
Tom put his money in his pocket.
汤姆把他的钱放在口袋里。

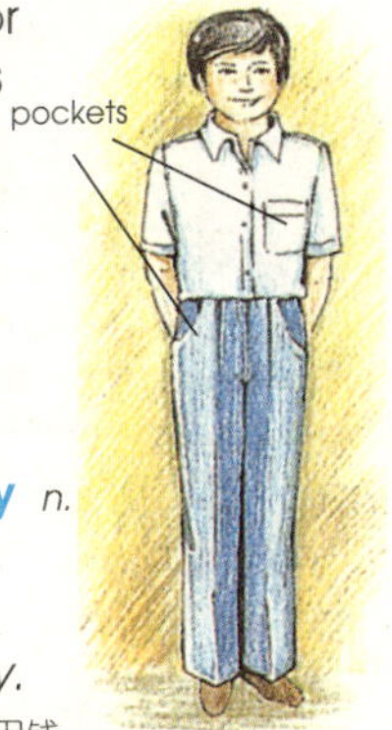

pocket-money *n.*
零用钱
Tom gets $50 pocket-money.
汤姆有五十港元零用钱。

poem /'po·em; 'pəʊɪm/ *n.*
piece of writing in lines which have a rhythm 诗
The teacher read a poem to the children.
老师给孩子们念了一首诗。

poet *n.* 诗人
The poet is writing a new poem.
那诗人正在写一首新的诗歌。

poetry *n.* 诗歌
Susan likes poetry.
苏珊喜欢诗歌。

point [1] /point; pɔɪnt/ *n.*
1 thin, sharp end 尖；尖端
Tom broke the point of his pencil.
汤姆把铅笔尖弄断了。
2 number that shows the score in a game 比赛的得分
The basketball team won by five points.
这支篮球队以五分的优势赢了。
3 exact place 地点
Mary went back to the point where she dropped her purse.
玛丽回到她丢了钱包的地点。
4 dot that shows part of a whole number 小数点
Half of five is two point five (2.5).
五的一半是二点五。

point [2] /point; pɔɪnt/ *v.*
use your finger, your arm or stick to show something 指着；指向
The teacher pointed to the blackboard.
老师指着黑板。
Baoling pointed at the dress.
宝玲指着那件连衣裙。

poison /'poi·son; 'pɔɪzn/ *n.*
something that will kill or hurt one if it gets inside one's body
毒药
You must be careful with poisons.
毒药必须小心处理。

poisonous *adj.* 有毒的
Some snakes are poisonous.
有些蛇是有毒的。

pole /pole; pəʊl/ *n.*
1 place on Earth that is furthest north or south 北极或南极
It is very cold at the North Pole.
北极非常寒冷。
2 long, thin piece of wood, metal or plastic 棒；柱；杆；竿
Peter put a flag on a pole.
彼得在杆上挂起一面旗子。

police /po·'lice; pə'liːs/ *n.*
(no plural)
group of men and women who stop people doing bad things 警察；警方
Mr Chen telephoned the police.
陈先生打电话报警。

policeman *n.* 男警察
The policeman caught the robber.
警察捉到了盗贼。

police-station *n.* 警察局
He took the robber to the police-station.
他把盗贼带到警察局去。

policewoman *n.* 女警察
The policewoman arrested the thief.
女警察拘捕了那个小偷。

polish [1] /'pol·ish; 'pɒlɪʃ/ *v.*
rub something so that it shines 擦亮
David polished his shoes.
戴维把鞋子擦亮。

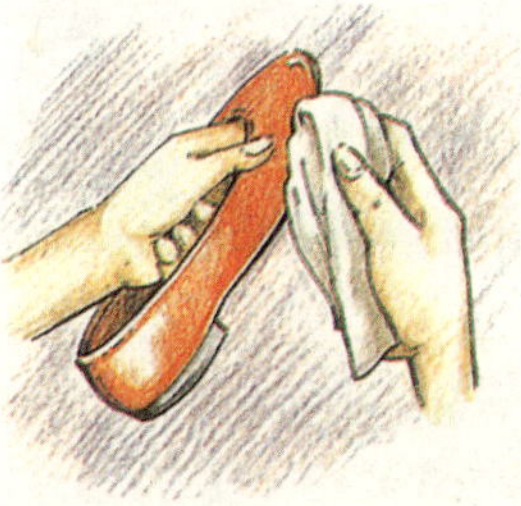

polish [2] /ˈpol·ish; ˈpɒlɪʃ/ *n.*
(**no plural**)
stuff that you rub into something so that it shines
擦亮剂
David bought a tin of shoe polish.
戴维买了一罐鞋油。

polite /po·ˈlite; pəˈlaɪt/ *adj.*
(**more polite, most polite**)
not rude 有礼貌的；客气的
The children are very polite.
孩子们都很有礼貌。
opp. 反义词：impolite, rude
不礼貌的
politely *adv.* 有礼貌地
The children always behave politely.
孩子们总是很有礼貌。

pollution /pol·ˈlu·tion; pəˈluːʃn/ *n.*
(**no plural**)
rubbish, smoke, etc. 污染
There is too much pollution in Hong Kong.
香港的污染太厉害。

pond /pond; pɒnd/ *n.*
piece of water; small lake
水池；池塘
Some ducks were swimming on the pond.
有些鸭子在池塘里游泳。

pony /ˈpo·ny; ˈpəunɪ/ *n.*
(two **ponies**)
small horse 小马
Susan had a ride on a pony.
苏珊骑着小马走了一会。

pool /pool; puːl/ *n.*
1 little water on the ground
小池；水坑
Sam's book fell in a pool of water.
萨姆的书掉到水坑里了。
2 place for swimming 游泳池
David had a swim in the pool.
戴维在游泳池里游了一会。

poor /poor; pɔː/ *adj.*
1 not having much money
贫穷的
The old man was very poor.
那个老人十分贫穷。
opp. 反义词：rich 富有的
2 bad 很坏的；很差的
Tom got poor marks in the exams.
汤姆的考试成绩很差。
3 sad 可怜的
The poor child has fallen down.
那可怜的孩子掉了下来。
the poor *n.* 穷人
John collected money for the poor.
约翰为穷人筹款。

popcorn /ˈpopcorn; ˈpɒpkɔːn/ *n.*
food made with corn 爆玉米花；爆谷（方言）
Sam likes popcorn.
萨姆爱吃爆玉米花。

pop group /ˈpop·group; ˈpɒp gruːp/ *n.*
group that plays modern music 流行乐队
The children liked the pop group.
孩子们喜欢那支流行乐队。
pop music *n.* 流行音乐
They like pop music.
他们喜欢流行音乐。
pop star *n.* 流行音乐歌星
They clapped the pop star.
他们为那流行音乐歌星鼓掌。

popular /ˈpop·u·lar; ˈpɒpjʊlə/ *adj.*
(**more popular, most popular**)
that many people like 大众化的；受大众欢迎的；通俗的
He is a popular singer.
他是个受欢迎的歌手。
opp. 反义词：unpopular 不受欢迎的

population /pop·u·ˈla·tion; pɒpjʊˈleɪʃn/ *n.*
number of people who live in

a place, country, etc. 人口
The population of Hong Kong is more than six million.
香港的人口有六百多万。

pork /pork; pɔːk/ *n.*
(**no plural**)
meat from a pig 猪肉
Peter likes sweet and sour pork.
彼得爱吃咕咾肉。

porridge /'por·ridge; 'pɒrɪdʒ/ *n.*
(**no plural**)
kind of food 麦片粥；粥
David does not like porridge.
戴维不喜欢吃麦片粥。

port /port; pɔːt/ *n.*
town by the sea, with a harbour 港口
Hong Kong is a busy port.
香港是个繁忙的港口。

possible /'pos·si·ble; 'pɒsəbl/ *adj.*
(**more possible, most possible**)
that can happen; that you can do 可能的
It's possible to fly round the world.
环绕地球飞行是可能的。
opp. 反义词：impossible 不可能的
possibly *adv.* 可能地
I can't possibly come tomorrow.
明天我不可能来了。

post [1] /post; pəʊst/ *n.*
1 tall piece of wood or metal that stands in the ground 柱；支柱
There was a notice on the post.
柱上有一张告示。
2 letters and parcels 邮件
The post comes at eight o'clock.
邮件每天八时送达。
lamp-post *n.* 灯柱
The car crashed into the lamp-post.
汽车撞到灯柱上了。
post-box *n.* 邮筒；邮箱
Susan put the letter in the post-box.
苏珊把信投入邮筒里。

postcard *n.* 明信片
Tom sent a postcard to Sam.
汤姆寄了一张明信片给萨姆。
post office *n.* 邮局
David went to the post office.
戴维到邮局去。

post [2] /post; pəʊst/ *v.*
send a letter or parcel 邮寄；投寄
Susan posted the letter.
苏珊寄了那封信。

poster /'post·er; 'pəʊstə/ *n.*
big piece of paper with a picture or words 海报
Susan has a poster of her favourite pop star.
苏珊有一张她最喜欢的流行音乐歌星的海报。

postman /'post·man; 'pəʊstmən/ *n.*
(two **postmen**)
man who takes letters and parcels to homes, offices, etc. 邮递员
The postman comes at eight o'clock.
邮递员八时来。

pot /pot; pɒt/ *n.*
deep, round dish for cooking or holding food 锅；盆；罐；壶；瓶
After dinner, Susan washed the pots.
吃完饭之后，苏珊把锅盆等洗干净。

potato /po·'ta·to; pə'teɪtəʊ/ *n.*
(two **potatoes**)
hard, round vegetable 马铃薯
Baoling does not like potatoes.
宝玲不喜欢吃马铃薯。

potatoes

pottery /'pot·ter·y; 'pɒtərɪ/ *n.*
(**no plural**)
pots, dishes, vases, etc. 陶器
Mrs Wang makes pottery.
王太太会做陶器。

pound (lb) /pound; paʊnd/ *n.*
measure of weight 磅
Anna bought a pound of grapes.
安娜买了一磅葡萄。

pour /pour; pɔ:/ *v.*
let liquid run out of a bottle, etc. 倒；流；注
Peter poured some orange juice in a glass.
彼得在一只玻璃杯里倒了一些橙汁。

powder /'pow·der; 'paʊdə/ *n.*
stuff like dust 粉；粉末
Janet bought a packet of soap powder.
珍妮特买了一包洗衣粉。

power /'pow·er; 'paʊə/ *n.*
being strong; being able to do something 力量；能力
The power of the wind blew the tree over.
风的力量把树吹倒了。

powerful *adj.* 有力的；强的
The wind was very powerful.
风力非常大。

practise /'prac·tise; 'præktɪs/ *v.*
(**practising, practised, practised**)
do something often so that you will do it well 练习；实习
John practises the guitar every day.
约翰天天练习吉他。

practice *n.* 练习
You need a lot of practice to play the guitar well.
要弹好吉他，需要经常练习。

praise /praise; preɪz/ *v.*
(**praising, praised, praised**)
say that someone or something is good 称赞；赞美；赞扬
The teacher praised Sam's work.
老师称赞萨姆的功课做得好。

prawn /prawn; prɔ:n/ *n.*
small sea animal 大虾
Peter likes steamed prawns.
彼得喜欢吃清蒸大虾。

pray /pray; preɪ/ *v.*
speak to one's god 祈祷；祷告
The people were praying in the church.
那些人在教堂里祈祷。

prayer *n.* 祷文
Mrs Chen was saying prayers.
陈太太在念祷文。

precious /'pre·cious; 'preʃəs/ *adj.*
(**more precious, most precious**)
valuable; worth a lot of money 宝贵的；贵重的
A diamond is a precious stone.
钻石是一种宝石。

prefer /pre·'fer; prɪ'fɜ:/ *v.*
(**preferring, preferred, preferred**)
like someone or something better 宁愿；较喜欢
Peter prefers tea to coffee.
彼得喜欢喝茶甚于喜欢喝咖啡。

prepare /pre·'pare; prɪ'peə/ *v.*
(**preparing, prepared, prepared**)
make something ready 准备；预备
Susan prepared lunch.
苏珊准备午饭。

present [1] /'pres·ent; 'preznt/ *adj.*

1 here 在场；到；出席
Tom was not present yesterday.
汤姆昨天没有到。
opp. 反义词：absent 不在场；缺席

2 being now 现在的
Who is the present leader of the country?
谁是这个国家的现任领袖？

at present 现在
Mr Chen is busy at present.
陈先生现在很忙。

present [2] /'pres·ent; 'preznt/ *n.*
something that you give to someone 礼物；赠品
Sam got a lot of presents for his birthday.
萨姆收到很多生日礼物。

president /'pres·i·dent; 'prezɪdənt/ *n.*
chief person in a country
总统；主席
He is the president of the country.
他是这个国家的总统。

press /press; pres/ *v.*
push something
按；压
Mary pressed the doorbell.
玛丽按门铃。

pretend /pre·'tend; prɪ'tend/ *v.*
make other people believe something that is not true
假装；伪装
She pretended that she was ill.
她假装生病。

pretty /'pret·ty; 'prɪtɪ/ *adj.*
(**prettier**, **prettiest**)
lovely 漂亮的；可爱的；美丽的
She is a very pretty girl.
她是个非常美丽可爱的女孩子。
syn. 同义词：beautiful
opp. 反义词：ugly 丑陋的；难看的

price /price; praɪs/ *n.*
money that you pay for something 价钱；价格
Susan asked the price of the dress.
苏珊询问这件连衣裙的价钱。

primary /'pri·ma·ry; 'praɪmərɪ/ *adj.*
first 首要的；基本的
The children are primary students.
孩子们都是小学生。

primary school *n.* 小学
Sam goes to primary school.
萨姆上小学。

prime minister /prime 'mi·ni·ster; praɪm 'mɪnɪstə/ *n.*
chief person in a government
首相；总理
He is the prime minister of the country.
他是这个国家的总理。

prince /prince; prɪns/ *n.*
son of a king or queen 王子
The prince visited Hong Kong.
王子访问香港。

princess /prin·'cess; prɪn'ses/ *n.*
(two **princesses**)
daughter of a king or queen
公主
The princess wore a beautiful dress.
公主穿了一件美丽的连衣裙。

principal /'prin·ci·pal; 'prɪnsəpl/ *n.*
man or woman in charge of a school 校长
The principal came into the classroom.
校长走进教室。

print /print; prɪnt/ *v.*
make words or pictures on paper with a machine 印刷
They print a lot of books in Hong Kong.
他们在香港印刷许多书。
printer *n.* 印刷商；印刷工人
Mr Li is a printer.
李先生是个印刷商。

prison /'pris·on; 'prɪzn/ *n.*
place where criminals must stay for a while 监狱
The judge sent the robber to prison.
法官判盗贼入狱。
prisoner *n.* 囚犯
The prisoners were building a road.
那些囚犯在筑路。

private /'pri·vate; 'praɪvɪt/ *adj.*
(more private, most private)
for one person; for a small group of people 私人的
That is a private garden.
那是个私人花园。
opp. 反义词：public 公众的；公共的

prize /prize; praɪz/ *n.*
present for the winner or best student 奖品；奖金
Peter won a prize in the maths competition.
彼得在数学比赛中得了奖。

probably /'prob·a·bly; 'prɒbəblɪ/ *adv.*
almost certainly 很可能
We shall probably visit Canada next year.
明年我们很可能到加拿大旅行。

problem /'prob·lem; 'prɒbləm/ *n.*
something that is difficult 问题；难题
Pollution is a big problem in Hong Kong.
在香港，污染是个很大的问题。

produce /pro·'duce; prə'dju:s/ *v.*
(producing, produced, produced)
make something 生产；制造
Hong Kong produces a lot of clothes.
香港生产许多成衣。
product *n.* 产品
Toys are a major Hong Kong product.
玩具是香港的主要产品。
production *n.* 生产；产量
The factory exports half its production.
这家工厂把一半的产品出口。

programme /'pro·gramme; 'prəugræm/ *n.*
1 list of things in a concert 节目表；程序表
Sam gave out programmes at the concert.
萨姆在音乐会上分发节目表。
2 something on the radio or television 节目
I saw a good programme on TV last night.
昨天晚上我看了一个很好的电视节目。

progress /'pro·gress; 'prəugres/ *n.*
(no plural)
getting better at school or work 进步；进展
The children were making good progress.
孩子们有很大的进步。

project /'pro·ject; 'prɒdʒekt/ *n.*
something you plan to do 计划；设计
Peter was working on a science project.
彼得正在进行一个科学研究计划。

promise[1] /'prom·ise; 'prɒmɪs/ *n.*
something that you say you will do 诺言；承诺
Sam made a promise to be good.
萨姆答应做个好孩子。
break one's promise 不守诺言
Tom broke his promise to come home early.
汤姆不守诺言，没有早些回家。
keep one's promise 履行诺言
Tom did not keep his promise to come home early.
汤姆不守诺言，没有早些回家。

promise[2] /'prom·ise; 'prɒmɪs/ *v.*
(promising, promised, promised)
say that you will do something 答应；承诺；应允
Tom promised to come home early.
汤姆答应早些回家。

pronoun /'pro·noun; 'prəunaun/ *n.*
word that takes the place of a noun 代词
'He' and 'she' are pronouns.
he 和 she 都是代词。

ɔronounce /pro·'nounce;
rə'naʊns/ *v.*
ɔronouncing, pronounced,
ɔronounced)
nake the sound of a letter or
vord 发音；读
'he word was difficult to
ɔronounce.
这个单词的音很难发。

ɔronunciation
pro·nun·ci·'a·tion; prənʌnsɪ'eɪʃn/ *n.*
ound of a letter or word 发音；
读音
'he pronunciation was
difficult.
这个音很难发。

ɔroof /proof; pru:f/ *n.*
hings that show that
omething is true 证据
'he police had proof that
he man stole the money.
警方有证据证明那人偷了钱。

ɔropeller /pro·'pel·ler;
rə'pelə/ *n.*
hing that makes a boat or
ɔlane move 推进器；螺旋桨
'he boat had two propellers.
那艘船有两个推进器。

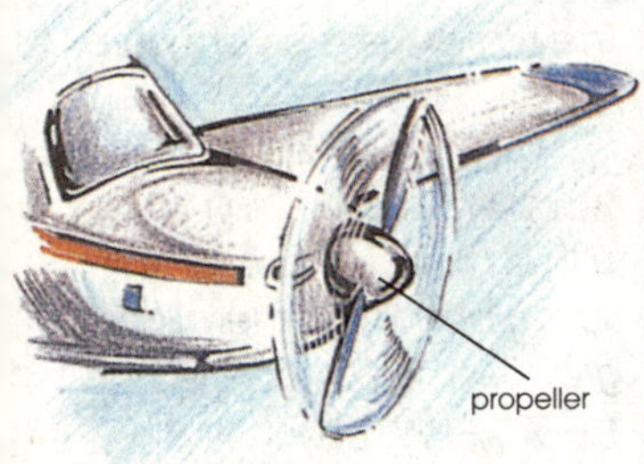

ɔroperly /'prop·er·ly; 'prɒpəlɪ/
adv.
correctly 适合地；正当地
Baoling always does her
homework properly.
宝玲总是把家庭作业做得好好的。

property /'pro·per·ty;
'prɒpətɪ/ *n.*
(**no plural**)
things that belong to you
财产；所有物
The children took care of
their property.
孩子们爱护自己的财物。

protect /pro·'tect; prə'tekt/ *v.*
keep a person or place safe
保护
The army protected the
border.
陆军保卫边界。

proud /proud; praud/ *adj.*
feeling pleased about
something you have or did
骄傲；自豪；得意
Sam is very proud of his new
bicycle.
萨姆因有一辆新自行车而感到十分自
豪。
proudly *adv.* 骄傲地；得意
洋洋地
Sam proudly rode his new
bicycle in the playground.
萨姆在操场上得意洋洋地骑他的新自
行车。

prove /prove; pru:v/ *v.*
(**proving, proved, proved**)
show that something is true
证明；证实
Can you prove that this is
your money?
你能证明这些钱是你的吗？

public /'pub·lic; 'pʌblɪk/ *adj.*
for all people 公共的；公众的
In Hong Kong, most people
use public transport.
在香港，大部分人使用公共交通工具。
opp. 反义词：private 私人的

public light bus /'pub·lic
light bus; 'pʌblɪk laɪt bʌs/ *n.*
(two **public light buses**)
small bus 小型公共汽车；小巴（方
言）
Sam took a public light bus
to school.
萨姆乘小型公共汽车上学。

public light buses

pull /pull; pʊl/ *v.*
move something towards
you; go forward moving a
vehicle behind you 拉；拖
The tractor was pulling a
cart.
拖拉机拖着一辆手推车。
opp. 反义词：push 推

pullover /'pull·ov·er;
'pʊləʊvə/ *n.*
piece of clothing made from
wool that you wear over a
shirt or blouse 套头毛衣
When it is cold, Mary wears
a pullover.
天气寒冷时玛丽会穿上套头毛衣。

pump [1] /pump; pʌmp/ *n.*
machine that moves water, air, etc., into or out of something 泵；抽水机；打气筒
The farmer switched on the pump.
那农民开动抽水机。

pump [2] /pump; pʌmp/ *v.*
move water, air, etc., into or out of something 抽水；打气
The farmer pumps water into his fields.
那农民把水抽到田里。

pumpkin /'pump·kin; 'pʌmpkɪn/ *n.*
large fruit 南瓜
The fairy changed the pumpkin into a coach.
那小仙子把南瓜变成一辆马车。

punctual /'punc·tu·al; 'pʌŋktʃuəl/ *adj.*
(**more punctual, most punctual**)
at the right time 准时；守时
Peter always tries to be punctual.
彼得总是尽量守时。

punctuation /punc·tu·'a·tion; pʌŋktʃu'eɪʃn/ *n.*
marks like (!) (,) (?) when you are writing 标点符号
Sam's punctuation is not very good.
萨姆的标点符号用得不太好。

puncture /'punc·ture; 'pʌŋktʃə/ *n.*
hole in a tyre 小孔
Mary's bicycle had a puncture.
玛丽的自行车轮胎上有一个小孔。

punish /'pun·ish; 'pʌnɪʃ/ *v.*
do something to someone because they were bad 惩罚；处罚
The man was punished for stealing.
那人因为偷窃而受到惩罚。
punishment *n.* 惩罚
The teacher gave the children a punishment.
老师给孩子们一次惩罚。

pupil /'pu·pil; 'pju:pl/ *n.*
someone who is learning something with a teacher 学生
There were thirty pupils in the class.
班里有三十个学生。

pupils

puppet /'pup·pet; 'pʌpɪt/ *n.*
toy like a small person or animal that can move when you pull strings or put your hand inside it 木偶
The children were making puppets.
孩子们正在制作木偶。

puppets

puppy /'pup·py; 'pʌpɪ/ *n.*
(two **puppies**)
young dog 小狗
The dog had two puppies.
那只狗有两只小狗。

pure /pure; pjuə/ *adj.*
(**purer, purest**)
with nothing else in it 纯净的；纯洁的
The water here is very pure.
这里的水很纯净。

purple /'pur·ple; 'pɜ:pl/ *adj.*
with a blue-red colour 紫色
Susan bought some purple grapes.
苏珊买了一些紫葡萄。

purpose /'pur·pose; pɜ:pəs/ *n.*
what you plan to do 目的；意图
The teacher told the pupils the purpose of the exercise.
老师告诉学生做这个练习的目的。
on purpose 故意
Tom did not break the vase on purpose.
汤姆不是故意打破花瓶的。

purr /purr; pɜ:/ *v.*
make the sound of a happy cat 猫儿愉快时发出的呜呜声
The cat was purring.
那只猫在呜呜地叫。

purse /purse; pɜ:s/ *n.*
small bag where you keep money 小钱包
Mary had fifty dollars in her purse.
玛丽的小钱包里有五十港元。

purses

push /push; pʊʃ/ *v.*
move something away from you; go forward, moving a vehicle in front of you 推
We had to push the car to the side of the road.
我们只好把汽车推到路边。
opp. 反义词：pull 拉

put /put; pʊt/ *v.*
(putting, put, put)
move something to another place 放置；摆放
Anna put her books on a shelf.
安娜把书籍放在书架上。
put on 打开（开关）
Mary put the light on.
玛丽开了电灯。
put out 关掉（开关）
Mary put out the light.
玛丽把电灯关掉。

puzzle /'puz·zle; 'pʌzl/ *n.*
game where you must find an answer 填字游戏；拼图
David likes doing puzzles.
戴维喜欢玩填字游戏。

puzzles

pyjamas /py·'ja·mas; pə'dʒɑ:məz/ *n.*
(plural)
loose jacket and trousers that you wear in bed 睡衣
Sam has some new pyjamas.
萨姆有几套新的睡衣。

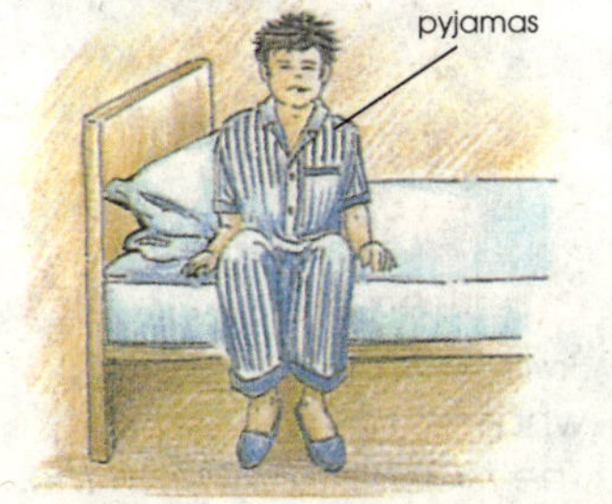

pyramid /'pyr·a·mid; 'pɪrəmɪd/ *n.*
solid shape that comes to a point at the top 金字塔
The shopkeeper made a pyramid of apples.
店主把苹果堆成金字塔形。

pyramids

quality /'qual·i·ty; 'kwɒlətɪ/ *n.*
(qualities)
how good or bad something is 质量
The shop has good quality fruit.
那家店的水果质量很好。

quantity /'quan·ti·ty; 'kwɒntətɪ/ *n.*
(quantities)
amount; how much there is of something 量
Hong Kong imports a large quantity of food.
香港进口大量食品。

quarrel [1] /ˈquar·rel; ˈkwɒrəl/ *n.*
fight with words 吵架；口角
The children had a quarrel in the playground.
孩子们在操场上吵架。

quarrel [2] /ˈquar·rel; ˈkwɒrəl/ *v.*
(**quarrelling, quarrelled, quarrelled**)
talk angrily because you cannot agree 吵架；争吵
The children were quarrelling about the toys.
孩子们为争玩具而吵起来。

quarry /ˈquar·ry; ˈkwɒrɪ/ *n.*
(two **quarries**)
place where you get stone, sand, etc., out of the ground
石料场；采石场
The quarry produces good stone.
这个采石场出产的石料很好。

quarter /ˈquar·ter; ˈkwɔːtə/ *n.*
one of four equal parts 四分之一
Mrs Chen cut the oranges into quarters.
陈太太把橙切成四份。

a quarter 四分之一
Mr Chen gave a quarter of the orange to Peter.
陈太太分了四分之一的橙给彼得。

a quarter past （指时间）过十五分
It's a quarter past eight.
现在是八时十五分。

a quarter to （指时间）差十五分
It's a quarter to twelve.
十二时差十五分。

three-quarters 四分之三
Mr Chen ate three-quarters of the orange.
陈先生吃了那个橙的四分之三。

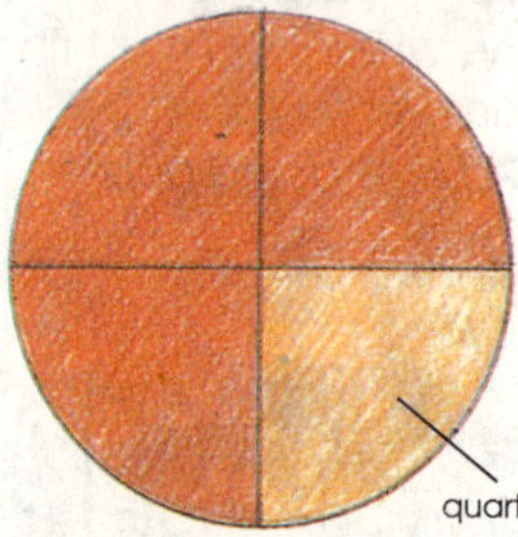

queen /queen; kwiːn/ *n.*
wife of a king; woman who rules a country 皇后；女王
Great Britain has a queen.
英国有女王。

question [1] /ˈques·tion; ˈkwestʃən/ *n.*
what you ask 问题
The teacher answered the children's questions.
教师回答孩子们的问题。
opp. 反义词：answer, reply 答案；答复

question [2] /ˈques·tion; ˈkwestʃən/ *v.*
ask things 问；询问
The teacher questioned the children.
教师问孩子们问题。
opp. 反义词：answer, reply 回答

question mark /ˈques·tion mark; ˈkwestʃən mɑːk/ *n.*
sign (?) that you put at the end of a sentence to show a question 问号

queue /queue; kjuː/ *n.*
line of people who are waiting to do something （排队等候的）一队人
There was a long queue at the bus-stop.
公共汽车站排了长长的一队人。

quick /quick; kwɪk/ *adj.*
fast; taking a little time 快的；迅速的
Susan is a quick runner.
苏珊跑得很快。
opp. 反义词：slow 慢的

quickly *adv.* 很快地
The children walked quickly to school.
孩子们快步走向学校。

quick

quiet /'qui·et; 'kwaɪət/ *adj.*
not loud; with little sound; with no sound 安静；寂静；宁静
In Hong Kong, the streets are never quiet.
香港的街道从来没有安静的时刻。
syn. 同义词：silent
opp. 反义词：noisy 吵闹；喧闹
be quiet 安静下来；不要吵
Be quiet! The baby is asleep.
不要吵，婴儿在睡觉呢。
quietly *adv.* 安静地；静静地
Do your work quietly.
静静地做你的工作吧。

quilt /quilt; kwɪlt/ *n.*
thick, warm cover for a bed
被子；棉被
Sam has a quilt on his bed in winter.
冬天时萨姆的床上有被子。

quite /quite; kwaɪt/ *adv.*
1 in every way 完全地
The teacher is quite right. Tom is a naughty boy.
老师说得完全对，汤姆是个顽皮的孩子。
2 rather 相当；颇
It's quite hot here in summer.
这里的夏天相当热。

quiz /quiz; kwɪz/ *n.*
(**two quizzes**)
game where you try to answer questions 问答比赛
Baoling won the spelling quiz.
宝玲在英语拼写比赛中获胜。

quotation marks
/quo·'ta·tion marks; kwəu'teɪʃn mɑːks/ *n.*
signs (' ') (" ") that you put around words to show what someone said or wrote 引号

rabbit /'rab·bit; 'ræbɪt/ *n.*
small animal with long ears 兔
David has a pet rabbit.
戴维养了一只兔子做宠物

rabbits

race [1] /race; reɪs/ *n.*
competition to see who can run, swim, ride, drive, etc., fastest 比赛；竞赛
Suan won the fifty-metre race.
苏珊在五十米赛跑中得了第一名。

race-course *n.* 赛马场
There are two race-courses in Hong Kong.
香港有两个赛马场。
race-horse *n.* 赛马用的马
Peter saw some race-horses in Shatin.
彼得在沙田看见一些赛马用的马。

race [2] /race; reɪs/ *v.*
(**racing, raced, raced**)
run, swim, ride, drive, etc., in a competition 竞赛
Peter raced David in the pool.
彼得和戴维在游泳池里比赛。

racket /'rack·et; 'rækɪt/ *n.*
thing for hitting a ball in tennis, badminton, etc. 球拍
Susan bought a new tennis racket.
苏珊买了一个新网球拍。

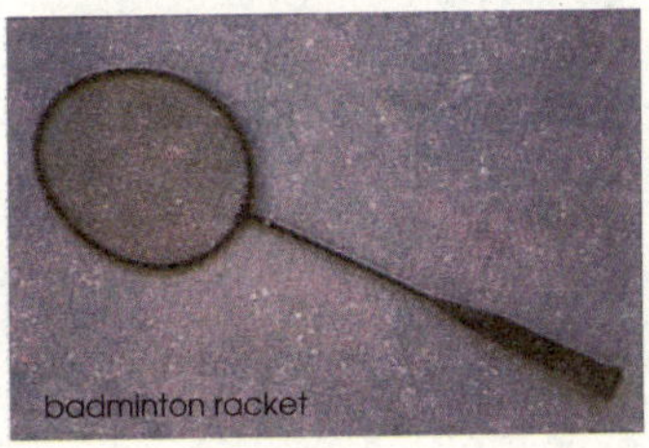
badminton racket

radio /'ra·di·o; 'reɪdɪəu/ *n.*
thing that brings voices and music from far away 收音机
Sam takes his radio to the beach.
萨姆把他的收音机带到海滩去。

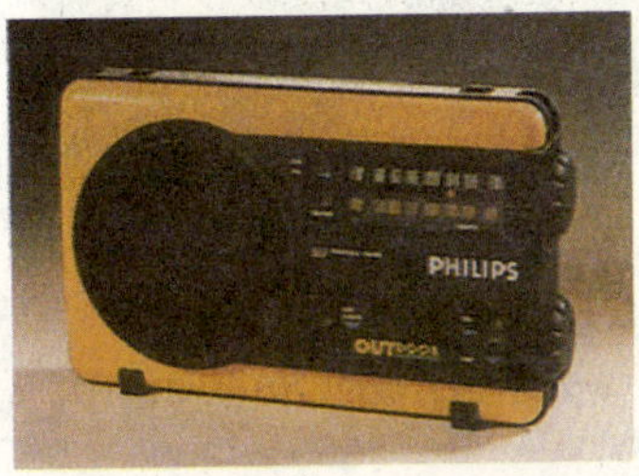

raft /raft; rɑːft/ *n.*
flat boat 筏
They sailed across the ocean on a raft.
他们乘筏漂洋过海。

rail /rail; reɪl/ *n.*
1 long piece of wood or metal fixed to a wall 扶手；栏杆
Hold the rail when you walk down the stairs.
下楼梯时要扶着扶手。
2 long piece of metal that makes a track for a train 路轨
You must not walk on the rails.
切勿在路轨上走。

railway /'rail·way; 'reɪlweɪ/ *n.*
track where a train runs 铁路
There are railways all over China.
中国到处都有铁路。

rain [1] /rain; reɪn/ *n.*
(no plural)
water that falls from the sky 雨
There was a lot of rain last month.
上个月下了很多雨。
rainbow *n.* 彩虹
There was a beautiful rainbow in the sky.
天空中有一道美丽的彩虹。
raincoat *n.* 雨衣
Mary put her raincoat on and went to school.
玛丽穿上雨衣上学去。

rainfall *n.* 雨量
The annual rainfall in Hong Kong is 2 225 mm.
香港全年的雨量是 2 225 毫米。
rain-water *n.* 雨水
Rain-water is collected in reservoirs.
雨水积聚在水库里。

rain [2] /rain; reɪn/ *v.*
water falling from the sky 下雨
It rains a lot in Hong Kong.
香港常下雨。
it is raining 下雨了

rainy /'rain·y; 'reɪnɪ/ *adj.*
(rainier, rainiest)
having rain 多雨的；下雨的
There were ten rainy days last month.
上个月有十天下雨。
opp. 反义词：dry 干燥的

raise /raise; reɪz/ *v.*
(raising, raised, raised)
lift someone or something 举起；升起
Raise your hand if you know the answer.
知道答案的请举手。
opp. 反义词：lower 放下；降低

ran /ran; ræn/ *v.*
p.t. of **run** run 的过去式
John ran to school.
约翰跑到学校去。

rang /rang; ræŋ/ *v.*
p.t. of **ring** ring 的过去式
Peter rang the bell.
彼得鸣钟。

rare /rare; reə/ *adj.*
(rarer, rarest)
not happening often; that you do not often see or hear 罕有的；稀有的
The panda is very rare.
熊猫是十分罕有的动物。
opp. 反义词：common 常见的
Usage note: A thing or animal that is *rare* may have been common — *The panda is now a rare animal. This stamp is rare now.*
用法：rare 的动物或东西以前可能是很常见的，例如 The panda is now a rare animal 及 This stamp is rare now。

rat /rat; ræt/ *n.*
animal like a big mouse 老鼠
The dog killed the rat.
那只狗弄死了那只老鼠。

rather /'rath·er; 'rɑːðə/ *adv.*
a little 相当
I'm rather tired.
我相当累了。
would rather 宁愿
Sam would rather play football than watch TV.
萨姆宁愿踢足球而不看电视。

raw /raw; rɔː/ *adj.*
not cooked 生的；未煮过的
Some raw vegetables are good for you.
有些未煮过的蔬菜对你有益。

ray /ray; reɪ/ *n.*
line of light 光线
A ray of sunshine came through the window.
一道日光透过窗户射进来。

reach /reach; riːtʃ/ *v.*
1 put your hand out and touch something 伸手触及
Sam could not reach the shelf.
萨姆触不到那架子。

2 arrive at 到达；抵达
They reached Shatin at ten o'clock.
他们十时到达沙田。

read /read; riːd/ *v.*
(reading, read, read)
understand written words; look at words and say them aloud 读；看懂；念
David reads a lot of books.
戴维看很多书。

reader /'read·er; 'riːdə/ *n.*
1 someone who is reading 看书的人；读者
David is a quick reader.
戴维看书看得很快。
2 book for reading in class 读本；读物
Our reader is very interesting.
我们的课本十分有趣。

ready /'read·y; 'redɪ/ *adj.*
(readier, readiest)
1 able to do something now 准备好
The family is ready to go on holiday.
这家人准备度假去了。
2 prepared 准备好的
Is dinner ready?
饭准备好了吗?
get ready 准备
Susan got ready to go to school.
苏珊准备上学去。

real /real; rɪəl/ *adj.*
true 真的；真正的
Susan's dress is real silk.
苏珊的连衣裙是真丝做的。

really /'re·al·ly; 'rɪəlɪ/ *adv.*
1 truly 真的
Have you really been to Australia?
你真的去过澳大利亚吗?
2 very 很；非常
The boys have been really naughty today.
这些男孩子今天实在非常顽皮。

rear /rear; rɪə/ *n.*
(no plural)
back 后部；背面
Tom sat at the rear of the bus.
汤姆坐在公共汽车的后排座位上。

reason /'rea·son; 'riːzn/ *n.*
why you do or say something 理由；原因
Sam had a good reason for being late.
萨姆迟到是有充分的理由的。

receive /re·'ceive; rɪ'siːv/ *v.*
(receiving, received, received)
get something 接受；接到
Mary received a letter from Susan.
玛丽接到苏珊寄来的信。
opp. 相反词：give, send 给；送

recently /'re·cent·ly; 'riːsntlɪ/ *adv.*
(more recently, most recently)
short time ago 最近
The family emigrated to Canada recently.
这家人最近移民加拿大。

recess /re·ˈcess; rɪˈses/ *n.*
(two recesses)
a break 休息时间；小憩
At school, we have a recess at ten o'clock.
学校十时正有一次小憩。

recite /re·ˈcite; rɪˈsaɪt/ *v.*
(reciting, recited, recited)
say a poem that you have learnt 背诵
Xiaofang recited a poem in class.
小芳在班上背诵了一首诗。

recognize, recognise
/ˈrec·og·nize, ˈrec·og·nise; ˈrekəgnaɪz, ˈrekəgnaɪz/ *v.*
(recognizing, recognized, recognized)
know someone when you see him again; know something because you have seen it or heard it before 认识；认出
I didn't recognize Mary without her glasses.
玛丽没有戴眼镜，我没认出她。

record [1] /ˈre·cord; ˈrekɔ:d/ *n.*
1 music disc 唱片
The children were playing records.
孩子们在放唱片。

2 things written down 纪录
The teacher keeps a record of the children's marks.
教师保存了一份孩子们的成绩纪录。

3 the best ever done 最高纪录
John broke the school record for the fifty-metre race.
约翰五十米赛跑的成绩破了学校纪录。

record-player *n.* 唱机
Susan has a record-player.
苏珊有一台唱机。

record [2] /re·ˈcord; rɪˈkɔ:d/ *v.*
put in writing, on tape or on film 记录；录音；录像
Mr Chen recorded the TV programme.
陈先生把那电视节目录了下来。

recorder /re·ˈcor·der; rɪˈkɔ:də/ *n.*
musical instrument 笛子
Anna plays the recorder.
安娜会吹笛子。

rectangle /ˈrec·tan·gle; ˈrektæŋgl/ *n.*
four-sided shape 长方形
Sam drew a rectangle.
萨姆画了一个长方形。

red /red; red/ *adj.*
(redder, reddest)
with the colour of blood
红色的
Xiaofang has a nice red dress.
小芳有一条很好看的红色连衣裙。

referee /ref·er·ˈee; refəˈri:/ *n.*
someone who makes sure that players are playing a game in the right way （球赛的）裁判员
The referee blew his whistle for the end of the match.
裁判员吹哨子，表示比赛结束。

reflect /re·ˈflect; rɪˈflekt/ *v.*
throw back light 反射；反映
The mirror reflected the sunlight.
镜子把阳光反射开来。

reflection /re·ˈflec·tion; rɪˈflekʃn/ *n.*
what you see in a mirror or something shiny 影像
Susan looked at the reflection in the window.
苏珊看着窗上反映出来的影像。

refreshments /re·'fresh·ments; rɪ'freʃmənts/ *n.* **(plural)**
food and drink that you can buy 点心；小吃
The children stopped at a café to get some refreshments.
孩子们在小餐馆前停下来买些点心吃。

refrigerator /re·'frig·er·a·tor; rɪ'frɪdʒəreɪtə/ *n.*
special cold cupboard for keeping food fresh 冰箱；雪柜（方言）
Mrs Chen put the drinks in the refrigerator.
陈太太把饮料放在冰箱里。
syn. 同义词：fridge

refugee /re·fu·'gee; refjʊ'dʒi:/ *n.*
someone who leaves his own country because he is in danger and tries to find a new safe home 难民
There were some refugees on the island.
岛上有些难民。

refuse /re·'fuse; rɪ'fju:z/ *v.* **(refusing, refused, refused)**
say 'no' when someone asks you to do something 拒绝
Mary refused to help Tom with his homework.
玛丽拒绝帮助汤姆做家庭作业。
opp. 反义词：agree 同意

register /'reg·is·ter; 'redʒɪstə/ *n.*
book in which the names of children are written 记录；注册簿
The teacher wrote the children's names in the register.
教师把孩子们的名字登记在注册簿上。

relation, relative /re·'la·tion, 'rel·a·tive; rɪ'leɪʃn, 'relətɪv/ *n.*
someone in your family 亲戚；亲属
Xiaofang visits her relatives at Chinese New year.
小芳在农历新年的时候去探访她的亲戚。

religion /re·'li·gion; rɪ'lɪdʒən/ *n.*
what you believe about your god or gods 宗教
There are many religions in the world.
世界上有许多种宗教。

remain /re·'main; rɪ'meɪn/ *v.*
1 stay in a place after a part has gone 留下；剩下
If you take six from ten, four remains.
十减六剩四。
2 stay in the same place 停留；逗留
Peter had to remain at school for an hour.
彼得要留在学校一小时。
3 not change 保持；无变化
Fish will not remain fresh for long.
鱼肉不能长久保持新鲜。

remainder /re·'main·der; rɪ'meɪndə/ *n.*
what is left 剩下来的
Tom ate most of the sweets and left the remainder for Peter.
汤姆吃了大部分的糖，剩下的就给彼得吃。

remember /re·'mem·ber; rɪ'membə/ *v.*
keep something in your mind 记得；记起
Susan always remembers her friends' birthdays.
苏珊总是记得她朋友们的生日。
opp. 反义词：forget 忘记

remind /re·'mind; rɪ'maɪnd/ *v.*
tell someone to keep something in their mind 提醒
Mrs Chen reminded Peter to do his homework.
陈太太提醒彼得做家庭作业。

remove /re·'move; rɪ'mu:v/ *v.* **(removing, removed, removed)**
take something away 拿开；取去；搬开
David removed his books from his desk.
戴维从书桌上拿走他的书。

rent[1] /rent; rent/ *n.*
money that you pay to use the building, car, land, etc., of another person 租金
How much rent do you pay for your flat?
你的公寓房租金是多少？

rent [2] /rent; rent/ *v.*
pay to use the building, car, land, etc., of another person
租用
On holiday, Mrs Wang always rents a car.
王太太在假日总是租用汽车。

repair [1] /re·'pair; rɪ'peə/ *v.*
mend something; make something good again 修理
The mechanic repaired Mrs Wang's car.
那个技工修理王太太的汽车
syn. 同义词：fix

repair [2] /re·'pair; rɪ'peə/ *n.*
making something good again 修理
Mr Wang's car needed a lot of repairs.
王先生的车子需要大修。

repeat /re·'peat; rɪ'pi:t/ *v.*
say or do something again
重说；重做；重复
Would you repeat the question, please?
请再说一遍你的问题好吗？

replace /re·'place; rɪ'pleɪs/ *v.*
(**replacing, replaced, replaced**)
1 put something where it was before 放回原处
Please replace the books on the shelves after you have read them.
请你把看过的书放回书架上。
2 put one thing in the place of another 代替
If you lose a book, you will have to replace it with a new one.
如果你把书丢了，就必须买一本新的来代替。

reply [1] /re·'ply; rɪ'plaɪ/ *v.*
(**replying, replied, replied**)
answer 回答
Susan replied to Anna's letter.
苏珊回信给安娜。
opp. 反义词：ask 问

reply [2] /re·'ply; rɪ'plaɪ/ *n.*
(two **replies**)
answer 答复
Anna received Susan's reply to her letter.
安娜接到了苏珊给她的回信。
opp. 反义词：question 问题

report /re·'port; rɪ'pɔ:t/ *n.*
1 piece of news; words in a newspaper, on television, etc., that tell people about something 报告；报道
Fishermen always listen to the weather report.
渔民经常听天气报告。
2 what your teachers write about you 学业成绩报告
Susan's school report was very good.
苏珊的成绩报告很好。
reporter *n.* 新闻记者
The reporter wrote about the typhoon.
记者写了有关台风情况的报道。

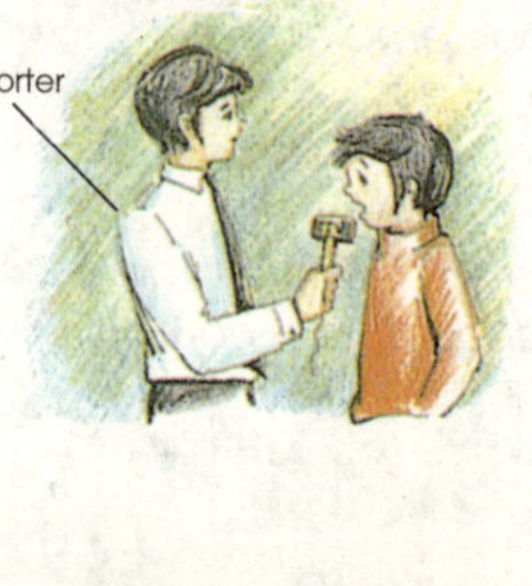

represent /re·pre·'sent; reprɪ'zent/ *v.*
do something in place of someone else 代表
Sam represented his school in the race.
萨姆代表学校参加比赛。

reptile /'rep·tile; 'reptaɪl/ *n.*
animal with cold blood
爬行动物；爬虫类动物
Snakes and lizards are reptiles.
蛇和蜥蜴都是爬行动物。

rescue /'res·cue; 'reskju:/ *v.*
(**rescuing, rescued, rescued**)
save someone or something from danger 救援
The fireman rescued the man from the burning building.
消防员把那个人从燃烧着的建筑物里救出来。
come to the rescue 救援；救助
The fireman came to the rescue and saved the man.
消防员前来抢救，把那人救了出来。

reservoir /'res·er·voir; 'rezəvwɑ:/ *n.*
lake where a town stores its water 水库；水塘

Hong Kong has some big reservoirs.
香港有一些大型水库。

respect /re·'spect; rɪ'spekt/ *v.*
feel that someone is good and admire him 尊敬
You should respect your parents.
你们应该尊敬父母。

responsible /re·'spon·sible; rɪ'spɒnsəbl/ *adj.*
having a duty and doing it 负责的
The man is responsible for guarding the bank.
那人负责守卫银行。

rest [1] /rest; rest/ *v.*
be still and quiet 休息
Mrs Chen works in the morning and rests in the afternoon.
陈太太上午工作，下午休息。

rest [2] /rest; rest/ *n.*
1 keeping still; not working 静止；休息
If you are tired, have a rest.
如果你累了，就休息一下吧。
2 what there is when some has gone; the other part 其余的；剩余的
David ate some of the sweets and Peter ate the rest.
戴维吃了部分的糖，剩下来的给彼得吃了。

restaurant /'res·tau·rant; 'restrɒnt/ *n.*
place where you buy a meal and eat it 餐馆；饭店
The family had a good meal in the restaurant.
那家人在饭店吃了一顿很好的饭。

result /re·'sult; rɪ'zʌlt/ *n.*
what happens because of another thing 结果
The accident was the result of bad driving.
这次事故是不小心驾驶的结果。

return [1] /re·'turn; rɪ'tɜ:n/ *v.*
1 come back; go back 回来；回去
Anna returned from Canada yesterday.
安娜昨天从加拿大回来。
2 give something back 归还
Sam returned a record to Susan.
萨姆把唱片还给苏珊。

return [2] /re·'turn; rɪ'tɜ:n/ *n.*
(no plural)
1 coming back; going back 回来；回去
Mrs Wang waited for the return of her husband.
王太太等她丈夫回来。
2 going and coming back 来回
David always buys a return ticket when he takes the ferry.
戴维搭乘渡轮总是买来回票。

reverse /re·'verse; rɪ'vɜ:s/ *v.*
(reversing, reversed, reversed)
go backwards 倒退
The car reversed into the road.
汽车倒退到马路上去。

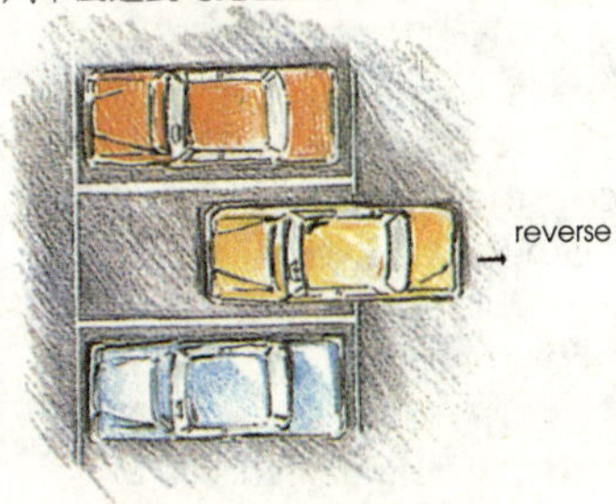

revise /re·'vise; rɪ'vaɪz/ *v.*
(revising, revised, revised)
learn something again 反复阅读；温习
Susan revised her history before the test.
苏珊在测验前温习历史。
revision *n.* 复习；温习
Sam did a lot of revision for the exam.
萨姆为准备考试而作了很多温习。

reward [1] /re·'ward; rɪ'wɔ:d/ *n.*
present or money to thank someone 报酬；酬金
Susan gave the boy a reward for finding her purse.
苏珊给了男孩一些报酬，感谢他找回她的钱包。

reward [2] /re·'ward; rɪ'wɔ:d/ *v.*
give a present or money to thank someone for something 酬谢
Susan rewarded the boy who found her purse.
苏珊酬谢那个给她找回钱包的男孩。

rhyme [1] /rhyme; raɪm/ *n.*
1 words that end with the same sound 押韵的词
'Look' and 'book' are rhymes.
look和book是押韵的词。
2 songs or poems with rhymes 儿歌；童谣
Mrs Li sang nursery rhymes to her children.
李太太唱儿歌给她的孩子们听。

rhyme [2] /rhyme; raɪm/ *v.*
have the same sound as another word 押韵
'Pen' rhymes with 'men'.
pen和men押韵。

rhythm /ˈrhy·thm; ˈrɪðəm/ *n.*
pattern of strong and weak sounds in music or words 节奏
The music has a very good rhythm.
这首乐曲的节奏很美妙。

ribbon /ˈrib·bon; ˈrɪbən/ *n.*
long, narrow piece of cloth 丝带
Xiaofang has a red ribbon in her hair.
小芳的头发上系了一条红丝带。

rice /rice; raɪs/ *n.*
(no plural)
plant with seeds that you can eat 米；饭
Peter likes chicken and rice.
彼得喜欢吃鸡饭。

rice

rich /rich; rɪtʃ/ *adj.*
with a lot of money, land, etc. 富有的；有钱的
The rich family has a big house with a swimming pool.
这个富有人家有一所带游泳池的大宅。
opp. 反义词：poor 贫穷的

rickshaw /ˈrick·shaw; ˈrɪkʃɔː/ *n.*
sort of cart for carrying people 人力车
The tourists had a ride in a rickshaw.
游客们坐了一次人力车。

rid, get rid of /rid, get ride of; rɪd, get rɪd əv/ *v.*
throw something away; make someone or something go away 清除；除去；扔掉
Mrs Wang got rid of some old furniture.
王太太把一些旧家具处理掉了。

riddle /ˈrid·dle; ˈrɪdl/ *n.*
game with words where you must find an answer; trick question 谜语；难解的问题
John guessed the answer to the riddle.
约翰猜出了谜语。

ride [1] /ride; raɪd/ *n.*
travelling on an animal, bicycle or motor-bike, or in a car, bus, train, etc. 骑；乘坐
Sam had a ride on David's bicycle.
萨姆骑过戴维的自行车。

rider *n.* 骑马的人；骑自行车的人
The rider fell off his horse.
骑马的人从马上摔了下来。
riding *n.* 骑马
Susan likes riding.
苏珊喜欢骑马。

ride [2] /ride; raɪd/ *v.*
(riding, rode, ridden)
1 travel on an animal, a bicycle or a motor-bike 骑（马、自行车、摩托车等）
Mr Chen rides a motor-bike.
陈先生骑摩托车。
2 travel in a car, bus, train, etc. 乘坐（汽车、公共汽车、火车等）
Laura rides to school in her mother's car.
劳拉坐妈妈的汽车上学。

right [1] /right; raɪt/ *adj.*
1 opposite of left 右的
You shake hands with your

right hand.
握手用右手。
opp. 反义词: left 左的
2 good 应该的; 正当的
It is not right to cheat.
欺骗是不应该的。
opp. 反义词: wrong 错误的
3 correct; with no mistakes
正确的; 对的
Are these shoes the right size?
这些鞋子大小合适吗?
opp. 反义词: wrong 错误的
be right 对的
You are right. The match is tomorrow.
你说得对，比赛是在明天举行。

right [2] /right; raɪt/ *adv.*
1 correctly 正确地; 对的
Sam did not do the work right.
萨姆的工作做得不对。
opp. 反义词: wrongly 错误的
2 on the right 向右
Turn right and you will come to the park.
向右一拐就到公园。
opp. 反义词: left 向左
right here 就在这里
The crash was right here.
那次撞车事故就是在这里发生的。
right now 现在; 立刻
I'm going to do my homework right now.
我立刻开始做家庭作业。

ring [1] /ring; rɪŋ/ *n.*
1 circle of metal one wears on one's finger 戒指; 指环
Mrs Wang has a diamond ring.
王太太有一枚钻石戒指。

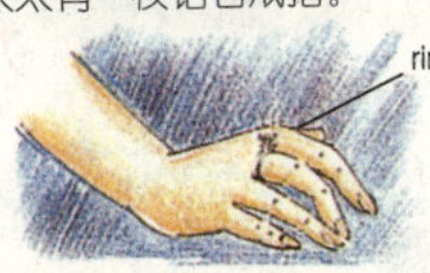

2 circle 圆圈
The children stood in a ring.
孩子们站成一个圆圈。

ring [2] /ring; rɪŋ/ *v.*
(ringing, rang, rung)
1 hit or press a bell 按(钟或铃)
Susan rang the bell.
苏珊按铃。
2 telephone someone 打电话
Peter rang David about the homework.
彼得打电话给戴维谈家庭作业。

ripe /ripe; raɪp/ *adj.*
(riper, ripest)
ready to pick and eat 成熟的
Mary bought some ripe pears.
玛丽买了些熟透了的梨子。

rise /rise; raɪz/ *v.*
(rising, rose, risen)
1 go up 升起
The sun rose at five o'clock.
太阳五时升起。
opp. 反义词: set 落下
2 get up 起床
Mr Chen rises at six o'clock.
陈先生六时起床。

risk [1] /risk; rɪsk/ *n.*
danger; chance that something bad may happen
危险; 冒险
Don't take any risks when you go swimming.
游泳时不要冒险。

risk [2] /risk; rɪsk/ *v.*
take the chance that something bad may happen
冒险
Don't risk swimming when the sea is rough.
海面浪大时不要冒险去游泳。

river /'riv·er; 'rɪvə/ *n.*
big stream of water that flows to the sea 河流; 江河
The Zhujiang River is very muddy.
珠江的水有很多泥沙。

road /road; rəud/ *n.*
way from one place to another where cars, animals and people can go 道路; 马路
The roads in Hong Kong are very busy.
香港的道路非常繁忙。

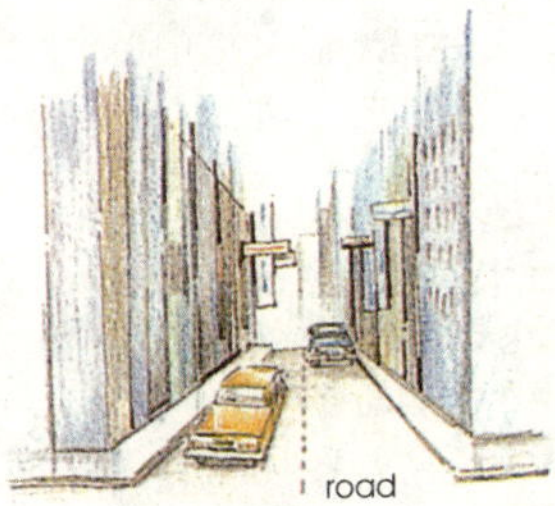

roar [1] /roar; rɔː/ *n.*
loud, deep sound 吼叫
The lion gave a loud roar.
狮子在大声吼叫。

roar [2] /roar; rɔː/ *v.*
make a loud, deep sound
吼叫
The lion roared loudly.
狮子大声地吼叫。

roast /roast; rəust/ *adj.*
meat or vegetables cooked in an oven 烤过的
Peter likes roast pork.
彼得喜欢吃烤猪肉。

rob /rob; rɒb/ *v.*
(robbing, robbed, robbed)
steal something from someone 抢劫
The men robbed the bank.
那几个人抢劫了银行。
robber *n.* 盗贼
The robbers ran out of the bank with some money.
盗贼带着钱逃出了银行。
robbery *n.* 抢劫案
There was a robbery at the bank.
银行发生了抢劫案。
Usage note: *Rob* is used about a place or person — *He robbed a bank. The man was robbed in the street. Steal* is used for things — *The man stole the money.*
用法：说某人或某地方被抢劫，我们用 rob，例如 He robbed a bank 或 The man was robbed in the street。
如果被偷去的是物件，我们用 steal，例如 The man stole the money。

robot /'ro·bot; 'rəubɒt/ *n.*
1 machine that does the work of a person 机器人（替代人操作的）自动机
The robots were making cars.
自动机在制造汽车。
2 machine that looks like a person 机器人
The robots attacked the soldiers.
机器人攻击那些士兵。

robots

rock /rock; rɒk/ *n.*
stone; very hard part of the earth 石；岩石
The children were playing on the rocks.
孩子们在石上玩耍。

rocket /'rock·et; 'rɒkɪt/ *n.*
1 big engine that pushes a spaceship into space 火箭
The spaceship had two big rockets.
太空船有两支大火箭。

2 firework that goes quickly into the air （火箭式）烟火
They fired lots of rockets at Chinese New Year.
农历新年时人们放许多烟火。

rode /rode; rəud/ *v.*
p.t. of **ride** ride 的过去式
Peter rode his bicycle to the park.
彼得骑自行车去公园。

roll[1] /roll; rəul/ *n.*
paper, cloth, etc., that has been rolled up一卷；卷（或筒）形物
Mrs Chen bought some toilet rolls.
陈太太买了几卷卫生纸。

roll[2] /roll; rəul/ *v.*
move along, turning over and over 滚动，转动
The ball rolled off the table.
球从桌上滚到地上去了。

roll

roll up 卷起
Tom rolled up the poster.
汤姆卷起了海报。

roller-skate /'rol·ler·skate; 'rəuləskeɪt/ *n.*
thing with four wheels that you tie to your foot 旱冰鞋
David has a pair of roller-skates.
戴维有一双旱冰鞋。
roller-skating *n.* 溜旱冰
David likes roller-skating.
戴维喜欢溜旱冰。

roller-skate

roof /roof; ru:f/ *n.*
top of a building or a car 屋顶；车顶
The cat climbed onto the roof.
猫爬到屋顶上去了。

roofs

room /room; ru:m/ *n.*
1 one of the parts inside a building 房间

Mrs Wang's flat has four rooms.
王太太住的公寓房有四个房间。

2 enough space 地方；空间
There is room for five people in Mrs Chen's car.
陈太太的车子可以坐五个人。

root /root; ru:t/ *n.*
part of a plant or tree that grows under the ground 根
The roots of the big tree went under the road.
那棵大树的根一直伸到马路下面。

rope /rope; rəup/ *n.*
very thick, strong string 缆；粗绳；索
The sailor threw the rope onto the ship.
水手把缆抛到船上。

rose[1] /rose; rəuz/ *v.*
p.t. of **rise** rise 的过去式
The sun rose at six o'clock.
太阳在六时升起。

rose[2] /rose; rəuz/ *n.*
sort of flower 玫瑰
Mr Chen bought some red roses for his wife.
陈先生买了些红玫瑰给太太。

rotten /'rot·ten; 'rɒtn/ *adj.*
(more rotten, most rotten)
bad 腐烂的；已变坏的
The apple was rotten.
那只苹果烂了。

rough /rough; rʌf/ *adj.*
1 not smooth or flat 粗糙的；不平滑的；崎岖不平的
The road was very rough.
路面崎岖不平。

2 not finished 粗略写成的；未经修饰的
Mary did a rough copy of the homework.
玛丽做家庭作业，打了一个草稿。
3 not gentle 粗野的；粗鲁的
Sam is a rough boy.
萨姆是个粗鲁的男孩。

roughly *adv.* 粗鲁地；大约
Sam plays roughly.
萨姆玩得很粗鲁。
Susan is roughly five feet tall.
苏珊大约五英尺高。

round[1] /round; raund/ *adj.*
like a ball or circle 球形的；圆形的
The earth is round.
地球是球形的。

round[2] /round; raund/ *adv.*
1 making a circle 成圆形地
The children danced round in a circle.
孩子们绕着圈子跳舞。
2 in the opposite direction; so that you are looking the other way 转身；回头
Sam turned round to watch the TV.
萨姆转过身来看电视。

round [3] /round; raund/ *n.*
stage in a competition (比赛的)一局；一回合；一场
The boxing match lasted six rounds.
这场拳击赛打了六个回合。

round [4] /round; raund/ *prep.*
to all or some parts of a place 到处；在各处
The visitors walked round the museum.
游客在博物馆内到处参观。

roundabout
/'round·a·bout; 'raundəbaut/ *n.*
1 circle that cars go round in the middle of the crossroads 环状交叉路，交叉口
The car came to a roundabout.
汽车驶到了环状交叉口。

2 round thing that people ride on at a fair or in a park 旋转木马
The children were playing on the roundabout.
孩子们在玩旋转木马
syn. 同义词：merry-go-round

row [1] /row; rəu/ *n.*
line of people or things 一行；一列；一排
The children were sitting in rows.
孩子们一排一排地坐着。

row [2] /row; rəu/ *v.*
move a boat through the water with oars 划(艇)
Mr Chen rowed across the harbour.
陈先生划艇横渡海港。
rowing-boat *n.* 划艇
Mr Chen has a rowing-boat in the harbour.
陈先生有一只划艇停在港内。

rowing-boats

royal /'roy·al; 'rɔɪəl/ *adj.*
of a king or queen 王室的；皇帝的
The royal family live in a palace.
王室成员住在王宫里。

rub /rub; rʌb/ *v.*
(rubbing, rubbed, rubbed)
move something across another thing many times 擦；擦净；擦干
Mrs Chen rubbed the lamp with a cloth.
陈太太用布来擦灯。
rub out 擦掉
Peter rubbed out his mistakes.
彼得擦掉写错的地方。

rubber /'rub·ber; 'rʌbə/ *n.*
1 **(no plural)** material used to make tyres, balls, etc. 橡胶；橡皮
Sam was playing with a rubber ball.
萨姆在玩橡皮球。
2 piece of rubber that takes away pencil marks 橡皮擦；擦胶(方言)
David borrowed Peter's rubber.
戴维借用彼得的橡皮擦。
syn. 同义词：eraser

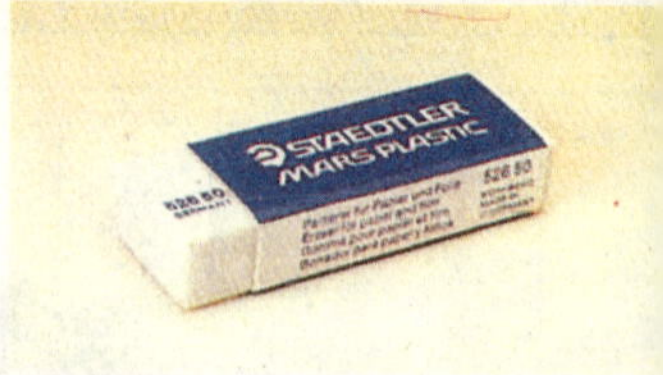

rubbish /'rub·bish; 'rʌbɪʃ/ *n.*
(no plural)
things that you throw away 垃圾；废物
Don't leave rubbish on the beach.
不要把垃圾留在海滩上。
syn. 同义词：litter

ruby /'ru·by; 'ru:bɪ/ *n.*
(two **rubies**)
red jewel 红宝石
Mrs Chen has a ring with a ruby.
陈太太有一枚红宝石戒指。

rude /rude; ru:d/ *adj.*
(ruder, rudest)
not polite; talking or doing things in a way that hurts other people 粗鲁无礼的
The naughty boy was rude to his father.
那顽皮的男孩对他爸爸没有礼貌。
opp. 反义词：polite 有礼貌的
rudely *adv.* 粗鲁无礼地
The naughty boy behaved rudely.
那顽皮的孩子行为粗鲁无礼。

rug /rug; rʌg/ *n.*
small carpet 小地毯
The cat was asleep on the rug.
那只猫在地毯上睡着了。

rule [1] /rule; ru:l/ *n.*
what you must and must not do in a game, at school, etc. 规则；规定
Susan is learning the rules of chess.
苏珊正在学习下棋的规则。

rule [2] /rule; ru:l/ *v.*
(ruling, ruled, ruled)
be in charge of a country 统治
The queen ruled the country.
女王统治这个国家。

ruler /'rul·er; 'ru:lə/ *n.*
1 leader of a country 统治者
The queen is the ruler of the country.
女王是这个国家的统治者。
2 long piece of wood or plastic that helps you to draw lines or measure things 尺
Tom measured his desk with a ruler.
汤姆用尺量他的书桌。

run [1] /run; rʌn/ *v.*
(running, ran, run)
1 move quickly with one's legs 跑
David ran to school.
戴维跑往学校。

2 flow 流
The river runs through the town.
这条河流经那个城镇。
3 hold 举行
The school is running a painting competition.
学校正举行一个绘画比赛。
4 go; make a journey 往来行驶
How often do the ferries run to Cheung Chau?
往长洲的渡轮隔多少时间开一班?
run away, run off 逃走
The thief ran away with the handbag.
小偷拿着提包逃走了。
run over 压过去，驶过
A car ran over Tom's bicycle.
一辆汽车从汤姆的自行车上压了过去。
run out of 用完了；没有了
Mr Chen's car ran out of petrol.
陈先生的汽车没有汽油了。

run [2] /run; rʌn/ *n.*
something you do with your legs 跑；跑步
Peter went for a run.
彼得跑步去了。

runner *n.* 赛跑运动员；跑步者
There were six runners in the race.
这次赛跑有六名运动员参加。

rung /rung; rʌŋ/ *v.*
p.p. of **ring** ring 的过去分词
Has the bell rung?
钟响了没有?

runway /'run·way; 'rʌnweɪ/ *n.*
long, wide road where planes take off and land （机场的）跑道
The plane landed on the runway.
飞机降落在跑道上。

rush /rush; rʌʃ/ *v.*
move or do something quickly; hurry 匆匆忙忙；赶快
Mary rushed home from school.
玛丽从学校匆匆忙忙赶回家。

rust /rust; rʌst/ *n.*
(no plural)
red powder on iron or steel 锈
Sam cleaned the rust off his bicycle.
萨姆把他的自行车上的锈擦掉。
rusty *adj.* 生锈的
Sam's bicycle was rusty.
萨姆的自行车生锈了。

Ss

sack /sack; sæk/ *n.*
big, strong bag 大袋
Mrs Chen bought a sack of rice.
陈太太买了一袋米。

sad /sad; sæd/ *adj.*
(**sadder, saddest**)
not happy 悲哀的；难过的
Susan was sad when her rabbit died.
苏珊的兔子死了，她很难过。
opp. 反义词：happy 快乐的
sadly *adv.* 悲哀地；伤心地
Susan sadly buried her rabbit.
苏珊伤心地把兔子埋葬了。

saddle /'sad·dle; 'sædl/ *n.*
seat on a bicycle or a horse, etc. 马鞍；自行车的车座
Mary put a saddle on the horse.
玛丽把鞍放在马背上。

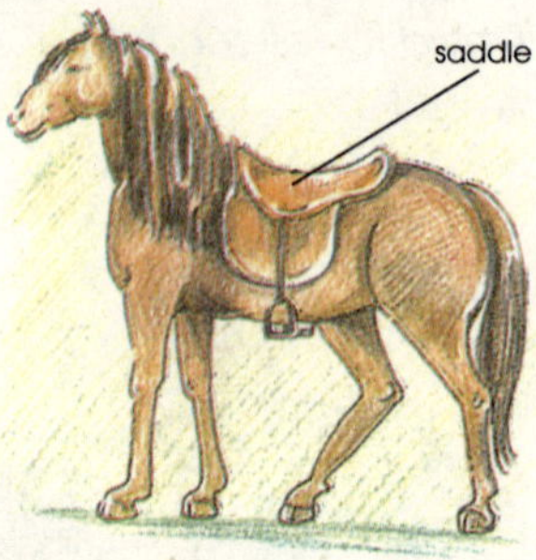

safe [1] /safe; seɪf/ *adj.*
(**safer, safest**)
not dangerous 安全的；没有危险的
The sea is quite safe for swimming.
在这海里游泳相当安全。
opp. 反义词：dangerous 危险的
safely *adv.* 安全地
The aeroplane landed safely.
飞机安全地降落了。

safe [2] /safe; seɪf/ *n.*
strong metal box where you can keep valuable things 保险箱
Mr Chen put the money in the safe.
陈先生把钱放在保险箱里。

safety /'safe·ty; 'seɪftɪ/ *n.*
(**no plural**)
being safe; with no danger 安全
The children learn about road safety.
孩子们学习道路安全规则。

said /said; sed/ *v.*
p.t. of **say** say 的过去式
The boy said his name was Tom.
那男孩说他名叫汤姆。

sail [1] /sail; seɪl/ *n.*
big piece of cloth on a boat to catch the wind 帆
The boat had two sails.
那艘船有两个帆。

sail [2] /sail; seɪl/ *v.*
travel on water 航行
The ferry sailed to Cheung Chau.
这艘渡轮开往长洲。
sailing *n.* 航海；航行
David likes sailing.
戴维喜欢航海。

sailor /'sail·or; 'seɪlə/ *n.*
someone who works on a boat or ship 海员；水手
Mr Qian is a sailor.
钱先生是个海员。

salad /'sal·ad; 'sæləd/ *n.*
mixture of raw vegetables or fruit 色拉；沙律（方言）
Mary made a tomato salad.
玛丽做了个番茄色拉。

salary /'sal·a·ry; 'sælərɪ/ *n.*
(two **salaries**)
money that you receive every month for your work
薪水

Ir Wang earns a small
alary.
E先生薪水很少。

ale /sale; seɪl/ *n.*
me when a shop sells things
or less money than usual
价；廉售
usan bought a dress in the
ale.
价时，苏珊买了一件连衣裙。

or sale 待售
Ars Chen's flat is for sale.
太太的公寓房正待出售。
alesman, saleswoman *n.*
店员；女店员
he saleswoman showed
Anna some shoes.
店员拿了些鞋子给安娜看。

alt /salt; sɔːlt/ *n.*
no plural)
tuff like white sand, which
ou put on food 盐

David put some salt on his
chicken.
戴维在鸡肉上放了些盐。
salty *adj.* 咸的
The vegetables were too
salty.
这些蔬菜味道太咸了。

same /same; seɪm/ *adj.*
not different; not another
one 一样的；相同的
Mr Chen has lived in the
same flat for fifty years.
陈先生在同一套公寓房里居住了五十年。
opp. 反义词：different 不同的

sampan /ˈsam·pan; ˈsæmpæn/ *n.*
small boat 舢板
There are lots of sampans in
the harbour.
海港内有许多舢板。

sand /sand; sænd/ *n.*
(no plural)
tiny bits of rock which you
find on the beach and in the
desert 沙
The children were playing in
the sand.
孩子们在沙地上玩耍。
sandy *adj.* 有沙的；沙状的
There was a long, sandy
beach round the island.
这个岛被一个长长的沙滩环绕着。

sandal /ˈsan·dal; ˈsændl/ *n.*
light, open shoe with straps
凉鞋
In summer, Susan always
wears sandals.
夏天时，苏珊总是穿凉鞋。

sandwich /ˈsand·wich; ˈsænwɪdʒ/ *n.*
(two **sandwiches**)
two pieces of bread with
other food between 三明治；
三文治（方言）
Tom had a ham sandwich
for his lunch.
汤姆午餐吃了一块火腿三明治。

sang /sang; sæŋ/ *v.*
p.t. of **sing** sing 的过去式
The children sang 'Happy
Birthday' to Peter.
孩子们向彼得唱“生日快乐”歌。

sank /sank; sæŋk/ *v.*
p.t. of **sink** sink 的过去式
The boat sank in the storm.
那船在暴风雨中沉没了。

sat /sat; sæt/ *v.*
p.t. of **sit** sit 的过去式
Tom sat at the back of the
classroom.
汤姆坐在教室的后排。

satellite /ˈsa·tell·ite; ˈsætəlaɪt/ *n.*
1 planet which moves around a bigger planet 卫星
The moon is a satellite of the earth.
月亮是地球的卫星。
2 machine which is sent into space 人造卫星
The rocket carried a satellite into space.
那支火箭把一颗人造卫星带上太空。
by satellite 通过人造卫星
The TV programme came by satellite.
那个电视节目通过人造卫星播送。

satisfactory /sat·is·ˈfac·to·ry; sætɪsˈfæktərɪ/ *adj.*
(**more satisfactory, most satisfactory**)
good enough 令人满意的
Tom's work is always satisfactory.
汤姆做事总是令人满意的。

Saturday /ˈSat·ur·day; ˈsætədɪ/ *n.*
day of the week 星期六
Sam played football last Saturday.
萨姆上星期六踢足球。

sauce /sauce; sɔːs/ *n.*
liquid that makes food taste better 酱汁
Peter likes soya sauce.
彼得吃东西喜欢蘸酱油。

saucepan /ˈsauce·pan; ˈsɔːspən/ *n.*
deep, round dish with a handle, for cooking 长柄有盖的深平底锅
Mrs Chen cooked some rice in a saucepan.
陈太太用平底锅煮了些饭。

saucer /ˈsau·cer; ˈsɔːsə/ *n.*
small plate that you put under a cup 茶碟
The coffee spilt into the saucer.
咖啡泼在茶碟里了。

sausage /ˈsaus·age; ˈsɒsɪdʒ/ *n.*
chopped meat in a long, thin shape 腊肠；香肠
The children cooked some sausages on the beach.
孩子们在海滩上烤香肠吃。

save /save; seɪv/ *v.*
(**saving, saved, saved**)
1 take something or someone away from danger 拯救；挽救
The lifeguard saved the drowning boy.
救生员救了那个溺水的男孩。
2 keep money or other things for a later time 储蓄；节省；存起
David is saving for his holiday.
戴维正为他的度假计划而存钱。

savings /ˈsa·vings; ˈseɪvɪŋz/ *n.*
(**plural**)
money that you save 储蓄
Mary went on holiday with her savings.
玛丽用她存储的钱来度假。

saw [1] /saw; sɔː/ *n.*
tool for cutting wood 锯子
Mr Chen cut the wood with a saw.
陈先生用锯把木头锯开。

saw [2] /saw; sɔː/ *v.*
1 p.t. of **see** see 的过去式
I saw Peter yesterday.
昨天我看见彼得。
2 use a saw 锯
Mr Chen was sawing a piece of wood.
陈先生正在锯一块木头。

say /say; seɪ/ *v.*
(**saying, said, said**)
make words with your mouth 说；讲
Peter said hello to Sam.
彼得对萨姆说了声"你好"。
Usage note: Note the difference between *say* and *tell* — *Peter said he was going to the cinema. Peter told his mother he was going to the cinema.*
用法：注意 say 和 tell 的不同，例如 Peter said he was going to the cinema 和 Peter told his mother he was going to the cinema。

scale /scale; skeɪl/ *n.*
machine for weighing things 天平；秤
Mary weighed the vegetables on a scale.
玛丽把蔬菜放在天平上称重量。

scarf /scarf; skɑːf/ *n.*
(two **scarves**)
piece of cloth that you wear

ɹnd your neck 围巾
vas cold so Mary put a
arf on.
气寒冷，因此玛丽围上围巾。

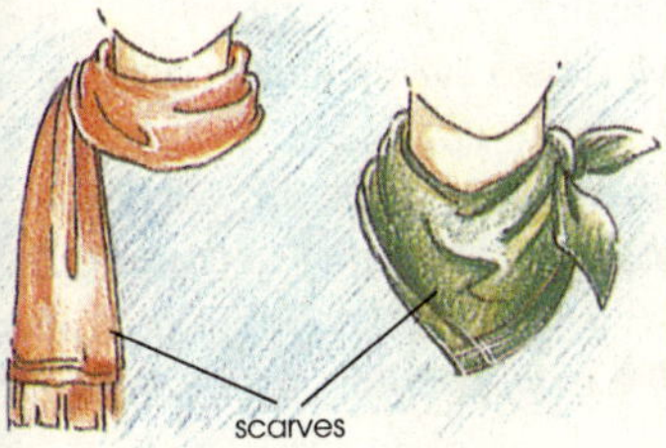

:hool /school; sku:l/ *n.*
ace where children go to
arn 学校
ere are three hundred
iildren in Tom's school.
姆的学校有三百个学生。

:hoolboy *n.* 男学生
m is a schoolboy.
姆是个男学生。

:hoolgirl *n.* 女学生
ary is a schoolgirl.
丽是个女学生。

:hool teacher *n.* 教师
'ary wants to be a school
acher.
丽想当教师。

age note: Use *the* before *hool* when you mean a hool building — *The school is Kowloon.* Don't use *the* when ɔu mean any school — *Mary ɔes to school.*
法：如果指明某所学校，school 前面加 the, 例如 The school is in ɔwloon。如泛指学校，school 前面不加 the, 例如 Mary goes to hool。

:ience /'sci·ence; 'saɪəns/ *n.*
ıding out how things work; ıbjects such as physics, ology, etc. 科学
avid is good at science.
维的科学课学得很好。

scientist *n.* 科学家
David wants to be a scientist.
戴维想做科学家。

scissors /'scis·sors; 'sɪzəz/ *n.*
(plural)
tool with two blades for cutting 剪刀
Mary cut the paper with scissors.
玛丽用剪刀剪纸。

pair of scissors 一把剪刀
Be careful! This pair of scissors is sharp.
当心! 这把剪刀很锋利。

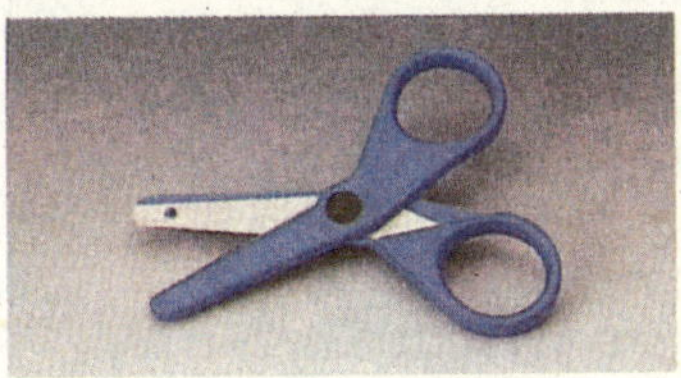

scold /scold; skəʊld/ *v.*
tell someone angrily that he has done wrong 骂；责备
The teacher scolded Tom for being late.
老师责备汤姆迟到。

score [1] /score; skɔ:/ *n.*
number of points that you win in a game 得分；分数
The score was 3 goals to 1.
双方得分是三比一。

score [2] /score; skɔ:/ *v.*
(scoring, scored, scored)
win a point 取得分数
Sam scored two goals.
萨姆踢进了两个球。

scout /'scout; 'skaʊt/ *n.*
member of a special club for boys 童子军
Peter and David are scouts.
彼得和戴维都是童子军。

scrape /scrape; skreɪp/ *v.*
(scraping, scraped, scraped)
rub something with a hard or rough thing 刮；擦
Sam scraped the mud off his football boots.
萨姆擦去足球靴上的泥浆。

scratch [1] /scratch; skrætʃ/ *v.*
1 cut or mark something with a sharp thing 抓
The cat scratched Mary.
那只猫抓玛丽。

2 rub to stop an itch 抓痒；搔
Don't scratch your mosquito bites.
别抓蚊子叮过的地方。

scratch [2] /scratch; skrætʃ/ *n.*
(two **scratches**)
mark that a sharp thing makes 抓痕
Mary had a scratch on her arm.
玛丽手臂上有一道抓痕。

scream [1] /scream; skri:m/ *v.*
cry loudly because you are hurt or afraid 尖叫
Baoling screamed when she saw the snake.
宝玲看见蛇便尖叫起来。

scream [2] /scream; skri:m/ *n.*
loud noise that you make because you are hurt or afraid 尖叫声
Baoling gave a loud scream when she saw the snake.
宝玲看见蛇便发出一声尖叫。

screen /screen; skri:n/ *n.*
flat thing where pictures are shown 银幕；屏幕
Mr Wang's TV has a big screen.
王先生的电视机屏幕很大。

screw [1] /screw; skru:/ *n.*
pointed piece of metal, which fixes things together
螺丝(钉)
The notice-board was fixed to the wall with screws.
布告板是用螺丝(钉)钉在墙上的。

screw [2] /screw; skru:/ *v.*
fix something with a screw
拧紧螺丝(把物件钉稳)
The man screwed the notice-board to the wall.
那人用螺丝把布告板钉在墙上。
opp. 反义词：unscrew 拧松螺丝

screw-driver *n.*
螺丝刀
The man used a screw-driver to fix the notice-board to the wall.
那人用螺丝刀把布告板钉在墙上。

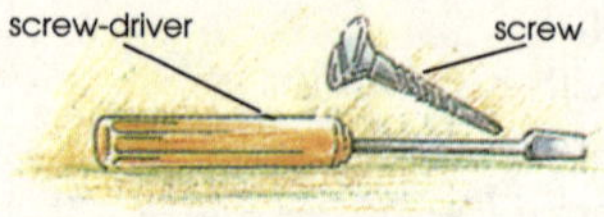

scrub /scrub; skrʌb/ *v.*
(**scrubbing, scrubbed, scrubbed**)
rub something with a brush and water to clean it 擦洗
Mary scrubbed the floor.
玛丽擦洗地板。

sculpture /ˈsculp·ture; ˈskʌlptʃə/ *n.*
statue of someone or something 雕刻；雕塑
There is a sculpture of a lion in the park.
公园里有一座狮子的雕塑。

sea /sea; si:/ *n.*
salty water that covers the earth where there is no land 海
David likes swimming in the sea.
戴维喜欢在海里游泳。

by sea 经海路；乘船
They travelled to Hong Kong by sea.
他们乘船去香港。

seafood *n.* 海鲜
You can buy good seafood on Cheung Chau.
你可以在长洲买到很好的海鲜。

seashore *n.* 海岸；海边
There were some shells on the seashore.
海边有一些贝壳。

seaside *n.* 海边，海滨
Mr Chen lives by the seaside.
陈先生住在海边。

seaweed *n.* 海草
There was a lot of seaweed on the beach.
海滩上有许多海草。

seal /seal; si:l/ *n.*
sea animal with fur 海豹
Mary saw some seals at the zoo.
玛丽在动物园里看见一些海豹。

search /search; sɜ:tʃ/ *v.*
try to find someone or something 寻找；搜寻
Sam was searching for a pen.
萨姆在找一支笔。

season /ˈsea·son; ˈsi:zn/ *n.*
one of the four parts of the year 季节
Autumn is the nicest season in Hong Kong.
在香港，秋天是天气最好的季节。

seat /seat; si:t/ *n.*
chair; place where you sit
座位
Please take a seat.
请坐。

seat-belt /'seat·belt; 'siːtbelt/ *n.*
belt that you wear in a car or aeroplane to keep you safe in an accident （交通工具座位上的）安全带
Please fasten your seat-belts.
请扣好你的安全带。

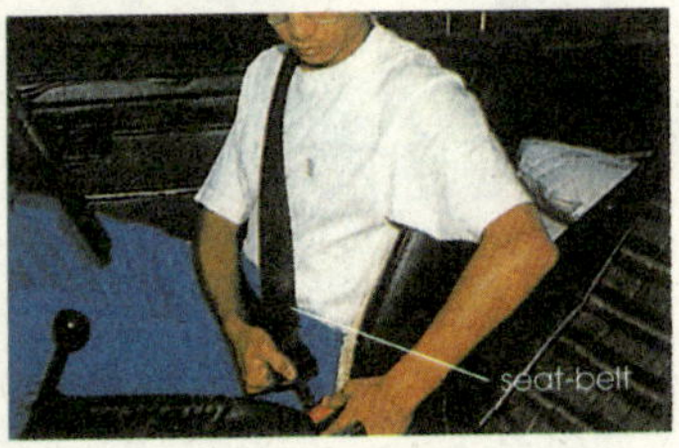

second [1] (2nd) /'sec·ond; 'sekənd/ *n. adj.*
next after first 第二
'B' is the second letter of the alphabet.
B是字母表中的第二个字母。

second [2] /'sec·ond; 'sekənd/ *n.*
measure of time 秒
There are sixty seconds in a minute.
一分钟有六十秒。

secondary school
/'sec·ond·ary school; 'sekəndrɪ skuːl/ *n.*
school for older pupils, after primary school 中学
David will go to secondary school next year, after he finishes primary school.
戴维明年念完小学后就要上中学了。

secret [1] /'se·cret; 'siːkrɪt/ *adj.*
(more secret, most secret)
that other people must not know 秘密的
David hides his money in a secret place.
戴维把钱放在一个秘密的地方。

secretly *adv.* 秘密地
Sam left the house secretly.
萨姆秘密地离开了那所房子。

secret [2] /'se·cret; 'siːkrɪt/ *n.*
something that you must not tell other people 秘密
Sam cannot keep a secret.
萨姆守不住秘密。

secretary /'sec·ret·ary; 'sekrətrɪ/ *n.*
(two **secretaries**)
someone who types letters, looks after papers and answers the telephone in an office 秘书
Mrs Wang is a secretary.
王太太是个秘书。

see /see; siː/ *v.*
(seeing, saw, seen)
1 learn about something with your eyes 看见；见到
David saw a panda at the zoo.
戴维在动物园里见到一只熊猫。
2 visit someone or something 探访
Susan went to see Mary.
苏珊去探望玛丽。
3 understand 明白；了解
Do you see what I mean?
你明白我的意思吗？
4 go to find out about something 查看
Mrs Li went to see what the children were doing.
李太太去看看孩子们在干什么。

seed /seed; siːd/ *n.*
little thing that grows into a new plant 种子
Anna planted some flower seeds in a pot.
安娜在花盆里播了些花的种子。

seem /seem; siːm/ *v.*
make you think that something is true 好像；看来是
Mary seems to be a quiet girl.
玛丽看来是个娴静的女孩子。
it seem 看来
It seems that Peter is ill.
看来彼得是病了。

seen /seen; siːn/ *v.*
p.p. of **see** see 的过去分词
Have you ever seen a panda?
你见过熊猫吗？

seesaw /'see·saw; 'siːsɔː/ *n.*
thing that children play on 跷跷板
Susan, Sally and Mary were playing on a seesaw.
苏珊、萨莉和玛丽在玩跷跷板。

selfish /'self·ish; 'selfɪʃ/ *adj.*
(more selfish, most selfish)
thinking too much about yourself; not thinking about other people 自私的
Don't be selfish! Share your sweets!
不要自私！把糖分给大家吃！

sell /sell; sel/ *v.*
(selling, sold, sold)
1 give something to someone who pays money for it 卖
Mr Qian sold his car to Mr Wang.
钱先生把车子卖给王先生。
2 have things that people can buy 出售；售卖
That shop sells clothes.
那家商店出售衣服。
opp. 反义词：buy 买

send /send; send/ *v.*
(sending, sent, sent)
make something or someone go somewhere 送；寄；派
Mrs Chen sent Baoling a birthday present.
陈太太送给宝玲一份生日礼物。
send for 请别人来；派人去拿
Peter was ill, so his mother sent for the doctor.
彼得生病，所以他妈妈把医生请来。

sense /sense; sens/ *n.*
(no plural)
what is the best thing to do 见识；理智
It is good sense to use pedestrian crossings.
过马路时走人行横道线是明智的做法。

sensible /'sen·si·ble; 'sensəbl/ *adj.*
(more sensible, most sensible)
knowing what is the best thing to do 明理的；明智的
Baoling is a sensible girl.
宝玲是个明理的女孩子。

sent /sent; sent/ *v.*
p.t. of **send** send 的过去式
David sent Peter a birthday card.
戴维送给彼得一张生日卡。

sentence /'sen·tence; 'sentəns/ *n.*
group of words that tells you something or asks a question 句子
Sam wrote ten sentences about his holidays.
萨姆写了十个句子来描述他的假期。

separate [1] /'sep·a·rate; 'seprət/ *adj.*
1 not together; not joined 分开的
Sam cut the apple into four separate pieces.
萨姆把苹果切成四份。
2 different 不同的
Tom and his brother go to separate schools.
汤姆和他哥哥上不同的学校。

separate [2] /'sep·a·rate; 'sepəreɪt/ *v.*
(separating, separated, separated)
1 be between two things 分隔
Victoria harbour separates Hong Kong island and Kowloon.
维多利亚港分隔了香港岛和九龙。
2 divide something into parts 分开
The teacher separated the children into four groups.
老师把孩子们分成四组。
opp. 反义词：join 连接

separate 2

September /Sep·'tem·ber; sep'tembə/ *n.*
ninth month of the year 九月
In September the weather is hot in Hong Kong.
香港的九月天气炎热。

serious /'se·ri·ous; 'sɪərɪəs/ *adj.*
(more serious, most serious)
1 very bad 严重的
Mr Chen had a serious accident at work.
陈先生工作时发生了严重事故。
2 sensible 严肃的
The teacher told Peter to be serious.
老师叫彼得严肃些。
3 meaning what you say 认真的
When Mary said she was angry, she was serious.
玛丽说她生气时，她是认真的。
seriously *adv.* 严重地
Mr Chen is seriously ill.
陈先生病情严重。

servant /'serv·ant; 'sɜ:vənt/ *n.*
someone who works in another person's house 仆人
The Chen family has a servant.
陈家有一个仆人。

serve /serve; sɜ:v/ *v.*
(serving, served, served)
1 sell things to someone in a shop 侍候；招待；为…服务
The salesman served Mrs Chen.
售货员招待陈太太。
2 give a meal to someone 送上饭菜
Mrs Chen serves chicken for dinner once a week.
每周一次陈太太做的晚饭总有鸡。

service /'serv·ice; 'sɜ:vɪs/ *n.*
something done to help you 服务
The service is slow in that restaurant.
那家餐厅的服务态度很怠慢。

set [1] /set; set/ *n.*
1 group of things that belong together （一）套
John has a set of Hong Kong stamps.
约翰有一套香港邮票。
2 machine 视听器材
Mary switched on the TV set.
玛丽开了电视机。

set [2] /set; set/ *v.*
(setting, set, set)
1 go down from the sky （太阳、月亮等）从天空上落下
The sun set at seven o'clock.
七时日落。
opp. 反义词：rise 升起
2 put something somewhere 放置
The children set the cups and plates on the table.
孩子们把杯碟放在桌子上。
3 become solid 凝固
Baoling put the jelly in the fridge to set.
宝玲把果冻放在冰箱里凝固。
set an example 做榜样
The teacher sets an example by coming to school early.
老师一早就来到学校，做个好榜样。
set fire to 点燃；放火
Sam set fire to the paper.
萨姆把纸烧着了。
set free 释放
Mr Wang opened the cage and set the bird free.
王先生打开鸟笼，把鸟儿放走了。
set off, set out 出发
The bus set off for Guangzhou at seven o'clock.
这班公共汽车七时出发，开往广州。

settle /'set·tle; 'setl/ *v.*
(settling, settled, settled)
go and live in a place 定居
The family settled in Canada.
那一家人定居加拿大。
settle down 安静下来
The teacher told the class to settle down.
老师叫班上学生安静下来。

seven (7) /'sev·en; 'sevn/ *n. adj.*
number 7 七
Tom will be seven years old tomorrow.
汤姆到明天就是七岁了。
seventh (7th) *n. adj.* 第七
Tom's seventh birthday is tomorrow.
明天是汤姆的七岁生日。

seventeen (17)
/sev·en·'teen; sevn'ti:n/ *n. adj.*
number 17 十七
Mr Chen left school when he was seventeen.
陈先生十七岁就不上学了。
seventeenth (17th) *n. adj.*
第十七
Anna got a ring for her seventeenth birthday.
安娜十七岁生日时收到的礼物是一枚戒指。

seventy (70) /'sev·en·ty; 'sevntɪ/ *n. adj.*
number 70 七十
Mr Chen will be seventy next year.
陈先生明年七十岁。
seventieth (70th) *n. adj.*
第七十
Mr Wang is in his seventieth year.
王先生已经七十岁了。

several /'sev·er·al; 'sevrəl/ *adj.*
some but not many 几个的；数个的
Baoling has been to Shanghai several times.
宝玲到过上海几次了。

sew /sew; səʊ/ *v.*
use a needle and thread, or a machine, to put pieces of cloth together 缝
Mary is sewing a dress.
玛丽正在缝制一件连衣裙。
sewing *n.* 缝纫
Mary likes sewing.
玛丽喜欢缝纫。
sewing-machine *n.* 缝纫机
Mary has a sewing-machine.
玛丽有一部缝纫机。

sh /sh; ʃ/ *int.*
word that you say when you want someone to be quiet
嘘！别作声！
Sh! The baby is asleep.
别作声！婴儿在睡觉呢。

shade [1] /shade; ʃeɪd/ *n.*
1 (**no plural**) place where it is dark because the sun does not shine there 阴凉处
It is too hot in the sun. Let's sit in the shade.
太阳底下太热了，我们到阴凉的地方坐吧。
2 cover for a lamp 灯罩
Mary bought a new shade for her lamp.
玛丽给她的灯买了个新灯罩。

shady *adj.* 阴凉的
The children sat under a shady tree.
孩子们坐在树阴下。

shade [2] /shade; ʃeɪd/ *v.*
(**shading, shaded, shaded**)
use crayons etc. to make part of a picture darker than the rest 在图画上加阴影
Tom shaded the sea on the map.
汤姆把地图上的海洋加上阴影。

shadow /'shad·ow; 'ʃædəʊ/ *n.*
dark shape that comes when someone or something is in front of the light 影子
The shadow of the buildings fell on the beach.
那些建筑物的影子投在海滩上。

shake /shake; ʃeɪk/ *v.*
(**shaking, shook, shaken**)
move something quickly many times 摇动
The wind is shaking the trees.
风把树木吹得摇来摇去。
shake hands 握手
Mr Chen shook hands with his friends.
陈先生和朋友们一一握手。
shake your head 摇头
When Tom asked to go out his mother shook her head.
汤姆想要出去，他妈妈摇头不答应。

shall /shall; ʃəl/ *v.*
1 word that shows something is going to happen 将会
I shall see Peter tomorrow.
明天我会见到彼得。
2 word that you say when you are asking what is the right thing to do …好吗；要不要…
Shall I serve the dinner now?
我现在开饭好吗？
opp. 反义词：shall not, shan't 不会；不要
Usage note: You can use *will* with *I* and *we* in the same way as *shall* — *I shall go to Canada next year. I will go to Canada next year.* Use *shall* in questions like — *Shall I lay the table?*
用法： I 和 we 之后可用 shall 或 will, 例如 I shall go to Canada next year 和 I will go to Canada next year。shall 亦可用于问题开首，例如 Shall I lay the table?

shallow /'shal·low; 'ʃæləʊ/ *adj.*
not deep; with a little water 浅的
In summer, the river is shallow.
夏天时，这条河很浅。

shame /shame; ʃeɪm/ *n.*
sad feeling because you have done someting wrong
羞耻；羞愧
When he realized what he had done, Tom was filled with shame.
汤姆对自己的所作所为感到很羞愧。
it's a shame 羞愧；令人惋惜
It's a shame that you have lost your purse.
你丢了钱包，真倒霉。

shampoo /sham·'poo; ʃæm'pu:/ *n.*
stuff you wash your hair with 洗发精
Mary washed her hair with shampoo.
玛丽用洗发精洗头发。

shan't /shan't; ʃɑ:nt/ *v.*
shall not 即 shall not

I shan't go there again.
我不会再到那里去。

shape /shape; ʃeɪp/ *n.*
how something looks 形状
A ball has a round shape.
球是圆形的。

share [1] /share; ʃeə/ *n.*
what each person gets 分得的一份
The children all got a share of the sweets.
孩子们各分得一份糖果。

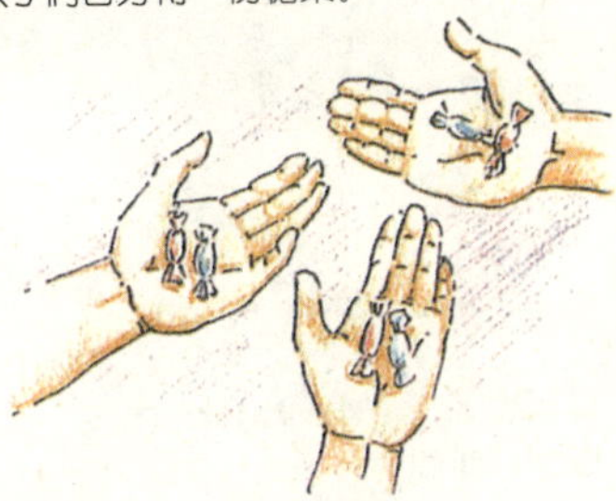

share [2] /share; ʃeə/ *v.*
(**sharing, shared, shared**)
1 divide something and give some to each person 分给；分摊
The children shared the sweets.
孩子们分了那些糖。
2 use something with another person 分享；共用
Mary forgot her book and had to share with Susan.
玛丽忘记了带书，只好和苏珊共用一本书。

shark /shark; ʃɑːk/ *n.*
dangerous fish 鲨鱼
The shark attacked the swimmers.
鲨鱼袭击游泳的人。

sharp /sharp; ʃɑːp/ *adj.*
1 with an edge that cuts easily 锋利的
The cook has a sharp knife.
这个厨师有一把锋利的刀。
2 with a good point 尖锐的
Have you got a sharp pencil?
你有削尖的铅笔吗?
opp. 反义词：blunt 钝的
sharpen *v.* 削尖；磨利
Susan sharpened her pencil.
苏珊把铅笔削尖。
sharpener *n.* 削尖或磨利的器具
Have you got a pencil sharpener?
你有铅笔刀吗?

shave /shave; ʃeɪv/ *v.*
(**shaving, shaved, shaved**)
cut hair off the face 刮胡子
Mr Wang shaves every morning.
王先生每天早上刮胡子。

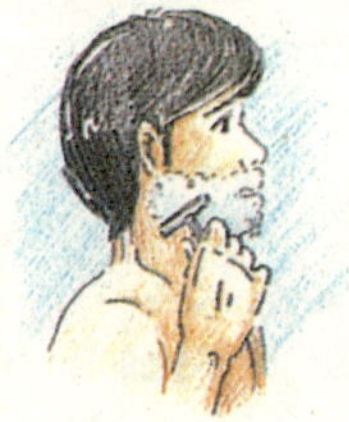

she /she; ʃiː/ *pron.*
word that shows a woman or girl 她
Where is Mary? She is late.
玛丽在哪里？她迟到了。

she'd /she'd; ʃiːd/
1 she had 即 she had
She said she'd been busy.
她说很忙。
2 she would 即 she would
She said she'd come.
她说会来的。

sheep /sheep; ʃiːp/ *n.*
(two **sheep**)
farm animal that you keep to eat and for wool 羊；绵羊
There were some sheep in the field.
田野上有些绵羊。

sheet /sheet; ʃiːt/ *n.*
piece of thin cloth to cover you in bed 被单；床单
Mrs Chen put clean sheets on the beds.
陈太太把干净的床单铺在床上。

sheet of paper 一张纸
The teacher gave Tom a sheet of paper to draw on.
老师给汤姆一张纸画图。

shelf /shelf; ʃelf/ *n.*
(two **shelves**)
flat piece of wood on a wall or in a cupboard to hold books, etc. 架子
Anna put the books on a shelf.
安娜把书放到书架上。

she'll /she'll; ʃiːl/
she will 即 she will
I hope she'll like the present.
我希望她会喜欢这份礼物。

shell /shell; ʃel/ *n.*
hard outside of birds' eggs, nuts and sea animals 壳；贝壳
A crab has a hard shell.
蟹有硬壳。

shells

shelter [1] /'shel·ter; 'ʃeltə/ *n.*
place where you will be safe 躲避处
The children used the shop as a shelter from the storm.
孩子们利用那商店作为躲避暴风雨的地方。
take shelter 躲避
The children took shelter from the rain.
孩子们躲雨。

shelter [2] /'shel·ter; 'ʃeltə/ *v.*
find a safe place from bad weather, danger, etc. 躲避
The children sheltered in a shop until the rain stopped.
孩子们在一家商店里躲雨，直到雨停止才离开。

shepherd /'shep·herd; 'ʃepəd/ *n.*
man who looks after sheep 牧羊人
The shepherd was looking after his sheep.
牧羊人在照料他的羊。

shepherds

she's /she's; ʃiːz/
1 she is 即 she is
She's very pretty.
她很漂亮。
2 she has 即 she has
She's finished the work.
她已完成工作。

shine /shine; ʃaɪn/ *v.*
(shining, shone, shone)
give out light; be bright 发光；照耀
The sun is shining today.
今天阳光灿烂。
shiny *adj.* 擦亮的；磨光的
Mary has a pair of shiny new shoes.
玛丽有一双擦得锃亮的新鞋。

ship /ship; ʃɪp/ *n.*
big boat that sails on the sea 船
There are a lot of ships in the harbour.
海港内有许多船只。

shirt /shirt; ʃɜːt/ *n.*
piece of thin clothing that a man wears on the top part of his body 衬衣
Tom spilt some tea on his shirt.
汤姆溅了些茶在他的衬衣上。

shirts

shiver /'shi·ver; 'ʃɪvə/ *v.*
shake because you are cold, ill or afraid 颤抖
The cold wind made Peter shiver.
冷风使彼得发抖。

shock [1] /shock; ʃɒk/ *n.*
bad surprise 震惊
Mr Chen had a shock when he saw the rubbish in the sea.
陈先生看见海里的垃圾，吓了一跳。

shock [2] /shock; ʃɒk/ *v.*
give someone a bad surprise 使人震惊
Mr Chen was shocked by the rubbish in the sea.
陈先生被海里的垃圾吓了一跳。

shoe /shoe; ʃuː/ *n.*
what you wear on your foot, over your sock 鞋
Mary bought some new shoes.
玛丽买了一些新鞋。
pair of shoes 一双鞋
Susan bought a pair of shoes.
苏珊买了一双鞋。
shoelace *n.* 鞋带
Tom tied his shoelaces.
汤姆结上鞋带。

shone /shone; ʃɒn/ *v.*
p.t. of **shine** shine 的过去式
The sun shone all day yesterday.
昨天整日都有阳光。

shook /shook; ʃʊk/ *v.*
p.t. of **shake** shake 的过去式
The wind shook the trees.
风把树木吹得摇来摇去。

shoot /shoot; ʃu:t/ *v.*
(shooting, shot, shot)
fire a weapon at someone or something 射击
The hunter shot a wild duck.
那猎人射中了一只野鸭。

shop 1 /shop; ʃɒp/ *n.*
building where you buy things 商店
On Sunday, Mary goes to the shops.
星期天玛丽到商店去。

shop 2 /shop; ʃɒp/ *v.*
(shopping, shopped, shopped)
buy things 买东西
Mrs Chen shops for food every day.
陈太太每天都要买食物。

shopkeeper *n.* 店主
Mr Qian is a shopkeeper.
钱先生是个店主。

shopping *n.* 购物；买好的东西
Mrs Chen carried her shopping to her car.
陈太太把买好的东西拿上她的汽车。

shore /shore; ʃɔ:/ *n.*
land by the sea or a lake 岸边
The children walked along the shore looking for shells.
孩子们沿着岸边走，寻找贝壳。

short /short; ʃɔ:t/ *adj.*
1 not tall 矮的
The girl was too short to reach the shelf.
那女孩子太矮，够不到那个架子。
opp. 反义词：tall 高的

2 not long 矮的
The dress was too short for Mary.
那件连衣裙对玛丽来说是太短了。
opp. 反义词：long 长的
3 for a little time 短暂的
The Wang family had a short holiday in Macao.
王家在澳门度过了一个短暂的假期。
opp. 反义词：long 长期的

short-sighted *adj.* 近视的
If you are short-sighted, you need glasses.
如果你患近视，就要戴眼镜。

shorten /'shor·ten; 'ʃɔ:tn/ *v.*
make shorter 改短
Mary shortened a dress.
玛丽把一件连衣裙改短。

shorts /shorts; ʃɔ:ts/ *n.*
(plural)
short trousers 短裤
When it is hot, Peter wears shorts.
天气炎热时，彼得穿短裤。
pair of shorts 短裤
Tom tore his new pair of shorts.
汤姆扯破了他的新短裤。

shot 1 /shot; ʃɒt/ *n.*
sound that a gun makes 枪声
Did you hear a shot?
你听到枪响了吗？

shot 2 /shot; ʃɒt/ *v.*
p.t. of **shoot** shoot 的过去式
The hunter shot a wild duck.
那猎人射中了一只野鸭。

should /should; ʃəd/ *v.*
p.t. of **shall** shall 的过去式
You should be careful when you cross the road.
过马路时应该小心。
opp. 反义词：should not, shouldn't 不应该

shoulder /'shoul·der; 'ʃəuldə/ *n.*
part where the arm joins the body 肩膀
The man carried the box on his shoulder.
那人肩膀上扛着箱子。

shouldn't /'should·n't; 'ʃʊdnt/ *v.*
should not 即 should not
You shouldn't run into the road.
你不应该在马路上乱闯。

shout [1] /shout; ʃaʊt/ *n.*
something said very loudly
叫声；呼喊声
The children heard a shout.
孩子们听见一声叫喊。

shout [2] /shout; ʃaʊt/ *v.*
say something very loudly
大叫；呼喊
David shouted to Peter.
戴维向彼得大声呼喊。

show [1] /show; ʃəʊ/ *n.*
something you go to see 戏；表演
There is a good show at the theatre.
戏院正上演一出好戏。

show [2] /show; ʃəʊ/ *v.*
(showing, showed, shown)
let someone see something
给(人)看；显示
Mary showed Susan her stamp collection.
玛丽把她收集的邮票给苏珊看。
show how 说明；指导
The teacher showed Sam how to do the maths.
老师指导萨姆做数学练习。

shower /'show·er; 'ʃaʊə/ *n.*
1 rain that falls for a short time 阵雨
There was a shower this morning.
今早下了一场阵雨。
2 place where you wash yourself under falling water
淋浴设备
There is a shower in our bathroom.
我们的浴室有淋浴设备。
3 washing yourself in a shower 淋浴
Sam takes a shower every morning.
萨姆每天早上洗淋浴。

shrimp /shrimp; ʃrɪmp/ *n.*
small sea animal with a shell
小虾
Mary put some shrimps in the fried rice.
玛丽在炒饭里放了一些小虾。

shrink /shrink; ʃrɪŋk/ *v.*
(shrinking, shrank, shrunk)
get smaller when washed
缩小
Tom's shirt shrank when he washed it.
汤姆的衬衣一洗就缩小了。

shroff /shroff; ʃrɒf/ *n.*
place where you pay for parking your car 收款处
Mr Chen paid for parking at the shroff.
陈先生在收款处缴付停车费。

shut /shut; ʃʌt/ *v.*
(shutting, shut, shut)
close something 关上；闭上
Please shut the door.
请把门关上。
opp. 反义词：open 开

shut

shy /shy; ʃaɪ/ *adj.*
not sure of yourself; not able to talk easily to other people
害羞的
Mary was too shy to sing at the concert.
玛丽害羞，不敢在音乐会上唱歌。
shyly *adv.* 害羞地
The children walked shyly onto the stage.
孩子们害羞地走上舞台。

sick /sick; sɪk/ *adj.*
ill; not feeling well 有病的
Peter was sick and could not go to school.
彼得生病了，不能上学。
be sick 呕吐
Sam was sick after eating too much cake.
萨姆吃了太多蛋糕，以致呕吐起来。
feel sick 作呕；想呕吐
Sam felt sick after eating some cake.
萨姆吃了些蛋糕后，就想呕吐。
Usage note: *To be sick* means to bring food up from the stomach. Before a noun it means ill — *She is a sick woman.*
用法：to be sick 可指呕吐。sick 用于名词前面则指患病，例如 She is a sick woman。

side /side; saɪd/ *n.*
1 one of the flat, outside parts of something （物体的一）面
Please write on both sides of the paper.
请在纸的两面书写。
2 edge; part away from the middle 边
The children camped at the side of a lake.
孩子们在湖边露营。

3 part that is not the front or the back 侧面；旁边
Please go through the door at the side of the building.
请从大厦旁边的门进出。。
4 part of your body near your arm （身体）旁边
Sam stood at the side of his father.
萨姆站在他父亲身边。
5 one of the two groups who are fighting or playing a game against each other （一）方；（一）队
Which side are you on?
你支持那一方？
on each side 每一边
There are trees on each side of the road.
路的每一边都有树。
on the other side 在另一边
Mary is on the other side of the road.
玛丽在路的另一边。
on this side 在这一边
Please stay on this side of the road.
请继续在路的这一边走。

sideways /'side·ways; 'saɪdweɪz/ *adv.*
moving or facing to the side 横着（移动）
A crab can run sideways.
蟹可以横行

sight /sight; saɪt/ *n.*
1 something that you see 景色
At night, the harbour is a beautiful sight.
晚上海港的景色很美。
2 (**no plural**) how you see 视力
Peter's sight is very good.
彼得的视力很好。

sign [1] /sign; saɪn/ *n.*
something that you say, write, draw, or do to tell people something 符号；记录；告示
The sign told people not to walk on the grass.
告示牌示意人们不要践踏草地。

signpost *n.* 路标
The signpost said Shek O five miles.
路标表示此处距离石澳有五英里。

sign [2] /sign; saɪn/ *v.*
write your name 签名
Would you sign the book please?
请在书上签名好吗？
signature *n.* 签名
Write your signature here, please.
请你在这里签名。

signal /'sig·nal; 'sɪgnəl/ *n.*
word, picture, or noise to tell people something 信号
They show the typhoon signal on TV.
他们在电视上打出台风信号。

silence /'si·lence; 'saɪləns/ *n.*
(**no plural**)
without noise 寂静；沉默
There was silence in the library.
图书馆里很安静。

silent /'si·lent; 'saɪlənt/ *adj.*
completely quiet; without any noise 寂静的；沉默的
The library was silent.
图书馆里很安静。
opp. 反义词：noisy 吵闹的；嘈杂的
silently *adv.* 静静地；默然
The children walked silently into the library.
孩子们静静地走进图书馆。

silk /silk; sɪlk/ *n.*
(**no plural**)
thin, soft cloth 丝绸
Mrs Chen bought some silk to make a dress.
陈太太买了些丝绸来做连衣裙。

silly /'sil·ly; 'sɪlɪ/ *adj.*
(sillier, silliest)
foolish; stupid 愚蠢的；傻的
The silly boy went out in the rain without an umbrella.
那傻男孩不拿伞就走到了雨里。
opp. 反义词：sensible 理智的；懂事的

silver [1] /'sil·ver; 'sɪlvə/ *n.*
(no plural)
shining, white metal 银
The teapot is made of silver.
这个茶壶是银做的。

silver [2] /'sil·ver; 'sɪlvə/ *adj.*
made of silver 银做的
I have a silver teapot.
我有一个银茶壶。

similar /'sim·i·lar; 'sɪmɪlə/ *adj.*
almost the same as another thing 相似的
Peter's bicycle is similar to David's.
彼得和戴维两人的自行车很相似。

simple /'sim·ple; 'sɪmpl/ *adj.*
(simpler, simplest)
1 easy to do or understand 简单的；容易的
Peter thinks mathematics is simple.
彼得认为数学很容易。
opp. 反义词：difficult 困难的
2 ordinary 一般的；平常的
Mr Wang prefers simple food.
王先生较喜欢吃简单的食物。
opp. 反义词：complicated 复杂的

since /since; sɪns/ *prep. conj. adv.*
from then until now 自从；从…以后
I have not seen Tom since last Saturday.
上星期六之后，我没见过汤姆。
I have known him since he came to Hong Kong.
他来香港以后，我就认识他了。
I ate some fish yesterday and I have felt ill ever since.
自从昨天我吃了些鱼后，直至现在仍感到不舒服。

sincerely /sin·'cere·ly; sɪn'sɪəlɪ/ *adv.*
truly; what you say at the end of a letter 真诚地；诚恳地
Yours sincerely, Tom.
你真诚的朋友汤姆上(信末签名前的用语)。

sing /sing; sɪŋ/ *v.*
(singing, sang, sung)
make music with your voice 唱
Mary sings in the school choir.
玛丽在学校合唱团中唱歌。
singer *n.* 歌手
Mary is a good singer.
玛丽的歌唱得很好。

single /'sin·gle; 'sɪŋgl/ *adj.*
1 one 单一的
I haven't a single clean shirt.
我一件干净的衬衣都没有。
2 for a journey to a place but not back again 单程的
Tom bought a single ticket to Shatin.
汤姆买了一张单程车票去沙田。
3 not married 未婚的
Mrs Chen's younger sister is still single.
陈太太的妹妹还没有结婚。

singular /'sin·gu·lar; 'sɪŋgjʊlə/ *adj.*
form of a word for one person or thing
单数的
'Chair' is singular. 'Chairs' is plural.
chair 是单数名词，chairs 是复数名词。

sink [1] /sink; sɪŋk/ *v.*
(sinking, sank, sunk)
go down under the water
沉下
The boat sank in the typhoon.
那艘船在台风中沉没。

sink [2] /sink; sɪŋk/ *n.*
place in the kitchen where you wash plates, etc. 洗涤槽
Mary put the dirty dishes in the sink.
玛丽把脏碟子放在洗涤槽里。

sir /sir; sɜ:/ *n.*
title for a man that you respect 先生
Can I help you, sir?
先生，我可以帮你忙吗？

sister /'sis·ter; 'sɪstə/ *n.*
girl or woman who has the same parents as another person 姐妹
Baoling's elder sister is called Xiaofang.
宝玲的姐姐叫小芳。

sit /sit; sɪt/ *v.*
(**sitting, sat, sat**)
est on your
oottom; put
ourself in a
eat 坐
Sit down,
please.
青坐。

sitting-room /'sit·ting·room;
sɪtɪŋru:m/ *n.*
oom in a house where you
can sit in comfortable chairs
客厅
Our TV set is in the sitting-
room.
我家的电视机放在客厅里。

six (6) /six; sɪks/ *n. adj.*
number 6 六
Mary's younger sister is six.
玛丽的妹妹六岁。
sixth (6th) *n. adj.* 第六
Tomorrow is Betty's sixth
birthday.
明天是贝蒂的六岁生日。

sixteen (16) /six·'teen;
sɪk'sti:n/ *n. adj.*
number 16 十六
Mrs Chen left school when
she was sixteen.
陈太太十六岁就离开学校了。
sixteenth (16th) *n. adj.*
第十六
We have a holiday on the
sixteenth of next month.
下个月十六日我们放假。

sixty (60) /'six·ty; 'sɪkstɪ/ *n.*
adj.
number 60 六十
Mr Wang stopped working
when he was sixty.
王先生六十岁就不工作了。
sixtieth (60th) *n. adj.* 第六十
Mr Chen had his sixtieth
birthday yesterday.
昨天是陈先生的六十岁生日。

size /size; saɪz/ *n.*
how big or small something is
大小；尺寸；尺码
What size shoes do you take?
你穿什么尺码的鞋子？

skate /skate; skeɪt/ *v.*
(**skating, skated, skated**)
move on ice with special
shoes 溜冰
Susan knows how to skate.
苏珊会溜冰。

pair of skates 溜冰鞋
Susan has a pair of skates.
苏珊有一双溜冰鞋。

skeleton /'ske·le·ton;
'skelɪtn/ *n.*
bones of a person or animal
骨骼
There is a skeleton in the
window of the medicine
shop.
这家药房的橱窗里摆放着一副骨骼。

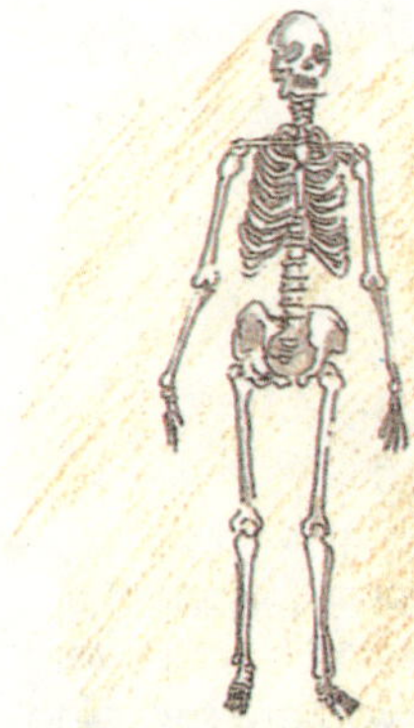

ski /ski; ski:/ *n.*
long, thin piece of wood or
plastic that you wear on your
feet to move over the snow
滑雪板
Mary put on her skis.
玛丽穿上她的滑雪板。
ski *v.* 滑雪
The man skied down the
mountain.
那人从山上滑雪而下。
skiing *n.* 滑雪
Mrs Li goes skiing every
year.
李太太每年都去滑雪。

skin /skin; skɪn/ *n.*
(no plural)
1 outside part of the body 皮肤
The sun burnt Peter's skin.
太阳把彼得的皮肤晒伤了。
2 outside part of some vegetables and fruit 蔬菜或水果的皮
Apples have a smooth skin.
苹果的皮很光滑。

skip /skip; skɪp/ *v.*
(skipping, skipped, skipped)
jump again and again over a rope that you are swinging 跳绳
Mrs Chen skips for exercise.
陈太太跳绳锻炼身体。

skirt /skirt; skɜːt/ *n.*
piece of clothing for a woman or girl, which hangs from the waist 裙子
The girls wear blue skirts for school.
那些女孩子穿蓝色的裙子上学。

sky /sky; skaɪ/ *n.*
(two skies)
space above the earth 天空
The skies are cloudy today.
今天天空上有很多云。

sleep [1] /sleep; sliːp/ *n.*
(no plural)
when you close your eyes and rest 睡觉
The baby had a long sleep.
那婴儿睡了很久。

sleep [2] /sleep; sliːp/ *v.*
(sleeping, slept, slept)
close your eyes and rest 睡觉
Tom sleeps for nine hours every night.
汤姆每晚睡九小时。

go to sleep 入睡
Tom goes to sleep at eight o'clock.
汤姆八时睡觉。
sleepy *adj.* 困了；想睡的
At eight o'clock, Tom feels sleepy.
八时汤姆就想去睡觉了。
sleeping bag *n.* 睡袋
The scouts took sleeping bags when they went camping.
那班童子军露营时都带睡袋。

sleeve /sleeve; sliːv/ *n.*
part of your clothes that covers your arm 衣袖
Mary bought a dress with short sleeves.
玛丽买了一件短袖连衣裙。

slept /slept; slept/ *v.*
p.t. of **sleep** sleep 的过去式
Tom slept well last night.
昨晚汤姆睡得很好。

slice /slice; slaɪs/ *n.*
thin piece you cut off meat, bread or other food 一片
Would you like a slice of melon?
要吃一片瓜吗?

slide [1] /slide; slaɪd/ *n.*
special thing where you can climb up steps and slide down the other side 滑梯
The children were playing on the slide.
孩子们在玩滑梯。

slide [2] /slide; slaɪd/ *v.*
(sliding, slid, slid)
move smoothly 滑动
The big rock slid down the hill.
那块大石从山上滑了下来。

slim /slim; slɪm/ *adj.*
(slimmer, slimmest)
not fat 苗条的
Baoling is very slim.
宝玲很苗条。

sling /sling; slɪŋ/ *n.*
piece of cloth which holds up a broken arm 吊带
Tom had his arm in a sling.
汤姆的手臂挂在吊带上。

lip /slip; slɪp/ *v.*
slipping, slipped, slipped)
all or nearly fall 滑倒
Peter slipped on the wet floor.
皮得在湿地板上滑倒了。

lipper /'slip·per; 'slɪpə/ *n.*
ght, soft shoe that you wear n the house 拖鞋
Mary bought her father a pair of slippers for his birthday.
玛丽买了一双拖鞋送给爸爸做生日礼物。

lippery /'slip·per·y; 'slɪpərɪ/ *adj.*
more slippery, most slippery)
very smooth; difficult to walk on 光滑的；湿滑的
After the rain, the roads were slippery.
雨后，路上很湿滑。

low /slow; sləu/ *adj.*
slower, slowest)
not fast; taking a long time 慢的
The traffic is very slow today.
今天路上的车辆走得很慢。
opp. 反义词：quick 快的
slowly *adv.* 缓慢地
The traffic is moving slowly today.
今天路上的车辆走得很慢。

small /small; smɔ:l/ *adj.*
not big; little 小的
The Chens live in a small flat.
陈家住在一套小公寓房里。
opp. 反义词：large 大的

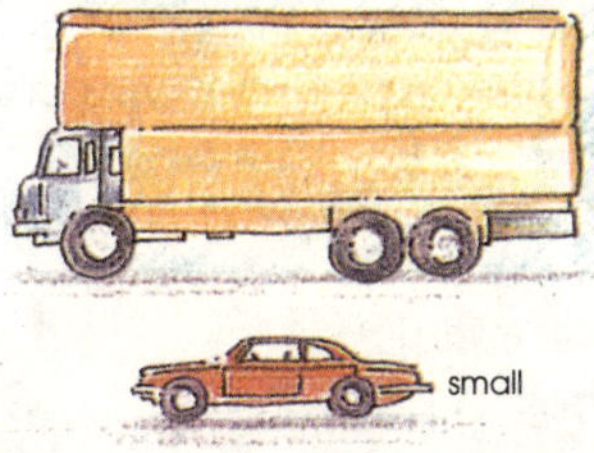

smart /smart; smɑ:t/ *adj.*
clean and neat 漂亮的；整齐的
When the children go to school they are very smart.
孩子们上学时总是很清洁整齐的。

smell [1] /smell; smel/ *n.*
something you learn about with your nose 气味
These flowers have a nice smell.
这些花有香味。
smelly *adj.* 有臭味的
The bad fish was very smelly.
变坏了的鱼有股很难闻的臭味。

smell [2] /smell; smel/ *v.*
(smelling, smelt, smelt)
learn about something with your nose 嗅；闻
Can you smell these flowers?
你闻到这些花的香味吗？

smile [1] /smile; smaɪl/ *n.*
look of happiness 微笑
Sam always has a smile on his face.
萨姆总是面带笑容。

smile [2] /smile; smaɪl/ *v.*
(smiling, smiled, smiled)
look happy 微笑
Sam is always smiling.
萨姆总是在微笑。

smoke [1] /smoke; sməuk/ *n.*
(no plural)
grey or black stuff that goes up into the air from a fire 烟
The kitchen was full of smoke.
厨房里满是烟。

smoke [2] /smoke; sməuk/ *v.*
(smoking, smoked, smoked)
have a burning cigarette or pipe in one's mouth 抽烟；吸烟
Mr Li smokes a pipe.
李先生抽烟斗。

smooth /smooth; smu:ð/ *adj.*
not rough; flat 平滑的；光滑的
Silk is very smooth.
丝绸非常光滑。
opp. 反义词：rough 粗糙的

snack /snack; snæk/ *n.*
small, quick meal 快餐；小吃；点心
Mr Wang has a snack at lunchtime.
王先生午饭时吃快餐。

snail /snail; sneɪl/ *n.*
small animal with a shell on its back 蜗牛
There was a snail on the cabbage.
卷心菜上有一只蜗牛。

snake /snake; sneɪk/ *n.*
long, thin animal with no legs 蛇
Susan does not like snakes.
苏珊不喜欢蛇。

snatch /snatch; snætʃ/ *v.*
take something roughly and quickly 抢；夺
It is rude to snatch things.
一把将东西夺去是没有礼貌的行为。

sneeze /sneeze; sni:z/ *v.*
(sneezing, sneezed, sneezed)
send air out of your nose and mouth with a sudden noise when you have a cold, etc. 打喷嚏
Peter's cold made him sneeze.
彼得着了凉，所以打起喷嚏来。

snore /snore; snɔ:/ *v.*
(snoring, snored, snored)
breathe noisily when you are asleep 打鼾；打呼噜
Mr Qian snores when he is asleep.
钱先生睡觉时打鼾。

snow [1] /snow; snəʊ/ *n.*
(no plural)
soft, white stuff that falls from the sky when it is very cold 雪
The ground was covered with snow.
地上满是雪。

snow [2] /snow; snəʊ/ *v.*
snow falling 下雪
It sometimes snows in Great Britain.
英国有时下雪。

so [1] /so; səʊ/ *adv.*
1 very 非常；很
Baoling is so clever.
宝玲真聪明。
2 also 也是
David is nine and so is Peter.
戴维九岁，彼得也是九岁。

so [2] /so; səʊ/ *conj.*
and because of this 因此；所以
There was a typhoon so we could not go to school.
台风来了，所以我们不能上学。

soak /soak; səʊk/ *v.*
make very wet 泡；浸湿
The heavy rain soaked the children.
大雨使孩子们浑身湿透。

soap /soap; səʊp/ *n.*
(no plural)
stuff that you use with water for washing 肥皂
David washed his hands with soap and water.
戴维用肥皂和水洗手。

sock /sock; sɒk/ *n.*
what you wear on your foot inside your shoe 袜
Susan wears white socks to school.
苏珊上学穿白袜子。
pair of socks 一双袜子
Mary bought a new pair of socks.
玛丽买了一双新袜子。

sofa /'so·fa; 'səʊfə/ *n.*
long, soft seat 沙发
Mary and Susan sat on the sofa.
玛丽和苏珊坐在沙发上。

sofa

soft /soft; sɒft/ *adj.*
1 not hard or rough; smooth and comfortable 柔软的；柔滑的
Sam's bed is very soft.
萨姆的床很软。
opp. 反义词：hard 硬的
2 quiet; not loud 低声的；轻柔的
Mr Wang likes soft music.
王先生喜欢轻柔的音乐。
opp. 反义词：loud 大声的；响亮的

softly *adv.* 轻轻地；轻柔地
Please talk softly.
谈话时请轻声点。

soft drink *n.* （不含酒精的）饮料
The children bought some soft drinks.
孩子们买了一些饮料。

soil /soil; sɔɪl/ *n.*
(no plural)
ground; earth 土地；土壤
Mary put some soil in a flower pot.
玛丽把一些泥土放进花盆里。

sold /sold; səuld/ *v.*
p.t. of **sell** sell 的过去式
Mr Chen sold his car yesterday.
昨天陈先生把他的车子卖掉了。

soldier /'sol·dier; 'səuldʒə/ *n.*
someone who is in the army 士兵
The soldiers marched through the town.
士兵齐步穿过那个城镇。

soldiers

solid /'sol·id; 'sɒlɪd/ *adj.*
hard; with no empty space inside 固体的；实心的
The statue was solid gold.
那雕像是用金子实心铸成的。
opp. 反义词：hollow 中空的

solve /solve; sɒlv/ *v.*
(solving, solved, solved)
find the answer to 解决
The police solved the mystery.
警方解开了那个谜。

some [1] /some; səm/ *adj.*
an amount of; a number of 一些；有些
Mary bought some oranges.
玛丽买了一些橙。

some [2] /some; sʌm/ *pron.*
an amount of; a number of 一些
I have got a bag of sweets. Have some.
我有一包糖果，请吃一些吧。
Usage note: Use *some* in positive sentences (when you mean yes) — *Mary bought some sweets.* Use *any* or *no* in negative sentences (when you mean no) — *He hasn't any sweets. He has no sweets.*
用法：指“有”的时候用 some，例如 Mary bought some sweets。指“没有”的时候用 any 或 no，例如 He hasn't any sweets 和 He has no sweets。

somebody, someone /'some·bo·dy, 'some·one; 'sʌmbədɪ, 'sʌmwʌn/ *pron.*
person 某人；有人
There's somebody in the house.
有人在房子里。

somehow /'some·how; 'sʌmhau/ *adv.*
in some way 用某种方法
I shall get home somehow.
我总得设法回家。

something /'some·thing; 'sʌmθɪŋ/ *pron.*
thing 一些东西
There is something on your face.
你脸上有些东西。

sometimes /'some·times; 'sʌmtaɪmz/ *adv.*
not often; not many times 有时
Peter sometimes goes to the cinema.
彼得有时会去看电影。

somewhere /'some·where; 'sʌmweə/ *adv.*
in some place 某地方
I left my umbrella somewhere.
我把雨伞遗留在某个地方了。

son /son; sʌn/ *n.*
boy child 儿子
Mr and Mrs Chen have two sons and a daughter.
陈先生夫妇有两个儿子和一个女儿。

song /song; sɒŋ/ *n.*
music that you make with your voice 歌曲
Susan liked the songs she heard at the concert.
苏珊喜欢在那个音乐会上听到的歌曲。

soon /soon; suːn/ *adv.*
short time after this 不久；很快
The bus will be here soon.
公共汽车很快就来。

sore /sore; sɔː/ *adj.*
(sorer, sorest)
giving pain 疼痛的
After walking all day, Peter had sore feet.
彼得走了一整天路，脚痛得很。

sorry /'sor·ry; 'sɒrɪ/ *adj.*
(sorrier, sorriest)
1 sad about something 难过的；可惜的
I'm sorry you do not feel well.
你病了，我很难过。
2 sad because you have done something bad 对不起；抱歉
Sam was sorry that he hurt Peter.
萨姆对于伤害彼得一事，感到很歉疚。

sort /sort; sɔːt/ *n.*
type; kind 种类
What sort of bicycle have you got?
你的自行车是哪一类型的？

sound[1] /sound; saʊnd/ *n.*
what you hear; noise 声音
We heard the sound of running water.
我们听到流水声。

sound[2] /sound; saʊnd/ *v.*
1 seem 听来
Your new friend sounds interesting.
你的新朋友听来很有趣。
2 make a noise 发出响声
The bell sounded.
钟响了。

soup /soup; suːp/ *n.*
liquid food that you eat with a spoon 汤
Sam likes chicken soup.
萨姆爱喝鸡汤。

sour /'s·our; 'saʊə/ *adj.*
1 with a taste that is not sweet 酸的
Lemons are sour.
柠檬是酸的。
2 with a taste that is not fresh 变酸了的
This milk is sour.
这牛奶变酸了。

south /south; saʊθ/ *n. adj. adv.*
word that shows where a place is 南方；南面的；向南
Peter lives in the south of Hong Kong Island.
彼得住在香港岛的南区。
Hong Kong is on the south coast of China.
香港位于中国南面的海岸上。
Birds fly south in the winter.
冬天鸟儿向南飞。

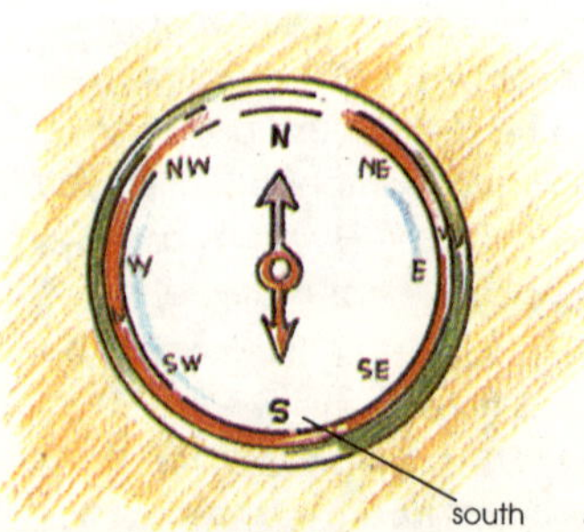

south-east *n.* 东南
The wind is blowing from the south-east.
风从东南面吹来。
southern *adj.* 南面的
We had a holiday in southern France.
我们在法国南部度假。

sow /sow; səʊ/ *v.*
(sowing, sowed, sown)
put seeds into the ground 播种
The farmer sowed some onion seeds.
那农民播下了一些洋葱种子。

soya bean /'soy·a bean; 'sɔɪə biːn/ *n.*
bean that you can eat 黄豆；大豆
The farmer grows soya beans.
那农民种黄豆。
soya sauce *n.* 酱油；豉油(方言)
Peter likes soya sauce.
彼得吃东西喜欢蘸酱油。

space /space; speɪs/ *n.*
1 place with nothing in it 空间；空位
There is space for two more people on the bus.
公共汽车上还有空位可多容纳两个人。
2 **(no plural)** place where the stars are 太空
The rocket went into space.
火箭进入太空。
spaceman *n.* 宇航员，航天员
Tom wants to be a spaceman.
汤姆希望成为宇航员。
spaceship *n.* 宇宙飞船
The spaceship went to the moon.
宇宙飞船飞往月球。

space shuttle *n.* 航天飞机
The space shuttle will return to earth.
航天飞机会飞回地球。

spacesuit *n.* 航天服，宇航服
Spacemen wear spacesuits.
宇航员穿着航天服。

spade /spade; speɪd/ *n.*
tool for digging earth 铲
The children were digging in the sand with spades.
孩子们用铲挖沙。

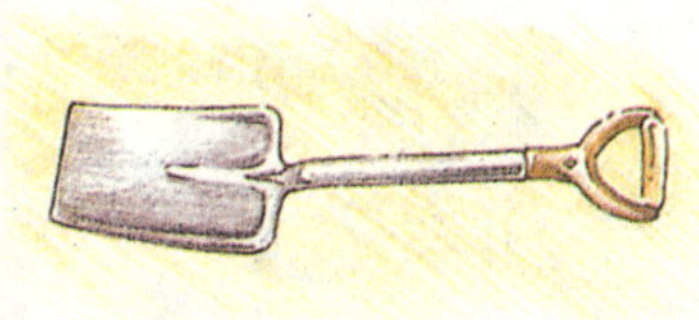

spaghetti /spa·'ghet·ti; spə'getɪ/ *n.*
(**no plural**)
food in long strings; noodles 意大利面条
Sam likes spaghetti and tomato sauce.
萨姆爱吃番茄酱意大利面条。

spanner /'span·ner; 'spænə/ *n.*
tool for turning things 扳手；扳钳
Tom fixed his bicycle with a spanner.
汤姆用扳手修理他的自行车。

spare /spare; speə/ *adj.*
kept for later use; extra 后备的
There is a spare tyre on a car.
汽车都带着一个后备轮胎。

sparrow /'spar·row; 'spærəʊ/ *n.*
small bird 麻雀
The trees were full of sparrows.
树上满是麻雀。

speak /speak; spi:k/ *v.*
(**speaking, spoke, spoken**)
1 talk; make words with your mouth 说话；谈话
I would like to speak to your father.
我想跟你父亲谈谈。
2 know how to talk in a language 会说某种语言
Mary can speak French.
玛丽会说法语。

special /'spe·cial; 'speʃl/ *adj.*
not like others; for one person only; for one time only 特别的；特殊的
Tomorrow is a special day for Tom. It's his birthday.
明天对汤姆来说是个特别的日子，那是他的生日。

spectacles /'spec·ta·cles; 'spektəklz/ *n.*
(**plural**)
glasses; pieces of glass or plastic that you wear over your eyes so that you can see better 眼镜
Peter wears spectacles for reading.
彼得看书时戴眼镜。

spectator /spec·'ta·tor; spek'teɪtə/ *n.*
someone who watches a game 观众
There were thousands of spectators at the football match.
这场足球赛有成千上万的观众。

speech /speech; spi:tʃ/ *n.*
1 (two **speeches**) special talk to a group of people 演讲
The mayor gave a speech on TV.
市长在电视里演讲。
2 (**no plural**) way of speaking 讲话方式
I could tell from his speech that he was from Beijing.
我听他说话就知道他是从北京来的。

speed /speed; spi:d/ *n.*
(**no plural**)
how fast someone or something goes 速度
What speed is the car doing?
这辆汽车现在的车速是多少？

spell /spell; spel/ *v.*
(**spelling, spelt, spelt**)
use the right letters to make a word 拼字
Peter can spell very well.
彼得拼字很棒。
spelling *n.* 拼字法
Peter is good at spelling.
彼得拼字很棒。

spend /spend; spend/ *v.*
(**spending, spent, spent**)
1 pay money for something 用钱
Tom spends his pocket money on sweets.
汤姆把他的零用钱都用来买糖果。

2 use time for something 度过；消磨
Mr Chen spent a month in Shanghai.
陈先生在上海逗留了一个月。

spider /'spi·der; 'spaɪdə/ *n.*
very small animal with eight long legs 蜘蛛
Mary is afraid of spiders.
玛丽怕蜘蛛。

spider

spill /spill; spɪl/ *v.*
(**spilling, spilt, spilt**)
let liquid fall out of a cup, etc., by mistake 使溢出；泼出
Mary spilt tea on her dress.
玛丽把茶泼在连衣裙上了。

spin /spin; spɪn/ *v.*
(**spinning, spun, spun**)
1 make cotton, silk, wool, etc., into thread 纺纱
The factory spins cotton.
那工厂把棉纺成纱。
2 turn round and round very fast 迅速旋转
The wheels spun round.
轮子快速旋转。

spirit /'spi·rit; 'spɪrɪt/ *n.*
1 how you feel 精神
The children were in good spirits.
孩子们的精神很好。
2 ghost 幽灵；鬼魂
Sam thought he saw a spirit.
萨姆认为自己看见了鬼魂。

spit /spit; spɪt/ *v.*
(**spitting, spat, spat**)
blow something out of your mouth 吐唾液；吐痰
You must not spit.
你不要随地吐痰。

splash [1] /splash; splæʃ/ *v.*
throw water or other liquid over someone or something 溅污；泼湿
The children splashed water over one another.
孩子们彼此往身上泼水。

splash [2] /splash; splæʃ/ *n.*
(two **splashes**)
what happens when something falls into water 飞溅；扑通声
Sam fell into the water with a big splash.
萨姆扑通一声掉进水里。

split /split; splɪt/ *v.*
(**splitting, split, split**)
break or tear open 裂开
Tom bent over and split his trousers.
汤姆弯腰时，裤子绽裂了。

spoil /spoil; spɔɪl/ *v.*
(**spoiling, spoilt, spoilt**)
make something less good than before 破坏；损坏；糟蹋
The rain spoilt Susan's new shoes.
这场雨把苏珊的新鞋弄坏了。

spoke /spoke; spəuk/ *v.*
p.t. of **speak** speak 的过去式
I spoke to Peter yesterday.
昨天我跟彼得谈过。

spoken *v.* speak 的过去分词
I have spoken to Peter.
我已经和彼得谈过了。

spoon /spoon; spu:n/ *n.*
tool with a round end for lifting food 匙
Sam ate his rice with a spoon.
萨姆用勺子吃饭。

spoonful *n.* 一匙的分量
Anna put two spoonfuls of sugar in her coffee.
安娜放了两匙糖在她的咖啡里。

sport /sport; spɔ:t/ *n.*
game 运动
Football is Sam's favourite sport.
足球是萨姆最喜爱的运动。

sports

sports ground *n.* 运动场
There is a sports ground near our school.
我们学校附近有个运动场。

spot /spot; spɒt/ *n.*
1 small, round mark 小圆点；斑点
The dog is white with black spots.
那只狗白底带有黑点。

2 place 地点
The children found a nice spot for a picnic.
孩子们找到一个野餐的好地方。

spray /spray; spreɪ/ *v.*
make liquid fall all over something 喷洒
Susan sprayed her plants with water.
苏珊用水喷洒她的植物。

spread /spread; spred/ *v.*
(spreading, spread, spread)
1 open something and lay it down 铺开
Susan spread a cloth on the table.
苏珊把一块桌布铺在桌子上。
2 put soft stuff all over something 抹开
Tom spread some butter on his toast.
汤姆在他的烤面包上抹上一些黄油。

spread 2

3 open something 展开
The bird spread its wings.
那鸟儿展开翅膀。
4 move to different parts 散开
The children spread around the room.
孩子们在房间里散开。

spring /spring; sprɪŋ/ *n.*
1 time of the year when plants begin to grow 春天，春季
Spring is my favourite season.
春天是我最喜欢的季节。
2 piece of metal or wire twisted round and round 弹簧
Mr Wang's car has a broken spring.
王先生的车子有一根弹簧断了。

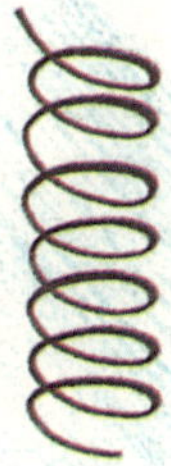

square [1] /square; skweə/ *adj.*
with the shape of a square 正方形的
Mrs Chen bought a square table.
陈太太买了一张正方形的桌子。

square [2] /square; skweə/ *n.*
1 shape with four equal, straight sides 正方形
Tom drew a square.
汤姆画了个正方形。
2 big space in a town 广场
There are some big trees in the square.
广场里有些大树。

squash [1] /squash; skwɒʃ/ *v.*
press something so that you make it flat 压扁
Peter squashed the tomato.
彼得压扁了那个番茄。

squash [2] /squash; skwɒʃ/ *n.*
kind of fruit drink 果汁饮料
Xiaofang drank a glass of orange squash.
小芳喝了一杯橙汁饮料。

squeeze /squeeze; skwi:z/ *v.*
(squeezing, squeezed, squeezed)
press something hard between other things 榨；挤压
Peter squeezed the juice out of some oranges.
彼得把一些橙榨汁。

squid /squid; skwɪd/ *n.*
sort of sea animal 鱿鱼
Sam likes fried squid.
萨姆爱吃炸鱿鱼。

squid

stadium /ˈsta·di·um; ˈsteɪdɪəm/ *n.*
place for sports with seats around the sides 运动场
There is a football match at the stadium.
那个运动场在举行足球比赛。

staff /staff; stɑ:f/ *n.*
(no plural)
group of people who work together 全体工作人员
The staff of the school are very good.
这个学校的全体员工都很好。

stage /stage; steɪdʒ/ *n.*
part of a hall or theatre where people stand to act, speak or sing 舞台
The choir came onto the stage.
那个合唱团走到舞台上。

stairs /stairs; steəz/ *n.*
(plural)
steps that go from one floor to the next floor 楼梯；阶梯
The children climbed the stairs.
孩子们上楼梯。

stairs

stalk /stalk; stɔ:k/ *n.*
part of a plant 茎；柄；梗
The flowers have long stalks.
那些花有长长的茎。

stall /stall; stɔ:l/ *n.*
small, open shop 售货摊
Mr Qian has a stall in the market.
钱先生在市场里有一个售货摊。

stamp [1] /stamp; stæmp/ *v.*
put your foot down hard 踏；踩；跺脚
Tom stamped on the beetle.
汤姆踩那只甲虫。

stamp [2] /stamp; stæmp/ *n.*
small piece of paper that you stick on a letter or a parcel to show that you have paid to send it 邮票
Mary collects stamps.
玛丽收集邮票。

stamps

stand /stand; stænd/ *v.*
(standing, stood, stood)

1 get up onto your feet 站起来
The class stood when the principal came in.
校长进来时，全班学生都站起来。
2 be on your feet 站立
The children were standing at the bus stop.
孩子们站在公共汽车站。
opp. 反义词：sit 坐
3 be in a certain place 在；位于
The house stands in a large garden.
那所房子建在一个大花园里面。
stand up 站起
Would you stand up, please?
请你站起来好吗？
stand still 站住
The teacher told the children to stand still.
老师叫孩子们站住。

stapler /'sta·pler; 'steɪplə/ *n.*
machine for pinning things together 钉书机
Peter fastened the papers together with a stapler.
彼得用钉书机把纸钉在一起。

star /star; stɑ:/ *n.*
1 one of the bright things that shine in the sky 星
The sky is covered with stars tonight.
今晚天空上满是星星。

star 1

2 famous actor, singer, etc. 明星
There were many stars in the film.
这部电影里有许多明星。

stare /stare; steə/ *v.*
(staring, stared, stared)
look at someone or something for a long time 盯着；注视
The children stared at the very tall man.
孩子们盯着那个高个子。

starfish /'star·fish; 'stɑ:fɪʃ/ *n.*
(two **starfish**)
sort of sea animal 海星
Tom found a starfish on the beach.
汤姆在海滩上找到一个海星。

start [1] /start; stɑ:t/ *n.*
beginning 开始
Peter missed the start of the race.
彼得错过了比赛的开始部分。
opp. 反义词：finish 结尾部分

start [2] /start; stɑ:t/ *v.*
1 begin to happen 开始
The film started half an hour ago.
电影在半小时前就开始了。
2 begin to do something 开始
Mr Wang starts work at seven o'clock.
王先生七时开始工作。
opp. 反义词：stop 停止

starve /starve; stɑ:v/ *v.*
(starving, starved, starved)
get ill or die because one has too little food 挨饿；饿死
Millions of people in that country are starving.
那个国家有数以百万计的人在挨饿。

station /'sta·tion; 'steɪʃn/ *n.*
1 place where trains stop so that people can get on or off 火车站
Tom catches a train at the Shatin station.
汤姆在沙田站上火车。

2 place for policemen, firemen, etc. 所；站；台
Mr Wang went to the police station.
王先生去了警察署。

stationery /'sta·tion·er·y; 'steɪʃənrɪ/ *n.*
(no plural)
pencils, paper, etc. 文具
Sam bought some stationery and wrote a letter.
萨姆买了些文具来写信。

statue /'sta·tue; 'stætʃu:/ *n.*
shape of a person or animal in stone, metal or wood 塑像；雕像
There is a statue of a famous man in the square.
广场上有一座名人的塑像。

stay /stay; steɪ/ *v.*
1 be in the same place; remain 逗留
We stay at home when there is a typhoon.
刮台风时，我们都留在家里。
2 not change; remain 维持；保持
Food will stay fresh in the fridge.
食物在冰箱里面可保持新鲜。
3 live somewhere for a time 小住
Peter stays with his grandmother for his holidays.
彼得放假时去祖母那里小住。
stay away 离开
David stayed away from school for a week.
戴维一星期没有回学校。
stay behind 留下来
The teacher made the children stay behind.
老师要孩子们留下来。
stay in 留在家
The children stay in when it rains.
下雨天孩子们都留在家里。
stay out 留在外面
The children do not stay out when there is a typhoon.
刮台风时，孩子们都不出去。

steak /steak; steɪk/ *n.*
thick piece of meat or fish for cooking 肉排；鱼块
David likes steak and chips.
戴维爱吃牛排和炸薯条。

steal /steal; sti:l/ *v.*
(stealing, stole, stolen)
take something that is not yours 偷
The thief stole a car.
那小偷偷了一辆汽车。

steam [1] /steam; sti:m/ *n.*
(no plural)
white cloud that rises from very hot water 水蒸气
The kitchen was full of steam.
厨房里满是水蒸气。

steam [2] /steam; sti:m/ *v.*
cook food in steam 蒸
Mrs Chen is steaming a chicken.
陈太太正在蒸鸡。

steel /steel; sti:l/ *n.*
(no plural)
sort of metal 钢
The pans are made of steel.
平底锅是用钢做的。

steep /steep; sti:p/ *adj.*
rising quickly from a low place to a high place 陡峭的
There was a steep path up the mountain.
有一条很陡的小路通到山上去。

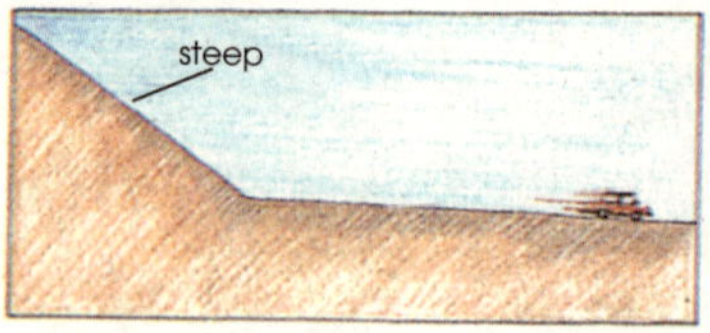

steer /steer; stɪə/ *v.*
turn a car, bike, etc. in the direction you want 驾驶
Tom steered the car into the garage.
汤姆把车开进车房里。
steering wheel *n.* 方向盘；驾驶盘
Tom turned the steering wheel of the car.
汤姆转动汽车的方向盘。

stem /stem; stem/ *n.*
part of a plant 茎；干
The flowers had long stems.
那些花有长长的茎。

step [1] /step; step/ *v.*
(stepping, stepped, stepped)
move your foot to go forward or backwards 踏步
David stepped on some glass on the beach.
戴维在海滩上踩着一些玻璃碎片。

step [2] /step; step/ *n.*
1 place to put your foot when you go up the stairs 楼梯；台阶
Peter slipped on the wet steps.
彼得在湿滑的楼梯上滑倒了。

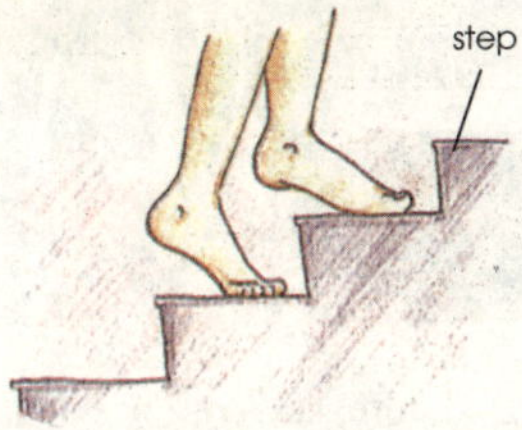

2 movement of your foot when walking, running, etc. 脚步
The baby took two steps.
那婴孩走了两步。

step by step 逐步
Mary followed the instructions step by step.
玛丽按着指示逐步来做。

step-mother /'step·moth·er; 'stepmʌðə/ *n.*
woman who is not one's mother married to one's father 继母
Cinderella had a wicked step-mother.
灰姑娘有一个心肠狠毒的继母。

stereo /'ste·re·o; 'steriəu/ *n.*
machine for listening to music 立体声唱机
Anna was playing records on her stereo.
安娜用她的立体声唱机放唱片。

stew /stew; stju:/ *n.*
dish of cooked meat and vegetables 炖煮的菜肴
Peter cooked a delicious beef stew.
彼得做了一道美味的炖牛肉。

stick [1] /stick; stɪk/ *n.*
thin piece of wood 枝；棍；棒
The children made a fire with sticks.
孩子们用柴枝生火。

walking stick *n.* 手杖
The old man uses a walking stick.
那老人拄手杖走路。

stick [2] /stick; stɪk/ *v.*
(**sticking, stuck, stuck**)
1 fix something onto another thing with glue 粘；贴
Anna stuck a picture of a horse on the wall of her bedroom.
安娜在她的卧室墙上贴了一张马的图片。
2 become fixed so that it cannot move 陷住不能动
The lorry stuck in the muddy field.
那货车陷在泥地里不能动。
3 push a sharp thing into something 插；刺
Sam stuck a pin in the balloon and burst it.
萨姆用针刺破了气球。

sticky /'stick·y; 'stɪkɪ/ *adj.*
(**stickier, stickiest**)
that becomes fixed to someone or something 黏性的
John likes sticky rice.
约翰爱吃黏米。

still [1] /still; stɪl/ *adj.*
not moving or making any sound 静止的；寂静的
The school was still after the children went home.
孩子们回家后，学校一片寂静。

keep still 静止不动
The children would not keep still.
孩子们不会静下来。

stand still 站着不动
The soldiers stood still.
士兵们站着不动。

still [2] /still; stɪl/ *adv.*
word that you use to show that something has not changed 仍然
Is Peter still working?
彼得仍在工作吗?

sting [1] /sting; stɪŋ/ *n.*
pain made by a bee, wasp, plant, etc. 刺伤处
Sam has a sting on his arm.
萨姆的手臂给刺伤了。

sting [2] /sting; stɪŋ/ *v.*
(**stinging, stung, stung**)
hurt someone with a sharp, poisonous point 刺；叮
A bee stung Sam.
萨姆给蜜蜂刺伤了。

stir /stir; stɜ:/ *v.*
(**stirring, stirred, stirred**)
move a spoon or stick round and round to mix something 搅动
Mary stirred the soup with a spoon.
玛丽用匙搅汤。

stitch [1] /stitch; stɪtʃ/ *n.*
(two **stitches**)
putting your needle once into cloth （一）针
The dress needed a lot of stitches.
这件连衣裙要缝很多针。

stitch [2] /stitch; stɪtʃ/ *v.*
fasten cloth with thread 缝
Susan was stitching a new dress.
苏珊在缝制一件新连衣裙。

stockings /'stock·ings; 'stɒkɪŋz/ *n.*
(**plural**)
long, thin socks 长袜
The nurses wear black stockings.
护士们穿着黑长袜。

stole /stole; stəʊl/ *v.*
p.t. of **steal** steal 的过去式
The thief stole some money.
那小偷偷了一些钱。

stolen *v.* steal 的过去分词
Someone has stolen Mr Wang's car.
有人偷了王先生的车子。

stomach /'stom·ach; 'stʌmək/ *n.*
part inside the body where food goes 胃
Sam had a stomach ache.
萨姆胃痛。

stone /stone; stəʊn/ *n.*
1 (**no plural**) very hard part of the ground; rock 石
The building is made of stone.
那房子是用石块建造的。
2 hard part in the middle of a fruit 果核
A peach has a large stone in it.
桃子有一个大核。
3 small piece of rock 小石块
David threw a stone into the sea.
戴维把一块石子扔进海里。

stood /stood; stʊd/ *v.*
p.t. of **stand** stand 的过去式
The children stood up.
孩子们站了起来。

stool /stool; stu:l/ *n.*
seat with no back 凳子
The children were sitting on stools.
孩子们坐在凳子上。

stop [1] /stop; stɒp/ *v.*
(**stopping, stopped, stopped**)
1 become still; finish what you are doing 停止
The train stops at Shatin.
这火车停在沙田。
opp. 反义词: start 开始
2 not allow someone to do something 阻止；制止
The teacher stopped the boys from fighting.
老师制止那些男孩打架。

stop [2] /stop; stɒp/ *n.*
place where buses, trams, etc., stop moving so that people can get on and off 车站
A lot of people were waiting at the bus-stop.
许多人在公共汽车站等车。

store [1] /store; stɔ:/ *n.*
big shop 百货商店
Mr Chen bought some new clothes at the store.
陈先生在百货商店买了些新衣服。

store [2] /store; stɔ:/ *v.*
(**storing, stored, stored**)
keep for later 储藏；储存
The company stored the rice.
那公司把米储存起来。

storey /'sto·rey; 'stɔ:rɪ/ *n.*
floor of a building 层
The building is forty storeys high.
那座建筑物有四十层高。

storm /storm; stɔ:m/ *n.*
time of strong wind and rain 暴风雨
The children sheltered from the storm.
孩子们躲避暴风雨。

story /'sto·ry; 'stɔ:rɪ/ *n.*
(two **stories**)
true or untrue things that someone tells you about 故事
The teacher told the children a story.
老师给孩子们讲了一个故事。

stove /stove; stəuv/ *n.*
hing on which you cook
ood 炉
Mrs Qian has an electric
stove.
伐太太有电炉。

straight [1] /straight; streɪt/ *adj.*
not bending; with no curve
直的
The road was very straight.
这条路非常直。

straight [2] /straight; streɪt/ *adv.*
by the shortest way; not
stopping 直接地
Mrs Chen told Tom to go
straight home.
陈太太吩咐汤姆直接回家。

strange /strange; streɪndʒ/
adj.
(**stranger, strangest**)
that you do not know; not
usual 陌生的；奇怪的
This is a strange place.
这是个陌生的地方。

stranger /ˈstran·ger;
ˈstreɪndʒə/ *n.*
someone you do not know
陌生人
The man was a stranger.
那是个陌生人。

straw /straw; strɔː/ *n.*
1 thin paper or plastic tube
for drinking 吸管
Mary was drinking orange
juice through a straw.
玛丽用吸管喝橙汁。
2 dry stalks of rice, wheat,
etc. 稻草
The roof was made of
straw.
那屋顶用稻草盖成。

strawberry /ˈstraw·ber·ry;
ˈstrɔːbrɪ/ *n.*
(two **strawberries**)
soft, red fruit 草莓
Peter likes strawberries.
彼得爱吃草莓。

stream /stream; striːm/ *n.*
small river 小河；小溪
There were some fish in the
stream.
小溪里有些鱼。

street /street; striːt/ *n.*
road in a town or village 街道
There were a lot of cars in the
street.
街道上汽车很多。

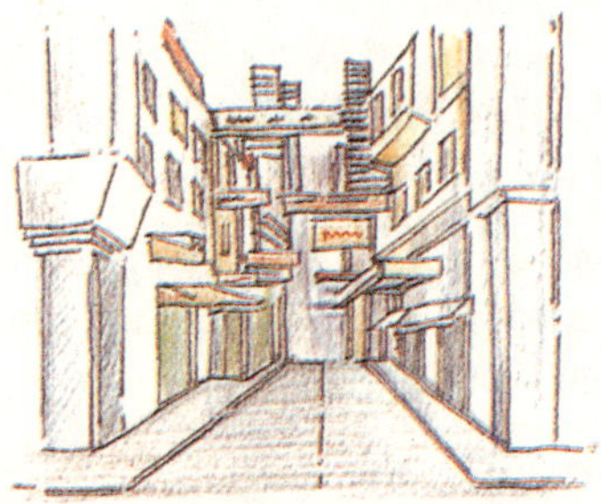

stretch /stretch; stretʃ/ *v.*
get bigger 伸展；拉长
Anna's pullover has stretched.
安娜的套头毛衣拉长了。

strict /strict; strɪkt/ *adj.*
makes you do what you are
told 严格
Miss Li is very strict with the
children.
李小姐对孩子非常严格。

strike /strike; straɪk/ *v.*
(**striking, struck, struck**)
1 hit 击；打
The ball struck Tom in the
face.
那球打中了汤姆的脸。
2 make the sound of a bell
敲响
The clock struck three.
那钟敲了三下。

string /string; strɪŋ/ *n.*
1 strong thread for tying
things 绳子
Mary tied the parcel with
a string.
玛丽用绳子把包裹捆好。
2 part of a musical
instrument 乐器的弦
A string broke on Mary's
guitar.
玛丽的吉他有一根弦断了。

strip /strip; strɪp/ *n.*
long narrow piece of
something 长条
There is a strip of grass round
the building.
环绕着这座建筑物四周的是长条形的
草地。

stripe /stripe; straɪp/ *n.*
line of colour 条纹
The dress has blue and white
stripes.
那件连衣裙有蓝白条纹。
striped *adj.* 有条纹的
The dress is striped.
这件连衣裙印有条纹。

strong /strong; strɒŋ/ *adj.*
1 with a powerful body 强壮的
The policeman was very strong.
那个警察身体非常强壮。
2 that will not break easily
坚固的；结实的
The old chair is not very strong.
那张旧椅子不太结实。
3 that you can see, smell, taste or feel very easily
强烈的；浓烈的
A strong wind blew the tree down.
强风把树吹倒了。
opp. 反义词：weak 弱的
strongly *adv.* 强烈地；极力地
The wind blew strongly.
风吹得很猛。

stuck /stuck; stʌk/ *v.*
p.t. of **stick** stick 的过去式
Mary stuck a picture in her exercise book.
玛丽在她的练习簿上贴了一张图片。

student /ˈstu·dent; ˈstju:dnt/ *n.*
someone who is learning something 学生
Tom's elder brother is a university student.
汤姆的哥哥是个大学生。

students

studio /ˈstu·di·o; ˈstju:dɪəʊ/ *n.*
place where films or television and radio programmes are made
播放室；广播室；录制室
Mrs Fang works in a TV studio.
方太太在电视录制室工作。

study /ˈstud·y; ˈstʌdɪ/ *v.*
(**studying, studied, studied**)
learn something 学习
The children are studying English.
孩子们在学英语。

stuff /stuff; stʌf/ *n.*
(**no plural**)
material; sort of thing 材料；东西
Silk is expensive stuff.
丝绸是昂贵的东西。

stung /stung; stʌŋ/ *v.*
p.t. of **sting** sting 的过去式
The bee stung Tom.
那蜜蜂刺伤了汤姆。

stupid /ˈstu·pid; ˈstju:pɪd/ *adj.*
(**more stupid, most stupid**)
not able to understand quickly; foolish 愚蠢的
The stupid boy ran into the road.
那傻男孩在马路上乱闯。
opp. 反义词：clever, wise 聪明的

subject /ˈsub·ject; ˈsʌbdʒɪkt/ *n.*
what you learn at school
科目；学科
History is Baoling's favourite subject.
历史是宝玲最喜欢的科目。

submarine /sub·ma·ˈrine; sʌbməˈri:n/ *n.*
ship that can travel under the sea 潜水艇
The submarine ran into the fishing net.
那艘潜水艇撞到鱼网上去了。

submarine

subtract /sub·ˈtract; səbˈtrækt/ *v.*
take one number away from another number 减
Subtract four from ten please.
请计算十减四得多少。
opp. 反义词：add 加
subtraction *n.* 减法
Tom thinks subtraction is difficult.
汤姆觉得减法很难。

subway /ˈsub·way; ˈsʌbweɪ/ *n.*
path under a road 地道；地下通道
Use the subway to cross that road.
请通过地道横穿马路。

succeed /suc·ˈceed; səkˈsi:d/ *v.*
do something that you wanted to do 成功
Mary succeeded in getting tickets for the concert.
玛丽买到音乐会的票子了。
opp. 反义词：fail 失败

success /suc·ˈcess; səkˈses/ *n.*
(two **successes**)
something done well; done with the right result 成功；成就
The choir was a big success at the concert.
音乐会上，那个合唱团的表演非常成功。

successful *adj.* 成功的
Mr Qian is a successful shopkeeper.
钱先生是个成功的店主。
successfully *adv.* 成功地
The spaceship landed successfully on the moon.
宇宙飞船成功登陆月球。

such /such; sʌtʃ/ *adj.*
word that makes another word stronger 这样的；如此的
She's such a nice girl.
她是这么好的一个女孩。
such as 例如；像
He likes to eat a lot of fruit such as oranges and bananas.
他爱吃的水果很多，如橙、香蕉等。

suck /suck; sʌk/ *v.*
take liquid with your mouth like a baby 吸；啜
Tom sucked the lemonade through a straw.
汤姆用吸管来啜柠檬水。

sudden /'sud·den; 'sʌdn/ *adj.*
(more sudden, most sudden)
happening quickly; that you do not expect 突然的；忽然的
A sudden storm sunk the boat.
突然而来的暴风雨把船弄沉了。
suddenly *adv.* 突然地
The tram suddenly stopped.
那电车突然停了下来。

sugar /'sug·ar; 'ʃugə/ *n.*
(no plural)
sweet stuff that comes from a plant 糖
Mary put two spoons of sugar in her coffee.
玛丽在她的咖啡里放了两匙糖。

sugar cane *n.* 甘蔗
Mrs Chen squeezed sugar cane to make a drink.
陈太太榨蔗汁做饮料。

suit /suit; su:t/ *n.*
jacket and trousers that you wear together 一套衣服
Mr Wang wears a blue suit to go to work.
王先生穿一套蓝西服上班。

suitcase /'suit·case; 'su:tkeɪs/ *n.*
thing with a lid and a handle that holds your clothes when you travel 手提衣箱
Tom packed his suitcase for his holidays.
汤姆把东西装进衣箱，准备度假去。

sum /sum; sʌm/ *n.*
piece of work in arithmetic 算术题
Xiaofang is good at sums.
小芳的算术很好。

summer /'sum·mer; 'sʌmə/ *n.*
one of the four seasons of the year 夏天
Summer is the hottest time of the year in Hong Kong.
在香港，夏天是一年最热的时候。

sun /sun; sʌn/ *n.*
the big round thing that shines in the sky 太阳；日
The sun rose at five o'clock.
太阳五时便升起来。

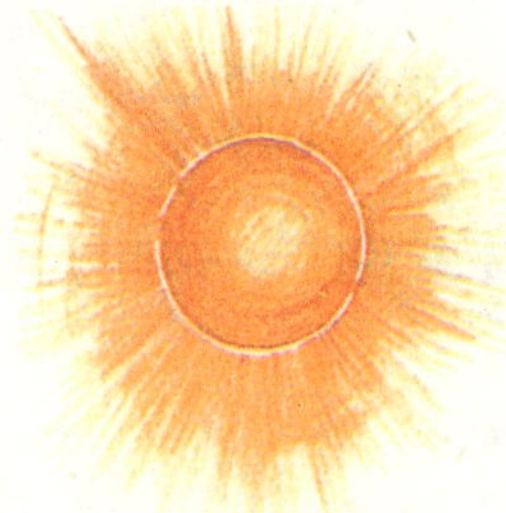

sunny *adj.* 有阳光的
It's sunny today.
今天阳光充沛。
sunbathing *n.* 日光浴
Sunbathing can be bad for your skin.
日光浴可能对你的皮肤有害。
sunglasses *n.* 太阳眼镜
When it is sunny, Tom wears sunglasses.
阳光普照时，汤姆会戴上太阳眼镜。
sunlight *n.* 阳光
Sunlight came into the room.
阳光照进房间里。
sunrise *n.* 日出
Sunrise is at five o'clock tomorrow.
明天五时日出。
sunset *n.* 日落
Sunset is at seven o'clock tomorrow.
明天七时日落。
sunshine *n.* 阳光
The old people were sitting in the sunshine.
那些老人家坐在阳光之下。

Sunday /'Sun·day; 'sʌndɪ/ *n.*
day of the week 星期日
We do not go to school on Sunday.
星期日我们不用上学。

supermarket
/'su·per·mar·ket; 'su:pəmɑ:kɪt/ *n.*
big food shop 超级市场
Mrs Chen shops at the supermarket.
陈太太在超级市场买东西。

supper /'sup·per; 'sʌpə/ *n.*
last meal of the day 晚饭；晚餐
Peter had fish for his supper.
彼得晚饭吃鱼。

sure /sure; ʃɔ:/ *adj.*
(**surer, surest**)
certain; knowing that something is true or may happen 一定；肯定；相信
The bus is sure to come soon.
公共汽车一定很快就来。
sure! *int.* 当然！
Would you like to come to the party? Sure!
你来参加聚会吗？当然来！
surely *adv.* 确实；必然
Surely the bus will come soon.
公共汽车一定很快就来。

surf /surf; sɜ:f/ *v.*
travel on the tops of waves on a long piece of wood, etc. 冲浪；滑浪(方言)
Mary likes to surf at the beach.
玛丽喜欢在海滩冲浪。
surfboard *n.* 冲浪板
Mary bought a new surfboard.
玛丽买了一块新的冲浪板。

surface /'sur·face; 'sɜ:fɪs/ *n.*
top part 表面
There was a lot of rubbish on the surface of the sea.
海面上有很多垃圾。

surname /'sur·name; 'sɜ:neɪm/ *n.*
name of your family 姓
David's surname is Li.
戴维姓李。

surprise [1] /sur·'prise; sə'praɪz/ *n.*
something that you do not expect 惊奇；意外
The present was a nice surprise.
那份礼物带来了惊喜。

surprise [2] /sur·'prise; sə'praɪz/ *v.*
(**surprising, surprised, surprised**)
do something that someone does not expect 使惊奇；使感到意外
The present surprised Peter.
那份礼物使彼得感到意外。
surprising *adj.* 使人惊奇的；出人意表的
The expensive present was surprising.
那份昂贵的礼物令人感到意外。

surround /sur·'round; sə'raʊnd/ *v.*
be or go all round something 包围；环绕
The police surrounded the building.
警方包围了那座建筑物。

swallow /'swal·low; 'swɒləʊ/ *v.*
take something into your mouth and down your throat 吞下；咽下
Susan swallowed the medicine.
苏珊把药吞了下去。

swam /swam; swæm/ *v.*
p.t. of **swim** swim 的过去式
David swam to the boat.
戴维向着那小船游去。

swan /swan; swɒn/ *n.*
large white water bird 天鹅
There were two swans on the lake.
湖上有两只天鹅。

sweat /sweat; swet/ *v.*
drops of water coming from your skin when you are hot or ill 出汗
On a hot day, we sweat.
在炎热的天气下，我们都出汗了。

sweater /'sweat·er; 'swetə/ *n.*
piece of thick woollen clothing that you wear on the top part of your body 毛衣
When it is cold, David wears a sweater.
天气寒冷时，戴维穿上毛衣。

sweep /sweep; swi:p/ *v.*
(**sweeping, swept, swept**)
clean with a brush, etc. 扫；打扫
Mary swept the classroom floor.
玛丽把教室的地板扫干净。

sweet [1] /sweet; swi:t/ *adj.*
1 with a taste of sugar 甜的
Sam likes sweet things.
萨姆爱吃甜食。
2 beautiful 可爱的；漂亮的
The baby is very sweet.
这婴儿很可爱。

sweet [2] /sweet; swi:t/ *n.*
small piece of sweet food 糖果
Children like sweets.
孩子们爱吃糖果。

swept /swept; swept/ *v.*
p.t. of **sweep** sweep 的过去式
Mrs Chen swept the flat.
陈太太打扫那套公寓房。

swim [1] /swim; swɪm/ *v.*
(**swimming, swam, swum**)
move your body through water 游泳
David swims every day.
戴维每天游泳。

swim [2] /swim; swɪm/ *n.*
moving your body through water 游泳
Let's go for a swim.
我们游泳去吧。
swimmer *n.* 游泳的人
David is a good swimmer.
戴维善于游泳。
swimming *n.* 游泳
David likes swimming.
戴维喜欢游泳。

swimming-pool *n.* 游泳池
The school has a swimming-pool.
学校有个游泳池。

swimming-pools

swimming-trunks *n.* 游泳裤
Sam put his swimming-trunks on and went to the beach.
萨姆穿了游泳裤便走向海滩。
swimsuit *n.* 游泳衣
Jenny did not swim because she forgot her swimsuit.
詹妮不游泳，因为她忘了带游泳衣。

swing [1] /swing; swɪŋ/ *v.*
(**swinging, swung, swung**)
hang and move through the air 摇荡；摆动
The sign was swinging in the wind.
那招牌在风中摇荡。

swing [2] /swing; swɪŋ/ *n.*
seat that hangs from ropes and moves through the air 秋千
Anna was playing on a swing in the park.
安娜在公园里玩秋千。

switch [1] /switch; swɪtʃ/ *n.*
(two **switches**)
small handle or knob that starts and stops electricity 开关
Where is the switch for the fan?
风扇的开关在哪里？

switch [2] /switch; swɪtʃ/ *v.*
turn electricity on or off 开或关
Switch on the lights, please.
请开灯。
Switch off the fan, please.
请关掉风扇。

sword /sword; sɔ:d/ *n.*
very long, sharp knife for fighting 剑；刀
The soldier had a sword.
那个军人有一把剑。

swum /swum; swʌm/ *v.*
p.p. of **swim** swim 的过去分词
David has swum across the harbour.
戴维已经游到海港的另一边了。

swung /swung; swʌŋ/ *v.*
p.t. of **swing** swing 的过去式
The gate swung open.
大门打开了。

syllable /ˈsyl·la·ble; ˈsɪləbl/ *n.*
part of a word 音节
The word 'vegetarian' has five syllables.
单词 vegetarian 有五个音节。

synonym /ˈsyn·o·nym; ˈsɪnənɪm/ *n.*
word or phrase that means almost the same thing as another word or phrase 同义词
The words 'small' and 'little' are synonyms.
small 和 little 是同义词。

table /ˈta·ble; ˈteɪbl/ *n.*
1 piece of furniture with a flat top 桌子；台子
Baoling put the food on the table.
宝玲把食物放在桌子上。
2 list of information 表
The children are learning their multiplication tables.
孩子们正在学习乘法表。

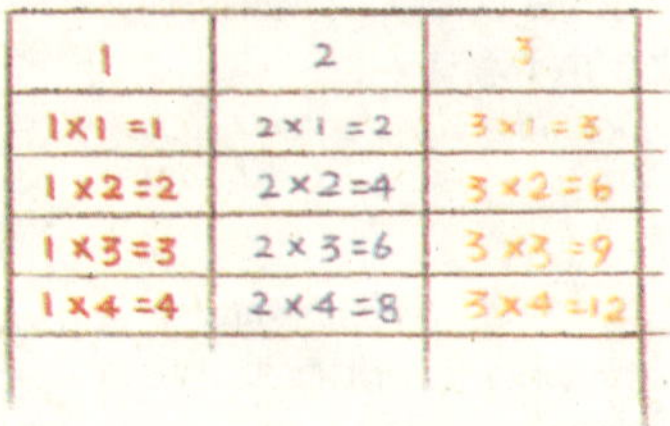

tablecloth /ˈta·ble·cloth; ˈteɪblklɒθ/ *n.*
cover for a table 桌布
Mary put a clean tablecloth on the table.
玛丽在桌上铺上一块干净的桌布。

table tennis /ˈta·ble ˈtennis; ˈteɪbl ˈtenɪs/ *n.*
(no plural)
game where players hit a small ball across a net on a big table 乒乓球
Peter and David are playing table tennis.
彼得和戴维在打乒乓球。
syn. 同义词：ping-pong

tablet /ˈtab·let; ˈtæblɪt/ *n.*
small, hard piece of medicine 药片
The doctor gave Peter some tablets.
医生给了彼得一些药片。

tail /tail; teɪl/ *n.*
part of the back of an animal, bird, or fish 尾巴
A monkey has a long tail.
猴子有一根长尾巴。

tailor /ˈtai·lor; ˈteilə/ *n.*
someone who makes clothes 裁缝
The tailor made a suit for Mr Wang.
裁缝替王先生做了一套衣服。

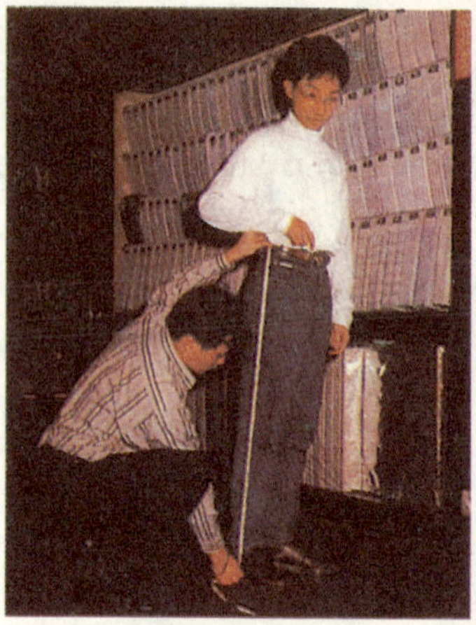

take /take; teɪk/ *v.*
(taking, took, taken)
1 carry something 拿；带
The children took some food to the beach.
孩子们带了些食物到海滩去。
2 remove something 拿走
Someone took David's bicycle.
有人拿走了戴维的自行车。
3 bring someone 带领
Mr Wang takes his children to school.
王先生带他的小孩上学。
4 go by taxi, bus, train, boat, or aeroplane 乘；搭
Sam takes a bus to school.
萨姆乘公共汽车上学。
5 need an amount 需要；花费
It takes Sam twenty minutes to get to school.
萨姆要走二十分钟才到学校。
6 choose 选择
Which road shall we take?
我们走哪一条路？

take a bath 洗澡
Peter takes a bath every day.
彼得天天洗澡。
take medicine 吃药
If you do not take the medicine, you will not get better.
如果你不吃药，你的病就不会好。
take off 起飞
The plane took off at five o'clock.
飞机五时起飞。
take something off 脱掉
Mary took off her coat.
玛丽脱掉她的外衣。

tale /tale; teɪl/ *n.*
story 故事
Peter read an interesting tale.
彼得看了一个有趣的故事。

talk [1] /talk; tɔːk/ *n.*
speaking with another person or other people 谈话
The teacher had a talk with David.
老师跟戴维谈过。

talk [2] /talk; tɔːk/ *v.*
speak; make words with your mouth 谈话
Please do not talk in the library.
图书馆内请勿谈话。

tall /tall; tɔːl/ *adj.*
(taller, tallest)
1 high; how far from bottom to top 高
The building is a hundred metres tall.
这座建筑物有一百米高。
2 high; going up a long way 高的
The building is very tall.
这座建筑物很高。
opp. 反义词：low, short 低的；矮的

tame /tame; teɪm/ *adj.*
(tamer, tamest)
not wild; that lives with people 驯服的
We saw a tame bear at the circus.
我们在马戏团见到一头驯服的熊。

tank /tank; tæŋk/ *n.*
1 large box that holds water 大桶；大箱；大槽
The tank is full of water.
槽里装满水。
2 strong machine, with guns, for fighting 坦克车
The tanks attacked the enemy.
坦克车向敌人进攻。

tap [1] /tap; tæp/ *n.*
1 handle that you turn to make water come out of a pipe （自来水或其他液体容器的）龙头
David turned on the tap and washed his hands.
戴维打开水龙头来洗手。

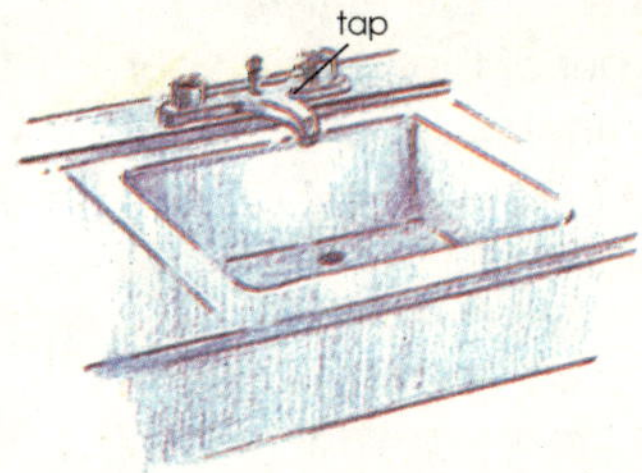

2 light knock 轻敲
Anna heard a tap on the window.
安娜听见轻敲窗户的声音。

tap [2] /tap; tæp/ *v.*
(tapping, tapped, tapped)
knock something lightly
轻敲；轻拍
Someone tapped at the door.
有人轻轻地敲门。

tape /tape; teɪp/ *n.*
1 long, thin piece of material 带子
Sam fastened the parcel with sticky tape.
萨姆用胶带把包裹捆起来。
2 special plastic strip that stores music, voices and pictures 录音带；录像带
David bought a tape of his favourite singer.
戴维买了一盒他最喜欢的歌手的录音带。

tape-recorder *n.* 录音机
The teacher has a tape-recorder.
老师有一台录音机。

taste [1] /taste; teɪst/ *n.*
flavour of the thing in your mouth 味道
Sugar has a sweet taste.
糖是甜的。
syn. 同义词：flavour
tasty *adj.* 美味的；可口的
The meal was very tasty.
这顿饭很可口。

taste [2] /taste; teɪst/ *v.*
(**tasting, tasted, tasted**)
give a feeling when you put it in your mouth 尝味道
The meal tasted good.
这顿饭很可口。

taught /taught; tɔ:t/ *v.*
p.t. of **teach** teach 的过去式
Peter taught Sam to swim.
彼得教萨姆游泳。

taxi /ˈtax·i; ˈtæksɪ/ *n.*
car with a driver which you can hire for short journeys
出租汽车；的士（方言）
Mr Wang took a taxi to the airport.
王先生乘出租汽车去飞机场。

tea /tea; ti:/ *n.*
(**no plural**)
1 drink that you make with special dry leaves and hot water 茶
Mary made some tea.
玛丽泡了点茶。
2 meal in the afternoon
下午茶
Peter has his tea at five o'clock.
彼得五时吃下午茶。
teacup *n.* 茶杯
Tom broke a teacup.
汤姆打破了一个茶杯。
teapot *n.* 茶壶
Mary put some hot water in the teapot.
玛丽把一些热水装进茶壶里。

teaspoon *n.* 茶匙
Mary used a teaspoon to stir her coffee.
玛丽用茶匙来搅动咖啡。

teach /teach; ti:tʃ/ *v.*
(**teaching, taught, taught**)
tell things to people who are learning; show people how to do something 教导
Miss Li teaches English.
李小姐教英语。

teacher /ˈteach·er; ˈti:tʃə/ *n.*
someone who tells things to people who are learning; someone who shows people how to do something 老师；教员
Miss Li is a teacher.
李小姐是教师。

team /team; ti:m/ *n.*
group of people who play on one side in a game（比赛中的）队伍
Sam plays for the school football team.
萨姆是学校足球队的队员。

tear [1] /tear; teə/ *v.*
(**tearing, tore, torn**)
make a rough hole in something; pull something into pieces 戳破；撕开
Sam tore his shirt on a nail.
萨姆的衬衣给钉子戳破了。

tear [2] /tear; tɪə/ *n.*
drop of water from your eye when you cry 眼泪
The girl's face was wet with tears.
那女孩泪流满面。

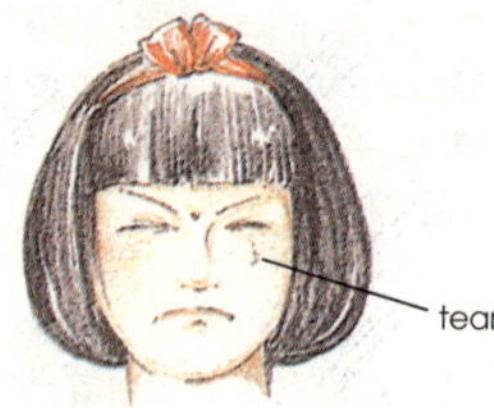

teddy bear /ˈted·dy bear; ˈtedɪ beə/ *n.*
toy bear 玩具熊
Susan bought a teddy bear for the baby.
苏珊给那婴儿买了一只玩具熊。

teenager /ˈteen·ag·er; ˈti:neɪdʒə/ *n.*
boy or girl between the ages of 13 and 19 青少年
The club is for teenagers.
这是个青少年人的俱乐部。

teeth /teeth; ti:θ/ *n.*
plural of **tooth** tooth 的复数
Sam has good teeth.
萨姆的牙齿很好。

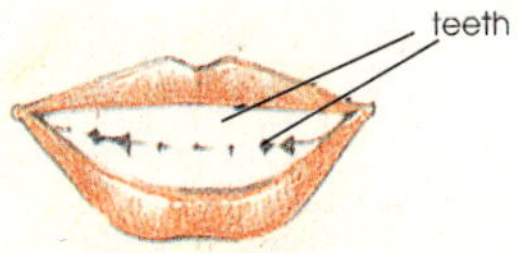

telephone [1] /ˈtel·e·phone; ˈtelɪfəʊn/ *n.*
thing that you use to speak and listen to someone in another place 电话；电话机
Mary answered the telephone.
玛丽接电话。
syn. 同义词：phone

telephone booth, telephone box *n.* 公用电话亭
Susan called Mary from a telephone box.
苏珊在一个电话亭打电话给玛丽。
telephone call *n.* (打进或打出的)电话
Mary answered Susan's telephone call.
玛丽接了苏珊打来的电话。
telephone directory *n.* 电话簿
Susan looked in the telephone directory for Mary's number.
苏珊在电话簿里找玛丽的电话号码。
telephone number *n.* 电话号码
What's your telephone number?
你的电话号码是什么？

telephone [2] /ˈtel·e·phone; ˈtelɪfəʊn/ *v.*
(**telephoning, telephoned, telephoned**)
use a thing to speak and listen to someone in another place 打电话
Susan telephoned Mary.
苏珊打电话给玛丽。

telescope /ˈtel·e·scope; ˈtelɪskəʊp/ *n.*
thing for seeing far away 望远镜
Sam looked at the moon through his telescope.
萨姆用他的望远镜看月亮。

television (TV) /ˈtel·e·vi·sion; ˈtelɪvɪʒn/ *n.*
pictures with voices and music from far away; machine like a box, which shows these pictures and sounds 电视；电视机
Mr Qian watches television every evening.
钱先生每天晚上都看电视。

tell /tell; tel/ *v.*
(**telling, told, told**)
1 speak to someone and give him information 告诉
Peter told Sam the answer to the question.
彼得告诉萨姆那个问题的答案。
2 say what someone must do 吩咐；命令
The teacher told Sam to stop talking.
老师吩咐萨姆停止说话。
tell a story 说故事
The teacher told the children a story.
老师给孩子们讲了一个故事。

temper /ˈtem·per; ˈtempə/ *n.*
how you feel 脾气；心情
Miss Li is in a bad temper.
李小姐脾气不好。
lose your temper 发脾气
Miss Li lost her temper with the naughty children.
李小姐对那些顽皮的孩子发脾气。

temperature /ˈtem·per·a·ture; ˈtemprətʃə/ *n.*
how hot or cold something is 温度
What's the temperature today?
今天气温是多少度？

temple /'tem·ple; 'templ/ *n.*
building where you pray
庙宇；寺
There is an old temple on Cheung Chau.
长洲有座古庙。

ten (10) /ten; ten/ *n. adj.*
number 10 十
Mary bought ten oranges.
玛丽买了十个橙。
tenth (10th) *n. adj.* 第十
October is the tenth month of the year.
October 是一年的第十个月。

tennis /'ten·nis; 'tenɪs/ *n.*
(**no plural**)
game where the players hit a ball over a net 网球
Xiaofang plays tennis.
小芳会打网球。
tennis court *n.* 网球场
There are some tennis courts in the park.
公园里有几个网球场。

tennis racket *n.* 网球拍
John bought a new tennis racket.
约翰买了一个新的网球拍。

tent /tent; tent/ *n.*
house made of cloth 帐篷
The scouts put up their tents.
那些童子军搭起了帐篷。

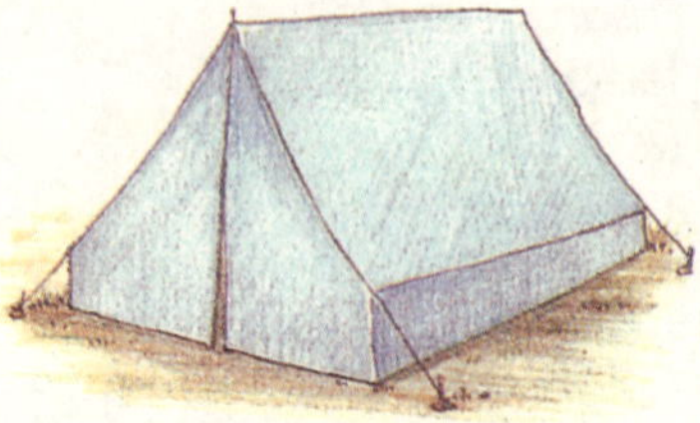

term /term; tɜ:m/ *n.*
part of a school year 学期
There are two terms in our school year.
我们一学年有两个学期。

terrible /'ter·ri·ble; 'terəbl/ *adj.*
(**more terrible, most terrible**)
very bad 可怕的
There was a terrible fire in Mong Kok.
旺角发生了一场可怕的火灾。

territory /'ter·ri·to·ry; 'terətrɪ/ *n.*
(two **territories**)
land that belongs to a government 领土；地方
Hong Kong is a small territory with more than six million people.
香港这个小地方有人口六百多万。

test [1] /test; test/ *n.*
question to find out how good something is 测验；考试
The class had an English test.
这个班级举行了一次英语测验。
syn. 同义词：examination

test [2] /test; test/ *v.*
ask questions to find out how good something is 测验；考验；试验
The teacher tested our English.
老师测验我们的英语。

textbook /'text·book; 'teksbʊk/ *n.*
book that teaches you about something 教科书；课本
The class has a new English textbook.
这一班有新的英语课本。

textbooks

than /than; ðən/ *conj.*
word that you use when you compare things or people 比
David is older than Sam.
戴维年纪比萨姆大。

thank /thank; θæŋk/ *v.*
tell someone that you are pleased with what they did or gave you 感谢；道谢
Susan thanked Mary for her birthday present.
苏珊感谢玛丽送她生日礼物。
thank you, thanks 谢谢；多谢
Susan said thank you to Mary for her present.
苏珊多谢玛丽送她礼物。

that [1] /that; ðət/ *adj.*
(**that** girl, **those** girls)
thing there; person there 那
Who is that boy?
那男孩子是谁?

that[2] /that; ðət/ *pron. conj.*
1 the one then 那
That was the day I was ill.
那天我病了。
2 word that joins two parts of a sentence 用来连接句子的两个部分
Tom said that he was hungry.
汤姆说他饿了。
3 word you use when you start to say more about something or someone
用来连接附加的形容语句
This is the dress that Mary made.
这就是玛丽缝制的连衣裙。

the /the; ðə/ *art.*
word before a definite person or thing; word before a person or thing that you know （用来特指人或物）那；这
The meal is on the table.
那些饭菜摆在那张桌子上。

theatre /'the·a·tre; 'θɪətə/ *n.*
place where you go to see plays 戏院；剧院
We saw an interesting play at the theatre.
我们在戏院看了一出有趣的戏。

their /their; ðeə/ *adj.*
of them 他们的；它们的
That is their car.
那是他们的车子。

theirs /theirs; ðeəz/ *pron.*
that belongs to them 属于他们的；属于它们的
That car is theirs.
那车子是他们的。

them /them; ðəm/ *pron.*
word that shows other people or things 他们；它们
I saw them in the park.
我在公园看见他们。

themselves /them·'selves; ðəm'selvz/ *pron.*
word for the same people or things that you have just talked about 他们自己；它们本身
The boys fell and hurt themselves.
那些男孩子跌伤了。
by themselves 独自；独力
The children are doing homework by themselves.
孩子们自己在做家庭作业。

then /then; ðən/ *adv.*
1 at that time 那时；当时
We lived on Lantau then.
那时我们住在大屿山。
2 next; after that 然后；以后
Tom did his homework and then he went to bed.
汤姆做完他的功课后便去睡觉。

there /there; ðeə/ *adv.*
in or to that place 在那里；往那里
Please sit there.
请坐在那里。
opp. 反义词：here 这里
there is, there's 有；那里是…
There is some rice in the cupboard.
橱里有些米。

therefore /'there·fore; 'ðeəfɔː/ *adv.*
because of this 因此
Tom was ill and therefore he had to stay in bed.
汤姆生病了，因此他要卧床休息。

thermometer
/ther·'mom·e·ter; θə'mɒmɪtə/ *n.*
thing that shows how hot or cold something is 温度计
The thermometer said 18℃.
温度计的读数是摄氏 18 度。

these /these; ðiːz/ *adj. pron.*
(**this** car, **these** cars)
things here; people here 这些
These books are mine.
这些书是我的。
These are mine.
这些是我的。

they /they; ðeɪ/ *pron.*
word that shows more than one person or thing 他们；它们
They had a barbecue on the beach.
他们在海滩上烧烤。
they'd, they had
They'd never been to Shanghai before.
他们从未到过上海。
they'd, they would
They'd like to visit Shanghai.
他们想到上海去。
they'll, they will
They'll visit Shanghai next year.
明年他们会到上海去。
they're, they are 他们是
They're members of the club.
他们是那个俱乐部的成员。
they've, they have 他们有；他们曾经
They've been to Shanghai before.
他们曾到过上海。

thick /thick; θɪk/ *adj.*
1 how far through from one side to the other 厚
The wall is a metre thick.
那堵墙有一米厚。
2 not thin; far from one side through to the other 厚的
The wall is very thick.
那堵墙很厚。
thickness *n.* 厚度
What is the thickness of the wall?
那堵墙有多厚?

thief /thief; θi:f/ *n.*
(two **thieves**)
someone who takes something that is not his 贼; 小偷
A thief stole Mr Wang's car.
窃贼偷走了王先生的车子。

thin /thin; θɪn/ *adj.*
(**thinner, thinnest**)
1 not fat; with little flesh 瘦的
Xiaofang is very thin.
小芳很瘦。
2 not thick; not far through from one side to the other 薄的
The walls of the flat are very thin.
那套公寓房的墙很薄。
Usage note: Sometimes *thin* may have a bad meaning -- *Mary is very thin because she was ill last week. Slim* has a good meaning -- *Susan is beautifully slim.*
用法: thin 有时含有贬义，例如 Mary is very thin because she was ill last week; slim 则有褒义，例如 Susan is beautifully slim。

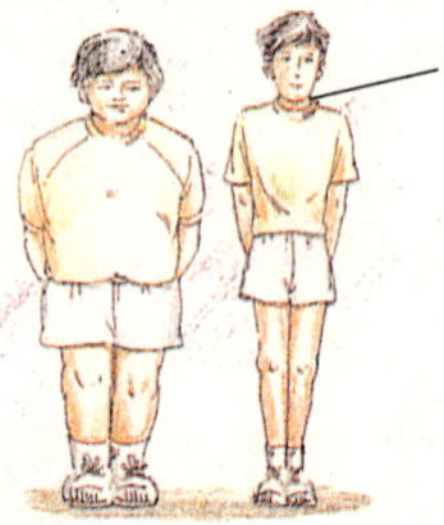

thing /thing; θɪŋ/ *n.*
any material object 东西
What's that thing in the tree?
树上的东西是什么?

think /think; θɪŋk/ *v.*
(**thinking, thought, thought**)
1 work with your mind 想
Think before you answer the question.
回答问题之前先想一想。
2 believe something 认为; 猜想
I think Peter is at home.
我看彼得是在家里。

third (3rd) /third; θɜ:d/ *n. adj.*
next after second 第三
Sam was third in the race.
萨姆在比赛中得了第三名。

thirsty /'thirst·y; 'θɜ:stɪ/ *adj.*
(**thirstier, thirstiest**)
wanting to drink 口渴的
The children were hot and thirsty.
孩子们又热又口渴。

thirteen (13) /thir·'teen; θɜ:'ti:n/ *n. adj.*
number 13 十三
Tony is thirteen years old.
托尼十三岁。
thirteenth (13 th) *n. adj.* 第十三
It's the thirteenth of October.
今天是十月十三日。

thirty (30) /'thir·ty; 'θɜ:tɪ/ *n. adj.*
number 30 三十
There were thirty children at the party.
这个聚会共有三十个孩子参加。
thirtieth (30 th) *n. adj.* 第三十
It's Mr Wang's thirtieth birthday.
今天是王先生的三十岁生日。

this /this; ðɪs/ *adj. pron.*
(**this** book, **these** books)
thing here; person here 这
I like this dress.
我喜欢这件连衣裙。
This is my book.
这是我的书。

those /those; ðəuz/ *adj. pron.*
(**that** car, **those** cars)
things there; people there 那些
Those books are mine.
那些书是我的。
Those are my books.
那些是我的书。

though /though; ðəu/ *conj.*
although 虽然
She went to the shop though she did not plan to buy anything.
虽然她没有打算买东西，但她仍到那商店去了。

thought /thought; θɔ:t/ *v.*
p.t. of **think** think 的过去式
I thought I saw Tom in the park.
我以为我在公园里见到过汤姆。

thousand (1 000) /'thou·sand; 'θauznd/ *n. adj.*
number 1 000 一千
The vase is a thousand years old.
这花瓶有一千年的历史。
thousandth (1 000th) *n. adj.*
第一千
Mary was the thousandth visitor to the exhibition.
玛丽是那展览会的第一千名观众。

thread /thread; θred/ *n.*
long, thin piece of cotton for sewing 线
Mary looked for a needle and thread.
玛丽找针和线。

three (3) /three; θri:/ *n. adj.*
number 3 三
John's younger sister is three.
约翰的妹妹三岁。

threw /threw; θru:/ *v.*
p.t. of **throw** throw 的过去式
David threw the ball to Peter.
戴维把球扔给彼得。

throat /throat; θrəut/ *n.*
front part of the neck 喉头；喉咙
Tom had a sore throat.
汤姆喉咙痛。

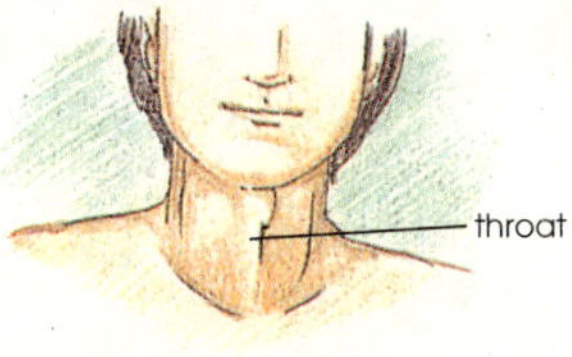

through [1] /through; θru:/ *prep.*
from one end to the other; from one side to the other
穿过；通过
The bus goes through the tunnel.
那辆公共汽车驶过隧道。

through [2] /through; θru:/ *adv.*
from the beginning to the end; from one side to the other 从(头)…到(尾)…
He slept the whole night through.
他睡了一整晚。

throw /throw; θrəu/ *v.*
(**throwing, threw, thrown**)
move your arm quickly to send something through the air 投；掷；扔
Tom threw a stone into the sea.
汤姆把一块石子扔进海里。

throw away 扔掉
Mrs Wang threw away her old furniture.
王太太把旧家具都扔掉了。

thumb /thumb; θʌm/ *n.*
the short, thick finger on your hand 拇指
Peter hurt his thumb.
彼得弄伤了拇指。

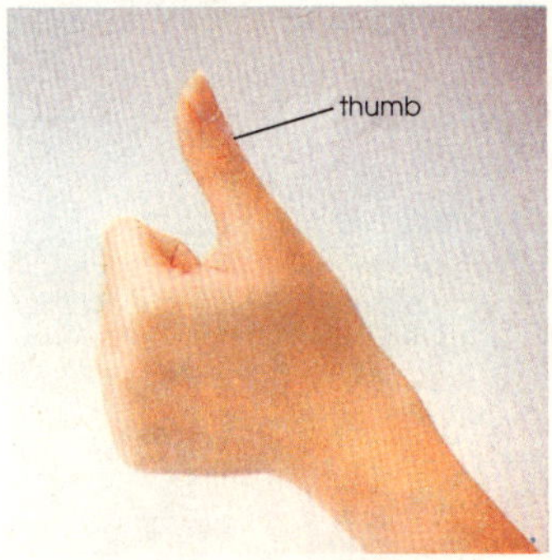

thunder /'thun·der; 'θʌndə/ *n.*
(**no plural**)
big noise in the sky in a storm 雷声
We heard the thunder.
我们听见了雷声。
thunderstorm *n.* 雷雨
There was a thunderstorm yesterday.
昨天有雷雨。

Thursday /'Thurs·day; 'θɜ:zdɪ/ *n.*
day of the week 星期四
We have a holiday next Thursday.
下星期四我们放假。

tick [1] /tick; tɪk/ *n.*
mark like this ✓ to show that something is right ✓号
The teacher put a tick on Tom's work.
老师在汤姆的作业上加上✓号。

tick [2] /tick; tɪk/ *v.*
make a mark like this ✓
加上✓号
The teacher ticked Tom's work.
老师在汤姆的作业上加上✓号。

ticket /'tick·et; 'tɪkɪt/ *n.*
small piece of paper that shows you have paid to go into a place, have a seat, etc. 票；券
Anna bought a ticket for the concert.
安娜买了一张音乐会票子。

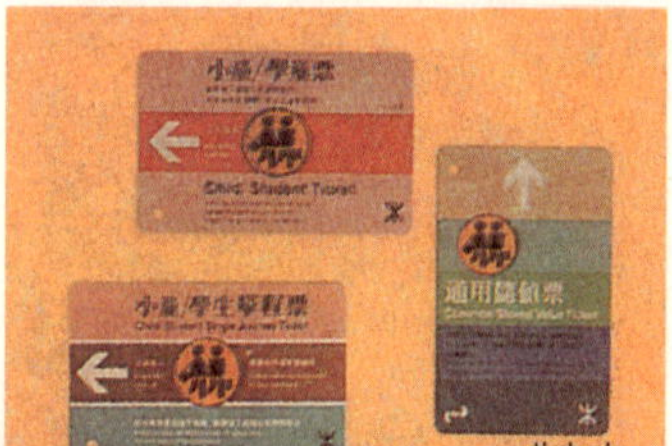
tickets

tide /tide; taɪd/ *n.*
rise and fall of the sea 潮；潮汐
The tide is coming in.
潮水在涨。

tidy /'ti·dy; 'taɪdɪ/ *adj.*
(tidier, tidiest)
neat; with everything in the right place 整洁的；整齐的
Susan's room is always tidy.
苏珊的房间总是整洁的。
opp. 反义词：untidy 不整洁的；不整齐的

tie [1] /tie; taɪ/ *n.*
long thin piece of cloth that a man wears round his neck
领带
Mr Wang always wears a tie to work.
王先生上班时总打上领带。

tie [2] /tie; taɪ/ *v.*
(tying, tied, tied)
fasten something with string, ribbon, rope, etc. 捆；缚；系；结
Mary tied a ribbon in her hair.
玛丽在头发上结上一条丝带。
opp. 反义词：untie 松开；解开
tie up 捆；捆绑
Susan tied up the parcel with string.
苏珊用绳子把包裹捆起来。

tiger /'ti·ger; 'taɪgə/ *n.*
big wild animal with stripes
老虎
The children saw a tiger at the zoo.
孩子们在动物园里看见一只老虎。

tigers

tight /tight; taɪt/ *adj.*
not loose; not easy to undo
紧的
These shoes are too tight.
这些鞋子太紧。

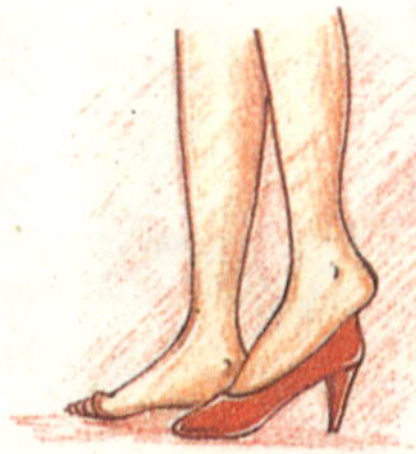

tighten *v.* 收紧；束紧
Tom tightened his belt.
汤姆束紧腰带。
tightly *adv.* 紧紧地
Mary tied the parcel tightly.
玛丽把包裹捆得紧紧的。

till [1] /till; tɪl/ *prep.*
until; up to the time when
直到…为止
Wait till your father comes home.
等到你父亲回家为止。

till [2] /till; tɪl/ *n.*
machine that holds money and adds up prices 钱柜
The shopkeeper put the money in the till.
老板把钱放进钱柜里。

time /time; taɪm/ *n.*
1 **(no plural)** seconds, minutes, hours, days, weeks, months, and years
时间
We waited a long time for the bus.
我们等公共汽车等了很久。
2 **(no plural)** hour of the day
时候
What time is it?
现在是什么时候了？

3 when something happens 次
Baoling has been to Shanghai three times.
宝玲到过上海三次。
on time 按时；准时
The bus came on time.
公共汽车准时到达。

ime to 是该…的时候
t's time to go to bed.
是该睡觉的时候了。
ell the time 说出时间
Sam can tell the time in English.
萨姆可以用英语说出时间。

imes /times; taɪmz/ *prep. n.*
word in arithmetic for multiplying numbers 乘
Two times five is ten (2 x 5 = 10).
二乘五得十。
This dictionary is three times as thick as the old one.
这本字典的厚度是那本旧的三倍。

imetable /'time·ta·ble; taɪmteɪbl/ *n.*
ist of times when something will happen 时间表
Mary got a timetable for the ferries to Lamma.
玛丽有一张往南丫岛的渡轮时间表。

in /tin; tɪn/ *n.*
1 (**no plural**) sort of metal 锡
The box is made of tin.
这箱子是锡做的。
2 metal container 金属罐；罐头
Mary bought a tin of fruit.
玛丽买了一听罐头水果。
tinned *adj.* 罐装的
Mary bought some tinned food for the picnic.
玛丽买了些罐装食物去野餐。
tin-opener *n.* 罐头刀
You will need a tin-opener to open the tins.
你需要一把罐头刀来开这些罐头。

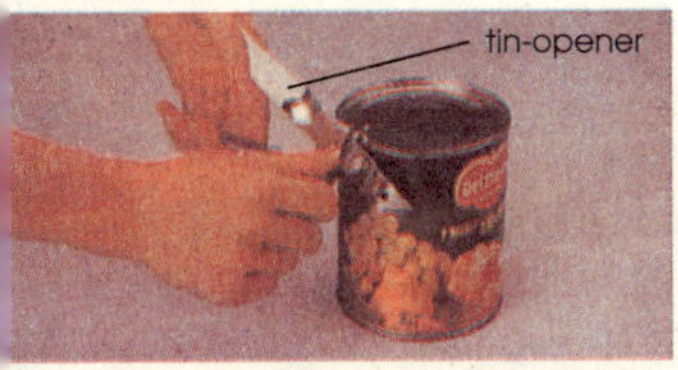

tiny /'ti·ny; 'taɪnɪ/ *adj.*
(**tinier, tiniest**)
very small 非常小的
Ants are tiny insects.
蚂蚁是非常小的昆虫。

tip /tip; tɪp/ *n.*
1 end of something 尖端
There is a fly on the tip of your nose.
你的鼻尖上有一只苍蝇。
2 extra money that you give to a waiter, etc. 小费
Mr Wang gave the waiter a large tip.
王先生给了那服务员很多小费。

tired /'tir·ed; 'taɪəd/ *adj.*
wanting to rest 疲倦的；累的
After playing football, Sam was very tired.
踢完足球之后，萨姆累得很。

tired of 厌倦；感到厌烦
Tom is tired of homework.
汤姆对做家庭作业感到厌烦。
tiring *adj.* 使人疲倦的
Running is very tiring.
跑步使人非常疲倦。

tissue /'tis·sue; 'tɪʃu:/ *n.*
piece of thin paper 纸巾；绵纸
Susan bought a box of tissues.
苏珊买了一盒纸巾。

a box of tissues

title /'ti·tle; 'taɪtl/ *n.*
1 name of a book, film, or picture 名称；题目；标题
What is the title of the film?
这部影片的片名是什么？
2 word that you put in front of a person's name
称号；尊称
'Miss', 'Mr' and 'Mrs' are titles.
"小姐"、"先生"、"太太"都是尊称。

to /to; tu:/ *prep.*
1 as far as a place; word that shows where someone or something is going 到；往
Peter always walks to school.
彼得总是步行上学。
2 until a time 至（某时间）
Mr Qian works from eight o'clock to five o'clock.
钱先生从八时工作至五时。
3 word that shows how far away something is 表示距离
It's ten kilometres to Shatin.
从这里到沙田有十公里远。
4 word that shows who is receiving something 给（某人）
Sam gave a sweet to Peter.
萨姆给彼得一颗糖。
5 word that shows why 为了
David came to the old lady's help.
戴维前来帮助老太太。
6 fixed 固定在
Mary pinned the poster to the wall.
玛丽把海报钉在墙上。

toast /toast; təʊst/ *n.*
(no plural)
bread that has been made brown and dry by heating it 烤面包
Peter likes toast for his breakfast.
彼得早餐爱吃烤面包。
toaster *n.* 烤面包机
Peter put some bread in the toaster.
彼得在烤面包机里放了些面包。

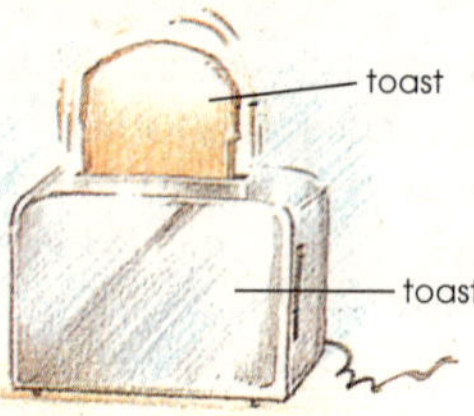

tobacco /to·'bac·co; tə'bækəʊ/ *n.*
(no plural)
special dry leaves that one can burn in cigarettes and pipes 烟草；烟叶；烟丝
The old man put some tobacco in his pipe.
那老人把一些烟丝放进他的烟斗里。

today /to·'day; tə'deɪ/ *n. adv.*
this day 今天
There is no school today.
今天学校停课。

toe /toe; təʊ/ *n.*
one of the parts of your foot 脚趾
Tom hurt his toe playing football.
汤姆踢足球时弄伤了脚趾。

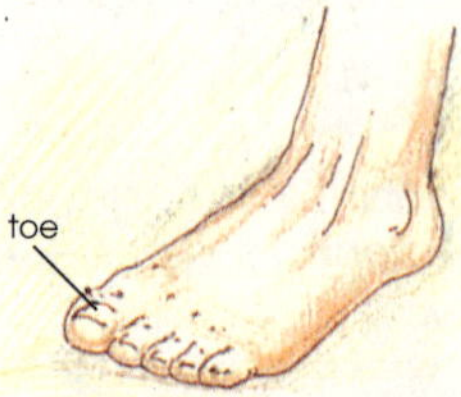

together /to·'geth·er; tə'geðə/ *adv.*
1 so that they are joined 在一起
Susan mixed some flour and water together.
苏珊把面粉和水混合在一起。
2 with each other 一同；一块儿
Peter and David play together.
彼得和戴维一同玩耍。

toilet /'toi·let; 'tɔɪlɪt/ *n.*
place to empty waste from the body 厕所；洗手间
Where is the toilet, please?
请问厕所在哪里？
syn. 同义词：lavatory

told /told; təʊld/ *v.*
p.t. of **tell** tell 的过去式
The teacher told the children to sit down.
老师吩咐孩子们坐下来。

tomato /to·'ma·to; tə'mɑːtəʊ/ *n.*
(two **tomatoes**)
round, red vegetable 番茄；西红柿
Susan bought a kilogram of tomatoes.
苏珊买了一千克番茄。

tomorrow [1] /to·'mor·row; tə'mɒrəʊ/ *n.*
day after today 明天
Tomorrow is Thursday.
明天是星期四。

tomorrow [2] /to·'mor·row; tə'mɒrəʊ/ *adv.*
day after today 明天
We have a holiday tomorrow.
明天我们放假。

tongue /tongue; tʌŋ/ *n.*
soft part inside your mouth that moves when you talk 舌头
It is rude to put out your tongue.
伸舌头是没有礼貌的。

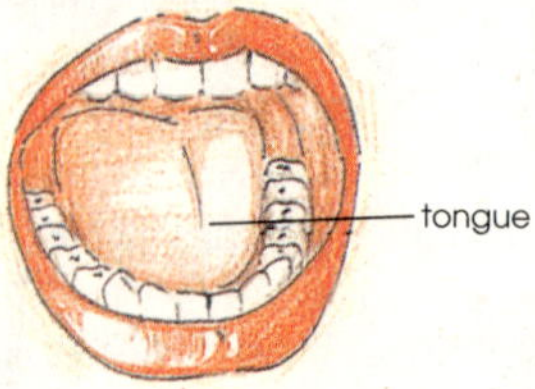

tonight [1] /to·'night; tə'naɪt/ *n.*
this night 今晚
Tonight is our choir practice night.
今晚我们的合唱团要练习。

tonight [2] /to·'night; tə'naɪt/ *adv.*
this night 今晚
We are going to the cinema tonight.
今晚我们要去看电影。

tonne /tonne; tʌn/ *n.*
measure of weight 吨
The truck weighs five tonnes.
这辆货车重五吨。

too /too; tuː/ *adv.*
1 also; as well 也；亦
David is going to the beach and Peter is going too.
戴维到海滩去，彼得也去。
2 more than you want; more than is good 太；过份

The sums were too hard for Sam.
那些算术题对萨姆来说是太难了。

took /took; tʊk/ *v.*
p.t. of **take** take 的过去式
Anna took the bus to school.
安娜乘公共汽车上学。

tool /tool; tu:l/ *n.*
thing that you use to do a job 工具
Mr Wang has some tools in his car.
王先生车里有些工具。

tooth /tooth; tu:θ/ *n.*
(two **teeth**)
one of the hard, white things in your mouth for biting and chewing 牙齿
Susan has nice, white teeth.
苏珊的牙齿洁白好看。

toothache *n.* 牙痛
Sam had toothache, so he went to the dentist.
萨姆牙痛，所以去看牙医。

toothbrush *n.* 牙刷
Mary bought a new toothbrush.
玛丽买了一个新牙刷。

toothpaste *n.* 牙膏
Susan cleans her teeth with toothpaste.
苏珊刷牙时用牙膏。

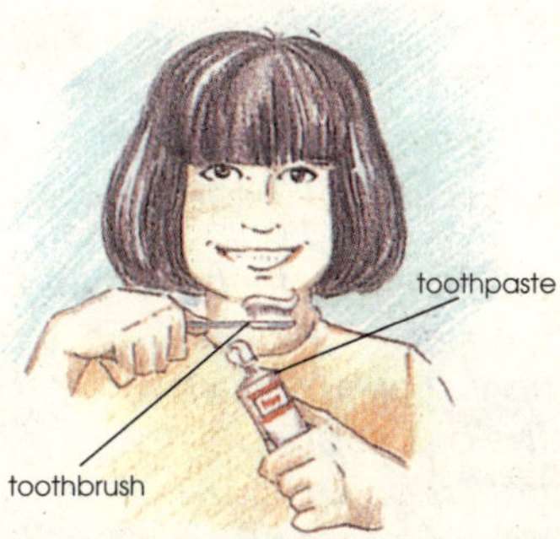

toothpick *n.* 牙签
Pass the toothpicks, please.
请把牙签递给我。

top [1] /top; tɒp/ *n.*
1 lid, cover 盖
Put the top on the bottle, please.
请把瓶盖盖好。
2 highest part 顶部
The children climbed to the top of the hill.
孩子们登上了山顶。
opp. 反义词：bottom 底部

top [2] /top; tɒp/ *adj.*
highest 顶部的；最高的
Your books are on the top shelf.
你的书放在最高的架子上。
opp. 反义词：bottom 底部的；最低的

torch /torch; tɔ:tʃ/ *n.*
(two **torches**)
small, electric lamp that you can carry 手电筒
David carries a torch at night.
戴维晚上带着手电筒。

tore /tore; tɔ:/ *v.*
p.t. of **tear** tear 过去式
Sam tore his shirt.
萨姆撕破了他的衬衣。

torn /torn; tɔ:n/ *v.*
p.p. of **tear** tear 的过去分词
Laura has torn her dress.
劳拉撕坏了她的连衣裙。

tortoise /'tor·toise; 'tɔ:təs/ *n.*
slow animal with a shell on its back 乌龟
Sam read a story about a tortoise.
萨姆读了一个关于乌龟的故事。

total [1] /'to·tal; 'təʊtl/ *adj.*
complete; with everyone or everything 总计的；全部的
What is the total number of children in the school?
全校学生的总数是多少？

total [2] /'to·tal; 'təʊtl/ *n.*
complete amount 总数
Add 20 and 15. What's the total?
二十加十五，总数是多少？

touch [1] /touch; tʌtʃ/ *v.*
put your finger or other part of your body against something 触摸；碰
Don't touch the wok. It's hot.
别碰这个锅，烫手的。

touch [2] /touch; tʌtʃ/ *n.*
putting your finger or other part of your body against something 触摸；接触
A snake is dry to the touch.
触摸一下就知道蛇(皮)是干的。

tough /tough; tʌf/ *adj.*
very hard 坚韧的；硬的；嚼不动的
This meat is very tough.
这块肉完全嚼不动。

tourist /'tour·ist; 'tʊərɪst/ *n.*
someone on holiday who travels to see many places
游客
Thousands of tourists visit Hong Kong.
很多游客来香港游览。
tour *n.* 旅游；游览
Mr Qian went on a tour to America.
钱先生到美国旅游去了。

toward, towards
/to·'ward, to·'wards; tə'wɔ:d, tə'wɔ:dz/ *prep.*
in the direction of 向着
The boat came towards us.
那艘船向着我们驶来。

towel /'tow·el; 'taʊəl/ *n.*
cloth for drying something 毛巾
Sam took a towel to the beach.
萨姆拿了一条毛巾到海滩去。

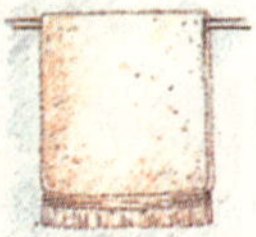

tower /'tow·er; 'taʊə/ *n.*
tall, narrow building; tall part of building 塔；高楼
The church has a tower.
那所教堂有一座高塔。

town /town; taʊn/ *n.*
place where there are many houses and other buildings
城镇；市镇
Shatin is a new town.
沙田是个新城镇。
town hall *n.* 市政厅
Shatin has a big town hall.
沙田有个很大的市政厅。

toy /toy; tɔɪ/ *n.*
something that a child plays with 玩具
Mary bought the baby a toy.
玛丽给那婴儿买了一个玩具。

toys

track /track; træk/ *n.*
1 special road for races 跑道
Peter ran round the track.
彼得绕着跑道奔跑。
2 rails where a train runs 火车轨道
The train came off the tracks.
火车出了轨。

tracksuit /'track·suit; 'træksu:t/ *n.*
special jacket and trousers that you wear for sport
长袖运动套装
Sam has a red tracksuit.
萨姆有一套红色的运动装。

tractor /'trac·tor; 'træktə/ *n.*
strong farm vehicle which pulls ploughs, etc. 拖拉机
The farmer has a tractor.
这个农民有一台拖拉机。

trade [1] /trade; treɪd/ *n.*
(no plural)
business; buying and selling
贸易；买卖
There is a lot of trade between Hong Kong and Shanghai.
香港与上海有许多贸易往来。

trade [2] /trade; treɪd/ *v.*
(trading, traded, traded)
do business; buy and sell
交易；买卖
Hong Kong trades with the world.
香港与世界各地进行贸易。

traffic /'traf·fic; 'træfɪk/ *n.*
(no plural)
all the cars, buses and people moving in the streets
交通
There is a lot of traffic today.
今天交通很繁忙。
traffic jam *n.* 交通阻塞
There was a traffic jam near the entrance to the tunnel.
隧道入口附近交通阻塞。
traffic lights *n.* 交通灯
The bus stopped at the traffic lights.
那辆公共汽车在交通灯前停了下来。

rain /train; treɪn/ *n.*
engine and several carriages which go on rails 火车
Sam took a train to Tai Po.
萨姆乘火车往大埔。

ram /tram; træm/ *n.*
electric bus that goes along rails 电车
There are trams in Hong Kong.
香港有电车。

ransport [1] /trans·'port; træn'spɔ:t/ *v.*
take people or goods from one place to another 运输
They transported the pigs to Hong Kong by train.
他们用火车把猪运来香港。

transport [2] /'trans·port; 'trænspɔ:t/ *n.*
(no plural)
1 taking people or goods from one place to another 运输
Air transport is expensive.
空中运输很昂贵。
2 aeroplanes, cars, ships, etc. 交通工具
There are many kinds of transport in Hong Kong.
香港有多种交通工具。

trap [1] /trap; træp/ *n.*
place or thing that one cannot get out of 陷阱
The rat was caught in a trap.
那只老鼠被困在陷阱里了。

trap [2] /trap; træp/ *v.*
(trapping, trapped, trapped)
catch in a thing from which there is no way out 设陷阱来捕捉；诱捕
The farmer trapped the rats.
农民设了陷阱来捕鼠。

travel [1] /'trav·el; 'trævl/ *v.*
(travelling, travelled, travelled)
go on a journey 旅行；去
Baoling travels to school by bus.
宝玲乘公共汽车去学校。

travel [2] /'trav·el; 'trævl/ *n.*
going on a journey 旅行
Travel to America is expensive.
到美国旅行要花很多钱。
traveller *n.* 旅客
The travellers arrived in Hong Kong.
那些旅客抵达了香港。

tray /tray; treɪ/ *n.*
flat piece of wood, metal, plastic, etc. for carrying things 托盘
Susan put some cups on a tray.
苏珊把一些杯子放在托盘上。

treasure /'treas·ure; 'treʒə/ *n.*
gold, silver, jewels, money or other valuable things 财宝；宝物
The divers found some treasure.
潜水员找到一些宝物。

treasure hunt *n.* 寻宝游戏
The children went on a treausre hunt.
孩子们玩寻宝游戏。

treat [1] /treat; tri:t/ *v.*
1 behave towards 对待
They treated us very well.
他们对我们很好。
2 handle 处理；医治
The doctor treated the illness.
医生治病。
3 give someone something nice 款待；请
Mr Chen treated his family to a holiday.
陈先生请家人去度假。

treat [2] /treat; tri:t/ *n.*
something nice that you get 乐事；请客
Mr Chen gave his family a treat.
陈先生请家人去游乐。

tree /tree; tri:/ *n.*
big plant with one tall stem 树
There are lots of trees in the park.
公园里有很多树。

triangle /'tri·an·gle; 'traıæŋgl/ *n.*
shape with three straight sides 三角形
David drew a triangle in his book.
戴维在他的书上画了一个三角形。

trick /trick; trık/ *n.*
1 lie or bad plan to cheat someone 诡计；计谋
The thief played a trick on the old man.
那小偷用诡计骗了那老人。
2 something done to amuse others 把戏；戏法
Sam can do card tricks.
萨姆会玩纸牌戏法。

tricycle /'tri·cy·cle; 'traısıkl/ *n.*
cycle with three wheels 三轮车
The little boy was riding his tricycle.
那小男孩正在骑三轮车。

tried /tried; traıd/ *v.*
p.t. of **try** try 的过去式
Peter tried to find Sam.
彼得尝试把萨姆找出来。

trip [1] /trip; trıp/ *v.*
(**tripping, tripped, tripped**)
fall or nearly fall over 绊倒
Sally tripped on the carpet.
萨莉给地毯绊倒了。

trip [2] /trip; trıp/ *n.*
journey 短途旅行
Sam went on a trip to Lantau.
萨姆去大屿山旅行。

trolley /'trol·ley; 'trɒlı/ *n.*
basket on wheels 手推车
Mrs Chen filled a trolley at the supermarket.
陈太太在超级市场买了满满一手推车的物品。

trouble /'trou·ble; 'trʌbl/ *n.*
1 problems; something that makes you sad or worried 麻烦
The teachers have a lot of trouble with that boy.
那男孩子给老师带来很多麻烦。
2 extra work and care 费力量；不怕辛苦
Baoling takes a lot of trouble with her homework.
宝玲很用心做家庭作业。

trousers /'trou·sers; 'traʊzəz/ *n.*
(**plural**)
piece of clothing for your legs 裤子
The boys wear shirts and trousers.
男孩子们都穿衬衣和裤子。

truck /truck; trʌk/ *n.*
lorry 货车
The truck was loaded with sand.
那货车装载沙子。

true /true; tru:/ *adj.*
(**truer, truest**)
correct; real; right 确实的；真的
The news about the war is true.
那则有关战事的新闻是确实的。
opp. 反义词：untrue, false 假的

trumpet /ˈtrump·et; ˈtrʌmpɪt/ *n.*
musical instrument that you blow 喇叭；小号
Peter is learning to play the trumpet.
彼得正在学吹小号。

trunk /trunk; trʌŋk/ *n.*
1 thick part of a tree 树干
The tree has a thick trunk.
这棵树的树干很粗。
2 elephant's nose 象鼻
The elephant sparyed water with its trunk.
大象用鼻子喷水。

trust /trust; trʌst/ *v.*
believe that someone is good, right and honest 信任
I don't trust that man.
我不信任那个人。

truth /truth; tru:θ/ *n.*
what is correct, real, or right 真理；真相；事实
Xiaofang always tells the truth.
小芳总是说真话。

try /try; traɪ/ *v.*
(trying, tried, tried)
1 work hard to do something 尝试；想法子
Sam tried to do the maths homework.
萨姆尝试做数学的家庭作业。
2 use something to find out if you like it 试试
Have you tried this new shampoo?
你用过这种新的洗发精吗？
try on 试穿
Mary tried the dress on.
玛丽试穿那件连衣裙。

T-shirt /ˈT·shirt; ˈti:ʃɜ:t/ *n.*
kind of shirt 短袖圆领衫；T 恤（方言）
Sam is wearing a T-shirt and shorts.
萨姆穿着短袖圆领衫和短裤。

tube /tube; tju:b/ *n.*
long thin thing, with a hole through the middle 管；筒
Mary bought a tube of toothpaste.
玛丽买了一管牙膏。

Tuesday /ˈTues·day; ˈtju:zdɪ/ *n.*
day of the week 星期二
The concert is on Tuesday.
音乐会在星期二举行。

tug /tug; tʌg/ *n.*
boat that pulls other boats 拖船
The tug was pulling a boat.
那拖船当时正在拖动着另一艘船。

tune /tune; tju:n/ *n.*
way a piece of music goes up and down 曲调；调子
Anna played a tune on the piano.
安娜用钢琴奏曲。

tunnel /ˈtun·nel; ˈtʌnl/ *n.*
long hole under the ground for a road or railway 隧道
There is a new tunnel under the harbour.
海港底下有一条新的隧道。

turkey /ˈtur·key; ˈtɜ:kɪ/ *n.*
kind of bird 火鸡
We had turkey at Christmas.
我们圣诞节吃火鸡。

turn [1] /turn; tɜ:n/ *v.*
1 move round 转动
The wheel turned.
轮子转动了。
2 move something round 转动
David turned the wheel.
戴维转动轮子。
3 move in another direction 转（方向）
The car turned right.
汽车向右转。
4 become different 转变
The leaves are turning brown.
树叶渐变成褐色。
turn into 将…变成
The fairy turned the mouse into a horse.
小仙子将老鼠变成马。
turn off 关掉
Turn off the light, please.
请关灯。
turn on 打开
Turn on the light, please.
请开灯。
turn over 翻过去
Turn over the page please.
请翻到下一页。

turn [2] /turn; tɜːn/ *n.*
time for you to do something
（轮流来的）一次
It is your turn to drive the car.
轮到你开车了。
in turn 轮流
The boys rode the bicycle in turn.
男孩子们轮流骑那辆自行车。

turtle /'tur·tle; 'tɜːtl/ *n.*
big sea animal with a shell on its back 海龟
The turtle laid its eggs in the sand.
海龟在沙里生蛋。

twelve (12) /twelve; twelv/ *n. adj.*
number 12 十二
There were twelve people in the bus.
公共汽车里有十二人。
twelfth (12th) *n. adj.* 第十二
It's David's twelfth birthday.
今天是戴维的十二岁生日。

twenty (20) /'twen·ty; 'twentɪ/ *n. adj.*
number 20 二十
The book cost twenty dollars.
这本书售价是二十港元。
twentieth (20th) *n. adj.* 第二十
Our holiday starts on the twentieth of June.
我们从六月二十日开始放假。

twice /twice; twaɪs/ *adv.*
two times 两次
Peter has been to Japan twice.
彼得到过日本两次。

twin /twin; twɪn/ *n.*
one of two children who are born at the same time to the same mother 孪生
The boys are twins.
这两个男孩是孪生兄弟。

twinkle /'twin·kle; 'twɪŋkl/ *v.*
(**twinkling, twinkled, twinkled**)
shine on and off 闪烁；闪耀
The stars twinkled in the sky.
星星在天空中闪闪发光。

twist /twist; twɪst/ *v.*
turn something strongly 转动；拧；扭
Peter twisted the knob on the radio.
彼得转动收音机的旋钮。

two (2) /two; tuː/ *n. adj.*
number 2 二
Mrs Chen has two children.
陈太太有两个孩子。

type [1] /type; taɪp/ *n.*
sort; kind 类型；种类
A rose is a type of flower.
玫瑰是花的一种。

type [2] /type; taɪp/ *v.*
(**typing, typed, typed**)
use a special machine to print letters and numbers 打字
Susan typed a letter to Mary.
苏珊打了一封信给玛丽。
typewriter *n.* 打字机
Susan has a typewriter.
苏珊有一部打字机。

typist *n.* 打字员
Susan is a typist.
苏珊是个打字员。

typhoon /ty·'phoon; taɪ'fuːn/ *n.*
dangerous storm with very big winds 台风
The boat sank in a typhoon.
那艘船在台风中沉没。
typhoon signal *n.* 台风信号
The typhoon signal was on TV.
电视上显示台风信号。

tyre /'ty·re; 'taɪə/ *n.*
rubber ring full of air round a wheel 轮胎
Mr Wang put new tyres on his car.
王先生给他的汽车换上了新的轮胎。

ugly /'ug·ly; 'ʌglɪ/ *adj.*
(**uglier, ugliest**)
not beautiful; not lovely 丑陋的；难看的
The furniture is very ugly.
这些家具很难看。
opp. 反义词：pretty 漂亮的；好看的

umbrella /um·ˈbrel·la; ʌmˈbrelə/ *n.*
special cover on a stick which you hold over your head to keep off the rain
雨伞
Mr Qian always carries an umbrella.
钱先生总是带着雨伞。

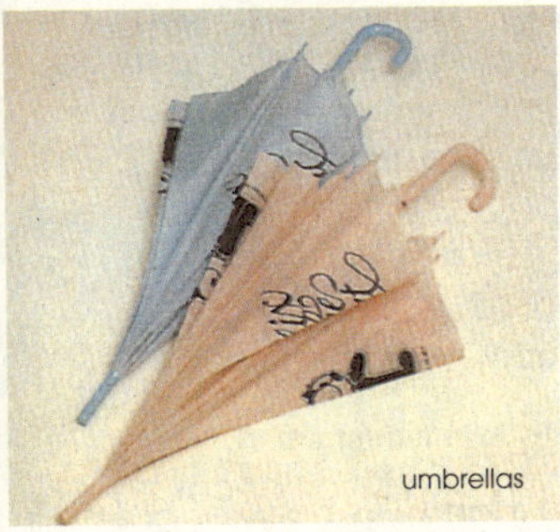
umbrellas

unable /un·ˈa·ble; ʌnˈeɪbl/ *adj.*
cannot do something
不能够的
Anna is unable to swim.
安娜不能游泳。
opp. 反义词：able 能够的
Usage note: *unable* is always followed by *to* — *Tom was unable to go to school because he was ill.*
用法：unable 后面通常用 to，例如 Tom was unable to go to school because he was ill。

uncle /ˈun·cle; ˈʌŋkl/ *n.*
brother of your father or mother; husband of your aunt 伯父；叔父；舅父；姑父；姨丈
Mary has three uncles.
玛丽有三个伯父。

uncomfortable /un·ˈcom·fort·able; ʌnˈkʌmftəbl/ *adj.*
(more uncomfortable, most uncomfortable)
not comfortable 不舒服的
This wooden chair is uncomfortable.
这张木椅坐起来不舒服。
opp. 反义词：comfortable 舒服的

uncomfortable

uncover /un·ˈcov·er; ʌnˈkʌvə/ *v.*
take a cover off something
移去遮盖物
Mr Yang uncovered his computer.
杨先生揭起电脑的外罩。
opp. 反义词：cover 遮盖

under /ˈun·der; ˈʌndə/ *prep.*
1 below someone or something 在…之下
Peter was sitting under a tree.
彼得坐在树下。

2 less than something 少于；不足
All the children are under twelve.
所有儿童都不足十二岁。
opp. 反义词：above, over 在…之上；超过

underground /ˈun·der·ground; ˈʌndəgraund/ *adj.*
below the ground 地下的
The MTR is an underground railway.
MTR 是地下铁路。

underline /un·der·ˈline; ʌndəˈlaɪn/ *v.*
(underlining, underlined, underlined)
put a line under 在…之下画线
Sam underlined the heading.
萨姆在标题下画线。

underneath /un·der·ˈneath; ʌndəˈniːθ/ *prep.*
under; below 在下面
There is a tunnel underneath the harbour.
海港底下有一条隧道。

understand /un·der·ˈstand; ʌndəˈstænd/ *v.*
(understanding, understood, understood)
know what something means; know why something happens 明白；了解
Sam did not understand the question.
萨姆不明白这个问题的意思。

underwear /ˈun·der·wear; ˈʌndəweə/ *n.*
(no plural)
clothes you wear next to your skin 内衣
Mary bought some underwear.
玛丽买了些内衣。

undo /un·'do; ʌn'du:/ *v.*
(**undoing, undid, undone**)
open something that was fastened 解开；松开
Sam undid the knots in his shoelaces.
萨姆解开了鞋带结。

undress /un·'dress; ʌn'dres/ *v.*
take off clothes 脱衣服
Mrs Chen undressed her baby.
陈太太为她的小宝宝脱衣服。
opp. 反义词：dress 穿衣服

unfair /un·'fair; ʌn'feə/ *adj.*
(**more unfair, most unfair**)
not fair; not treating all people in the same way 不公平的
Sam got more food than Jenny. Jenny thought that this was unfair.
萨姆比詹妮得到较多的食物，詹妮觉得不公平。
opp. 反义词：fair 公平的

unfriendly /un·'friend·ly; ʌn'frendlɪ/ *adj.*
(**unfriendlier, unfriendliest**)
not kind or helpful; showing that you do not like another person 不友善的；有敌意的
The man was very unfriendly.
这个男子很不友善。
opp. 反义词：friendly 友善的

unhappy /un·'hap·py; ʌn'hæpɪ/ *adj.*
(**unhappier, unhappiest**)
sad 不高兴的；不愉快的
Mary was unhappy when she lost her bag.
玛丽丢了袋子，很不高兴。
opp. 反义词：happy 高兴的

unhealthy /un·'health·y; ʌn'helθɪ/ *adj.*
(**unhealthier, unhealthiest**)
1 not well; often ill 不健康的；体弱的
Sally is an unhealthy child.
萨莉是个体弱的孩子。
2 that can make you ill 对身体有害的
It is unhealthy to smoke.
抽烟对身体有害。
opp. 反义词：healthy 健康的；对身体有益的

uniform /'u·ni·form; 'ju:nɪfɔ:m/ *n.*
special clothes for all the people in a school or job 制服
Their uniforms are green.
他们的制服是绿色的。

uniforms

unimportant /un·im·'por·tant; ʌnɪm'pɔ:tnt/ *adj.*
(**more unimportant, most unimportant**)
not important 不重要的
His job is unimportant.
他的职务并不重要。
opp. 反义词：important 重要的

unit /'u·nit; 'ju:nɪt/ *n.*
1 part of a book or course 单元；部分
There are twelve units in the book.
这本书有十二个单元。
2 numbers 0 to 9 in arithmetic 最小整数；个位数
Eleven is one ten and one unit.
十一是一个十位一加一个最小整数一。

university /u·ni·'ver·si·ty; ju:nɪ'vɜ:sətɪ/ *n.*
(two **universities**)
place where you can go to learn more after you leave school 大学
Tom's brother goes to university.
汤姆的哥哥上大学了。

unkind /un·'kind; ʌn'kaɪnd/ *adj.*
not kind 不友善的；冷酷的
Don't be unkind to animals.
不要对动物太凶。
syn. 同义词：cruel
opp. 反义词：kind 友善的

unless /un·'less; ən'les/ *conj.*
if not; except if something happens 除非
I won't go to the beach unless it is sunny.
除非天气晴朗，否则我不去海滩玩。

unlike /un·'like; ʌn'laɪk/ *adj. prep.*
(**more unlike, most unlike**)
not like; not the same as
不像；与…不同
David is very unlike his father.
戴维很不像他爸爸。
Unlike Sam, Susan works hard.
苏珊不像萨姆，她很用功。

unload /un·'load; ʌn'ləud/ *v.*
take things off a vehicle or ship 卸货
The men unloaded the truck.
那些人卸下卡车上的货物。
opp. 反义词：load 装载货物

unlock /un·'lock; ʌn'lɒk/ *v.*
open a door, box or case with a key 把锁打开
Mary unlocked the door.
玛丽把门锁打开。
opp. 反义词：lock 锁上

unlucky /un·'luck·y; ʌn'lʌkɪ/ *adj.*
(**unluckier, unluckiest**)
not lucky 不幸的；倒霉的
The unlucky man lost his money.
那倒霉的男人把钱丢了。
unluckily *adv.* 不幸地
Unluckily, the ball hit Tom in the face.
真倒霉，那球正好打中汤姆的脸。
opp. 反义词：lucky 幸运的

unnecessary
/un·'nec·es·sar·y; ʌn'nesəsrɪ/ *adj.*
that you do not need; not important 无用的；不必要的
When it is hot, coats are unnecessary.
天热时外衣就用不着了。
opp. 反义词：necessary 必要的

unpack /un·'pack; ʌn'pæk/ *v.*
take things out of a suitcase, etc. 从手提箱等取出东西
David unpacked his suitcase.
戴维打开手提箱，把东西拿出来。
opp. 反义词：pack 包装

unpleasant /un·'plea·sant; ʌn'pleznt/ *adj.*
(**more unpleasant, most unpleasant**)
not pleasant; not nice 不愉快的；可厌的
The smell of rubbish is very unpleasant.
垃圾的气味非常难闻。
opp. 反义词：pleasant 愉快的；可爱的

unpopular /un·'po·pu·lar; ʌn'pɒpjʊlə/ *adj.*
(**more unpopular, most unpopular**)
that many people do not like
不受欢迎的
Tom is unpopular among his classmates.
汤姆不受同学欢迎。
opp. 反义词：popular 受欢迎的

unscrew /un·'screw; ʌn'skru:/ *v.*
take out screws 拧松螺丝
Peter unscrewed the lock.
彼得拧松螺丝，把锁拆下。

unsuccessful
/un·suc·'cess·ful; ʌnsək'sesfl/ *adj.*
(**more unsuccessful, most unsuccessful**)
not doing something well; with the wrong result 不成功的；失败的
Peter was unsuccessful in the competition.
彼得在比赛中输了。
opp. 反义词：successful 成功的

untidy /un·'ti·dy; ʌn'taɪdɪ/ *adj.*
(**untidier, untidiest**)
not tidy; with things in the wrong place 不整洁的；凌乱的
Sam's room is always untidy.
萨姆的房间总是乱糟糟的。
opp. 反义词：tidy, clean 整洁的

untidy

untie /un·'tie; ʌn'taɪ/ *v.*
(untying, untied, untied)
undo a knot or bow 解开；松开
Susan untied the shoelaces.
苏珊解开鞋带。
opp. 反义词：tie 缚紧

until /un·'til; ən'tɪl/ *prep. conj.*
up to the time when 直至…为止
Mr Chen works until six o'clock.
陈先生天天工作到六时。
We stayed on the beach until it was dark.
我们在海滩逗留至天黑。

untrue /un·'true; ʌn'tru:/ *adj.*
not correct; not right 不真实的；假的
The story about Sam was untrue.
关于萨姆的传闻并不是真的。
syn. 同义词：false
opp. 反义词：true 真实的

unusual /un·'us·u·al; ʌn'ju:ʒl/ *adj.*
(more unusual, most unusual)
strange; that does not happen often 奇异的；不寻常的；罕有的
Mary found an unusual butterfly.
玛丽发现了一只罕见的蝴蝶。
opp. 反义词：ordinary, common 寻常的；常见的

unwell /un·'well; ʌn'wel/ *adj.*
(more unwell, most unwell)
ill; sick; not feeling well 生病的；身体不舒服的
Mrs Li is unwell.
李太太身体不舒服。

unwrap /un·'wrap; ʌn'ræp/ *v.*
(unwrapping, unwrapped, unwrapped)
take off the paper, etc., that is round something 解开；拆去包装
Baoling unwrapped the parcel.
宝玲解开了包裹。
opp. 反义词：wrap 包装

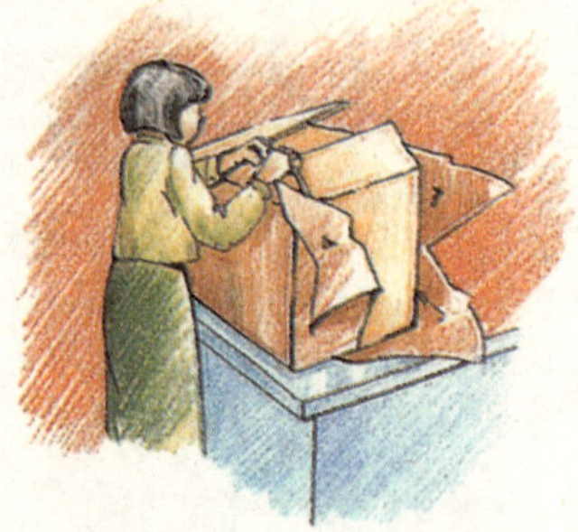

up /up; ʌp/ *adv. prep.*
from a lower to a higher place 起来；往上去
Sam gets up at seven o'clock.
萨姆七时起床。
Sam climbed up the tree.
萨姆爬到树上去。
opp. 反义词：down 下来

up to 到；至
The teacher walked up to Peter.
老师走到彼得跟前。
I can count up to 100.
我可以数到100。

upon /up·'on; ə'pɒn/ *prep.*
on 在…之上
Peter stood upon the chair.
彼得站在椅子上。

upper /'up·per; 'ʌpə/ *adj.*
that is above another 在上的
Sam sat on the upper deck of the bus.
萨姆坐在公共汽车的上层。
opp. 反义词：lower 在下的

upset /up·'set; ʌp'set/ *v.*
(upsetting, upset, upset)
1 knock over so that something spills 打翻；弄翻
David upset a cup of coffee.
戴维打翻了一杯咖啡。
2 make unhappy 令人不高兴；令人不快
David's bad exam results upset his mother.
戴维考试成绩不好，使妈妈不高兴。

upside-down
/up·side·'down; ʌpsaɪd'daʊn/ *adj. adv.*
with the top part at the bottom 倒转；倒置

The picture was upside-down.
那幅画挂反了。
Laura is holding her book upside-down.
劳拉把书倒过来拿。

upstairs /up·'stairs; ʌp'steəz/ *adv.*
in or to a higher part of a building 在楼上；往楼上
Mary went upstairs to her room.
玛丽上楼去她的房间。
opp. 反义词：downstairs 在楼下；往楼下

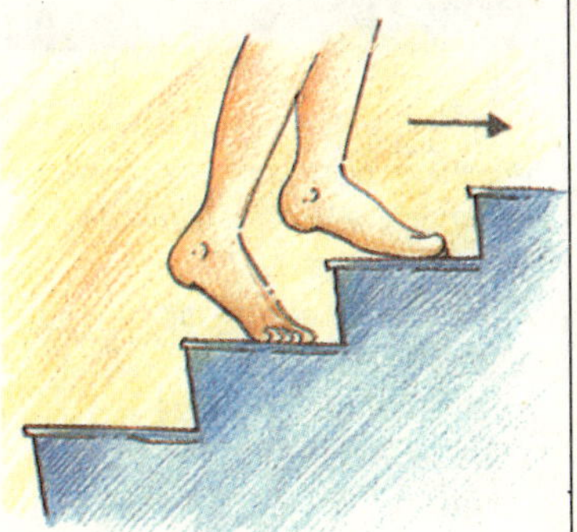

us /us; əs/ *pron.*
word that you say when you talk about yourself and other people together 我们
When we are late, the teacher punishes us.
我们如果迟到，老师就会责罚我们。

use [1] /use; ju:z/ *v.*
(using, used, used)
do a job with something 用；利用
Peter used a screwdriver to open the box.
彼得用螺丝刀把盒子打开。
use up 用完；用尽
Sam used up all the sugar to make a cake.
萨姆把糖全用来做蛋糕。

use [2] /use; ju:s/ *n.*
what you can do with something 用途；用处
Oil has many uses.
油的用处很多。

used to [1] /'used to; 'ju:st tu:/ *adj.*
know something well because you have done it or had it often 惯于
Mr Qian is used to getting up early.
钱先生惯于早起。
Usage note: *be used to* and *get used to* are followed by a noun, a pronoun or a verb that ends with 'ing' — *Jenny is used to cold weather. David soon got used to his new school. Baoling is used to driving a car.*
用法：be used to 和 get used to 后面用名词、代词或是以 'ing' 结尾的动词，例如 Jenny is used to cold weather, 又如 David soon got used to his new school, 或如 Baoling is used to driving a car。

used to [2] /'used to; 'ju:s tu:/ *v.*
words that show something happened in the past 以前是
David used to live in Shatin.
戴维以前住在沙田。

Usage note: We use *used to* to show what happened in the past, but doesn't happen any more — *Anna used to walk to school.* If something still happens, we don't use *used to* — *Anna walks to school. Used to* is not the same as *be used to* or *get used to.*
用法：used to 是用来描述过去发生的事情，而这些事情现在已不再发生，例如 Anna used to walk to school; 如果这些事情现在仍然存在，就不能用 used to, 例如 Anna walks to school。used to 跟 be used to 和 get used to 的意思和用法都不同。

useful /'use·ful; 'ju:sfl/ *adj.*
(more useful, most useful)
good for a job; helpful 有用的；有帮助的
A dictionary is very useful.
字典非常有用。
opp. 反义词：useless 无用的

useless /'use·less; 'ju:slɪs/ *adj.*
(more useless, most useless)
not good for anything 无用的
The broken TV was useless.
那台坏了的电视机没有用了。
opp. 反义词：useful 有用的

usual /'u·su·al; 'ju:ʒl/ *adj.*
(more usual, most usual)
normal; that happens often 平常的；通常的
Sam had his usual breakfast of toast and jam.
萨姆吃了他常吃的早餐——烤面包和果子酱。
opp. 反义词：unusual 不寻常的
usually *adv.* 通常地
We usually go for a walk on Sundays.
星期天，我们通常会去散步。

Vv

vacation /va·'ca·tion; və'keɪʃn/ *n.*
a rest away from home; holiday 度假；休假
Mr Wang had a vacation in Canada.
王先生在加拿大度假。

vacuum cleaner /'vac·u·um 'clea·ner; 'vækjuəm 'kli:nə/ *n.*
machine that takes dust and dirt from the floor 真空吸尘器
Mary cleaned the carpet with a vacuum cleaner.
玛丽用真空吸尘器把地毯弄干净。

valley /'val·ley; 'vælɪ/ *n.*
low land between hills 山谷
The village is in a valley.
那村庄位于山谷中。

valuable /'val·u·a·ble; 'væljuəbl/ *adj.*
(more valuable, most valuable)
worth a lot 贵重的
This diamond ring is very valuable.
这枚钻石戒指很贵重。

value /'val·ue; 'vælju:/ *n.*
how much something is worth 价值
Do you know the value of this ring?
你知道这枚戒指值多少钱吗？

van /van; væn/ *n.*
big car for carrying things; small lorry 小型客货两用车
The man put the chairs in his van.
那人把椅子放进小型客货两用车里。

vanilla /va·'nil·la; və'nɪlə/ *n.*
(no plural)
sort of flavour 香草香精
I like vanilla ice-cream.
我喜欢吃香草冰淇淋。

vase /vase; vɑ:z/ *n.*
pot for holding flowers 花瓶
This vase is very valuable.
这个花瓶很贵重。

vegetable /'veg·e·ta·ble; 'vedʒtəbl/ *n.*
plant that you eat 蔬菜
Susan fried some vegetables.
苏珊炒了些蔬菜。

vegetarian /veg·e·'ta·ri·an; vedʒɪ'teərɪən/ *n. adj.*
1 someone who only eats vegetables 素食者
Susan is a vegetarian.
苏珊是素食者。
2 vegetables only 素食的
Susan likes vegetarian meals.
苏珊喜欢吃素食。

vehicle /'ve·hi·cle; 'vɪəkl/ *n.*
thing on wheels that carries people or goods 车辆
There are lots of vehicles on the roads.
马路上车辆很多。

verb /'verb; vɜ:b/ *n.*
word that tells you what someone or something is doing 动词
The words 'read' and 'write' are verbs.
read 和 write 这两个词都是动词。

verse /'verse; vɜ:s/ *n.*
group of lines in a poem 诗节
The poem had ten verses.
这首诗共有十节。

vertical /'ver·ti·cal; 'vɜ:tɪkl/ *adj.*
standing up straight 垂直的
The building was not vertical.
这幢建筑物并不是垂直的。

very /'ver·y; 'verɪ/ *adv.*
word that makes another word stronger 非常；很
Baoling is very clever.
宝玲很聪明。
Usage note: Use *very* with adjectives — *Baoling is very happy.* Use *very much* with verbs — *Peter likes football very much.*
用法： very 与形容词连用，例如 Baoling is very happy。very much 与动词连用，例如 Peter likes football very much。

vest /'vest; vest/ *n.*
piece of clothing that you wear on the top part of your body under your other clothes 汗衫；背心
Sam wears a vest when it is cold.
天气寒冷时萨姆会穿上背心。

video /'vi·de·o; 'vɪdɪəʊ/ *n.*
tape that stores pictures and sounds; machine that puts television programme on tape 录像带；录像机
We watched a video last night.
我们昨晚看了一盒录像带。
video-cassette recorder (VCR) *n.* 录像机
We have a video-cassette recorder.
我们有一台录像机。

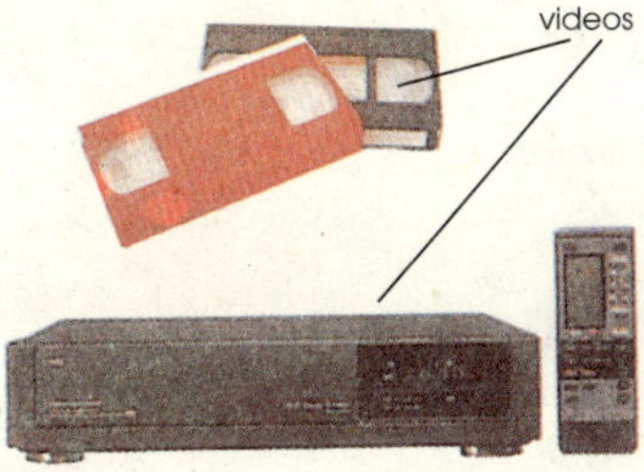

view /'view; vju:/ *n.*
(no plural)
what you can see when you stand far away from a place 景色；视野
We have a view of the harbour from our flat.
从我们的公寓房可以看到海港景色。

village /'vil·lage; 'vɪlɪdʒ/ *n.*
small town 乡村；村庄
Kam Tin is a village.
锦田是个乡村。

vinegar /'vin·e·gar; 'vɪnɪgə/ *n.*
(no plural)
liquid with a sour taste and smell that you use in cooking 醋
Pass the vinegar, please.
请把醋传过来。

violin /vi·o·'lin; vaɪə'lɪn/ *n.*
musical instrument with strings 小提琴
Susan plays the violin.
苏珊拉小提琴。

visit [1] /'vis·it; 'vɪzɪt/ *v.*
go to see a person or place 探访；访问；参观
The children visited the zoo.
孩子们参观动物园。

visit [2] /'vis·it; 'vɪzɪt/ *n.*
going to see someone or something 去探访某人；去看某物
Mary paid a visit to her grandmother.
玛丽探望祖母。

visitor /'vis·i·tor; 'vɪzɪtə/ *n.*
someone who goes to see a person or place 访客；参观者；游客
The zoo has lots of visitors.
动物园里有很多游客。

vitamin /'vi·ta·min; 'vɪtəmɪn/ *n.*
things in food that you need to be healthy 维生素；维他命
Fresh fruit has lots of vitamins.
新鲜水果含有许多维生素。

vocabulary /vo·'cab·u·la·ry; və'kæbjʊlərɪ/ *n.*
(two **vocabularies**)
words 词汇；语汇
Xiaofang writes English vocabulary in a book.
小芳把英语词汇写在一本本子上。

voice /voice; vɔɪs/ *n.*
sound from your throat when you speak or sing 说话声；歌唱声
Mary has a nice voice.
玛丽的声音很好听。

volcano /vol·'ca·no; vɒl'keɪnəʊ/ *n.*
(two **volcanoes**)
mountain which sometimes sends out hot gas, smoke and rock 火山
There are some volcanoes in Japan.
日本有些火山。

volley-ball /'vol·ley·ball; 'vɒlɪbɔ:l/ *n.*
game where players hit a big ball over a high net 排球
Xiaofang plays volley-ball.
小芳会打排球。

volume /'vol·ume; 'vɒlju:m/ *n.*
1 how much something holds 体积
David worked out the volume of the cube.
戴维算出这立方体的体积。
2 (**no plural**) loudness of a radio 音量；音响
The radio is too loud. Please turn down the volume.
收音机声音太大，请把音量调低。

vote /vote; vəʊt/ *v.*
(**voting, voted, voted**)
choose someone or something by putting up your hand or writing on a piece of paper 举手选举；投票选举
The class voted for a monitor.
那班学生举手选举一名班长。

vowel /'vow·el; 'vaʊəl/ *n.*
certain sound in a language 元音；元音字母
'A', 'e', 'i', 'o' and 'u' are vowels.
a、e、i、o、u都是元音字母。

voyage /'voy·age; 'vɔɪɪdʒ/ *n.*
journey by water, air, or in space 航行
The ship made a voyage to Japan.
那艘船去了一趟日本。

wage /wage; weɪdʒ/ *n.*
money that you receive every week for your work 工资；薪水
The factory pays good wages.
这家工厂给的薪水很高。
Usage note: *Wages* are paid every week or every day. A *salary* is paid every month.
用法： wages是指按周或按日发的工资；salary是指按月发的工资。

waist /waist; weɪst/ *n.*
part round the middle of the body 腰
Mary put a belt round her waist.
玛丽在腰部围上皮带。

wait [1] /wait; weɪt/ *v.*
stay in one place until something happens 等候
Sam waited at the bus stop for an hour.
萨姆在公共汽车站等了一个小时。

wait [2] /wait; weɪt/ *n.*
time you stay in one place until something happens
等待；等候的时间
We had a long wait for the bus.
我们等公共汽车等了很久。

waiter /'wait·er; 'weɪtə/ *n.*
man who brings your food in a restaurant or hotel
服务员
The waiter brought the menu.
服务员送上菜单。

waitress /'wait·ress; 'weɪtrɪs/ *n.*
(two **waitresses**)
woman who brings your food in a hotel or a restaurant
女服务员；女招待
Mrs Qian is a waitress in a restaurant.
钱太太是一家餐厅的女服务员。

wake /wake; weɪk/ *v.*
(**waking, woke, woken**)
1 stop sleeping and open your eyes 醒来
Peter woke at six o'clock.
彼得六时醒来。
2 make someone stop sleeping 唤醒
Mrs Wang woke David at seven o'clock.
王太太七时唤醒戴维。
wake up 醒来
What time do you wake up?
你通常什么时候睡醒？

walk [1] /walk; wɔːk/ *v.*
go on your feet, but not run
行走；步行
Anna walks to school.
安娜步行上学。
walking-stick *n.* 手杖
Old Mr Chen uses a walking-stick.
陈老先生拄着手杖走路。

walk [2] /walk; wɔːk/ *n.*
going on your feet, but not running 步行；散步
Mr Wang goes for a walk every Sunday.
王先生每星期日都去散步。

wall /wall; wɔːl/ *n.*
1 side of a building or room 墙
The classroom has pictures on the walls.
教室的墙上有些图片。
2 something you build with stones, bricks, etc. round a garden, town, etc. 围墙；城墙
Many tourists visit the Great Wall of China.
很多游客到中国的万里长城游览。

wallet /'wal·let; 'wɒlɪt/ *n.*
purse for paper money 钱包
David has a hundred dollars in his wallet.
戴维的钱包里有一百港元。

walnut /'wal·nut; 'wɔːlnʌt/ *n.*
sort of nut 胡桃；核桃
The children bought some walnuts at the market.
孩子们在市场上买了些核桃。

wand /wand; wɒnd/ *n.*
magic stick in stories 魔杖
The fairy waved her magic wand and changed the mice into horses.
小神仙挥动魔杖，把那些老鼠变成了马。

wander /'wand·er; 'wɒndə/ *v.*
go from place to place 漫游；漫步
Sam and David wandered through the park.
萨姆和戴维在公园里漫步。

want /want; wɒnt/ *v.*
1 wish for something 希望得到
Peter wants a bicycle for his birthday present.
彼得希望得到的生日礼物是一辆自行车。
2 need something 需要
How many books does the class want?
那班学生需要多少本书?
Usage note: When you offer something to someone or invite them to go somewhere, it is better to use *like* instead of *want* — *Would you like some cake?*
用法：如果你向人建议一些事情或邀请别人到某处，用 like 比用 want 好，例如 Would you like some cake?

war /war; wɔ:/ *n.*
fighting between countries 战争
Many people died in the war.
很多人在战争中死去。
opp. 反义词：peace 和平

ward /ward; wɔ:d/ *n.*
room in a hospital with several beds 医院里的病房
Mary was in the children's ward of the hospital.
玛丽住在医院的儿童病房。

wardrobe /'ward·robe; 'wɔ:drəub/ *n.*
cupboard where you keep your clothes
衣柜；衣橱
Mary put her dress in the wardrobe.
玛丽把衣服挂在衣柜里。

warehouse /'ware·house; 'weəhaus/ *n.*
big building where many things are stored 仓库；货仓
The warehouse was full of toys.
仓库里堆满玩具。

warm /warm; wɔ:m/ *adj.*
a little hot 温暖的
The weather is warm in October.
十月的天气很温暖。
opp. 反义词：cool 凉快的

warn /warn; wɔ:n/ *v.*
tell someone about something bad that may happen 警告；告诫；提醒
The teacher warned the children to be careful when they crossed the road.
老师提醒孩子们过马路要小心。
warning *n.* 警告；告诫；提醒
The teacher gave the children a warning about crossing the road.
老师提醒孩子们过马路要小心。

was /was; wɒz/ *v.*
1st and 3rd person singular past tense of **be** be 的第一和第三人称单数过去式
Sam was at school yesterday.
萨姆昨天在学校。
opp. 反义词：was not, wasn't 不是

wasn't /'was·n't; 'wɒznt/ *v.*
was not 即 was not
Peter wasn't at school yesterday.
彼得昨天不在学校。

wash /wash; wɒʃ/ *v.*
clean someone or something with water 洗；洗涤
Mary washed her school uniform.
玛丽洗校服。

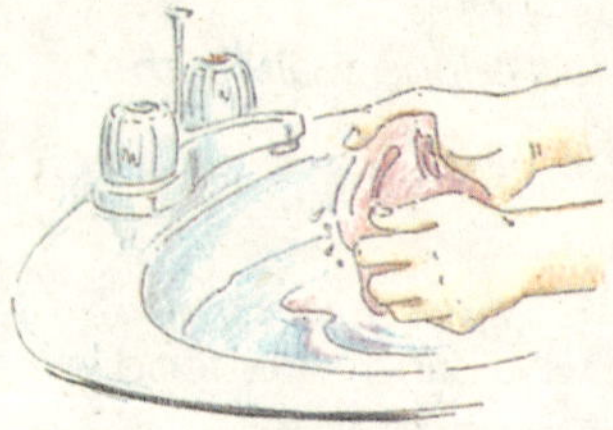

wash up 洗餐具；洗碗碟
Susan always washes up after dinner.
苏珊在饭后总是把餐具洗净。

washing /'wash·ing; 'wɒʃiŋ/ *n.*
(**no plural**)
clothes that you are cleaning, will clean or have cleaned
洗的衣物
Anna hung the washing on the line.
安娜把洗好的衣服晾在绳子上。

washing-machine *n.* 洗衣机
Anna put some clothes in the washing-machine.
安娜把衣服放入洗衣机。
washing powder *n.* 洗衣粉
Mrs Chen bought a packet of washing powder.
陈太太买了一包洗衣粉。

wasp /wasp; wɒsp/ *n.*
flying insect that can sting you 黄蜂；胡蜂
A wasp stung Sam.
一只黄蜂刺伤了萨姆。

waste [1] /waste; weɪst/ v.
(wasting, wasted, wasted)
not use something in the best way 浪费
You should not waste water.
不要浪费水。

waste [2] /waste; weɪst/ n.
1 not using something in the best way 浪费
Watching TV is sometimes a waste of time.
看电视有时是浪费时间。
2 useless things that you throw away 废物
Please put your waste in a bin.
请把废物放入垃圾箱。

waste-paper basket
/waste·'pa·per'bas·ket; weɪst'peɪpə 'bɑ:skɪt/ n.
container for papers, etc., that you do not want 废物篓；字纸篓
Please put that paper in the waste-paper basket.
请把那张纸放入废纸篓内。

watch [1] /watch; wɒtʃ/ n.
small clock that you wear on your arm 手表
My watch tells me the day and date.
我的手表显示星期和日期。

watch [2] /watch; wɒtʃ/ v.
1 look at someone or something 注视；看
Mary watches TV every evening.
玛丽每晚都看电视。
2 guard someone or something 监视；看守
Can you watch my things while I go for a swim?
我游泳时你替我看管一下我的物件好吗？

watchman /'watch·man; 'wɒtʃmən/ n.
(two **watchmen**)
someone who guards a building 警卫员
The building has a watchman.
这座建筑物有个警卫员。

water [1] /'wa·ter; 'wɔ:tə/ n.
liquid in rivers, lakes, seas, etc. 水
Sam drank a glass of water.
萨姆喝了一杯水。
water-bottle n. 水瓶
Sam takes a water-bottle to the beach.
萨姆带了一个水瓶去海滩。

water [2] /'wa·ter; 'wɔ:tə/ v.
put water on plants, etc. 浇水
Mrs Chen is watering her plants.
陈太太正在给植物浇水。

waterfall /'wa·ter·fall; 'wɔ:təfɔ:l/ n.
place where water goes over a cliff 瀑布
Sam saw a waterfall in Canada.
萨姆在加拿大看到瀑布。

water-melon
/'wa·ter·mel·on; 'wɔ:təmelən/ n.
sort of big round fruit 西瓜
Mary cut the water-melon into slices.
玛丽把西瓜切成很多片。

waterproof /'wa·ter·proof; 'wɔ:təpru:f/ adj.
that water cannot get into or through 防水的；不透水的
This coat is waterproof.
这件外衣是防水的。

water-skiing
/'wa·ter·ski·ing; 'wɔ:təski:ɪŋ/ n.
(**no plural**)
travelling over water on skis 滑水
David went water-skiing in Tai Tam Bay.
戴维去大潭湾滑水。

wave [1] /wave; weɪv/ v.
(**waving, waved, waved**)
1 move your hand in the air to say hello or goodbye 挥手示意
Susan waved to her friends.
苏珊向朋友挥手。
2 moving in the air 挥舞；飘动
The flags are waving in the wind.
旗帜在风中飘动。

wave [2] /wave; weɪv/ *n.*
part of the sea or a lake when it moves 水波；波浪
A big wave came into the boat.
一个巨浪打进船里。

wax /wax; wæks/ *n.*
(**no plural**)
sort of stuff for making candles and crayons 蜡
Candles are made of wax.
蜡烛是蜡做的。

way /way; weɪ/ *n.*
1 road, street or path 道路；街；径
Can you tell me the way to the post office?
请告诉我往邮局该怎么走。
2 how far it is; distance 距离
Is it a long way to the post office?
邮局距离这儿远吗？
3 how you do something 方法
What is the best way to cook chicken?
用什么方法煮鸡最好呢？
by the way 顺便说；附带提一下
By the way, I saw Susan today.
附带提一下，我今天看见苏珊了。
lose your way 迷路
The children lost their way in the country park.
孩子们在郊野公园迷了路。
on the way home 在回家路上
On his way home, David saw an accident.
戴维在回家路上见到一起事故。
on the way back 在回来的路上
On the way back from school, Peter lost his key.
彼得在从学校回来的路上把钥匙丢了。

we /we; wiː/ *pron.*
word that you say when you talk about yourself and other people together 我们
Mary and I are friends. We walk to school together.
玛丽和我是朋友，我们一起步行上学。
we'd, we had 我们是
We'd better go home now.
我们最好现在就回家。
we'd, we would 我们想
We'd like a menu, please.
我们想要一份菜单。
we'll, we will 我们将会
We'll visit Canada next year.
明年我们会到加拿大去。
we're, we are 我们是
We're always busy in the morning.
早上我们总是很忙碌。
we've, we have 我们有
We've got some kittens in our room.
我们的房间内有些小猫。

weak /weak; wiːk/ *adj.*
1 not strong; not having a powerful body 身体虚弱的
The boy was too weak to lift a suitcase.
那男孩身体太弱，连衣箱也拿不动。
2 not good at 不擅长的；不好的
Mary is weak at maths.
玛丽的数学不好。
opp. 反义词：strong 强壮的；擅长的

weapon /'weap·on; 'wepən/ *n.*
thing for fighting 武器
The soldiers had weapons.
士兵们都携带武器。

wear /wear; weə/ *v.*
(**wearing, wore, worn**)
have clothes on your body 穿着
Susan is wearing a new dress.
苏珊身穿一件新连衣裙。
wear out 穿破；用坏
Sam's shoes were worn out.
萨姆的鞋穿破了。

weather /'weath·er; 'weðə/ *n.*
how hot, cold, wet, or dry it is 天气
The weather is good in November in Hong Kong.
香港的十一月份天气很好。

wedding /'wed·ding; 'wedɪŋ/ *n.*
time when a man and a woman marry 婚礼
Susan is going to her sister's wedding next Saturday.
苏珊下星期六会参加姐姐的婚礼。

Wednesday /'Wednes·day; 'wenzdɪ/ *n.*
day of the week 星期三
Sam plays football on Wednesday afternoons.
萨姆每星期三下午踢足球。

week /week; wiːk/ *n.*
seven days from Sunday to the next Saturday; seven days 星期；周
Mr Chen went to Singapore for a week.
陈先生去了新加坡一个星期。

weekday /'week·day; 'wi:kdeɪ/ *n.*
Monday to Friday （星期六、日以外的）周日；工作日
Peter goes to bed early on weekdays.
彼得工作日很早就睡觉。

weekend /'week·end; 'wi:kend/ *n.*
Saturday and Sunday 周末（指星期六、日）
Peter goes to bed late at the weekend.
每逢周末彼得很晚才睡觉。

weekly /'week·ly; 'wi:klɪ/ *adj. adv.*
done or happening every week 每周
David buys a weekly magazine.
戴维买一本周刊。
He buys a magazine weekly.
他每周都买一本杂志。

weigh /weigh; weɪ/ *v.*
1 how heavy something is 重量是
The bananas weigh 500 grams.
这些香蕉重 500 克。

2 measure how heavy something is 称重量
They weigh your suitcase at the airport.
在机场他们替你的衣箱称重量。

weight /weight; weɪt/ *n.*
how heavy something is 重量
What is the weight of this suitcase?
这个衣箱有多重?

welcome [1] /'wel·come; 'welkəm/ *adj.*
gladly seen 受欢迎的
Visitors are welcome at the zoo.
到动物园来的游客都受到欢迎。

welcome [2] /'wel·come; 'welkəm/ *v.*
(welcoming, welcomed, welcomed)
show that you are glad to see someone 欢迎
Miss Li welcomed the new students.
李小姐欢迎新来的学生。

well [1] /well; wel/ *n.*
deep hole for getting water from under the ground 井
The well was full of water.
这口井的水很满。

well [2] /well; wel/ *adj.*
(better, best)
not ill, healthy 健康的；安好的
The children look very well.
孩子们看来很健康。

well [3] /well; wel/ *adv.*
(better, best)
in the right way; in a good way 对；好
Baoling works very well at school.
宝玲在学校表现出色。
opp. 反义词：badly 坏；不好地
well done 干得好
Your work is very good. Well done!
你的工作做得很好，干得好!
well-known 著名的；人所共知的
She is a well-known singer.
她是著名的歌手。

went /went; went/ *v.*
p.t. of **go** go 的过去式
Sam went to the beach yesterday.
昨天萨姆去海滩玩。

were /were; wɜ:/ *v.*
p.t. of **be** be 的复数和第二人称单数的过去式
Where were you yesterday?
昨天你在哪里?
opp. 反义词：were not, weren't 不是

weren't /were·n't; wɜ:nt/ *v.*
were not 即 were not
You weren't at school yesterday.
昨天你不在学校。

west /west; west/ *n. adj. adv.*
where the sun goes down in the evening 西方；西面的；向西
Our sitting-room faces the west.
我们的客厅对着西方。
The west wind is blowing.
西风在吹。
The house faces west.
这房子朝西。
opp. 反义词：east 东方；东面的；向东
western *adj.* 西方的
John lives in the western part of the island.
约翰住在岛的西部。

wet /wet; wet/ *adj.*
(**wetter, wettest**)
1 covered with water or other liquid 湿的
Sam changed his wet clothes.
萨姆换掉了湿衣服。

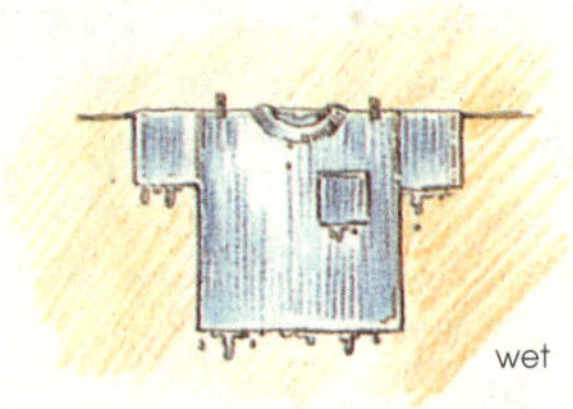

2 with rain 潮湿的；有雨的
The weather is very wet.
天气很潮湿。
opp. 反义词：dry 干燥的

whale /whale; weɪl/ *n.*
big sea animal 鲸鱼
The sailors saw a huge whale.
水手们看见一条巨大的鲸鱼。

what [1] /what; wɒt/ *adj.*
word that you use when you ask about something 什么
What time is it?
现在是什么时候？

what [2] /what; wɒt/ *pron.*
the thing that …的东西
Have you seen what Susan has bought?
你看见苏珊买了些什么东西吗？
what about 好不好；怎么样
What about going to the beach?
去海滩玩，怎么样？

what's, what has 已经…什么
What's she bought?
她买了些什么？
what's, what is 是什么
What's the time?
是什么时候了？

wheat /wheat; wi:t/ *n.*
(**no plural**)
plant like grass with seeds that we make into flour 小麦
They grow a lot of wheat in Canada.
加拿大种植许多小麦。

wheel /wheel; wi:l/ *n.*
round thing that turns to move something 轮；车轮
The truck had six wheels.
那辆货车有六个轮子。

wheelchair *n.* 轮椅
After an accident Mr Li was in a wheelchair for six months.
一次事故之后，李先生坐了六个月的轮椅。

when /when; wen/ *adv. conj.*
1 at what time 什么时候；何时
When is your birthday?
什么时候是你的生日？
2 at the time that 当…的时候
It was raining when Sam went to school.
萨姆上学的时候，天正在下雨。

where /where; weə/ *adv. conj.*
1 in what place 什么地方；何处
Where do you live?
你住在哪里？
2 in which 在那里
This is the street where we live.
我们就住在这条街上。

whether /'wheth·er; 'weðə/ *conj.*
if 是否；会否；能否
Do you know whether Sam is at home?
你知道萨姆在家吗？

which /which; wɪtʃ/ *adj. pron.*
1 word that you use when you ask about someone or something 哪一个；哪一些
Which dress do you like?
你喜欢哪一件连衣裙？
2 word that joins two parts of a sentence 用来连接句子的两个部分
That is the dress which Susan bought.
那就是苏珊买的连衣裙。

while [1] /while; waɪl/ *n.*
short time 一会儿
Will you stay here for a while?
你能在这里逗留一会儿吗？

while [2] /while; waɪl/ *conj.*
at the same time that 当…的时候
While you are in school, you must work hard.
你在学校的时候必须努力学习。

whisker /'whis·ker; 'wɪskə/ *n.*
long hair on the face 须
The cat has long whiskers.
那只猫有长长的须。

whisper [1] /'whis·per; 'wɪspə/ *v.*
speak very softly 低声说
Susan whispered something to Mary.
苏珊跟玛丽低声说了些话。

whisper [2] /'whis·per; 'wɪspə/ *n.*
speaking very softly 低声说的话
Susan spoke in a whisper.
苏珊低声地说话。

whistle [1] /'whis·tle; 'wɪsl/ *n.*
small thing that you blow
哨子
The referee blew his whistle.
裁判员吹哨子。

whistle [2] /'whis·tle; 'wɪsl/ *v.*
(whistling, whistled, whistled)
make a sound like a bird with your mouth or an instrument
吹口哨；吹哨子
The referee whistled for the end of the match.
裁判员吹哨子结束比赛。

white /white; waɪt/ *adj.*
(whiter, whitest)
with the colour of milk 白色的
Susan was wearing a white dress.
苏珊穿了一件白色连衣裙。

who /who; hu:/ *pron.*
1 word that you use when you ask about someone 谁
Who is in the classroom?
谁在教室里？
2 word that joins two parts of a sentence 用来连接句子的两个部分
That is the boy who broke the window.
就是那个男孩打碎了玻璃窗。
who's, who has 谁曾
Who's taken my pencil?
谁拿了我的铅笔？
who's, who is 是谁；谁是
Who's that girl?
那女孩子是谁？

whole [1] /whole; həʊl/ *adj.*
total; with everyone or everything 全部的；整个的
The whole school watched the match.
全校都去看这场比赛。

whole [2] /whole; həʊl/ *n.*
(no plural)
total; everyone or everything
全部；整个
The whole of the school was at the match.
全校都出席观看那场比赛。
opp. 反义词：part 部分

whom /whom; hu:m/ *pron.*
1 word that you use when you ask about someone 谁
Whom did you give the book to?
你把那本书给了谁？
2 wrod that joins two parts of a sentence 用来连接句子的两个部分
That's the boy to whom I gave the book.
我把书给了那个男孩。
Usage note: *Whom* is now usually used in writing. In speaking we use *who* — *The man who you met is a film star.*
用法：现在 whom 通常用作书面语；口语用 who，例如 The man who you met is a film star。

whose /whose; hu:z/ *pron.*
of which person 谁的
Whose book is this?
这本书是谁的？

why /why; waɪ/ *adv.*
for what reason 为什么
Why are you late?
你为什么迟到？

wicked /'wick·ed; 'wɪkɪd/ *adj.*
(more wicked, most wicked)
very bad 坏的；恶意的
He is a wicked man.
他是个坏蛋。
opp. 反义词：good 好的
Usage note: *Wicked* is not used much in speaking. You read it in stories.
用法：口语中很少用 wicked，这个单词多出现于故事中。

wide [1] /wide; waɪd/ *adj.*
1 how far from one side to the other 宽
The road is fifty metres wide.
这条马路有五十米宽。
2 far from one side to the other 宽阔的；广阔的
The road is very wide.
这条马路很宽。
opp. 反义词：narrow 狭窄的

wide[2] /wide; waɪd/ *adv.*
far 张得很大；远远；广阔地
He opened the doors and windows wide.
他把窗和门都大大打开。

width /width; wɪdθ/ *n.*
how far from one side to the other 宽度
What is the width of the room?
那个房间的宽度是多少？

wife /wife; waɪf/ *n.*
(two **wives**)
woman who has a husband 妻子；太太
Mr Chen bought some flowers for his wife.
陈先生买了些花给妻子。

wig /wig; wɪg/ *n.*
false hair 假发
Mrs Qian wears a wig.
钱太太戴假发。

wild /wild; waɪld/ *adj.*
that lives or grows in the country, away from people
野生的；荒野的
There are some wild animals in the country parks.
郊野公园里有些野生动物。
opp. 反义词：tame 驯服的

will /will; wɪl/ *v.*
1 word that shows something is going to happen 将会；将要
Sam will visit his grandmother next Sunday.
下星期日萨姆会去探望他的祖母。
2 word that shows what happens if you do something 就会
If you don't get up you will be late for school.
如果你还不起床上学，你就会迟到。

willing /'will·ing; 'wɪlɪŋ/ *adj.*
(**more willing, most willing**)
ready 乐意的；自愿的
The children are always willing to help.
那些小孩子总是乐意帮忙。

win /win; wɪn/ *v.*
(**winning, won, won**)
1 do best in a game 赢；获胜
Do you think your football team will win?
你看你那支足球队会赢吗？
2 receive something because you did well 赢得
Mary won a prize in the music competition.
玛丽在音乐比赛中赢得了奖项。
opp. 反义词：lose 输；失去

wind[1] /wind; wɪnd/ *n.*
air that moves 风
The wind blew a tree down.
风把一棵树吹倒了。
windy *adj.* 大风的
It's windy today.
今天的风很大。

wind[2] /wind; waɪnd/ *v.*
(**winding, wound, wound**)
turn a handle round and round; move or go in curves
上弦；绕
I have forgotten to wind my watch.
我忘了给手表上弦。

window /'win·dow; 'wɪndəʊ/ *n.*
hole in a wall, with glass 窗
Our flat has large windows.
我们那套公寓房的窗很大。

wine /wine; waɪn/ *n.*
sort of drink 酒
Mr Chen bought a bottle of wine.
陈先生买了一瓶酒。

wing /wing; wɪŋ/ *n.*
part of a bird, insect, or aeroplane that helps it to fly
翼；翅膀
The bird had big wings.
那鸟儿有大翅膀。

winner /'win·ner; 'wɪnə/ *n.*
someone who wins 胜利者；优胜者
Mary was the winner in the competition.
玛丽是该项比赛的优胜者。

winter /'win·ter; 'wɪntə/ *n.*
time of the year when it is cold 冬天
Susan does not go swimming in winter.
苏珊冬天不游泳。

wipe /wipe; waɪp/ *v.*
(**wiping, wiped, wiped**)
rub something with a cloth to clean or dry it 擦；拭；揩
David wiped the dishes.
戴维把碟子揩干净。

wire /'wire; 'waɪə/ *n.*
metal formed into a long, thin thread 金属线；金属丝
The fence is made of wire.
栅栏是用金属丝做的。

wise /wise; waɪz/ *adj.*
(**wiser, wisest**)
knowing many things; knowing what is right and good 博学的；有智慧的；聪明的
It is not wise to stay up too late.
太晚睡觉是不明智的。
syn. 同义词：clever, intelligent
opp. 反义词：foolish, stupid 愚蠢的
wisely *adv.* 聪明地；明智地
Baoling always behaves wisely.
宝玲处事总是很精明。

wish [1] /wish; wɪʃ/ *v.*
want to have or do something 希望
Sam wishes he had a bicycle.
萨姆希望有一辆自行车。

wish [2] /wish; wɪʃ/ *n.*
(two **wishes**)
what you want to have or do 希望；愿望
Tom made a wish.
汤姆许了一个愿。

witch /witch; wɪtʃ/ *n.*
(two **witches**)
wicked woman in stories 巫婆
The witch flew through the air.
那巫婆从空中飞过。

with /with; wɪð/ *prep.*
1 having something 有；带有
They have a house with a garden.
他们有一所带有花园的房子。
2 using something 用
Mary cut the string with scissors.
玛丽用剪刀剪断绳子。
3 word showing that things or people are together 和…一起
Susan walks to school with Mary.
苏珊和玛丽一起步行上学。
opp. 反义词：without 没有；不用
agree with 同意
Tom always agrees with his mother.
汤姆总是同意他妈妈的话。
quarrel with 和…吵架
Sam is quarrelling with Peter.
萨姆正在和彼得吵架。

without /with·'out; wɪ'ðaʊt/ *prep.*
not having; not using; not together 没有；不用
You can't write without a pen or a pencil.
没有钢笔或铅笔就不能写字。
opp. 反义词：with 有；用

wizard /'wiz·ard; 'wɪzəd/ *n.*
someone who does magic in stories 巫师；术士
The wizard changed the prince into a frog.
那巫师把王子变成一只青蛙。

wok /wok; wɒk/ *n.*
pan with a round bottom for cooking 铁锅；镬（方言）
Susan cooked some vegetables in a wok.
苏珊用铁锅煮蔬菜。

woke /woke; wəuk/ *v.*
p.t. of **wake** wake 的过去式
A noise woke Tom.
一阵响声吵醒了汤姆。
woken *v.* wake 的过去分词
A noise has woken the baby.
一阵响声把婴儿吵醒了。

wolf /wolf; wulf/ *n.*
(two **wolves**)
wild animal like a big dog 狼
The man killed the wolf.
那人把狼打死了。

woman /'wom·an; 'wumən/ *n.*
(two **women**)
female person who is not a child 女人
Tom helped an old woman to carry her shopping.
汤姆帮老太太拿她买的东西。

won /won; wʌn/ *v.*
p.t. of **win** win 的过去式
Who won the match?
那场比赛是谁赢了？

wonder /'won·der; 'wʌndə/ *v.*
ask yourself; want to know 想知道
I wonder where Tom is?
我想知道汤姆究竟在哪里。

wonderful /'won·der·ful; 'wʌndəfl/ *adj.*
(**more wonderful, most wonderful**)
very good 很好的；令人惊叹的
Mary cooked a wonderful meal.
玛丽做了一顿很好的饭。

wood /wood; wud/ *n.*
1 (**no plural**) hard part of a tree 木
The table is made of wood.
这桌子是木做的。
2 some trees 树林
Baoling saw some rabbits in the wood.
宝玲在树林里看见一些兔子。

wooden *adj.* 木做的
This is a wooden table.
这是一张木桌子。
woodcutter *n.* 樵夫；伐木工人
The woodcutter went into the forest.
樵夫走进森林里。

wool /wool; wul/ *n.*
(**no plural**)
hair on sheep; thread made from this 羊毛；毛线
Susan bought a ball of wool.
苏珊买了一团毛线。
woollen *adj.* 羊毛的
Susan made a woollen sweater.
苏珊编织了一件毛衣。
woolly *adj.* 羊毛的；毛茸茸；
Mary is wearing a woolly sweater.
玛丽穿着一件毛衣。

word /word; wɜ:d/ *n.*
group of letters that have a meaning 词
What does that word mean?
这个词是什么意思？

wore /wore; wɔ:/ *v.*
p.t. of **wear** wear 的过去式
The bride wore a white dress.
新娘穿了一件白色连衣裙。

work [1] /work; wɜ:k/ *n.*
what you do to earn money; what you do at school 工作；功课
The teacher marked the children's work.
老师给孩子们的功课评分。

work [2] /work; wɜ:k/ *v.*
1 do something to earn money; learn at school 工作；做事；念书

Mrs Qian works in a factory.
钱太太在一家工厂工作。

2 go correctly 正常操作
My watch is not working.
我的手表坏了。

workbook /'work·book; 'wɜ:kbʊk/ *n.*
book where you write answers 练习册
The children were writing in their workbooks.
孩子们在练习册上写字。

worker /'work·er; 'wɜ:kə/ *n.*
someone who works 工人；工作人员
The company has a thousand workers.
这家公司有一千名工人。

workman /'work·man; 'wɜ:kmən/ *n.*
(two **workmen**)
man who works with his hands or with machines 工人；劳动者
The workmen dug a hole in the road.
工人在路上挖了一个洞。

workshop /'work·shop; 'wɜ:kʃɒp/ *n.*
place where you make or mend things 工厂；工场；车间
Mr Wang makes furniture in his workshop.
王先生在工场里做家具。

world /world; wɜ:ld/ *n.*
all the countries and people on the earth 世界
Mr Wang has travelled round the world.
王先生游遍世界各地。

worm /worm; wɜ:m/ *n.*
very small animal, with no legs, which lives in the earth 虫
The bird pulled a worm out of the earth and ate it.
那鸟儿从地下拉出一条虫吃掉了。

worn /worn; wɔ:n/ *v.*
p.p. of **wear** wear 的过去分词
Susan has not worn her new dress yet.
苏珊还没有穿过她那件新连衣裙。

worry [1] /'wor·ry; 'wʌrɪ/ *v.*
(**worrying, worried, worried**)
feel that something is wrong 担心；不安
Mrs Chen worries when her children are late.
如孩子晚回家，陈太太就会很担心。
worried *adj.* 担心的；不安的
Mrs Chen was worried when Sam was late.
萨姆晚回家，令陈太太很担心。

worry [2] /'wor·ry; 'wʌrɪ/ *n.*
(two **worries**)
feeling that something is wrong 担忧牌不安
Worry made Mrs Chen ill.
陈太太忧虑成疾。

worse /worse; wɜ:s/ *adj.*
less good 较差的
Tom's work is worse than Peter's.
汤姆的功课比彼得差。
opp. 反义词：better 较好的

worst /worst; wɜ:st/ *adj.*
especially bad; worse than all the others 最差的
Tom is the worst student in the class.
汤姆是班上最差的学生。
opp. 反义词：best 最好的

worth /worth; wɜ:θ/ *v.*
having a value of 值
The flat is worth a million dollars.
这套公寓房价值一百万港元。

would /would; wəd/ *v.*
1 p.t. of **will** will 的过去式
Mary said she would be late.
玛丽说她会迟到。
opp. 反义词：would not, wouldn't 不会
2 word you say when you ask a polite question 用来礼貌地问问题
Would you like to come in?
请进来好吗？

wouldn't /'would·n't; 'wʊdnt/ *v.*
would not 即 would not
Mary wouldn't like to touch a snake.
玛丽不喜欢碰蛇。

wound /wound; wu:nd/ *n.*
cut or injury to the body 伤
The soldier died from his wounds.
那士兵伤重而死。
Usage note: A *wound* is usually the result of something done on purpose — *He was wounded in the battle. Injure* is used for accidents — *He was injured in a car crash.*
用法： wound 通常指蓄意造成的伤害，例如 He was wounded in the battle, 而 injure，则指意外造成的伤害，例如 He was injured in a car crash.

wrap /wrap; ræp/ *v.*
(**wrapping, wrapped, wrapped**)
cover something with paper, etc. 包；裹
Mr Chen wrapped up the gift in colourful paper.
陈先生用彩纸把礼物包起来。

wreck /wreck; rek/ *n.*
broken ship 失事船只
The wreck was on the beach.
那艘失事的船只被弃在海滩上。

wrist /wrist; rɪst/ *n.*
place where the hand joins the arm 手腕
Mary had a gold bracelet on her wrist.
玛丽手腕上戴了一个金镯子。

write /write; raɪt/ *v.*
(**writing, wrote, written**)
1 make words with a pen, pencil, chalk, etc. 写
The teacher wrote some sentences on the blackboard.
老师在黑板上写了几个句子。
2 make a book, story, etc. 写作
Mary wrote a letter to Susan.
玛丽写了一封信给苏珊。
writer *n.* 写字的人；作家
Mary is a good writer.
玛丽的文章写得很好。

writing /'writ·ing; 'raɪtɪŋ/ *n.*
making words with a pen or pencil; what you have written 笔迹
The teacher can't read Tom's writing.
老师看不清楚汤姆写的东西。

written /'writ·ten; 'rɪtn/ *v.*
p.p. of **write** write 的过去分词
Mary has written to Susan.
玛丽已经给苏珊写了一封信。

wrong /wrong; rɒŋ/ *adj.*
1 bad; not right 错的；不对的
It is wrong to tell lies.
说谎是不对的。
2 with mistakes; not correct 错误的；不对的
David's answer was wrong.
戴维的答案是错的。
wrongly *adv.* 错误地
David answered the question wrongly.
这个问题戴维答错了。

wrote /wrote; rəut/ *v.*
p.t. of **write** write 的过去式
Mary wrote a letter to Susan.
玛丽写了一封信给苏珊。

Xx

Xmas /'X·mas; 'krɪsməs/ *n.*
short for **Christmas**
Christmas 的缩写形式
Happy Xmas!
圣诞快乐!

x-ray [1] /'x·ray; 'eksreɪ/ *n.*
picture of things inside your body X光照片
The doctor took an x-ray of Peter's hand.
医生给彼得的手拍X光照片。

x-ray [2] /'x·ray; 'eksreɪ/ *v.*
take a photo of the inside of a body 拍X光照片
The doctor x-rayed Peter's chest.
医生给彼得的胸部拍X光照片。

xylophone /'xy·lo·phone; 'zaɪləfəun/ *n.*
sort of musical instrument 木琴
David is learning to play the xylophone.
戴维在学敲木琴。

Yy

yacht /yacht; jɒt/ *n.*
sort of boat with sails 快艇；游艇
There were some yachts in the harbour.
海港内有一些快艇。

yam /yam; jæm/ *n.*
sort of vegetable 薯蓣；番薯
Peter likes yams.
彼得喜欢吃薯蓣。

yard /yard; jɑ:d/ *n.*
1 measure of length 码
Mrs Qian bought three yards of silk.
钱太太买了三码丝绸。
2 piece of hard ground with a fence or wall around it, near a building 院子
The children were playing in the yard.
孩子们在院子内玩耍。

yawn /yawn; jɔ:n/ *n.*
open your mouth wide because you are tired 打呵欠
It was late and Mary was yawning.
时候不早了，玛丽已在打呵欠了。

year /year; jɜ:/ *n.*
twelve months from January to December; twelve months 年
Mr Wang lived in Canada for three years.
王先生在加拿大住了三年。
yearly *adj. adv.* 每年一次；一年一度
It is a yearly festival.
这是一年一度的节日。
The festival is held yearly.
这个节日每年一次。

yell /yell; jel/ *v.*
shout; cry loudly 叫喊；嚷
The policeman yelled at the naughty boys.
警察朝那些顽皮的男孩子叫喊。

yellow /ˈyel·low; ˈjeləʊ/ *adj.*
colour of lemons 黄色的
Anna is wearing a yellow dress.
安娜穿了一件黄色连衣裙。

yes /yes; jes/ *adv.*
word to show that you agree 是
Yes. I do like ice-cream.
是的，我的确喜欢吃冰淇淋。
opp. 反义词：no 不是

yesterday /ˈyes·ter·day; ˈjestədɪ/ *n. adv.*
day before today 昨天
Yesterday was Monday.
昨天是星期一。
David went to the beach yesterday.
昨天戴维到海滩去。

yet /yet; jet/ *adv.*
up to this time; up to that time 还；尚；仍然
Have you been to Canada yet?
你还未去过加拿大吗？

yoghurt /ˈyogh·urt; ˈjɒgət/ *n.*
(no plural)
soft food made from milk
酸乳酪
Sam eats yoghurt for his breakfast.
萨姆早餐吃酸乳酪。

yolk /yolk; jəʊk/ *n.*
middle, yellow part of an egg 蛋黄
The egg had two yolks.

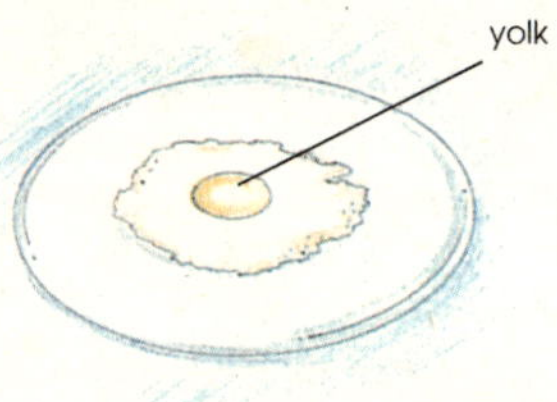

you /you; ju:/ *pron.*
person or people I am talking to 你
Would you like some tea?
你要喝点茶吗？
you'd, you had 你有；你已经
I thought you'd finished your work.
我以为你已经做完了功课。
you'd, you would 你会
You'd like this book.
你会喜欢这本书的。
you'll, you will 你将会
You'll have a holiday next week.
你将会在下星期放假。
you're, you are 你是
You're the only boy in the party.
你是这次聚会中唯一的一个男孩。
you've, you have 你有；你已经
You've seen the film, haven't you?
你已经看过这部电影了，是不是？

young /young; jʌŋ/ *adj.*
not old; in the early part of life 年轻的；年幼的
The young people had a barbecue on the beach.
那些年轻人在海滩烧烤。
opp. 反义词：old, elderly 年老的；年长的

your /your; jɔː/ *adj.*
of you 你的
Is this your book?
这是你的书吗？

yours /yours; jɔːz/ *pron.*
thing that belongs to you
属于你的
Is this book yours?
这本书是你的吗？
Usage note: *Yours* is also a way to end a letter to a good friend — *Yours, Peter.*
用法：yours 亦可用于信末，以表示亲切的态度，例如 Yours, Peter。

yourself /your·'self; jɔː'self/ *pron.*
1 word for you, when someone has just talked about you 你自己
Did you see the accident yourself?
你是亲眼看见这次事故的吗？
2 on your own; with nobody else 你自己
You must do the homework yourself.
你一定要自己做家庭作业。
by yourself 你独自
Did you do the work by yourself?
这功课是你自己做的吗？

yourselves /your·'selves; jɔː'selvz/ *pron.*
plural of yourself 你们自己
Susan and Mary, did you do this work yourselves?
苏珊和玛丽，这些功课是你们自己做的吗？
by yourselves 你们自己
Now children, work by yourselves.
孩子们，自己做自己的功课吧。

youth /youth; juːθ/ *n.*
young people; time when you are young 年轻人；青少年时代
Sam belongs to a youth club.
萨姆生在教堂结婚。部的成员。

yo-yo /'yo-yo; 'jəujəu/ *n.*
round piece of wood or plastic which goes up and down on a string 溜溜球
David was playing with a yo-yo.
戴维在玩溜溜球。

zebra /'ze·bra; 'zebrə/ *n.*
wild animal like a horse with stripes 斑马
Sam saw a zebra at the zoo.
萨姆在动物园里看到斑马。

zebra crossing /'ze·bra 'cros·sing; 'zebrə 'krɒsɪŋ/ *n.*
path of black and white stripes over a road, where you can cross safely 斑马线
Use the zebra crossing when you cross the road.
过马路要走斑马线。

zero (0) /'ze·ro; 'zɪərəu/ *n.*
nothing 零
Sam got zero in the test.
萨姆测验得了零分。

zigzag /'zig·zag; 'zɪgzæg/ *n.*
pattern shaped like a z
之字形
The boat travelled in a zigzag.
那船之字形航行。

zip [1] /zip; zɪp/ *n.*
long, metal thing that fastens clothes, bags, etc. 拉链
The zip on Mary's bag broke.
玛丽袋子上的拉链坏了。

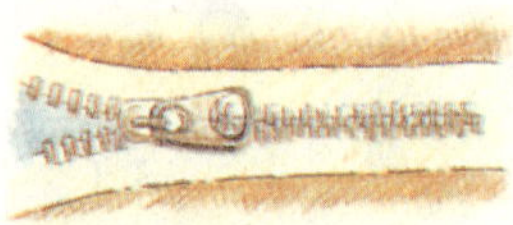

zip [2] /zip; zɪp/ *v.*
(zipping, zipped, zipped)
close a zip 拉开或拉上拉链
Peter zipped up his jacket.
彼得拉上短上衣的拉链。

zoo /zoo; zuː/ *n.*
place where you can see wild animals in cages 动物园
The children saw some elephants at the zoo.
孩子们在动物园里看见一些大象。

zoom /zoom; zuːm/ *v.*
move very fast with a loud noise 快速并喧闹地移动
The jet zoomed over our heads.
那喷气式飞机快速地从我们头上飞过，发出巨响。
zoom lens *n.* 可变焦距镜头
David's camera has a zoom lens.
戴维的照相机带有可变焦距镜头。

Appendices 附录

1 Our body 我们的身体

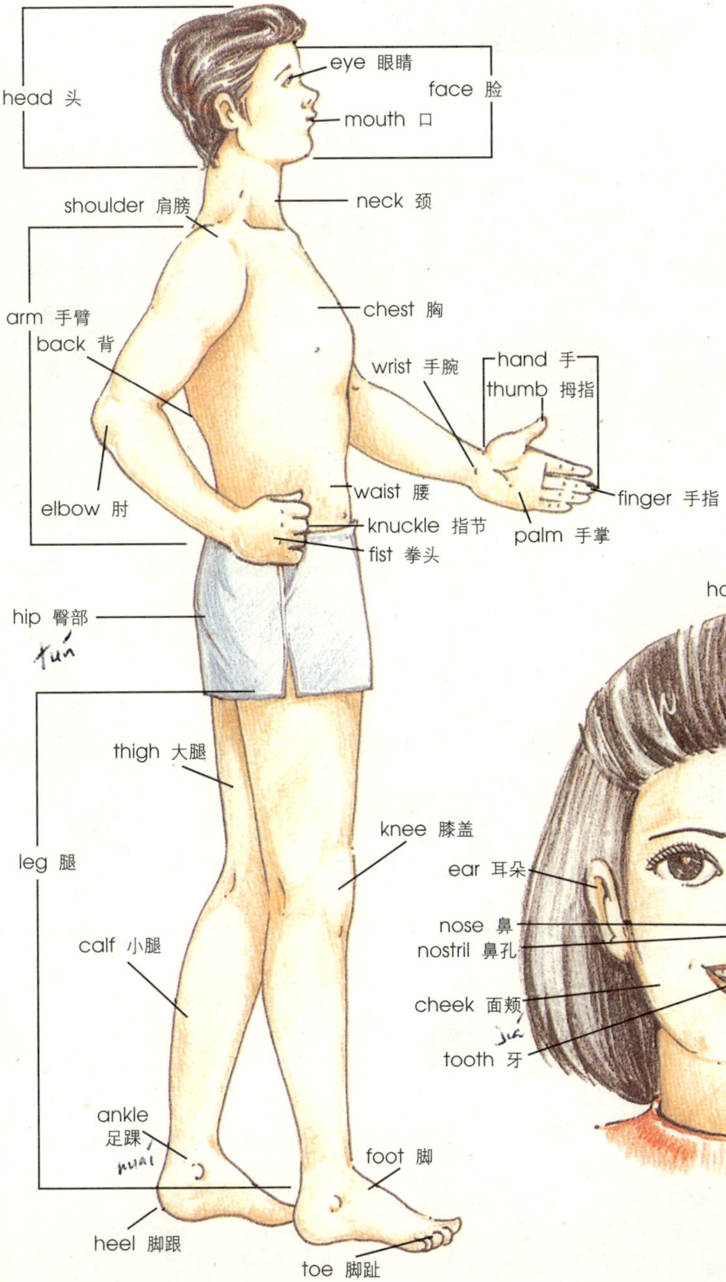

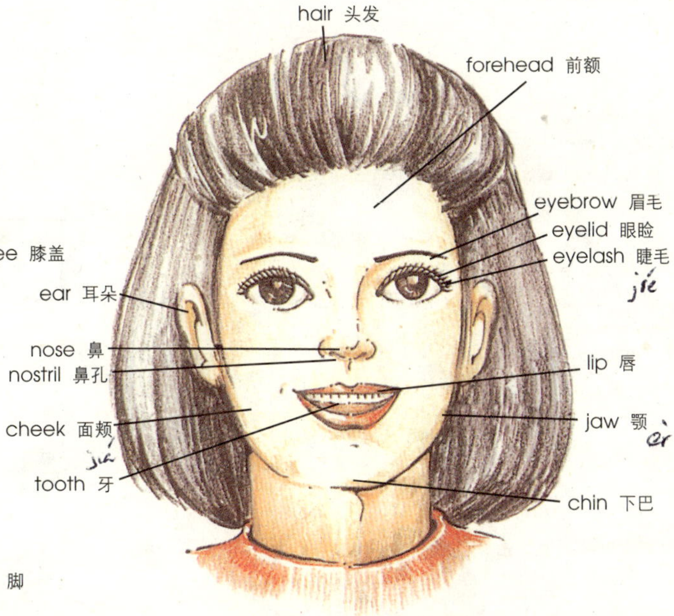

2 Colours 颜色

BLACK 黑
BLUE 藍
BROWN 棕
GREEN 綠、青
GREY 灰
ORANGE 橙
PINK 粉紅
WHITE 白
PURPLE 紫
RED 紅
YELLOW 黃

3 Lines and Shapes 线和形状

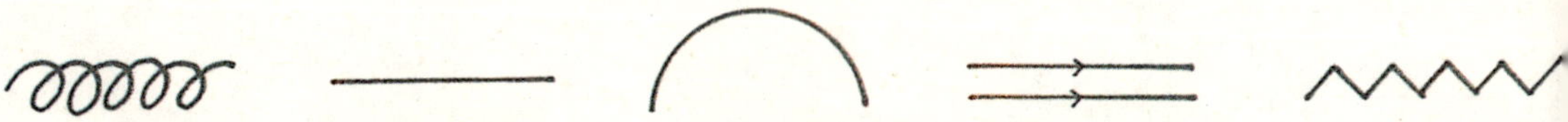

spiral 螺线 | straight line 直线 | curve 曲线 | parallel lines 平行线 | zigzag 之字线

wavy line 波浪纹 | circle 圆形 | oval 椭圆形 | triangles 三角形 | square 正方形

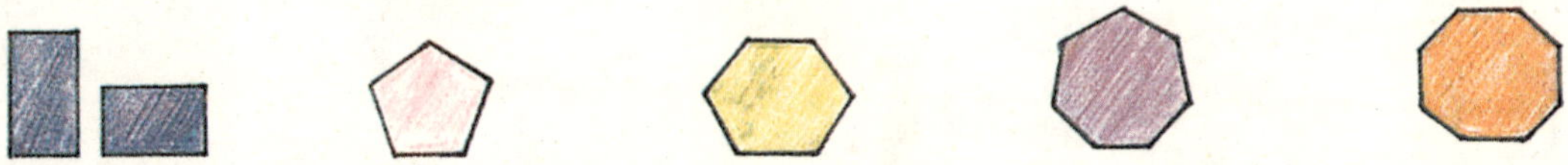

rectangles 长方形 | pentagon 五角形 | hexagon 六角形 | heptagon 七角形 | octagon 八角形

sphere 球体 | hemisphere 半球体 | cylinder 圆柱体 | cone 圆锥体

pyramid 角锥体 | cube 立方体 | cuboid 长方体 | spiral 螺旋形

4 Directions 方向

North 北

North-west 西北

North-east 东北

West 西

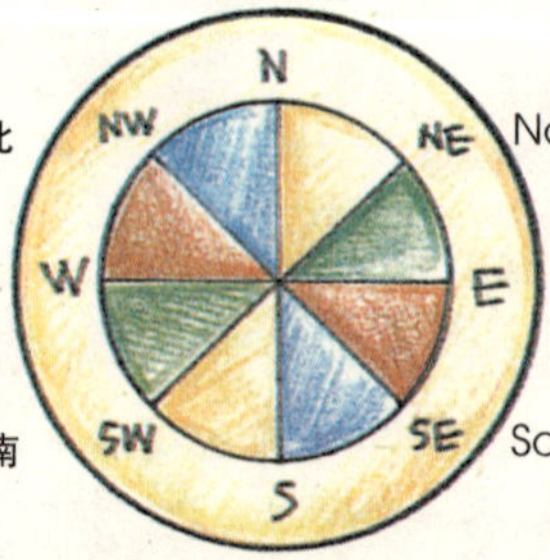

East 东

South-west 西南

South-east 东南

South 南

5 Money 货币（港元）

Ten cents
(10¢) 一毫

Two dollars
($2) 两元

Tweyth cents
(20¢) 两毫

Five dollars
($5) 五元

Fifty cents
(50¢) 五毫

One dollar
($1) 一元

Ten dollars
($10) 十元

6 Numbers 数字

0 zero, nought 零
1 one 一
2 two 二
3 three 三
4 four 四
5 five 五
6 six 六
7 seven 七
8 eight 八
9 nine 九
10 ten 十
11 eleven 十一
12 twelve 十二
13 thirteen 十三
14 fourteen 十四
15 fifteen 十五
16 sixteen 十六
17 seventeen 十七
18 eighteen 十八
19 nineteen 十九
20 twenty 二十
21 twenty-one 二十一
22 twenty-two 二十二
30 thirty 三十
40 forty 四十
50 fifty 五十
60 sixty 六十
70 seventy 七十
80 eighty 八十
90 ninety 九十
100 one hundred 一百
101 one hundred and one 一百零一
1 000 one thousand 一千
1 000 000 one million 一百万

1st first 第一
2nd second 第二
3rd third 第三
4th fourth 第四
5th fifth 第五
6th sixth 第六
7th seventh 第七
8th eighth 第八
9th ninth 第九
10th tenth 第十
11th eleventh 第十一
12th twelfth 第十二
13th thirteenth 第十三
14th fourteenth 第十四
15th fifteenth 第十五
16th sixteenth 第十六
17th seventeenth 第十七
18th eighteenth 第十八
19th nineteenth 第十九
20th twentieth 第二十
21st twenty-first 第二十一
22nd twenty-second 第二十二
30th thirtieth 第三十
40th fortieth 第四十
50th fiftieth 第五十
60th sixtieth 第六十
70th seventieth 第七十
80th eightieth 第八十
90th ninetieth 第九十
100th one hundredth 第一百
101st one hundred and first 第一百零一
1 000th one thousandth 第一千
1 000 000th one millionth 第一百万

7 Measuring things 度量物件

1 centimetre (cm) 厘米 = 10 millimetres (mm) 毫米
1 metre (m) 米 = 100 centimetres (cm) 厘米
1 kilogram (kg) 千克, 公斤 = 1 000 grams (g) 克
1 litre (l) 升 = 1 000 millilitres (ml) 毫升
1 square metre (m^2) 平方米 = 10 000 square centimetres (cm^2) 平方厘米
1 cubic metre (m^3) 立方米 = 1 000 000 cubic centimetres (cm^3) 立方厘米
a half (1/2) 一半, 二分之一
a quarter (1/4) 四分之一
one third (1/3) 三分之一
two thirds (2/3) 三分之二

8 Time 时间

1 hour 小时 = 60 minutes 分　　1 minute 分 = 60 seconds 秒

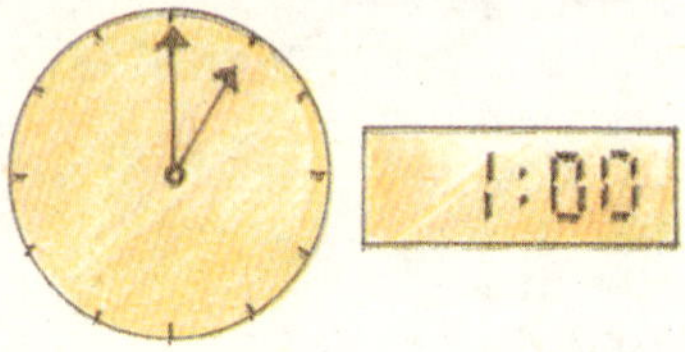

one o'clock 一时

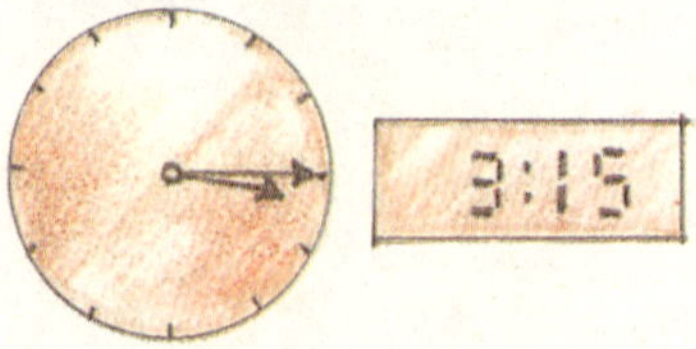

quarter past three, three fifteen
三时十五分

twenty to five, four forty
四时四十分

five past two 二时零五分

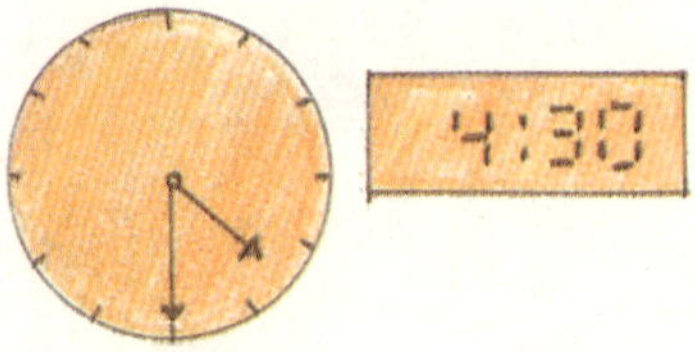

half past four, four thirty
四时三十分

quarter to six, five forty-five
五时四十五分

a.m. 上午　　p.m. 下午
morning 上午　　afternoon 下午
evening
傍晚(日落后至睡眠前的一段时间)
night
晚上(日落后至次日日出前的一段时间)
day 日　　week 周
fortnight 两周　　month 月
year 年　　century 世纪

Seasons 季节
spring 春　　summer 夏
autumn 秋　　winter 冬

Months of the year 月份
January 一月　　July 七月
February 二月　　August 八月
March 三月　　September 九月
April 四月　　October 十月
May 五月　　November 十一月
June 六月　　December 十二月

Days of the week 星期
Sunday 星期日
Monday 星期一
Tuesday 星期二
Wednesday 星期三
Thursday 星期四
Friday 星期五
Saturday 星期六

9 Things to say 常用口语

Classroom Phrases 教室内用语
Stand up 站立。
Sit down 坐下。
Come here, please. 请过来。
Go to your seat. 请回座位。
Open your books. 打开课本。
Close your books. 合上课本。
Listen. 听着。
Repeat. 再来一遍。
Good. 好。
Very good. 很好。
Good boy. 好(男)孩子。
Good girl. 好(女)孩子。
You say it. 你说吧!
Quiet, please. 请静一静。
Pencils down. 放下铅笔。
Hands up. 请举手。
Hands down. 请把手放下。
Read. 读出来。
Write. 写下来。
Draw. 画出来。
Go to... 去…
Give me... 给我…
Show me... 给我看…
Point to... 指出…
Together/Everyone. 全部人一起。
Come in. 进来。
Go out. 出去。
Open/Shut the door/ window, please. 请打开/关上门/窗。
Hold this, please. 请拿着。
Thank you. 谢谢。
Hello. 你好。
How are you? 你好吗?
I am fine. 我很好。
Goodbye. 再见。

Introduce yourself 介绍自己
My name is... 我的名字是…
I study at...school. 我在…学校念书
I am in Primary... 我念小学…年级。
I live in... 我住在…
I am...years old. 我…岁。
My favourite food is... 我最喜欢吃的是…
I like to play... 我喜欢玩…

10 At school 在学校

Classroom 教室

1 blackboard 黑板
2 book 书
3 chair 椅子
4 chalk 粉笔
5 eraser 黑板擦
6 crayon 蜡笔
7 desk 书桌
8 exercise book 练习簿
9 glue 胶水
10 map 地图
11 notice-board 布告板
12 pen 笔
13 pencil 铅笔
14 pencil-case 铅笔盒
15 pencil-sharpener 铅笔刀
16 pupil 学生
17 ruler 尺
18 scissors 剪刀
19 teacher 老师
20 wastepaper basket 废纸篓
21 workbook 练习册

playground 运动场

hall 礼堂

toilet 厕所

teachers' room 教员室

11 At home 在家中

Living-room 客厅

1 air-conditioner （冷暖）空调
2 clock 时钟
3 curtain 窗帘
4 cushion 软垫
5 lamp 台灯
6 wall unit 组合柜
7 sofa 沙发
8 coffee table 咖
9 telephone 电话
10 television 电视机

Bathroom 浴室

1 shampoo 洗发
2 shower cap 淋
3 shower head 莲
4 shower curtain 淋浴帘
5 soap 肥皂
6 sponge 海绵
7 tap 水龙头
8 toilet 厕所
9 toothbrush 牙刷
10 toothpaste 牙膏
11 towel 毛巾

Bedroom 卧室

1 bed 床
2 blanket 毛毯
3 blinds 卷帘
4 coat-hanger 挂衣架
5 drawer 抽屉
6 hook 钩
7 pillow 枕头
8 pillowcase 枕头套
9 mirror 镜子
10 sheet 被单
11 wardrobe 衣柜

Kitchen 厨房

1 bowl 碗
2 chopsticks 筷子
3 cupboard 碗橱
4 dishwashing liquid 洗洁精
5 freezer 冷冻格
6 ice-tray 冰格
7 kettle 水壶
8 pan 平底锅
9 plates 碟
10 pot 锅
11 refrigerator 冰箱
12 rice-cooker 电饭锅
13 scouring pad 刷锅用网垫
14 sink 洗涤槽
15 wok 铁锅
16 toaster 烤面包机

12 Clothes 衣服

1 belt 腰带
2 blouse （女用）短上衣；女衬衫
3 cap 鸭舌帽
4 cardigan 开襟毛外衣
5 coat 大衣
6 dress 连衣裙
7 hat 帽子
8 jacket 短外套
9 jeans 牛仔裤
10 jumper, pullover, sweater 套头毛衣
11 pants 内裤
12 pyjamas 睡衣
13 scarf 围巾
14 shirt 衬衣
15 shoes 鞋
16 shorts 短裤
17 skirt 裙子
18 slippers 拖鞋
19 socks 短袜
20 stockings 长袜
21 suit 一套衣服
22 T-shirt T恤
23 tie 领带
24 trousers 长裤
25 waistcoat(vest) 背心

13 Flowers and plants 花和植物

carnation 康乃馨

rose 玫瑰

poinsettia 圣诞红（圣诞花）

lily 百合

chrysanthemum 菊

daisy 雏菊

hyacinth 风信子

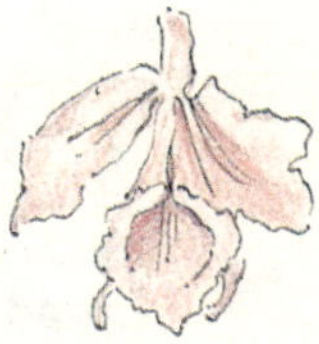
orchid 兰

dandelion 蒲公英

tulip 郁金香

wheat 小麦

maize 玉蜀黍（玉米）

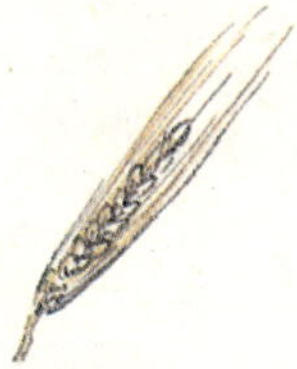
barley 大麦

oats 燕麦

cactus 仙人掌

14 Vegetables 蔬菜

cucumber 黄瓜

eggplant 茄子

carrots 胡萝卜

peppers 辣椒

lettuce 生菜

cabbages 卷心菜，椰菜

cauliflower 花椰菜

Chinese cabbage 白菜

potatoes 马铃薯

peas 豌豆

beans 豆

mushrooms 蘑菇

tomatoes 番茄

present tense 现在式	present participle 现在分词	past tense 过去式	past participle 过去分词
accuse	accusing	accused	accused
ache	aching	ached	ached
achieve	achieving	achieved	achieved
admire	admiring	admired	admired
admit	admitting	admitted	admitted
advertise	advertising	advertised	advertised
advise	advising	advised	advised
agree	agreeing	agreed	agreed
amuse	amusing	amused	amused
apologize	apologizing	apologized	apologized
argue	arguing	argued	argued
arrange	arranging	arranged	arranged
bake	baking	baked	baked
bathe	bathing	bathed	bathed
be	being	was/were	been
beat	beating	beat	beaten
become	becoming	became	become
beg	begging	begged	begged
begin	beginning	began	begun
behave	behaving	behaved	behaved
believe	believing	believed	believed
bend	bending	bent	bent
bite	biting	bit	bitten
blow	blowing	blew	blown
bounce	bouncing	bounced	bounced
break	breaking	broke	broken
breathe	breathing	breathed	breathed
bring	bringing	brought	brought
build	building	built	built
burn	burning	burnt	burnt
burst	bursting	burst	burst
bury	burying	buried	buried
buy	buying	bought	bought
capture	capturing	captured	captured
care	caring	cared	cared
carry	carrying	carried	carried
catch	catching	caught	caught
cause	causing	caused	caused
change	changing	changed	changed
charge	charging	charged	charged
chase	chasing	chased	chased
choke	choking	choked	choked
choose	choosing	chose	chosen
chop	chopping	chopped	chopped
circle	circling	circled	circled
clap	clapping	clapped	clapped
close	closing	closed	closed
come	coming	came	come

present tense 现在式	present participle 现在分词	past tense 过去式	past participle 过去分词
compare	comparing	compared	compared
complete	completing	completed	completed
continue	continuing	continued	continued
control	controlling	controlled	controlled
copy	copying	copied	copied
cost	costing	cost	cost
creep	creeping	crept	crept
cry	crying	cried	cried
cure	curing	cured	cured
cut	cutting	cut	cut
cycle	cycling	cycled	cycled
damage	damaging	damaged	damaged
dance	dancing	danced	danced
dare	daring	dared	dared
decide	deciding	decided	decided
decorate	decorating	decorated	decorated
decrease	decreasing	decreased	decreased
describe	describing	described	described
deserve	deserving	deserved	deserved
dial	dialling	dialled	dialled
die	dying	died	died
dig	digging	dug	dug
dilute	diluting	diluted	diluted
dip	dipping	dipped	dipped
disagree	disagreeing	disagreed	disagreed
disguise	disguising	disguised	disguised
dislike	disliking	disliked	disliked
dive	diving	dived	dived
divide	dividing	divided	divided
do	doing	did	done
double	doubling	doubled	doubled
drag	dragging	dragged	dragged
draw	drawing	drew	drawn
dream	dreaming	dreamt	dreamt
drink	drinking	drank	drunk
drip	dripping	dripped	dripped
drive	driving	drove	driven
drop	dropping	dropped	dropped
dry	drying	dried	dried
eat	eating	ate	eaten
educate	educating	educated	educated
emigrate	emigrating	emigrated	emigrated
encourage	encouraging	encouraged	encouraged
equal	equalling	equalled	equalled
escape	escaping	escaped	escaped
examine	examining	examined	examined
exchange	exchanging	exchanged	exchanged
excuse	excusing	excused	excused

present tense 现在式	present participle 现在分词	past tense 过去式	past participle 过去分词
exercise	exercising	exercised	exercised
explode	exploding	exploded	exploded
explore	exploring	explored	explored
face	facing	faced	faced
fall	falling	fell	fallen
feed	feeding	fed	fed
feel	feeling	felt	felt
fight	fighting	fought	fought
find	finding	found	found
fire	firing	fired	fired
fit	fitting	fitted	fitted
fly	flying	flew	flown
forbid	forbidding	forbade	forbidden
force	forcing	forced	forced
forget	forgetting	forgot	forgotten
forgive	forgiving	forgave	forgiven
freeze	freezing	froze	frozen
fry	frying	fried	fried
gamble	gambling	gambled	gambled
get	getting	got	got
give	giving	gave	given
glue	gluing	glued	glued
go	going	went	gone
grab	grabbing	grabbed	grabbed
grow	growing	grew	grown
grumble	grumbling	grumbled	grumbled
guide	guiding	guided	guided
gum	gumming	gummed	gummed
handle	handling	handled	handled
hang	hanging	hung	hung
hate	hating	hated	hated
have	having	had	had
hear	hearing	heard	heard
hide	hiding	hid	hidden
hike	hiking	hiked	hiked
hire	hiring	hired	hired
hit	hitting	hit	hit
hold	holding	held	held
hop	hopping	hopped	hopped
hope	hoping	hoped	hoped
hum	humming	hummed	hummed
hurry	hurrying	hurried	hurried
hurt	hurting	hurt	hurt
ignore	ignoring	ignored	ignored
imagine	imagining	imagined	imagined
immigrate	immigrating	immigrated	immigrated
improve	improving	improved	improved
include	including	included	included

present tense 现在式	present participle 现在分词	past tense 过去式	past participle 过去分词
increase	increasing	increased	increased
injure	injuring	injured	injured
introduce	introducing	introduced	introduced
invade	invading	invaded	invaded
investigate	investigating	investigated	investigated
invite	inviting	invited	invited
keep	keeping	kept	kept
kidnap	kidnapping	kidnapped	kidnapped
kneel	kneeling	knelt	knelt
knit	knitting	knitted	knitted
know	knowing	knew	known
lace	lacing	laced	laced
lay	laying	laid	laid
lead	leading	led	led
lean	leaning	leant	leant
leap	leaping	leapt	leapt
learn	learning	learnt	learnt
leave	leaving	left	left
lend	lending	lent	lent
let	letting	let	let
lie	lying	lay	lain
lie	lying	lied	lied
light	lighting	lit	lit
like	liking	liked	liked
live	living	lived	lived
lose	losing	lost	lost
love	loving	loved	loved
magnify	magnifying	magnified	magnified
make	making	made	made
manage	managing	managed	managed
marry	marrying	married	married
mean	meaning	meant	meant
measure	measuring	measured	measured
meet	meeting	met	met
move	moving	moved	moved
multiply	multiplying	multiplied	multiplied
name	naming	named	named
nod	nodding	nodded	nodded
notice	noticing	noticed	noticed
organize	organizing	organized	organized
owe	owing	owed	owed
paddle	paddling	paddled	paddled
paste	pasting	pasted	pasted
pay	paying	paid	paid
phone	phoning	phoned	phoned
pin	pinning	pinned	pinned
pity	pitying	pitied	pitied
place	placing	placed	placed

present tense 现在式	present participle 现在分词	past tense 过去式	past participle 过去分词
plan	planning	planned	planned
practise	practising	practised	practised
praise	praising	praised	praised
prefer	preferring	preferred	preferred
prepare	preparing	prepared	prepared
produce	producing	produced	produced
promise	promising	promised	promised
pronounce	pronouncing	pronounced	pronounced
prove	proving	proved	proved
put	putting	put	put
quarrel	quarrelling	quarrelled	quarrelled
race	racing	raced	raced
raise	raising	raised	raised
read	reading	read	read
receive	receiving	received	received
recite	reciting	recited	recited
recognize	recognizing	recognized	recognized
refuse	refusing	refused	refused
remove	removing	removed	removed
replace	replacing	replaced	replaced
reply	replying	replied	replied
rescue	rescuing	rescued	rescued
reverse	reversing	reversed	reversed
revise	revising	revised	revised
ride	riding	rode	ridden
ring	ringing	rang	rung
rise	rising	rose	risen
rob	robbing	robbed	robbed
rub	rubbing	rubbed	rubbed
rule	ruling	ruled	ruled
run	running	ran	run
save	saving	saved	saved
say	saying	said	said
score	scoring	scored	scored
scrape	scraping	scraped	scraped
scrub	scrubbing	scrubbed	scrubbed
see	seeing	saw	seen
sell	selling	sold	sold
send	sending	sent	sent
separate	separating	separated	separated
serve	serving	served	served
set	setting	set	set
settle	settling	settled	settled
shade	shading	shaded	shaded
shake	shaking	shook	shaken
share	sharing	shared	shared
shave	shaving	shaved	shaved
shine	shining	shone	shone

present tense 现在式	present participle 现在分词	past tense 过去式	past participle 过去分词
shoot	shooting	shot	shot
shop	shopping	shopped	shopped
show	showing	showed	showed
shrink	shrinking	shrank	shrunk
shut	shutting	shut	shut
sing	singing	sang	sung
sink	sinking	sank	sunk
sit	sitting	sat	sat
skate	skating	skated	skated
skip	skipping	skipped	skipped
sleep	sleeping	slept	slept
slide	sliding	slid	slid
slip	slipping	slipped	slipped
smell	smelling	smelt	smelt
smile	smiling	smiled	smiled
smoke	smoking	smoked	smoked
sneeze	sneezing	sneezed	sneezed
snore	snoring	snored	snored
solve	sloving	solved	solved
sow	sowing	sowed	sown
speak	speaking	spoke	spoken
spell	spelling	spelt	spelt
spend	spending	spent	spent
spill	spilling	spilt	spilt
spin	spinning	spun	spun
spit	spitting	spat	spat
split	splitting	split	split
spoil	spoiling	spoilt	spoilt
spread	spreading	spread	spread
squeeze	squeezing	squeezed	squeezed
stand	standing	stood	stood
stare	staring	stared	stared
starve	starving	starved	starved
steal	stealing	stole	stolen
step	stepping	stepped	stepped
stick	sticking	stuck	stuck
sting	stinging	stung	stung
stir	stirring	stirred	stirred
stop	stopping	stopped	stopped
store	storing	stored	stored
strike	striking	struck	struck
study	studying	studied	studied
surprise	surprising	surprised	surprised
sweep	sweeping	swept	swept
swim	swimming	swam	swum
swing	swinging	swung	swung
take	taking	took	taken
tap	tapping	tapped	tapped

present tense 现在式	present participle 现在分词	past tense 过去式	past participle 过去分词
taste	tasting	tasted	tasted
teach	teaching	taught	taught
tear	tearing	tore	torn
telephone	telephoning	telephoned	telephoned
tell	telling	told	told
think	thinking	thought	thought
throw	throwing	threw	thrown
tie	tying	tied	tied
trade	trading	traded	traded
trap	trapping	trapped	trapped
travel	travelling	travelled	travelled
trip	tripping	tripped	tripped
try	trying	tried	tried
twinkle	twinkling	twinkled	twinkled
type	typing	typed	typed
underline	underlining	underlined	underlined
understand	understanding	understood	understood
undo	undoing	undid	undone
untie	untying	untied	untied
unwrap	unwrapping	unwrapped	unwrapped
upset	upsetting	upset	upset
use	using	used	used
vote	voting	voted	voted
wake	waking	woke	woken
waste	wasting	wasted	wasted
wave	waving	waved	waved
wear	wearing	wore	worn
welcome	welcoming	welcomed	welcomed
whistle	whistling	whistled	whistled
win	winning	won	won
wind	winding	wound	wound
wipe	wiping	wiped	wiped
worry	worrying	worried	worried
wrap	wrapping	wrapped	wrapped
write	writing	wrote	written
zip	zipping	zipped	zipped